petroff defence

WITHDRAWN

by A. Raetsky
& M. Chetverik

EVERYMAN CHESS

Gloucester Publishers plc   www.everymanchess.com

First published in 2005 by Gloucester Publishers plc (formerly Everyman Publishers plc), Northburgh House, 10 Northburgh Street, London EC1V 0AT

British Library Cataloguing-in-Publication Data
A catalogue record for this book is available from the British Library.

ISBN 1 85744 378 0

Distributed in North America by The Globe Pequot Press, P.O Box 480, 246 Goose Lane, Guilford, CT 06437-0480.

All other sales enquiries should be directed to Everyman Chess, Northburgh House, 10 Northburgh Street, London EC1V 0AT
tel: 020 7253 7887 fax: 020 7490 3708
email: info@everymanchess.com
website: www.everymanchess.com

EVERYMAN CHESS SERIES (formerly Cadogan Chess)
Chief advisor: Garry Kasparov
Commissioning editor: Byron Jacobs
General editor: John Emms

Typeset and edited by First Rank Publishing, Brighton.
Cover design by Horatio Monteverde.
Production by Navigator Guides.
Printed and bound in the US by Versa Press.

CONTENTS

1 e4 e5 2 ♘f3 ♘f6

BIBLIOGRAPHY

Books

Fashionable Variation in the Petroff Defence, Raetsky and Chetverik (Voronezh 1992)

Modnyi variant russkoi partii, Raetsky and Chetverik (Voronezh 1990)

Russische Partie, Schwarz (Hamburg 1986)

Russische Verteidigung, Konikowski and Siebenhaar (Germany 1992)

The Cochrane Gambit, Matsukevich (Moscow 1994)

The Petroff, Janjgava (Gambit 2001)

The Petroff Defence, Forintos and Haag (Batsford 1991)

The Petroff Defence, Yusupov (Olms 1999)

Periodicals

Chess Informant 1-90

New in Chess Yearbook 1-72

Software

Chess Assistant 7.1

INTRODUCTION

The entire theory of chess openings is divided into the Petroff Defence and the rejected Petroff Defence (1 d4, 1 c4 and other lines). — Alexander Raetsky

The Petroff Defence has been one of the most fashionable 'open games' in the last decade, but it also has a long history. After 1 e4 e5 2 ♘f3, instead of defending his e5-pawn, Black prepares a counterattack on White's e4-pawn with 2...♘f6. Lucena mentioned this idea as far back as 1479, while in 1512 Damiano analysed 3 ♘xe5 ♘xe4 and, of course, after 4 ♕e2 reached conclusions that were discouraging for Black. No wonder the symmetrical opening was forgotten for many centuries after that! However, in 1824 Russian maestro, Alexander Petroff, found out that 3 ♘xe5 could be met by 3...d6!, and only after that should Black capture the e4-pawn. In 1842 another Russian expert, Jaenisch, published valuable analysis in *Palamede*. The opening was given a name of the Petroff or the Russian Defence (in Russia, Germany and Scandinavia).

It is quite natural that two Russian masters write about the Petroff Defence for the publisher Everyman Chess. Just like ballet, the Russian Defence could be labelled as property of the Russians. Grandmaster Artur Yusupov is an outstanding theoretical expert of this opening, while Russian champions Smyslov, Karpov and Kramnik often use it in practice. Raetsky and Chetverik have not made a substantial contribution to the theory of the Petroff Defence so far. However, it's worth pointing out that our first published articles and booklets were devoted to this opening in the early 1990s. Alexander Raetsky has considered the Petroff Defence to be his favourite opening for more than twenty years and can be proud, at least, of the quantity of his games played in the Petroff Defence (about 200, including 60 correspondence games), if not the quality.

Emotional players are scared off by the symmetrical trend in the Petroff Defence; they are afraid of the drawish aspirations of weaker opponents who play White. But what can be more symmetrical than the initial position in chess, which has not yet been ruined by the notorious 'draw death' despite Capablanca's indications? A more skilful strategic player triumphs in the Petroff Defence regardless of the colour of his pieces and the position's symmetry. The healthy strategical foundation of this opening allows Black to defend a lot of systems in the Petroff Defence even while playing against stronger opponents. Even the lines declared 'doubtful' by theory are normally better than their reputation.

Apart from minor alternatives (see Chapter 10), White has to choose between 3 d4 and 3 ♘xe5. The authors believe that after 3 d4, the move 3...♘xe4 is stronger than 3...exd4. Here the sharp variations like 4 dxe5 ♗c5!? and 4 ♗d3 d5 5 ♘xe5 ♘d7 6 ♘xd7 ♗xd7 7 0-0 ♕h4!? can replace the popular, solid, but uninteresting alternatives (4 dxe5 d5 and 4 ♗d3 d5 5 ♘xe5 ♘d7 6 ♘xd7 ♗xd7 7 0-0 ♗d6 respectively). After 3 ♘xe5 it is more difficult for Black to initiate an open battle and the positional niceties of the fight come to the fore.

One final advantage for the fans of the Petroff Defence: you don't have to study numerous complicated openings like the Ruy Lopez, Two Knights Defence, Italian Game and Scotch Game! After 2 ♘f3 ♘f6 you are home and dry!

Finally, some acknowledgements. Special thanks go to the founder of the Petroff Defence, Mr Petroff, and many thanks to our Danish/Scottish friend Jacob Aagaard for his technical help. Also thanks go to Zoya Nayshtut for her excellent translation into English and also to Mr Yusupov for his great book on the Petroff Defence – the real bible for people from our 'cast' (Petroff Defence players).

Play the Petroff Defence and be happy!

Alexander Raetsky & Maxim Chetverik,
Voronezh,
January 2005

CHAPTER ONE

3 ♘xe5: The Main Line with 8 c4

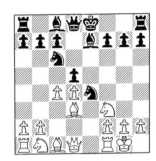

1 e4 e5 2 ♘f3 ♘f6 3 ♘xe5 d6 4 ♘f3 ♘xe4 5 d4 d5 6 ♗d3 ♗e7 7 0-0 ♘c6 8 c4

After 1 e4 e5 2 ♘f3 ♘f6 3 ♘xe5 d6 4 ♘f3 ♘xe4 5 d4 d5 6 ♗d3 Carl Jaenisch suggested the system 6...♗e7 7 0-0 ♘c6 as far back as the 19th century. This line is still very popular today, especially with regard to the immediate attack on the centre with 8 c4, the subject of this chapter.

Let's see how this line has developed over the years. The oldest reply, 8...♗e6, is not very good in view of 9 cxd5 ♗xd5 10 ♘c3 (by the way, the Löwenthal-Morphy game can be considered a model – see the notes to Game 11) or 9 ♖e1 ♘f6 10 c5. After the more aggressive development of the bishop with 8...♗g4, White should prefer 9 ♘c3 to simplifying the play in the centre with 9 cxd5 ♕xd5 10 ♘c3 ♘xc3 11 bxc3 (again see the notes to Game 11).

With 8...♘f6 Black protects the d5-square and strengthens his kingside at the same time. In the case of 9 ♘c3 ♗e6 (Game 11), White has a pleasant choice between 10 cxd5 and 10 c5, so Black should refrain from the development of the c8-bishop. If 9...0-0 10 h3 Black appears to equalise by means of 10...dxc4 11 ♗xc4 ♘a5 12 ♗d3 ♗e6. If we start with 9 h3 (Game 12), castling is again

effective, but White maintains an initiative after 9...♘b4, hassling the d3-bishop.

The ...♘c6-b4 raid is more appropriate when the other knight is still placed on e4, i.e. 8...♘b4 (Games 1-10). One option for White is simply to ignore this attack: 8...♘b4 9 cxd5 ♘xd3 10 ♕xd3 ♕xd5 11 ♖e1 ♗f5 (Games 9-10). In these games White tries to take advantage of the hanging position of the black pieces with ♘b1-c3 (immediately or after 12 g4 ♗g6) or 12 ♘e5.

Instead of 9 cxd5 White more often retreats his bishop to a safe place with 9 ♗e2 (Games 1-8), a line that has become fashionable owing to Karpov. The line 9...dxc4 10 ♗xc4 0-0 (Game 8) leads to a standard position with an isolated pawn on d4. Instead Black usually prefers to maintain pressure in the centre by means of with ...0-0 and ...♗e6 or ...♗f5. However, the order of the moves is important here. After 9...♗e6 the queen exchange 10 ♕a4+ ♕d7 11 ♕xd7+ ♔xd7 12 ♘c3 is interesting, and 10 c5!? followed by an attack on the queenside is even more so (see the notes to Game 6).

9...0-0 is preferable to 9...♗e6 because after 10 ♘c3 Black has several possible ways to develop his light-squared bishop. In Game 7 Black plays 10...b6 followed by ...♗b7. One of the main lines is 10...♗e6, against which

White can play 11 ♘e5 (Games 3-4) and 11 ♗e3 (Games 5-6).

The most fashionable line at the moment is 10...♗f5, which was utilised by Kramnik in his 2004 World Championship match with Leko. This move is discussed in Games 1-2.

Game 1
Leko-Kramnik
World Ch. (Game 1), Brissago 2004

---

1 e4 e5 2 ♘f3 ♘f6 3 ♘xe5 d6 4 ♘f3 ♘xe4 5 d4 d5 6 ♗d3 ♘c6 7 0-0 ♗e7 8 c4 ♘b4 9 ♗e2

Of course saving the bishop is the most popular option. Alternatives are studied in Games 9-10.

9...0-0 10 ♘c3 ♗f5

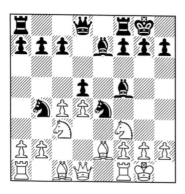

11 a3

This is the natural move but we should also consider two others:

a) 11 ♘e5 c5 and now:

a1) 12 dxc5 is not a clear error but it does allow pressure on f2: 12...♗xc5 13 ♘xd5 (White must be careful: if 13 a3? then 13...♘xf2! 14 ♖xf2 ♘c2 15 ♖a2 ♖e8 16 ♘d3 ♗xf2+ 17 ♘xf2 dxc4 and Black has a clear advantage) 13...♘xd5 14 ♕xd5 ♕xd5 15 cxd5 ♖ad8 16 ♗c4 ♖fe8 17 ♘f3 h6 18 ♗d2 ♘xd2 19 ♘xd2 ♗d4 with an unclear position.

a2) 12 a3 cxd4 13 ♘xe4 dxe4 14 axb4 f6 15 ♘g4 (15 ♘f3?! d3 16 ♗xd3 – J.Polgar-

Pavasovic, Istanbul Olympiad 2000 – and here Pavasovic claims an edge for Black after 16...exd3 17 ♕b3 ♕d7) 15...d3 16 ♘e3 dxe2 17 ♕xe2 ♗e6 18 ♖d1 ♕c7, which Pavasovic regards as unclear.

b) 11 ♕b3 leads fairly directly to a draw: 11...dxc4 12 ♗xc4 ♘f6 13 ♘e5 ♕xd4 (Bologan pointed out the error 13...♘c2? 14 ♘xf7 ♖xf7 15 ♗xf7+ ♔f8 16 ♗e3 when White is much better) 14 ♗xf7+ ♔h8 15 ♘f3 ♕d7 16 ♘e5 ♕d4 17 ♘f3 ♕d7 was agreed drawn in Bologan-Zarnicki, Buenos Aires 2000.

11...♘xc3 12 bxc3 ♘c6

13 ♖e1

After 13 cxd5 ♕xd5 White has a few choices:

a) 14 ♖e1 ♖fe8 transposes to the main game.

b) 14 ♗e3 ♖fd8 15 ♖e1 ♘a5 16 ♘e5 f6! (16...♕b3? is just a blunder: 17 ♗c4! ♕xd1 18 ♗xf7+ ♔f8 19 ♖axd1 ♘c6 20 ♘c1 ♘xe5 21 ♖xe5 ♗g4 22 ♖de1 ♗f6 23 ♖5e4 and White has won a clear pawn, Movsesian-P.Nielsen, Bundesliga 1999) 17 ♘d3 ♗d6 18 ♘b4 ♕f7 is unclear.

c) 14 c4 ♕d6 15 d5 ♘e5 16 ♘d4 ♗d7 17 a4 c6!? 18 ♖b1 (perhaps White should prefer 18 ♕b3 cxd5 19 cxd5 ♕b4 20 ♕xb4 ♗xb4, when his d-pawn is marginally more of a strength than a weakness) 18...cxd5 19 cxd5 ♕xd5 20 ♘f5 ♕e6 21 ♘xe7+ ♕xe7 22 ♖xb7 ♕e6 was level in Van Den Doel-Schandorff, Esbjerg 2001.

d) 14 ♗f4 ♘a5 15 ♗xc7 b6 16 ♗f4 ♖ac8 17 ♗d2 ♗d6 18 ♖e1 h6 19 a4 ♖c7 20 h3 ♕b3 21 ♗b5 (Krakops-Illescas, Leon 2001). Now Black could have played 21...♕xd1 22 ♖exd1 ♘b3 23 ♖a2 ♘xd2 24 ♘xd2 ♖xc3 with equality.

13...♖e8

A simple, sensible developing move but Black has other options.

13...♗f6 is probably not quite good enough to equalise: 14 ♗f4 ♘a5 15 cxd5 ♕xd5 16 ♕a4 (if 16 ♗xc7 ♖ac8 17 ♗xa5 ♕xa5 18 c4 ♖fd8 Black has pleasant compensation) 16...b6 17 ♘d2 ♗d7 18 ♕d1 and White had an edge in Short-Bologan, Skandenborg 2003. This advantage grew after 18...♖ac8 19 ♗d3 ♗f5 20 ♘e4 ♗e7 21 ♕h5 ♗xe4 22 ♕xd5 ♗xd5 23 ♖xe7 ♖fe8 24 ♖ae1 ♔f8 25 ♖xe8+ ♖xe8 26 ♖xe8+ ♔xe8 27 ♗xc7.

13...dxc4 14 ♗xc4 has been well tested:

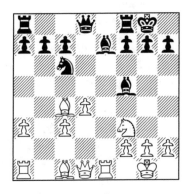

a) 14...♗f6 15 ♗f4 ♕d7 16 ♗a2 ♖fe8 17 ♘g5!? (this is Ftacnik's suggestion; 17 ♕d2 b5 18 ♗g5 ♗g6 19 ♗xf6 gxf6 20 ♘h4 ♗g7 21 f4 ♘e7 22 ♕f2 ♘f5 23 g4 ♘xh4 24 ♕xh4 f5 was unclear in Adams-Karpov, Dortmund 1999) 17...♖xe1+ 18 ♕xe1 ♗g5 19 ♗xg5 ♖e8 20 ♕d2 h6 21 ♗f4 ♘d8 22 d5 b5 and White has a nagging edge.

b) 14...♗d6 15 ♗g5 ♕d7 16 ♘h4 ♘a5 17 ♗a2 with a further branch:

b1) Black should avoid 17...b5?! 18 a4! a6 19 axb5 axb5 20 ♘xf5 ♕xf5 21 ♗e7 ♖fb8

22 g4! ♕f4 (even worse is 22...♕d7?! 23 ♗xf7+! ♔h8 – the point is 23...♔xf7 24 ♖xa5! ♖xa5 25 ♕b3+ ♔g6 26 ♖e6+ when Black will soon have to give up his queen – 24 ♗xd6 ♕xf7 25 ♗c5 and White was close to victory in Karpov-Portisch, Torino 1982) 23 ♗xd6 ♕xd6 24 ♕f3 ♕d7 25 ♖e2 ♘c4 26 ♖ae1 and White has a strong initiative, especially since 26...♖e8?? loses to 27 ♖e7!.

b2) 17...♗e6 18 ♗xe6 fxe6 19 ♘f3 ♖ae8 20 ♗h4 ♕c6 21 ♕c2 h6 and Black is just active enough to hold equality: 22 ♗g3 ♕d5 23 a4 ♘c4 24 ♖e4 a6 25 ♕e2 ♕c6 26 ♖e1 ♗xg3 27 hxg3 ♘d6 28 ♖xe6 ♕xc3 29 ♖e5 ♕b3 was now agreed drawn in Adams-Anand, FIDE World Championship, New Delhi 2000.

14 cxd5

14 ♗f4 is discussed in Game 2.

14...♕xd5 15 ♗f4

White has a minor alternative in 15 ♗e3 ♗f6 (also fine is 15...♘a5!? 16 ♘d2 ♕d7 17 ♗f3 ♗d6 18 c4 c6 19 ♕a4 ♗c7 with an unclear position) 16 ♘d2 ♖ad8 17 ♗c4 ♕d7 18 ♘b3 ♗e7 19 a4 ♗d6 20 ♕d2 (Bologan-Degraeve, Belfort 2002) ands here Bologan gives 20...♘e7! 21 ♗f4 b6 as equal.

15...♖ac8

16 h3

16 ♗d3 is a serious alternative. 16...♕d7 17 ♖b1 ♗xd3 18 ♕xd3 b6 19 d5 ♗f6 20 c4 h6 21 h3 ♖e7 22 ♖bd1 ♖d8 (if 22...♖ce8 23 ♖xe7 ♘xe7 24 ♖e1 ♖d8 25 ♗e5 White has

the more comfortable game) 23 ♖xe7 ♘xe7 24 ♘e5 ♗xe5 25 ♗xe5 ♖e8 26 ♗g3 ♘f5 27 ♗xc7! ♕xc7 28 ♕xf5 ♕xc4 29 d6 and White's strong passed pawn gave him the edge in Leko-Anand, Linares 2003.

A few days after this main game Leko tried 16 c4 ♕e4 17 ♗e3 and now:

a) 17...♕c2!? (Kramnik's novelty) 18 d5 ♘a5 19 ♘d4 ♕xd1 20 ♖exd1 (if 20 ♖axd1 Potkin analysed 20...♗d7 21 ♘b5 b6!? 22 ♘xa7 ♖a8 23 ♘b5 ♗xb5 24 cxb5 ♗xa3 as equal) 20...♗d7 21 ♗d2 ♗f6 22 ♗xa5 ♗xd4 23 ♖xd4 ♖xe2 ½-½ Leko-Kramnik, World Championship (Game 3), Brissago 2004.

b) Also reasonable is 17...♗f6 18 ♖a2 b6 19 h3 ♘a5 with a further split:

b1) 20 ♗d2 ♘b7!? (20...♕b1?! leads to a very unpleasant ending: 21 ♕xb1 ♗xb1 22 ♖xb1 ♖xe2 23 ♔f1 ♖ce8 24 ♘g1 ♖2e4 25 ♗xa5 bxa5 26 ♖e2, Kotronias-Marjanovic, Kallithea 2003) 21 ♕a4 ♗e6 22 d5 ♘c5 23 ♕xa7 ♗d7 when White's awkwardly placed queen provides Black with compensation for the pawn.

b2) 20 g4 ♗g6 21 g5 ♗e7 22 ♘e5 ♗d6 23 ♘xg6 hxg6 24 c5 ♗f8 (Kasparov analysed 24...bxc5 25 dxc5 ♗f4 26 ♗g4 ♖cd8 27 ♖d2 ♗xg5 28 ♗d7 ♖e5 29 ♖d4 as slightly better for White) 25 ♗g4 ♖cd8 26 ♖ae2 ♕c6! 27 ♕c2 (27 cxb6 was immediately abandoned as a draw in Anand-Adams, Linares 2002) 27...bxc5 28 dxc5 ♕d5 29 ♕c3 ♘c6 is equal according to Dokhoian.

Brissago (3) 2004.

16...♗e4!?

Previously 16...♗f6 had been played: 17 ♘h2!? ♕a5 18 ♗d2 ♘e7 (or 18...♖cd8 19 ♗f3 h6 20 ♘g4 ♗xg4 21 hxg4 ♗g5 22 ♗xg5 hxg5 – Kramnik-Anand, Wijk aan Zee 2003 – and here Huzman gives 23 ♕c1! ♖xe1+ 24 ♕xe1 ♔f8 25 ♖b1 ♖e8 26 ♕c1 as clearly better for White) 19 ♘g4 ♗xg4 20 ♗xg4 ♖cd8 when Anand believes White is slightly better.

17 ♗e3 ♘a5

Another try is 17...♖cd8 18 ♘d2 ♗g6 19

♗f3 ♕d7 20 ♕a4 ♘e5 21 ♕xd7 ♘xf3+ 22 ♘xf3 ♖xd7 23 ♘e5 ♖d5 as in Leko-Bologan, Dortmund (rapid) 2004. Igor Zaitsev now suggests 24 c4 ♖dd8 25 ♘xg6 fxg6 26 d5 ♔f7 27 ♖f1 ♖d7 28 ♖ab1 b6 29 ♖b3 as a way for White to gain an edge.

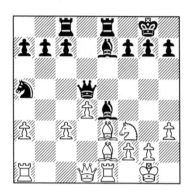

18 c4?!

This allows Black the chance to give up his queen for a definite equality. A better try for the advantage is 18 ♘d2!? ♗f5 (18...♗xg2? may look worrying for White, but I. Zaitsev provided the clever refutation: 19 c4 ♕c6 20 d5 ♕g6 21 ♗h5 ♗f3+ 22 ♗xg6 ♗xd1 23 ♗f5) 19 ♗f3 ♕d7 20 ♘b3 ♘xb3 21 ♕xb3 c6 when White has the merest of edges.

18...♘xc4! 19 ♗xc4 ♕xc4 20 ♘d2 ♕d5 21 ♘xe4 ♕xe4 22 ♗g5 ♕xe1+ 23 ♕xe1 ♗xg5 24 ♕a5 ♗f6 25 ♕xa7 c5 26 ♕xb7 ♗xd4 27 ♖a2

Belov gives 27 ♖d1 ♖b8 28 ♕d7 ♖e2 29 ♖xd4 cxd4 30 ♕xd4 as equal.

27...c4

Black must avoid the back rank trick 27...♖c7? 28 ♖e2!.

28 ♖e2 ♖ed8 29 a4?!

White should have played 29 ♖d2 ♗e5 30 f4! ♗f6 (not 30...♗xf4?! 31 ♖xd8+ ♖xd8 32 ♕c6 h5 33 ♕xc4 ♗g3 34 ♔f1 ♖e8 35 ♕c3 h4 36 a4 when White has some winning chances) 31 ♖xd8+ ♖xd8 32 ♕c7 c3 33 a4 g6 34 a5 ♖d2 35 a6 ♖a2 36 ♔h2 c2 37 a7 after which the game would have been drawn.

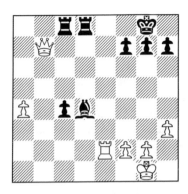

29...c3 30 ♕e4 ♗b6!

Now Black can think about trying to win.

31 ♕c2

White has to blockade: 31 ♕b4?! ♗xf2+ 32 ♔xf2 c2.

31...g6 32 ♕b3 ♖d6

The careless 32...♖d2? would spoil everything: 33 ♖e7 ♖xf2 34 ♕xb6 c2 35 ♖c7! and White wins.

33 ♖c2 ♗a5 34 g4 ♖d2 35 ♔g2 ♖cd8 36 ♖xc3! ♗xc3 37 ♕xc3 ♖2d5 38 ♕c6 ♖a5 39 ♔g3 ♖da8 40 h4 ♖5a6 41 ♕c1 ♖a5 42 ♕h6 ♖xa4 43 h5 ♖4a5 44 ♕f4?

A disastrous slip. Instead 44 hxg6 hxg6 45 f3 g5 46 ♕d6 and White holds the draw.

44...g5! 45 ♕f6 h6!

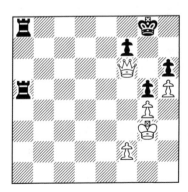

Now the win is just a matter of time.

46 f3

The point is that 46 ♕xh6? ♖8a6 traps the queen.

46...♖5a6 47 ♕c3 ♖a4 48 ♕c6 ♖8a6 49 ♕e8+ ♔g7 50 ♕b5 ♖4a5 51 ♕b4 ♖d5 52 ♕b3 ♖ad6 53 ♕c4 ♖d3 54 ♔f2 ♖a3 55 ♕c5 ♖a2+ 56 ♔g3 ♖f6 57 ♕b4 ♖aa6 58 ♔g2 ♖f4 59 ♕b2+ ♖af6 60 ♕e5 ♖xf3 61 ♕a1 ♖f1 62 ♕c3 ♖1f2+ 63 ♔g3 ♖2f3+ 64 ♕xf3 ♖xf3+ 65 ♔xf3 ♔f6 0-1

Game 2
Grischuk-Adams
Halkidiki 2002

---

1 e4 e5 2 ♘f3 ♘f6 3 ♘xe5 d6 4 ♘f3 ♘xe4 5 d4 d5 6 ♗d3 ♘c6 7 0-0 ♗e7 8 c4 ♘b4 9 ♗e2 0-0 10 ♘c3 ♗f5 11 a3 ♘xc3 12 bxc3 ♘c6 13 ♖e1 ♖e8 14 ♗f4

The main alternative to 14 cxd5.

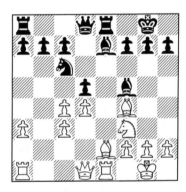

14...dxc4 15 ♗xc4 ♗d6 16 ♖xe8+ ♕xe8 17 ♘g5 ♗g6 18 ♗xd6 cxd6 19 h4 ♕e7

Anand demonstrated the following clever variation: 19...h6?! 20 h5 ♗xh5 21 ♕xh5 hxg5 22 ♔h2! ♖c8 23 ♖e1! ♘e7 24 ♗d3 g6 25 ♕xg5 ♖c7 26 ♖e3 and White is obviously better.

20 ♕g4 h6 21 ♘h3

21 h5 has also been tried, but led only to a draw in Movsesian-Gelfand, Bled Olympiad 2002 after 21...♗xh5 22 ♕xh5 hxg5 23 ♖d1 ♖f8 24 ♖d3 ♕e1+ 25 ♔h2 ♕xf2 26 ♖h3 ♕f4+ 27 ♔g1 ♕c1+ 28 ♔h2 ♕f4+.

21...♕e4

This is okay, but an interesting possibility

is 21...♕f6 22 ♖e1 ♗f5 23 ♕f3 ♔f8 24 ♘f4 (Anand-Karpov, Prague 2002). Anand now gives 24...♕xh4!? 25 ♗xf7 ♕g4 26 ♕xg4 ♗xg4 27 ♗d5 ♘e7 28 ♗xb7 ♖b8 as offering Black enough compensation.

22 ♕g3

Black can also defend against 22 ♘f4 ♘e5 23 dxe5 ♕xc4 24 exd6 ♕xc3 25 ♖f1 ♗e4! (not 25...♖d8? 26 ♘xg6 fxg6 27 d7 ♕c6 28 ♖d1 b5 29 h5! gxh5 30 ♕xh5 when White has a huge advantage, Mortensen-M.Andersson, Sweden 2003) 26 ♘e6 ♗d3 27 ♕f3! fxe6 28 ♖d1 ♕xa3 29 ♖xd3 ♕c1+ 30 ♔h2 ♕c6 31 ♕xc6 bxc6 32 ♖c3 – the rook ending is drawn.

22...♘a5 23 ♗a2 ♕d3 24 ♖f1 ♕xg3 25 fxg3 ♖c8 26 h5! ♗d3

Black avoids the obvious double attack: 26...♗xh5? 27 ♖f5 b6 28 ♖xh5 ♖xc3 29 ♖f5 when White should win.

27 ♗xf7+ ♔f8

27...♔h7?! is too passive: 28 ♖f3 ♗e4 29 ♖e3 d5 30 ♘f4 ♘c4 31 ♖e2 ♘xa3 32 ♗xd5 ♗xd5 33 ♘xd5 and White has good winning chances.

28 ♖f2

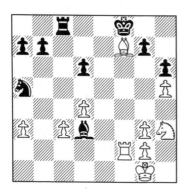

28...♔e7?

A fatal slip. After 28...♖xc3 29 ♗g6+ ♔g8 White has no more than a draw.

29 ♗d5 ♖f8

The problem with 29...♖xc3 is 30 ♖f3! ♖c1+ 31 ♔h2 ♗c4 32 ♖f7+ ♔d8 33 ♗xc4 ♖xc4 34 ♖xg7 ♖xd4 35 g4, when White's

kingside pawns decide the game.

30 ♘f4 ♗h7 31 ♗a2 ♔d7 32 ♘e6 ♖xf2 33 ♔xf2 ♗g8 34 ♘f8+ ♔e8 35 ♗xg8 ♔xf8 36 ♗d5!

White has kept the extra pawn and now dominates the knight: Black's position is hopeless.

36...♔e7 37 ♔e3 ♔f6 38 ♔f4 ♘c6 39 ♗xc6 bxc6 40 c4 ♔e6 41 g4 ♔e6 42 g5+ hxg5+ 43 ♔g4 1-0

Game 3
Anand-Shirov
Moscow 2001

---

1 e4 e5 2 ♘f3 ♘f6 3 ♘xe5 d6 4 ♘f3 ♘xe4 5 d4 d5 6 ♗d3 ♘c6 7 0-0 ♗e7 8 c4 ♘b4 9 ♗e2 0-0 10 ♘c3 ♗e6

11 ♘e5

Apart from 11 ♗e3, which is studied in Games 5-6, there are two alternatives to note:

a) 11 ♗f4 c5 12 ♖e1 ♗f6 13 ♘b5? (this expedition fails to some brilliant resources; White should prefer 13 ♕a4 ♘xc3 14 bxc3 ♘c6 15 ♖ab1 ♕d7 with an unclear position) 13...dxc4 14 ♘c7 ♘d5! 15 ♘xe6 fxe6 16 ♗g3 (Adams-Shirov, Dortmund 1998). Shirov now analysed 16...♘xg3 17 hxg3 b5! 18 a4 cxd4 19 ♘xd4 ♕b6! 20 ♘f3 (the beautiful point is 20 ♘xb5? ♕xf2+! 21 ♔xf2 ♗d4 mate!) 20...♗xb2 21 ♖b1 ♘c3! 22 ♕c2 ♘xa4 23 ♖xb2 ♘xb2 24 ♕xb2 ♖ac8 when Black's excellent pawns promise a clear advantage.

b) 11 a3 is safe but unthreatening. For example, 11...♘xc3 12 bxc3 ♘c6 13 cxd5 ♗xd5 14 ♘d2 ♘a5 15 ♗d3 b6 16 ♕c2 h6 17 ♗b2 ♗b7 18 ♘e4 b5! 19 a4 (if 19 ♗xb5 f5 20 ♕a4 c6 21 ♗c4+ ♘xc4 22 ♕xc4+ ♕d5 23 ♘d2 ♗g5 24 ♕d3 c5 Black's active bishops provide ample compensation) 19...a6 20 axb5 axb5 21 ♗xb5 f5 22 ♘c5 ♗xc5 23 dxc5 ♕d5 24 c6 ♘xc6 25 ♕d3 ♘e5 26 ♕xd5+ ♗xd5 with an equal position, Leko-Kramnik, Dortmund 1999.

11...c5

This early break gives White the chance to advance in the centre. The alternative 11...f6 is the subject of Game 4.

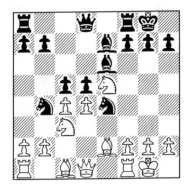

12 ♘xe4

If 12 ♗e3 cxd4 13 ♗xd4 ♘xc3 14 bxc3 ♘c6 15 ♘xc6 bxc6 16 ♕a4 c5 17 ♗e3 d4 Black equalises comfortably according to Yusupov.

12...dxe4 13 d5 ♗c8

Black must retreat since after 13...♗d6?! 14 a3 ♗xe5 15 axb4 ♗f5 16 bxc5 White's pawns are too strong. Baklan-Timman, Neum 2000 continued 16...♕c7 17 g3 ♕xc5 18 ♗e3 ♕d6 19 c5 ♕f6 20 ♕b3 ♗xb2 21 ♖a4! (Baklan pointed out that 21 ♖ab1 ♗d4 22 ♕xb7 ♗h3 23 ♖fd1 ♗xe3 24 fxe3 ♕c3 is just unclear) 21...♗e5 22 ♕xb7 ♗h3 23 ♖e1 a5 24 d6 and the pawns promise White an obvious advantage.

14 a3 ♘a6 15 ♕c2

Attacking the pawn is White's natural plan. 15 f4 was tried in Anand-Leko, Leon 2001, the game being level after 15...f6 16 ♘g4 ♗xg4 17 ♗xg4 f5 18 ♗e2 ♗f6 19 ♖b1 ♗d4+ 20 ♔h1 ♘c7 21 b4 b6 22 ♖b3 ♘e8 23 ♗e3 ♗xe3 24 ♖xe3 ♘d6 25 ♖b3 ♕f6 26 bxc5 bxc5 27 ♕a1 ♕xa1 28 ♖xa1 ♔f7.

15 f3!? is more enticing. Motylev analysed 15...♕c7 16 ♗f4! ♗d6 17 fxe4 ♖e8 (of course the idea is 17...♗xe5 18 d6) 18 ♕a4 ♗e7 19 ♘d3 ♖xe4 20 ♗xd6 ♕xd6 21 ♗f3 with a slight edge for White.

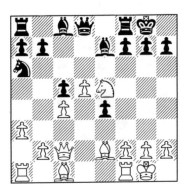

15...f6

Black threatens the knight at a moment when it has no choice but to retreat. Instead 15...♗d6 16 f4 f6 gives White the additional option of 17 ♕xe4!? ♖e8 (if Black takes the piece with 17...fxe5 18 fxe5 ♖e8 White has strong passed pawns and an attack as compensation after 19 ♗d3 g6 20 e6) 18 ♗h5 ♖e7 19 ♗f7+ (Morgado assessed 19 ♘f7 ♕c7 20 ♘xd6 ♖xe4 21 ♘xe4 as unclear) 19...♔h8 20 ♘g6+ hxg6 21 ♕xg6 ♗g4 22 f5! ♖xf7 23 ♕xf7 ♕c7 24 ♕xc7 ♗xc7 25 ♗f4 and Black's minor pieces cannot find any activity so White has an edge.

16 ♘g4

The play is certainly complicated, but White seems to have the better of it.

16...♕d6

In Topalov-Shirov, FIDE World Championship, Moscow 2001 Black tried 16...♗d6 17 f4 exf3 (or 17...♗xg4 18 ♗xg4 f5 19 ♗e2 ♗e7 20 ♗e3 ♗f6 21 ♖ad1 and White's advantage is small but definite) 18 ♗xf3 ♕c7 19 g3 ♗d7 20 ♘f2 b5 21 b3 ♖ae8 22 ♔g2 ♗e5 23 ♖b1 ♗d4 24 ♗d2 and White retained the usual nagging edge.

17 f3

White tries to destroy his opponent's centre. Anand also analysed 17 g3 f5 18 ♗f4 ♕b6 19 ♘e3 ♗f6 (not 19...g5?! 20 ♗e5 f4 21 gxf4 gxf4 22 ♔h1! and it is White who attacks along the g-file) 20 h4 ♕xb2 21 ♕xb2 ♗xb2 22 ♖a2 when White has some compensation but no definite advantage.

17...f5 18 ♘f2 ♗f6

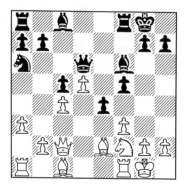

Black is more interested in the attack than mere pawns.

19 fxe4 ♗e5 20 h3 ♗d4 21 e5!?

Similarly, White would rather return the pawn than allow the f8-rook into the game.

21...♕xe5 22 ♔h1 ♗d7

Black's queen bishop settles for a modest square. 22...f4 gains the f5-square but only at the expense of surrendering g4: 23 ♘d3 ♗f5 24 ♗g4! (not 24 ♘xe5?! ♗xc2 25 ♗d3 ♗xd3 26 ♘xd3 g5 27 h4 h6 28 hxg5 hxg5 29 g3 b5, when White's centre collapses) 24...g5 25 ♗d2 and White retains the initiative.

23 ♘d3 ♗a4 24 ♕xa4 ♕xe2 25 ♖f3 ♖ae8

Again this is simple, sensible development. Black had a tricky try in 25...b5 26 cxb5 ♘b4!? 27 axb4 c4. The idea is to kick the knight and follow with ...♕e1+ and ...♗e5+, but White keeps control and a clear advan-

tage with the calm 28 ♕a3.

26 ♗f4

Now this simple move is enough to confirm a solid advantage.

26...h6 27 ♗d6!

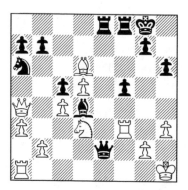

Not 27 ♖e1? ♕xe1+ 28 ♘xe1 ♖xe1+ 29 ♔h2 g5 and Black escapes with a draw.

27...♖f6 28 ♘f4 ♕e4 29 ♘e6 ♖exe6 30 dxe6 ♕xe6 31 ♗g3 ♗xb2 32 ♖e1 ♕f7 33 ♗h4 ♖e6 34 ♖xe6 ♕xe6 35 ♕c2 ♗d4 36 ♕xf5 ♕xc4 37 ♔h2 ♕e2

If Black tries 37...♕c1 White wins with 38 ♕d5+ ♔h7 39 ♕e4+ ♔g8 40 ♗e7!.

38 ♗g3!

Covering e5 from checks ensures the win.

38...♕d1 39 ♖f1 ♕b3 40 ♕e4 ♕b5

If 40...♗f6 then 41 ♖xf6! gxf6 42 ♕g6+ forces mate. For example, 42...♔h8 43 ♕xf6+ ♔h7 44 ♕f5+ and the bishop will soon join the attack with check.

41 ♕e6+ ♔h7 42 ♕f5+ ♔g8 43 ♕c8+ ♔h7 44 ♖f8 1-0

Game 4
Leko-Grischuk
Wijk aan Zee 2002

---

1 e4 e5 2 ♘f3 ♘f6 3 ♘xe5 d6 4 ♘f3 ♘xe4 5 d4 d5 6 ♗d3 ♘c6 7 0-0 ♗e7 8 c4 ♘b4 9 ♗e2 0-0 10 ♘c3 ♗e6 11 ♘e5 f6 12 ♘f3

This simple retreat causes Black the most problems.

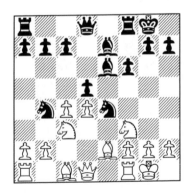

If 12 ♗g4, variation 'b' is the most accurate:

a) 12...♗c8 13 ♗xc8 ♖xc8 14 ♘f3 c6 (or 14...c5 15 ♕e2 cxd4 16 ♘xd4 ♖e8 17 ♗e3 ♗c5 18 ♖ad1 and White has an edge) 15 ♖e1 ♘xc3 16 bxc3 ♘a6 17 ♖b1 ♖c7 18 c5 ♖d7 19 ♗f4 and White was a bit better in Fressinet-Brodsky, Bucharest 2001.

b) 12...♗xg4 13 ♘xg4 f5 14 ♘e3 (14 a3 ♘c6 15 cxd5 ♘xc3 16 bxc3 ♕xd5 17 ♘e3 ♕f7 is unclear) 14...dxc4 15 ♘xc4 c5 16 ♕b3 ♔h8 17 ♘e5 ♕e8 (Black has the interesting alternative option of 17...cxd4!? 18 ♘xe4 fxe4 19 ♘f7+ ♖xf7 20 ♕xf7 ♕e8 with unbalanced play) 18 a3 ♘c6 19 ♘xc6 ♕xc6 20 ♘xe4 ♕xe4 (Minakov-Morgado, correspondence 1999) and here Morgado gives the equalising line 21 ♗d2 ♕xd4 22 ♕xb7 ♕xd2 23 ♕xe7 c4.

12...♔h8

Stepping away from any future trouble on the a2-g8 diagonal.

12...c5?! is premature: 13 ♗e3 ♖c8 14 dxc5 ♗xc5 15 ♗xc5 ♖xc5 16 ♕b3 a5 17 a3!? (17 ♖ad1 is less clear: 17...♕e7 18 ♘a4 ♗f7 19 ♕e3 ♖c7 20 a3 ♘a6 21 cxd5 ♘d6 22 ♕xe7 ♖xe7 23 ♗xa6 bxa6 is very messy but Black seems to have compensation, Khalifman-Karpov, Denpasar 2000) 17...♘xc3 (17...dxc4 allows White to play a very convincing queen 'sacrifice': 18 ♘xe4 cxb3 19 ♘xc5 ♗f7 20 axb4 axb4 21 ♗d1 and White has a healthy material advantage) 18 ♕xc3

♘c6 19 b4 axb4 20 axb4 d4 21 ♕b2 ♖xc4 22 ♗xc4 ♗xc4 23 ♖fd1 when Morgado claims a clear advantage for White.

A more worthwhile alternative is 12...♖e8. For example, 13 ♗e3 ♗f8 14 a3 ♘xc3 15 bxc3 ♘c6 16 cxd5 ♗xd5 17 c4 ♗f7 18 ♕c2 ♘a5 19 ♗d3 g6 20 ♗d2 (Morgado suggests White can gain an edge with 20 h4!? c5 21 dxc5 ♕c7 22 ♗d4 ♗xc5 23 ♗xf6 ♕f4 24 ♗g5 ♕g4 25 ♘h2 ♕e6 26 ♕c3 ♘xc4 27 ♖ae1 ♕d5 28 ♘g4) 20...c5 21 d5 (Timman assesses the variation 21 ♕a4 ♘c6 22 d5 ♘d4 23 ♘xd4 cxd4 24 ♗b4 b6! as equal) 21...b5 22 ♗xa5 ♕xa5 23 cxb5 ♗xd5 24 ♘d2 ♖ad8 25 ♖fd1 ♔g7 with a double-edged position, Adams-Timman, Wijk aan Zee 2001.

13 a3

White has various alternatives:

a) 13 cxd5 is too simple: 13...♘xc3 14 bxc3 ♘xd5 15 ♗d3 c5! (but not 15...♘xc3?? 16 ♕e1 with a winning double attack) 16 c4 ♘b4 17 d5 ♘xd3 18 ♕xd3 ♗d6! (of course taking on e6 would still lose the queen) 19 ♕b3 ♗g4 20 h3 ♗h5 21 a4 ½-½ Anand-Adams, Dortmund 2001.

b) 13 h3 is a bit too slow: 13...f5 14 a3 ♘c6 15 cxd5 (15 ♘xd5?! was tried in Ivanchuk-Ponomariov, FIDE World Championship, Moscow 2002, but after 15...♗xd5 16 cxd5 ♕xd5 17 ♕a4 ♗f6 18 ♖d1 ♖ad8 19 ♗e3 f4! 20 ♗xf4 ♘xd4 21 ♘xd4 ♗xd4 22 ♗e3 c5 Black was already a bit better) 15...♗xd5 16 ♗f4 ♘xc3 17 bxc3 ♗d6 Black has comfortable equality.

c) 13 ♖e1, however, is a reasonable alternative to 13 a3. 13...c5 14 ♗e3 f5 15 a3 f4 (Grischuk assesses 15...♘xc3 16 bxc3 ♘c6 17 cxd5 ♗xd5 18 dxc5 f4 19 ♗d4 as slightly better for White) 16 ♗d2 ♘c6 17 ♘xe4 dxe4 18 d5 ♗xd5! 19 cxd5 exf3 20 dxc6 fxe2 21 ♕xe2 bxc6 22 ♗xf4 and White's better structure gives him a small advantage, Grischuk-Motylev, FIDE World Championship, Moscow 2001.

13...♘xc3 14 bxc3 ♘c6

15 ♘d2

White must try to control c4. Instead 15 cxd5 ♗xd5 16 ♗e3 ♘a5 17 ♕a4 c6 18 ♕c2 ♘c4 gives Black easy equality.

15...f5

Making f6 available to the bishop. 15...♘a5!? is interesting but probably not quite good enough to equalise: 16 cxd5 ♗xd5 (or 16...♕xd5 17 ♗b2 ♕g5 18 c4 ♗d6 19 ♗c3 and White has the easier game) 17 c4 ♗f7 18 ♗b2 and now:

a) If 18...♗d6 White must be a bit careful. 19 ♕c2 (supporting c4 is essential; not 19 ♗d3?! ♗f4! 20 d5 c6 and White's centre collapses disastrously) 19...♗g6 20 ♗d3 ♗xd3 21 ♕xd3 and White has an edge (Belov).

b) 18...f5 19 ♗c3 c5 20 d5 ♗f6 21 ♕c2 b6 22 ♗d3 ♗xc3 23 ♕xc3 ♘b7 24 ♘f3 ♘d6 25 ♘e5 and the protected passed pawn makes White's position preferable, Kasimdzhanov-Adams, FIDE World Championship, Tripoli 2004.

16 ♖e1 ♗f6 17 a4

Trying to gain space on the queenside. 17 ♘b3 has also been tried: 17...b6 (an intriguing alternative is 17...dxc4 18 ♘c5 ♗c8 19 ♗xc4 ♘xd4!? 20 cxd4 ♕xd4 21 ♕xd4 ♗xd4 22 ♗e3 ♗xa1 23 ♖xa1 with equality) 18 ♗f3 ♗g8 19 cxd5 ♗xd5 20 ♗f4 ♖c8 (or 20...♘e7 21 ♗e5 c6 22 ♗xf6 ♖xf6 23 ♘c1 ♘g6 24 ♘d3 h6 – Leko-Kramnik, Dortmund 2000 – and now Galkin suggests that White gains an edge with 25 ♘b4 ♗xf3 26 ♕xf3) 21 ♗e5

♕d7 22 ♗xf6 ♖xf6 23 ♘c1 ♖e6 24 ♖xe6 ♕xe6 25 ♘d3 ♖e8 26 h3. Here the game is level and a draw was agreed in Galkin-Motylev, Dubai 2001.

17...♗g8 18 c5 ♖e8 19 ♘f3 h6?!

This is unnecessary. The direct 19...b6!? 20 cxb6 axb6 21 ♗b5 ♖xe1+ 22 ♕xe1 ♘a5 is equal.

20 ♖b1 ♖b8 21 ♗d3 ♖xe1+ 22 ♕xe1 ♕d7 23 ♗f4 ♖e8?

This overlooks a nasty trick. 23...♗h7 24 ♗b5 ♖e8 25 ♕d1 restricts White to an edge.

24 ♕d2 g5

This desperate lunge is forced. If 24...b6? then 25 cxb6 axb6 26 ♗xh6! wins immediately.

25 ♖xb7!

Crucially, this undermines the c6-knight.

25...♖c8

If 25...gxf4 White wins with 26 ♕xf4 ♗g5 (or 26...♗d8 27 ♕xh6+ ♗h7 28 ♗b5) 27 ♕xc7 ♕xc7 28 ♖xc7 (Leko).

26 h4?

This is a clever idea but there was an instant win with 26 ♗b5! gxf4 27 ♖xa7 as Black cannot escape the pin.

26...gxf4 27 ♕xf4 ♗g7 28 ♕xf5 ♕d8?

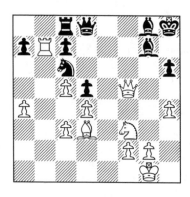

Now White is winning again. After 28...♕e8 29 ♕f4 ♕e7 30 ♗b5 ♕e6 31 ♗xc6 ♕xc6 32 ♖xa7 White has only a small advantage.

29 ♘g5!! hxg5 30 hxg5 ♕f8

This is the only move to save the king.

31 ♕h3+ ♗h6 32 ♗f5

The simple 32 gxh6 ♖e8 33 ♖xc7 ♖e1+ 34 ♗f1 ♘e7 35 ♖xa7 is also winning.

32...♖e8 33 ♖xc7 ♖e1+ 34 ♔h2 ♘e7 35 g4! ♗e6

Leko supplies the neat winning variation 35...♖e6 36 ♔g2 ♖a6 37 c6!? ♖xc6 38 ♖xc6 ♘xc6 39 ♕xh6+ ♕xh6 40 gxh6.

36 ♕xh6+ ♕xh6+ 37 gxh6 ♘xf5 38 gxf5 ♗xf5 39 ♖f7

White's pawns win easily.

39...♗g6 40 ♖xa7 ♖c1 41 ♔g3 ♖xc3+ 42 ♔f4 ♗h5 43 ♔e5 ♖f3 44 c6 ♗g4 45 a5 ♖xf2 46 a6 ♖c2 47 ♖c7 1-0

Game 5
Shirov-Gelfand
Leon 2001

---

1 e4 e5 2 ♘f3 ♘f6 3 ♘xe5 d6 4 ♘f3 ♘xe4 5 d4 d5 6 ♗d3 ♗e7 7 0-0 ♘c6 8 c4 ♘b4 9 ♗e2 0-0 10 ♘c3 ♗e6 11 ♗e3 ♗f5

11...f5 is a good alternative. For example, 12 a3 ♘xc3 13 bxc3 ♘c6

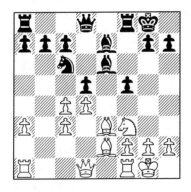

and now:

a) 14 cxd5 ♗xd5 15 c4 ♗xf3 16 ♗xf3 f4 17 ♗d5+ ♔h8 18 ♗c1 ♘xd4! 19 ♖b1 (19 ♗b2 does not alter the assessment: 19...c5 20 ♗xd4 cxd4 21 ♗xb7 ♖b8 22 ♗d5 ♗c5 is equal) 19...♗c5 20 ♖xb7 f3! 21 ♗xf3 ♘xf3+ 22 gxf3 ½-½ Hübner-Yusupov, Rotterdam 1988.

b) 14 ♕a4 has also been tried but Black has no real problems: 14...f4 15 ♗d2 ♔h8 16 ♖ab1 ♖b8 17 ♖fe1 dxc4 18 ♗xc4 ♗g4 19 ♗e2 a6 20 h3 ♗h5 21 ♘g5?! (now the tactics work out in Black's favour; White should have settled for 21 ♘h2 ♗xe2 22 ♖xe2 ♕d5 with equality) 21...♗xe2 (21...♗xg5?! is not the answer: 22 ♗xh5 f3?! 23 ♗xg5 ♕xg5 24 ♗xf3! ♖xf3 25 ♕xc6! ♖xf2 26 ♖e8+ ♖f8 27 ♖xb8 ♕e3+ 28 ♔h1 ♖xb8 29 ♕xc7 and White should win this ending) 22 ♘e6 ♕d5 23 ♖xe2 (if 23 ♘xf8 f3 Black is already much better because 24 gxf3 ♗xf3 25 ♘e6 ♕f5 gives a winning attack) 23...f3 24 ♖ee1 fxg2! and Black was clearly better in Rohde-Seirawan, Estes Park 1986.

12 ♕b3

Increasing the central pressure. 12 ♖c1 is the subject of Game 6, while a worthwhile option is 12 ♘e5. For example, 12...♗f6 (Short assesses 12...♘xc3 13 bxc3 ♘c2 14 ♖c1 ♘xe3 15 fxe3 ♗e4 as unclear) 13 g4 ♗e6 14 f4 ♘xc3 15 bxc3 ♘c6 16 ♗f3 ♗xe5 17 dxe5 d4 (White has the initiative after 17...dxc4 18 f5 ♗c8 19 ♗c5 ♕xd1 20 ♖axd1 ♖e8 21 ♖fe1) 18 cxd4 ♗xc4 19 d5 ♘e7 20 ♗c5 ♗xf1 21 ♔xf1 ♕d7 22 ♕b3 and White's bishops and impressive centre provide adequate compensation, Short-Anand, Amsterdam 1993.

12...c6

Choosing to bolster the centre but 12...dxc4 is also acceptable: 13 ♗xc4 a5 14 ♘xe4 (14 a3 can lead to a neat draw by repetition after 14...♘d2! 15 ♗xd2 ♗c2 16 ♗xf7+ ♖xf7 17 ♕e6 ♗f5 18 ♕b3 ♗c2 19 ♕e6) 14...♗xe4 15 a3 a4 16 ♕d1 ♘c2 17 ♖c1 ♘xe3 18 fxe3 ♗d6 19 ♗b5 ♕f6 20 ♖c3 ♕h6 is unclear, Barua-Manesh, Raipur 2002.

13 cxd5

White has various alternatives:

a) 13 c5 ♘xc3 14 bxc3 ♘c2 15 ♕xb7 ♘xa1 16 ♖xa1 ♕e8 17 ♕a6 f6 18 ♘e1 ♕c8 (Kramnik states that White has compensation after 18...♕d7 19 ♘d3 ♗xd3 20 ♗xd3) 19 ♕xc8 ♗xc8 20 ♗f4 ♗d8 21 ♘c2 ♖e8 22

♗d3 a5 is unclear, Topalov-Kramnik, Tilburg 1998.

b) 13 ♘e5 a5 14 g4 ♗e6 15 ♘xe4 dxe4 16 a3 f6 17 axb4 fxe5 18 d5 cxd5 19 cxd5 ♗xd5 20 ♗c4 ♗xc4 21 ♕xc4+ ♔h8 22 bxa5 ♖xa5 23 ♕xe4 ♖b5 and the simplifications have led to equality, Topalov-Shirov, FIDE World Championship 2001.

c) The wild option is 13 g4!? ♗xg4 14 c5 (the point of 13 g4!? is that Black no longer has the resource ...♘xc3, bxc3, ...♘c2) 14...a5 15 a3 ♘a6 16 ♕xb7 ♘xc3 17 bxc3 ♘c7 18 ♖ab1 ♘b5 with an unbalanced position, Topalov-Shirov, FIDE World Championship 2001.

13...♘xc3

13...cxd5 14 ♖ac1 a5 15 ♘a4 ♖b8 16 ♘c5 ♗d6 17 ♖fd1 (Shirov-Topalov, FIDE World Championship 2001) is a safe equalising line. Now the simplest for Black is 17...♖e8 18 ♗b5 ♖e7.

14 bxc3 ♘xd5

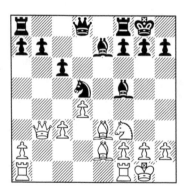

15 ♕xb7

White can play safe with 15 c4 ♘xe3 16 fxe3 ♕c7 17 ♗d3 ♗xd3 18 ♕xd3 ♖fe8 with an equal game.

15...♘xc3 16 ♗c4 ♖b8

If 16...♗e4? then 17 ♘e5 ♖b8 18 ♕xa7 ♖a8 19 ♕b7 ♖b8 20 ♕d7 and White's queen escapes with a clear extra pawn.

17 ♕xc6 ♗e4 18 ♗xf7+ ♖xf7 19 ♕xc3 ♗b4

Black also has compensation after

19...♗xf3!? 20 gxf3 ♗d6 21 ♕c6 ♖b6 22 ♕e4 ♕b8.

20 ♕c4 ♗d5 21 ♕d3 ♖xf3!? 22 gxf3 ♕d7 23 ♖fb1

Gelfand mentioned 23 ♗f4!? ♖f8 24 ♗g3 ♖xf3 25 ♕e2 with a murky position.

23...♕h3 24 ♗f4 ♖f8 25 ♖xb4

Or 25 ♗g3 a5 26 a3 ♖xf3 27 ♕f1 ♕h6! 28 ♕e2 (28 axb4 allows a clear draw after 28...♖xg3+! 29 fxg3 ♕e3+ 30 ♕f2 ♕e4 and White can only avoid the mate by allowing a perpetual check) 28...♕h5 29 ♖b2 ♗f8 and Black still has dangerous play – Gelfand.

25...♖xf4 26 ♖b8+ ♔f7

With 27...♖g4+ threatened White seems to be lost. However...

27 ♖b7+!

Now if Black takes the rook, ♕b3+ wins the bishop.

27...♔g8 28 ♖b8+ ½-½

Game 6
Kotronias-Motylev
Moscow 2004

1 e4 e5 2 ♘f3 ♘f6 3 ♘xe5 d6 4 ♘f3 ♘xe4 5 d4 d5 6 ♗d3 ♘c6 7 0-0 ♗e7 8 c4 ♘b4 9 ♗e2 ♗e6

10 ♘c3

Now this game simply transposes to the main line. However, the move order with 9...♗e6 gives White interesting additional options:

a) 10 ♕a4+ is tempting but Black can defend: 10...♕d7 11 ♕xd7+ ♔xd7 12 ♘c3 ♖hd8! (this is the way to equalise: after 12...♘xc3 13 ♘e5+ ♔e8 14 bxc3 ♘c6 15 cxd5 ♗xd5 16 ♗c4 Shirov claims an edge for White) 13 a3 ♘xc3 14 ♘e5+ ♔e8 15 bxc3 ♘c6 16 ♘xc6 bxc6 17 cxd5 ♗xd5 18 ♖e1 ♔f8 19 ♗f4 ♗d6 20 ♗xd6+ cxd6 21 ♗d3 g6 22 f3 ♖db8 23 ♖eb1 ♔e7 and in this dead level position a draw was agreed, Rausis-Bacrot, France 2003.

b) After 10 c5!? Black must defend against ideas with ♕b3.

b1) The natural 10...0-0?! runs straight into trouble after 11 ♕b3! a5 12 a3 ♘a6 13 ♕xb7. The attempt to trap the queen with 13...♘axc5 14 dxc5 ♘xc5 15 ♕c6 ♖b8 is met by 16 ♗g5!. White already has a pleasant advantage, but 16...f6?! just makes things worse: 17 ♗f4 ♗d6 18 ♘d4 ♗f7 19 b4 axb4 20 axb4 ♖xb4 21 ♗xd6 cxd6 22 ♘b5 and White is winning (Nataf).

b2) 10...a5 defends the knight but White keeps the initiative: 11 ♘e5 f6 12 ♘d3 0-0 13 ♘f4 ♗f7 14 ♗g4! g6 15 ♘e6 ♗xe6 16 ♗xe6+ ♔g7 17 a3 ♘c6 18 ♘c3 ♖e8 (Nataf points out the clever trick 18...♘a6? 19 ♘xd5! ♘xd4 20 ♕xd4 ♖xe6 21 ♘f4! ♖e5 22 ♕xe5!) 19 ♘xd5 ♗xc5 20 dxc5 ♖xe6 21 ♗f4 ♘e5 22 ♖c1 with an edge, Nataf-Topalov, Cannes 2002.

b3) 10...♘c6 11 ♗b5 ♗f6 (fighting for control of the key e5-square; 11...0-0 allows White to seize the initiative in simple fashion with 12 ♗xc6 bxc6 13 ♘e5 ♗d7 14 f3 ♘g5 15 ♘c3) 12 ♗xc6+ (after 12 ♗f4!? 0-0 13 ♗xc6 bxc6 14 ♘e5 ♕b8 15 ♕c1 ♗xe5 16 ♗xe5 f6 17 ♗f4 White was a bit better in Adams-Bacrot, Cap d'Agde [rapid] 2003) 12...bxc6 13 ♕a4 ♗d7 14 ♗f4 0-0 15 ♘c3 (trying to grab the c7-pawn with 15 ♕a5 allows Black counterplay: 15...♕b8 16 b3 ♖e8! 17 ♘e5 – if 17 ♗xc7 ♕b7 18 ♗e5 ♗d8 19 ♕a3 ♕b5 White's awkward development gives Black enough compensation – 17...♕b7 18 f3 ♘g5 19 ♗xg5 ♗xg5 20 f4 ♗f6 21 ♘c3

♖e7 and the position is finely balanced) 15...♖b8 16 ♕xa7 (defending the b-pawn with 16 ♖ab1 has other drawbacks: 16...♗f5 17 ♖bc1 g5!? 18 ♗g3 g4 19 ♘e5 ♖xb2 20 ♘xe4 ♗xe4 21 ♘xg4 ♗g7 with an unclear game) 16...♖xb2 17 ♘a4 (or 17 ♘xe4 dxe4 18 ♕a3 ♖e2 19 ♘e5 ♗xe5 20 ♗xe5 f6 21 ♗f4 ♗g4 with a messy position) 17...♖b4 18 a3 (White must be careful with his a4-knight; instead 18 ♖ab1!? ♕b8! 19 ♕xb8 ♖fxb8 and White was losing in Al-Modiahki-Iordachescu, Dubai 2004) 18...♗c4 19 ♘b2 ♖xd4 20 ♗e3 ♖c4 21 ♘xc4 ♗xa1 22 ♖xa1 dxc4 with an 'unclear' verdict from Iordachescu.

10...0-0 11 ♗e3 ♗f5 12 ♖c1 dxc4 13 ♗xc4

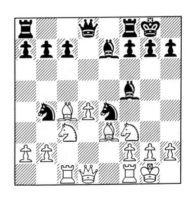

13...c6

Preparing a retreat to d5 for the b4-knight. White can achieve an edge after 13...♘xc3: 14 bxc3 ♘c6 15 ♗d3 ♗xd3 16 ♕xd3 ♕d7 17 ♖b1 (instead 17 c4 ♗f6 18 ♖fd1 ♖fe8 19 ♕b1 b6 20 h3 ♘e7 was only equal in G.Kuzmin-Huzman, Rethymnon 2003) 17...b6 18 ♖fe1 ♖fe8 19 ♗f4.

14 ♘e5 ♘xc3 15 bxc3 ♘d5 16 ♕f3

Also interesting is 16 ♕b3 f6 17 ♘f3 b5 (Ivanchuk suggests that 17...♕d7!? leads to an unclear position after 18 ♖fe1 ♔h8 19 ♗d2 ♗d6 20 ♗f1 ♘f4) 18 ♗e2 ♔h8 19 ♗d2 ♘b6 20 ♖fe1 ♕d7 21 c4 bxc4 22 ♗xc4 ♘xc4 23 ♕xc4 ♖fc8 24 ♘h4 ♗f8 and White has a very faint edge, Kir.Georgiev-Ivanchuk,

Debrecen 1992.

16...♗e6 17 ♗d2

The other way to play is 17 ♗d3 when Black has three main replies:

b) 17...♗f6 18 ♗d2 ♕d6 19 ♖fe1 ♖ad8 20 c4!? is Nijboer's suggestion (20 h4 c5 21 h5 cxd4 22 cxd4 ♘e7 23 h6 ♘g6 24 hxg7 ♗xg7 led to a messy position in Nijboer-Fressinet, Leon 2001). After 20...♘e7 21 ♗a5 ♖c8 22 ♗c3 ♘g6 White's space advantage makes his position preferable.

b) 17...♘xe3 18 fxe3 ♗d6 19 ♘c4 ♗c7 20 e4 f6 is unclear – Black's bishop pair compensates for White's centre.

c) 17...♗d6 18 ♗d2 ♕h4 19 ♖fe1 ♘f6 20 a4 ♘g4 21 ♗f4 ♗d5 22 ♗g3 ♘xe5 23 dxe5 ♕h6 (Hübner pointed out the blunder 23...♕xa4? 24 ♗xh7+! ♔xh7 25 ♕h5+ ♔g8 26 exd6) 24 ♗e4 ♗xe4 25 ♕xe4 ♗c7 is equal, Klimov-Smikovski, Toljatti 2003.

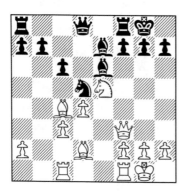

17...f6

Less accurate is 17...♗g5 18 ♗xg5 ♕xg5 19 ♖fe1 ♖ae8 20 g3 ♕f5 21 ♕d1 ♘b6 (White has a promising initiative after 21...♖e7 22 ♗d3 ♕f6 23 c4 ♘b6 24 ♖e4 – Topalov) 22 ♗d3 ♕f6 23 ♕c2 g6 24 ♖b1 ♗c8 25 ♖e2 ♖e7 26 ♖be1 and White had some pressure in Topalov-Akopian, Linares 1995.

18 ♘g4

Or 18 ♘d3 ♕d7 19 ♖fe1 ♗d6 20 h3 ♗f7 21 ♗b3 ♖ae8 22 ♕g4 ♖xe1+ 23 ♖xe1 ♖d8 24 ♕xd7 ♖xd7 25 ♘e5 ♗xe5 26 dxe5 fxe5

27 ♖xe5 ♘f6 and despite White's creative efforts the position was still level in Topalov-Ivanchuk, Novgorod 1996.

18...♕d7 19 h3 ♘f4

Exploiting the loose bishop on c4. Black could also play the simple 19...b5 20 ♗d3 ♖fe8 21 ♖fe1 ♗d6 22 ♘e3 ♘xe3 23 ♗xe3 ♗d5 24 ♕e2 ♕f7 with equality.

20 ♗b3

White ambitiously keeps the tension. The quiet 20 ♗xe6+ ♘xe6 21 ♘e3 ♖fe8 22 ♘f5 ♗f8 is level.

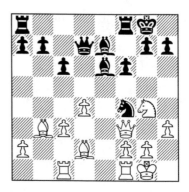

20...♗xb3 21 axb3 ♘g6 22 ♖fe1 ♗d6 23 ♘e3 ♖ae8 24 ♘f5 ♘e7

A sharp try is 24...♗f4!? 25 ♕g4 ♗xd2 26 ♘h6+ gxh6 27 ♕xd7 ♗xe1 28 ♕xb7 ♖e2 with an interesting and unbalanced position.

25 ♘xd6 ♕xd6 26 c4 ♘g6

The greedy 26...♕xd4?! allows a deadly pin: 27 ♗b4 ♖f7 28 ♖e6.

27 ♕f5 ♕xd4 28 ♗b4 ♘h4

Black has to play creatively to survive. If 28...♖xe1+ 29 ♖xe1 ♖d8 30 ♕e6+ ♔h8 31 ♕e8+ ♘f8 32 ♕f7 Black's weak back rank costs him the game.

29 ♕h5 g6 30 ♕a5

Motylev points out that 30 ♕c5 ♕xc5 31 ♗xc5 ♖xe1+ 32 ♖xe1 ♖d8 33 ♗xa7 ♔f7 is equal.

30...♖e5!

Once again 30...♖xe1+ leads to back rank problems: 31 ♖xe1 ♖f7 32 ♗c5 ♕b2 33 ♕d8+ ♔g7 34 ♔h2 (one clever preparatory move is required; instead 34 ♖e8?! allows Black to escape with a draw with 34...♕c1+ 35 ♔h2 ♘f3+! 36 gxf3 ♕f4+ – the king must go to h1 and allow a perpetual because moving to the g-file allows ...♕g5+ and ♕xc5) 34...♘f5 35 ♖e8 and White has a dangerous attack (Motylev).

31 ♖cd1!

Now White has to be careful. If 31 ♖xe5?! fxe5 32 ♗xf8 ♕e4 33 ♔f1 ♕xg2+ 34 ♔e2 ♕e4+ 35 ♔d2 ♘f3+ 36 ♔c3 ♕d4+ 37 ♔b4 ♔xf8 Black's position is preferable: two pawns and White's exposed king provide more than enough compensation for the exchange.

31...♕xd1 32 ♕xe5 fxe5

After 32...♕xb3 Black's exposed king allows White to draw with 33 ♕d6 ♖f7 34 ♖e8+ ♔g7 35 ♖e7 g5 36 ♖xf7+ ♔xf7 37 ♕e7+ ♔g6 38 ♕e4+.

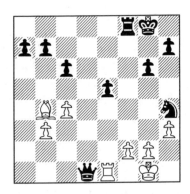

33 ♖xd1 ♖f7 34 ♖d8+ ♔g7 35 ♗d6 e4?!

This allows White's bishop too much scope. Instead 35...♔f6 36 ♖e8 ♖d7 37 ♗xe5+ ♔f7 is equal.

36 ♗c5

Now White has a tiny edge.

36...b6 37 ♗d4+ ♔h6 38 ♗e3+ ♔g7 39 ♗g5 ♘f5 40 g4 ♘h6

40...h6? is a horrible blunder: after 41 ♗c1 Black must lose a piece to avoid mate. 40...♘e7 is reasonable but White still has a pull after 41 b4 c5 42 ♖e8 ♘c6 43 bxc5 bxc5 44 ♖xe4.

41 b4 ♖f3 42 ♖d7+ ♘f7 43 ♗e3 ♖xh3 44 ♖xa7 ♔f6 45 ♗xb6

After the alternative 45 ♖a6 ♘e5 46 ♖xb6 ♔e6 47 b5 ♖h4 48 g5 ♔f5 49 bxc6 ♘f3+ Black's counterplay arrives just in time to save the draw.

45...♘e5 46 ♗d8+ ♔e6 47 ♔g2 ♖b3 48 ♖e7+ ♔d6 49 ♖xh7 ♘xc4 50 ♗g5 ♘e5 51 ♖g7 ♔d5 52 ♗f4 ♘xg4 53 ♖xg6 ♘xf2 54 ♖d6+ ♔c4 55 ♔xf2 ♖f3+ 56 ♔e2 ♖xf4 57 ♔e3 ♖h4 58 ♖xc6+ ♔xb4 59 ♖e6 ♔c4 60 ♖xe4+ ♖xe4+ 61 ♔xe4 ½-½

> ### Game 7
> ## Kasparov-Anand
> *Linares 2000*

---

1 e4 e5 2 ♘f3 ♘f6 3 ♘xe5 d6 4 ♘f3 ♘xe4 5 d4 d5 6 ♗d3 ♘c6 7 0-0 ♗e7 8 c4 ♘b4 9 ♗e2 0-0 10 ♘c3 b6

11 a3

11 cxd5 allows the interesting line 11...♗f5!? 12 ♕b3 a5 with unclear play.

11 ♘e5 is certainly direct but Black can defend: 11...♗b7 12 ♖e1 (12 a3 was tried in Shirov-Anand, Linares 2000, but led only to a draw after 12...♘xc3 13 bxc3 ♘c6 14 ♗f3 ♘a5 15 c5 c6 16 ♖e1 ♗f6 17 ♘g4 ♗c8 18 cxb6 axb6 19 a4 ♘c4 20 ♘xf6+ ♕xf6 21 ♗a3 ♘xa3 22 ♖xa3 ♗e6 23 ♕b3) and now:

a) 12...dxc4 13 ♗xc4 ♘xc3 14 bxc3 ♘d5 15 ♕f3 c6 (Hracek-Yusupov, Bundesliga

2000). Here Hracek suggests that 16 ♗d3 is worth an edge, the point being 16...♘xc3?! 17 ♘xf7! ♕d5 18 ♖xe7 ♕xf3 19 ♘h6+ gxh6 20 ♗xh7+ ♔h8 21 gxf3 ♗a6 22 ♗xh6 when White is clearly better.

b) 12...c5!? (the aggressive approach is best) 13 ♗f3 cxd4 14 ♘xd5 f5 15 ♘xe7+ ♕xe7 16 a3 ♘c2!? 17 ♘g6!? hxg6 18 ♕xc2 ♕h4 and after some very sharp play the position remains unclear.

11...♘xc3 12 bxc3 ♘c6 13 cxd5 ♕xd5 14 ♖e1

The simple 14 ♗f4 is only level after 14...♗d6 15 ♗xd6 cxd6 16 c4 ♕a5.

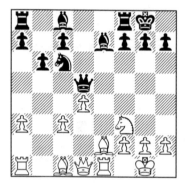

14...♗b7 15 ♗d3 ♖ae8 16 c4

It is wisest to hit the queen now. If 16 ♕c2 Black has two reasonable replies:

a) 16...h6 17 ♗h7+ ♔h8 18 ♗e4 (Kasparov-Kramnik, Linares 2000) and here Kasparov analysed the equalising line 18...♕h5 19 ♘e5 ♗d6 20 ♗f3 ♕h4 21 ♘xf7+ ♔g8 22 ♘xh6+ ♔h8.

b) The dangerous 16...♕h5!? is a good reason to avoid 16 ♕c2 here: 17 ♖b1 ♘xd4! (Black targets the h2 square) 18 cxd4 (White must avoid the back rank trick 18 ♘xd4? ♗d6) 18...♗xf3 19 gxf3 ♗d6 and Black has a threatening attack (Rogers).

16...♕d8

If Black again tries 16...♕h5 then White is better placed to meet the threats to h2: 17 d5 ♗d6!? 18 dxc6 ♖xe1+ 19 ♕xe1 ♗xc6 20 ♗e2! ♗xf3 21 ♗xf3 ♕xh2+ 22 ♔f1 ♕h1+

23 ♔e2 ♕h4 24 g4 h5 25 ♗e3 hxg4 26 ♗d5 (Kasparov) when White escapes the attack and has a good advantage.

17 d5 ♘b8

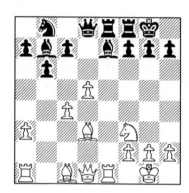

18 ♕c2

Possibly this commits the queen too early. Instead 18 ♘e5!? may be the best choice, Kasparov-H.Olafsson, Kopavogur (rapid) 2000 continuing 18...♗f6 19 ♗b2 g6 (or 19...c6 20 d6 g6 21 c5 and White's pawns are very strong) 20 ♕d2 ♘d7 21 ♘xd7 ♗xb2 22 ♘xf8 ♗xa1 23 ♘xg6 ♖xe1+ 24 ♕xe1 hxg6 25 ♕xa1 c6 26 dxc6 ♗xc6 27 ♕c3 and Kasparov was clearly better. After 18...♗d6 19 ♗b2 ♕f6 20 ♖e3 White is building a strong attack, the tactical justification being 20...♖xe5?! 21 ♗xe5 ♗xe5 22 ♕h5 ♖e8 23 ♖ae1 g5 24 h4 when White is already close to victory.

18...g6 19 ♘e5 ♗f6 20 ♗b2 ♘d7 21 f4

If 21 ♘g4 then 21...♗xb2 22 ♕xb2 h5 23 ♘e3 ♘c5 24 ♗c2 c6 is just unclear.

21...♗g7 22 ♕f2 ♘c5

This is fine but 22...c6!? 23 d6 ♘c5 24 ♖ad1 ♖e6 with a hard fight ahead was also reasonable.

23 ♗c2 ♕d6 24 ♖e3 f6 25 ♘g4 ♖xe3 26 ♕xe3 ♗c8 27 f5 ♗xf5 28 ♗xf5 gxf5 29 ♘f2

The alternative 29 ♘h6+ also leads to equality after 29...♗xh6 30 ♕xh6 ♘e4.

29...♘e4 30 ♘xe4 ½-½

Here the players agreed a draw. Kasparov

gives the variation 30...fxe4 31 ♕e4 f5 31 ♕c2 ♕c5+ 33 ♔h1 ♗xb2 34 ♕xb2 ♕xc4 35 ♕e5.

Game 8
Grischuk-Pavasovic
Istanbul 2003

---

1 e4 e5 2 ♘f3 ♘f6 3 ♘xe5 d6 4 ♘f3 ♘xe4 5 d4 d5 6 ♗d3 ♘c6 7 0-0 ♗e7 8 c4 ♘b4 9 ♗e2 dxc4

Immediately clarifying the situation in the centre to give White an IQP.

10 ♗xc4 0-0 11 ♘c3

Also possible is the straightforward 11 ♘e5. For example, 11...c6 12 ♘c3 ♘xc3 13 bxc3 ♘d5 14 ♕b3 (14 ♕d3 ♗d6 15 ♗b3 ♕f6 16 ♕g3 ♗e6 is also murky) 14...♕c7 15 ♗xd5 cxd5 16 ♗f4 (Sax-Pavasovic, Baden 1999). Now 16...♕a5 17 ♖fe1 ♗f6 leads to unclear play.

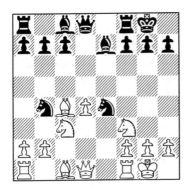

11...♘xc3

Exchanging is natural but retreating is also possible:

a) 11...♘f6 is rather passive. After 12 ♘e5 c6 13 ♗g5 ♘fd5 14 ♗xe7 ♕xe7 15 ♖e1 ♗e6 16 ♗xd5 ♘xd5 17 ♘xd5 cxd5 18 ♕b3 White's superior minor piece is enough for an edge.

b) More active is 11...♘d6 12 ♗b3 ♗f6 and now:

b1) 13 h3 (simply preventing ...♗g4) 13...♗f5 14 ♗e3 ♖e8 15 a3 ♘d3 (15...♘c6!?

is also fine: after 16 d5 ♘e5 17 ♘xe5 ♗xe5 Black has strong, active piece play) 16 ♖b1 c5 17 dxc5 ♘e4 (the tricky 17...♘xb2?! backfires after 18 ♖xb2 ♗xc3 19 cxd6 ♗xb2 20 ♗xf7+! ♔xf7 21 ♕d5+ ♔f8 22 ♕xf5+ ♕f6 23 ♕xh7 when White is clearly better) 18 ♗c2! ♘xb2 (after 18...♘g3?! 19 fxg3 ♖xe3 Black appears to be very active but a few accurate moves from White defuse the danger: 20 ♕d2 ♗d4 21 ♘xd4 ♕xd4 22 ♔h2 ♗g6 23 ♘d5! ♖e5 24 ♘f4 ♕e3 25 ♕xe3 ♖xe3 26 ♗xd3 ♖xd3 27 ♖be1 and White is simply a pawn up) 19 ♕xd8 ♖axd8 20 ♖xb2 ♗xc3 21 ♖xb7 ♘xc5 22 ♗xc5 ♗xc2 and White still holds a slight advantage, Karpov-Kasparov, World Championship (Game 41), Moscow 1984.

b2) Direct action with 13 ♘e5 is also possible: 13...♘c6 (not 13...♘f5? 14 ♘xf7! ♖xf7 15 ♗xf7+ ♔xf7 16 ♕b3+, a fairly common tactical theme in this line) 14 ♗f4 ♘f5 (Black should prefer 14...♘a5!? 15 ♗c2 ♗f5 with unclear play) 15 ♘xc6 bxc6 16 d5 c5 17 ♘a4 ♗a6 18 ♖e1 (A.Sokolov-Agzamov, Riga 1985). Now Black should try 18...c4 19 ♗c2 ♘d6 20 ♘c5 ♗c8 21 ♗e5, but White still has the initiative.

12 bxc3 ♘d5

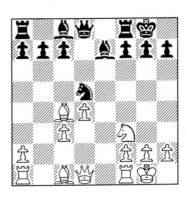

13 ♕c2

13 ♕b3 only wastes time. After 13...♘b6 14 ♗d3 c5 15 ♕c2 h6 Black has equalised comfortably.

13...♗e6

It is best to develop this bishop immediately. Delaying with 13...c6 14 &d3 h6 15 &b1 &e8 16 &e5 would make it difficult for Black to complete his development.

14 &d3 h6 15 &b1 b6 16 &h7+ &h8 17 &e4 &c8

Black steps out of the pin rather than blocking it with 17...c6. After 18 &e5 &d6 19 &d2 &ac8 20 c4 &f6 21 &f5 White keeps a nagging initiative.

18 c4 &f6

Black could have exploited the c-file lineup with 18...c6!?. After 19 &e1 &d6 the position is complex.

19 &b7 &b8 20 &c6 &d6 21 &d1

Advancing with 21 c5 does not achieve any clear after 21...&e7 22 &e1 bxc5 23 &xb8 &xb8 24 dxc5 &b4 25 &e3.

21...&c8 22 &b3 &f5 23 &b2 &d7 24 &e5 &xc6 25 &xc6 &g4!

This excellent move is forced. If 25...&a8?! then 26 &xh6! gxh6 27 d5 opens the long diagonal with decisive effect.

26 &f3

Playing to win material with 26 f3 leads only to a messy position after 26...&h5 27 g4 &xg4 28 &xb8 &xb8 29 c5 &xh2+ 30 &g2 &h4 31 fxg4 &xg4+ 32 &xh2 &xd1.

26...&be8 27 &xa7!?

This pawn may seem poisoned, but White has seen deeply into the position. Also interesting is 27 &xh6!? &e4 28 &e5 &xe5 29 dxe5 &g4 30 &f4 with an unclear position.

27...&h5 28 h3 &a5

Threatening mate on e1 as well as the knight, but there is a solution.

29 &d2! &xa7 30 &xf6

This sacrifice is enough for a draw.

30...gxf6 31 &xh6+ &g8 32 &h4 &a5 ½-½

Black cannot escape the checks.

Game 9
Anand-I.Sokolov
Dortmund 1999

1 e4 e5 2 &f3 &f6 3 &xe5 d6 4 &f3 &xe4 5 d4 d5 6 &d3 &c6 7 0-0 &e7 8 c4 &b4 9 cxd5 &xd5 10 &d3 &xd5

This is much more reliable than 10...&f6, which gives White the useful option of 11 &b5+ and now:

a) 11...&d7?! 12 &b3 and Black cannot regain the pawn. Timman-Kovacevic, Zagreb 1985 continued 12...0-0 13 &c3 b5 14 &g5 b4 (now Black's kingside is shattered but even if 14...&b8 15 &fe1 b4 16 &xf6 &xf6 17 &e4 &e7 18 &c5 his position is very unpleasant) 15 &xf6 gxf6 16 &e4 &h8 17 &fe1 a5 18 &ac1 &b5?! (it was already bad but now Black is lost) 19 &h4 &g8 20 d6! &xd6 21 &xf7 &f4 22 &c5 &g7 23 &xf6 &xf6 24 &xf6 and Black could resign.

b) Black should play 11...&d7 but White still has an edge after 12 &xd7+ &xd7 13 &c3 0-0-0 14 &e1 &de8 15 &e5 &b4 16

♗d2 ♖hf8 17 ♖ac1.

11 ♖e1 ♗f5

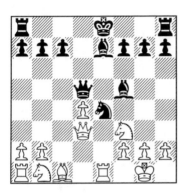

12 g4

This prevents Black from blocking the e-file with a later ...♗e6, but the weakening of White's kingside is obvious.

The solid option is 12 ♘c3 ♘xc3 13 ♕xc3 and now:

a) The natural 13...c6?! allows a beautiful tactic: 14 ♗h6! ♗e4 (the point is 14...gxh6 15 ♖e5 ♕d7 16 ♖ae1 ♗e6 17 d5! cxd5 18 ♖xe6 fxe6 19 ♕xh8+ ♗f8 20 ♕f6 and White wins) 15 ♗xg7 ♖g8 16 ♖xe4 ♕xe4 17 ♖e1 ♕xe1+ 18 ♘xe1 ♖xg7 19 d5 and White is much better.

b) After 13...♗e6 Black will be able to castle without any great difficulty:

b1) 14 ♖e5 looks aggressive but Black has two acceptable replies.

b11) 14...♕c4?? is an ugly blunder: 15 ♕xc4 ♗xc4 16 b3 ♗e6 17 d5 and White will win a piece.

b12) 14...♕c6 15 ♕e1!? 0-0-0 16 ♗g5 ♗xg5 17 ♘xg5 ♖he8 18 ♖c1 ♕d7 19 ♕a5 ♔b8 20 ♘xe6 ♖xe6 21 ♖xe6 fxe6 22 ♕e5 g6 23 g3 ♕d6 was equal in Milos-Zarnicki, Villa Martelli 1998.

b13) 14...♕d7 15 ♗g5 f6 16 ♖e2 fxg5 17 ♖ae1 0-0 18 ♖xe6 ♗f6 is unclear.

b2) 14 ♕xc7 (White wins a pawn, but Black will have strong compensation based on his bishop pair and light square control) 14...♗d6 15 ♕c3 (15 ♕c2 leads to similar

play, for example 15...0-0 16 ♗d2 ♗f5 17 ♕b3 ♕xb3 18 axb3 f6 19 ♗c3 ♔f7 20 ♘d2 ♖fd8 21 ♘e4 ♗f8 22 b4 b6 23 ♘g3 ♗d3 and Black has adequate compensation, Hübner-Smyslov, Velden 1983) 15...0-0 16 ♗d2 ♖fc8 17 ♕e3 h6 18 ♗c3 b5 (it is not clear that this advance achieves anything; the simple 18...♖e8!? 19 ♕d2 ♕b5 would have given Black reasonable compensation) 19 a3 a5 20 ♕d2 ♕b3 21 d5! ♕xd5 (there is nothing better: 21...♗xd5? loses neatly to 22 ♗xg7! ♔xg7 23 ♘d4!, threatening both the queen and ♘f5+) 22 ♗xa5 ♕xd2 23 ♗xd2 ♖c2 24 ♗c3 ♗c5 25 ♘d4 ♗xd4 26 ♗xd4, Rogers-Volkmann, Bled Olympiad 2002. White has a clear extra pawn, but the presence of opposite-coloured bishops gives Black drawing chances.

12...♗g6 13 ♘c3 ♘xc3 14 ♕xc3 f6

Since ...♗e6 is no longer an option, Black must find a different way to escape the pin on the e-file, and here he prepares to unpin with ...♔f7. An interesting alternative is 14...♕d6!?, for example 15 ♗g5 f6 16 ♗h4 c6 17 ♗g3 ♕d7 with an unclear position.

15 ♕xc7

Taking the pawn does not force an advantage, but neither do the alternatives:

a) 15 ♗f4 ♖d8 16 ♗e3 ♔f7 17 ♕xc7 ♖d7 18 ♕c3 ♖hd8 19 a3 ♗e4 20 ♘d2 (the solid way out is 20 ♖d1 ♗xf3 21 ♖xf3 ♕e4 22 ♖e1 ♕xd4 with dead equality – Varavin) 20...♗h1! 21 ♕b3 ♕xb3 22 ♘xb3 ♗c6 23

♖c3 h5 and Black has plenty of compensation, Varavin-Egin, Kaluga 1998.

b) 15 b3 ♔f7 16 ♕xc7 ♖he8 17 ♕c4 ♕xc4 18 bxc4 b6! (fixing then c-pawn as a target; Motylev points out that 18...♖ec8?! 19 c5 b6 20 ♗a3 bxc5 21 ♖ac1 gives White a clear advantage) 19 ♗b2 ♖ac8 20 ♖ac1 ♗d6 21 ♖xe8 ♖xe8 22 c5 ♗f4 (Zhang Pengxiang-Motylev, Shanghai 2001). Motylev now suggested that White should play 23 ♖e1 ♖xe1+ 24 ♘xe1 bxc5 25 dxc5 ♔e6 26 ♘g2 ♗d2 27 ♘e3 ♔d7, assessing the position as equal.

15...0-0 16 ♖xe7

This leads to sharp play. Black has the usual good compensation after 16 ♕c3 ♗d6 17 ♕b3 ♕xb3 18 axb3 ♗f7 19 ♖e3 ♖fd8.

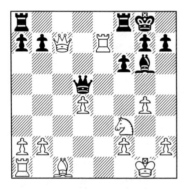

16...♕xf3 17 ♖xg7+ ♔h8 18 ♗h6 ♕xg4+

White's mating threat is demonstrated by 18...♗e4?? 19 ♖xh7+.

19 ♕g3 ♕xd4 20 ♖xg6!

White very wisely heads for a draw. Instead 20 ♖xb7? allows Black a deadly attack on the g-file with 20...♖g8 21 ♖e1 ♕d5! (21...♗f7?! fails to make the most of Black's chances: 22 ♖xf7 ♖xg3+ 23 hxg3 ♖g8 is only unclear) 22 ♖ee7 ♕d1+ 23 ♔g2 ♗e4+ 24 ♖xe4 ♖xg3+ 25 hxg3 ♕d5 26 ♖be7 f5 27 ♖7e5 ♕xe4+ 28 ♖xe4 fxe4 and Black should win this ending.

20...hxg6 21 ♕h3 ♔g8 22 ♗xf8 ♖xf8

Another drawing path is 22...♕xb2 23 ♖d1 ♖xf8 24 ♕h6 ♕c2 25 ♖d7 ♕b1+ 26

♔g2 ♕e4+ with a perpetual check.

23 ♕b3+ ♖f7 24 ♖d1 ♕g4+ 25 ♔f1 ♔g7 26 h3 ♕e4 27 ♕d5 ♕c2 28 ♖d2 ♕c1+ 29 ♔g2 ♖e7 30 ♕d8 ♕c6+ 31 ♕d5 ♕xd5+ ½-½

Game 10
Nyysti-M.Rychagov
Gothenburg 2003

---

1 e4 e5 2 ♘f3 ♘f6 3 ♘xe5 d6 4 ♘f3 ♘xe4 5 d4 d5 6 ♗d3 ♘c6 7 0-0 ♗e7 8 c4 ♘b4 9 cxd5 ♘xd3 10 ♕xd3 ♕xd5 11 ♖e1 ♗f5 12 ♘e5

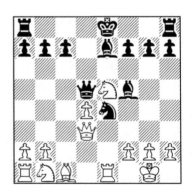

This is certainly a threatening-looking move, but Black has convincing replies.

12...0-0-0

Alternatively:

a) Black must avoid the losing blunder 12...♗h4? 13 g3 ♘xg3 (there is no hope in retreating: 13...♗e7 14 ♕f3 g6 15 g4! and White wins a piece) 14 ♕f3! ♘e4 15 ♘c3 ♘xc3 16 bxc3 ♕xf3 17 ♘xf3+ ♗e7 18 ♗a3 ♗e6 19 ♗xe7 ♔xe7 20 d5 and White wins easily, Zuidema-Barendregt, Amsterdam 1966.

b) 12...f6?! is more complicated but still bad: 13 ♘c3 (13 ♕f3 is only enough for equality after 13...g6 14 ♘c3 ♘xc3 15 bxc3 ♕xf3 16 ♘xf3 ♔d7) 13...♘xc3 14 ♕xf5 ♘b5 15 ♕g4 ♘xd4 (of course Black would like to take the piece with 15...fxe5 but after 16 ♖xe5 ♕xd4 17 ♖xe7+ ♔xe7 18 ♗g5+ ♔d6 19 ♖d1 White is clearly better) 16 ♘d3 and the pin causes Black immense difficulty:

b1) 16...♔f7 17 ♘f4! ♕f5 18 ♖xe7+! ♔xe7 19 ♕xg7+ ♔d6 20 ♗e3 ♖hg8 21 ♕f7 c5 (if 21...b6 then 22 ♗xd4 ♕xf4 23 ♗xb6! clears the d-file and continues the attack) 22 ♕xb7 ♖gb8 23 ♕a6+ ♖b6 24 ♕a3 and White's attack was obviously progressing well in Jonsson-Schandorff, Panormo 2001.

b2) If 16...♘c2 White must find 17 ♘b4! ♘xb4 18 ♕xb4 c5 19 ♕g4 ♔f7 20 ♗h6! gxh6 21 ♖ad1 with a massive attack, De Firmian-Plaskett, Copenhagen 1985. 17 ♖xe7+ leads to a draw after 17...♔xe7 18 ♕e2+ ♔f7 19 ♕xc2 ♖ad8 20 ♘e1 ♕d1 21 ♕xc7+ ♔g6 22 ♕g3+, as the pins force White to settle for a perpetual.

c) A reasonable alternative is 12...g6 13 ♕f3 (not 13 g4?! ♘xf2! 14 ♕f1 ♕h1+ 15 ♔xf2 ♗h4+ when White is in trouble) 13...♕xd4 14 ♘c3 ♕xe5 15 ♗f4 (or 15 ♘xe4 0-0-0 16 ♗f4 ♕a5 17 ♖ac1 ♖d7, when the game is unclear) 15...♕a5 16 b4!? ♕a3! (this is the best way to contain White's initiative; 16...♕xb4?! is obviously bad after 17 ♘d5, while 16...♗xb4 is not a clear mistake but after 17 ♖xe4+ ♗e6 18 ♗e5 White's initiative is very dangerous) 17 ♘d5 ♕xf3 18 gxf3 ♗d8 19 fxe4 ♗e6 20 ♘xc7+ ♗xc7 21 ♗xc7 (the game has fizzled out to equality) 21...f6 22 a3 ♖c8 23 ♖ac1 ♔f7 ½-½ Beliavsky-Smyslov, Reggio Emilia 1986.

13 ♕f3 g6 14 g4

14 ♘c3 is a solid option. However, after 14...♘xc3 15 bxc3 ♕xf3 16 gxf3 Black has no problems. For example, 16...♖de8!? 17 ♘xf7 ♖hf8 18 ♘e5 ♗h3 with compensation.

14...♗h4

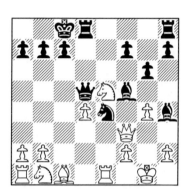

15 ♘d3

After this White seems to be in trouble. Following 15 ♘c3 there are many paths but White cannot force more than equality: 15...♘xc3 16 bxc3 ♗e6 17 g5 (or 17 ♕xd5 ♗xd5 18 g5 f6 19 gxf6 ♗xf6 with a balanced game) 17...♖he8 18 c4 ♕xd4 19 ♖b1 c6 20 ♗f4 (if 20 ♘xc6 Black bails out to a draw with 20...♕xf2+! 21 ♕xf2 ♗xf2+ 22 ♔xf2 bxc6) 20...♕c5 21 ♘xc6 ♖d3! 22 ♖xe6 (after 22 ♕xd3 Black can force a draw with 22...♕xf2+ 23 ♔h1 ♗d5+ 24 ♕xd5 ♖xe1+ 25 ♖xe1 ♕xe1+ 26 ♔g2 ♕e2+ 27 ♔h3 ♕f1+ 28 ♔xh4 ♕xf4+; instead 22 ♖e3 continues the fight: 22...♖xe3 23 ♘xa7+ ♕xa7 24 ♗xe3 ♕b8 25 ♕e4 ♗xg5 26 ♗xg5 and with opposite bishops and both kings vulnerable, the position is totally unclear) 22...fxe6 23 ♕xd3 ♕xf2+ 24 ♔h1 ♕xf4 25 ♘xa7+ ♔b8 26 ♘c6+ ♔c7 27 ♘a5 ♖d8 28 ♕e2 ♖d2 29 ♖xb7+ ♔d8 30 ♖b8+ ♔c7 ½-½ Wahls-Yusupov, Germany 1992.

15...♘xf2

This neat trick turns the game in Black's favour. Another attractive choice is 15...♖hg8!? 16 ♗e3 h5 17 h3 hxg4 18 hxg4 ♗e6 when Black has a dangerous initiative.

16 ♕xd5 ♘h3+ 17 ♔g2 ♖xd5 18 gxf5

♗xe1 **19 ♘xe1 ♖e8 20 ♘f3 ♖xf5 21 ♔g3?!**

White should prefer 21 ♘c3, but after 21...♘f4+ 22 ♗xf4 ♖xf4 Black is still obviously on top.

21...♘g1! 22 ♘bd2

The point is that if 22 ♘xg1 then 22...♖f1 23 ♘d2 ♖xg1+ 24 ♔f3 ♖ee1 25 ♘b3 f5 leaves White hopelessly tied up.

22...♘e2+

Another way to win is 22...♖e3!? 23 ♔f2 ♖exf3+ 24 ♔xg1 ♖g5+ 25 ♔h1 ♖f2.

23 ♔g2 g5 24 ♘b3 g4 25 ♘e1

There is also little hope after 25 ♘e5 ♘xd4 26 ♘xd4 ♖fxe5 27 ♔g3 f5.

25...♘xc1 26 ♖xc1 ♖e2+ 27 ♔g3 ♖f1

Perhaps even simpler was 27...h5 28 ♘c5 ♖f1 29 ♘cd3 f5.

28 ♘g2 ♖f3+ 29 ♔xg4 ♖xb3 30 ♘f4 h5+! 0-1

This little trick enables Black to save both rooks, so White resigned.

Game 11
Shirov-Gelfand
Astana 2001

1 e4 e5 2 ♘f3 ♘f6 3 ♘xe5 d6 4 ♘f3 ♘xe4 5 d4 d5 6 ♗d3 ♗e7 7 0-0 ♘c6 8 c4 ♘f6

8...♗e6 possibly commits the bishop too early:

a) 9 cxd5 is interesting: 9...♗xd5 10 ♘c3 ♘xc3 11 bxc3 0-0 12 ♗f4 ♗d6 13 ♗xd6 ♕xd6 14 ♘g5 h6 (14...f5 15 c4 ♗xg2! 16 ♔xg2 ♕g6 17 f4 h6 18 d5 ♘d8 19 h4 hxg5 20 hxg5 was a bit better for White in Löwenthal-Morphy, London 1858) 15 ♕h5 ♗xg2! 16 ♗h7+ ♔h8 17 ♔xg2 ♕d5+ 18 ♗e4 ♕xg5+ 19 ♕xg5 hxg5 20 ♖ab1 ♖ab8 21 ♖b5 and White has good compensation.

b) 9 ♖e1 is natural and probably best: 9...♘f6 10 c5!? 0-0 11 ♘c3 (preventing ...♗g4 with 11 h3!? may be best: 11...♘b4 12 ♘c3 ♘xd3 13 ♕xd3 h6 14 ♘e5 is good enough for an edge) 11...♗g4 12 ♗e3 ♗xc5!? (now Black has counterplay) 13 dxc5 d4 14 ♗xd4 (14 h3 ♗xf3 15 ♕xf3 dxc3 16 ♖ad1 ♘e5 17 ♕f5 ♘xd3 18 ♖xd3 ♕e7 19 ♖xc3 ♖ad8 is equal) 14...♘xd4 15 ♗xh7+ ♘xh7 16 ♕xd4 ♗xf3 17 ♕xd8 ♖fxd8 18 gxf3 ♘g5 with a level position, Short-Smyslov, Hastings 1988/89.

Also possible is 8...♗g4 9 ♘c3 (9 cxd5 is too simple an approach: 9...♕xd5 10 ♘c3 ♘xc3 11 bxc3 0-0 12 ♖e1 ♗xf3 13 ♕xf3 ♕xf3 14 gxf3 ♗d6 15 ♖b1 ♖ab8 16 ♗e3 b6 17 f4 ♘e7 18 c4 c6 19 ♔g2 ♖fd8 and Black had equalised in Kotronias-Langrock, Hamburg 2001) 9...♘xc3 (9...♘f6 transposes to 8...♘f6 9 ♘c3 ♗g4) 10 bxc3 0-0 11 ♖e1 dxc4 12 ♗xc4 ♕d6 13 ♖b1 ♖ab8 14 ♖b5 and White has his usual edge.

9 ♘c3

Black is okay in the variations after 9 cxd5 ♘xd5. For example, 10 ♘c3 0-0 11 ♖e1 ♘f6 12 a3 ♗g4 13 d5 ♘d4 14 ♗xh7+ ♘xh7 15 ♕xd4 ♗xf3 16 gxf3 ♗f6 17 ♕d3 ♕d7 18 ♗f4 ♘g5 (it is important to improve the badly placed knight immediately; instead in Svidler-Ovetchkin, Tomsk 2001 Black played 18...♖fe8 when 19 ♘e4 stranded the knight on h7 – White was a touch better after 19...b6 20 ♖e2 c5 21 ♖ae1 ♗d4 22 d6) 19 ♗xg5 ♗xg5 20 ♖e4 ♕f5 and White's weakened structure means that Black has no problems.

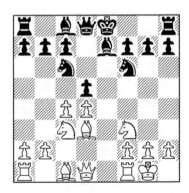

9...♗e6

9...♗g4 exerts less influence on d5, so it's logical for White to continue 10 cxd5. For example, 10...♘xd5 11 ♗e4 ♗e6 12 ♕d3 ♘cb4 13 ♕b1 c6 14 a3 ♘a6 15 ♘xd5 ♗xd5 16 ♖e1 ♘c7 17 ♗g5 ♗e6 18 ♗xe7 ♕xe7 19 ♘e5 0-0-0 20 ♕c2 ♖xd4?! (20...♕d6 21 ♖ad1 is better, after which White has only a small advantage) 21 ♗xc6! ♕d6 22 ♗d7+!

♗xd7 23 ♘xf7 ♕f8 24 ♘xh8 ♕xh8 (Sutovsky-Huzman, Tel Aviv 2000). Now White should have continued 25 ♕c5 ♖d2 26 ♕c3 ♖d5 27 ♖e7 with a clear advantage.

10 c5

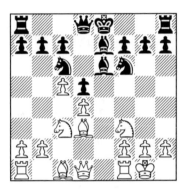

Ensuring a space advantage at the expense of taking the pressure off Black's centre. With the bishop already on e6, 10 cxd5 seems less logical but it is by no means bad. For example, 10...♘xd5 11 ♖e1 0-0 12 ♗e4 ♗f6 13 a3 h6 14 ♕d3 ♘ce7 15 ♗d2 c6 16 ♖ad1 ♖c8 17 h3 ♘xc3 18 bxc3 b5 19 ♗f4 ♗d5 20 ♘d2! ♖e8 21 ♕g3 ♔h8 22 ♗c2!? (clearing the way to centralise the knight; instead 22 ♕g4 ♗e6 23 ♕h5 ♘g8! 24 ♗b1 g6 25 ♕f3 ♗d5 26 ♕g3 ♗g7 was equal in Movsesian-Yusupov, Batumi 1999) 22...♕d7 23 ♘e4 and White's position is mildly preferable.

10...♗g4 11 ♗b5 0-0 12 ♗xc6 bxc6 13 h3 ♗xf3 14 ♕xf3 ♖e8 15 ♗e3 ♕b8

Black can provoke many exchanges with 15...♘e4 but after 16 ♘xe4 dxe4 17 ♕xe4 ♗xc5 18 ♕xc6 ♗xd4 19 ♖ad1 ♕f6 20 ♕xf6 ♗xf6 21 b3 White's better structure is a significant factor.

16 ♖ab1 ♗f8 17 ♖fe1 ♕b4

17...♘e4 still does not help. Gelfand analyses 18 ♗f4 ♘xc3 19 bxc3 ♖xe1+ 20 ♖xe1 ♕b2 21 ♖e2 as clearly better for White.

18 a3

18 ♕f4!? ♖ac8 19 ♖e2 also keeps an edge.

18...♕c4 19 ♖bc1

Again there was a good alternative: 19 ♕g3 ♖e7 20 ♖ed1 g6 21 ♗g5 ♗g7 22 ♕f4 ♘h5 23 ♕d2 and White has a pull.

19...♖ab8

If 19...♖e6 then 20 ♕g3 reminds Black of the weakness of c7.

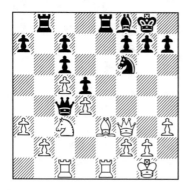

20 ♕f5

Now Black is able to fix b2 as a weakness. 20 b4 was required to keep a small advantage: 20...a5 21 bxa5 ♖b3 22 ♘b1!; or 20...♕b3 21 ♗g5 ♕xa3 22 ♗xf6 gxf6 23 b5 cxb5 24 ♕g4+ ♔h8 25 ♘xd5 and White has a strong attack.

20...♕b3 21 ♗g5 ♘e4

The bold 21...♕xb2 is also possible. 22 ♗xf6 gxf6 (but not 22...♖xe1+ 23 ♖xe1 ♕xc3 24 ♖e3 ♕c1+ 25 ♔h2 ♕b1 26 ♕d7! gxf6 27 ♖g3+ ♗g7 28 ♕g4 ♕g6 29 ♕f4 when Black has to surrender his queen) 23 ♕d3 ♗h6 24 ♖xe8+ ♖xe8 25 ♖c2 ♕xa3. Notkin analysed this variation but understandably stopped now with the assessment of 'unclear'.

22 ♘xe4 dxe4 23 ♖xe4 ♕d3 24 ♖ce1 ♖xb2

It's clear that White has lost control of the position.

25 ♕f4

Or 25 ♕f3 ♖xe4 26 ♕xd3 ♖xe1+ 27 ♔h2 h5 with a murky, unbalanced position.

25...♖xe4 26 ♕xe4 ♕xe4 27 ♖xe4 f6 28 ♗f4 ♔f7 29 ♗xc7 ♖a2

29...♖b3 was another way to draw after 30

♗d6 ♗xd6 31 cxd6 ♖b7.

30 ♗d6 ♖xa3 31 ♗xf8 ♔xf8 32 ♖e6 ♖d3 33 ♖xc6 ♖d1+ 34 ♔h2 ♖xd4 35 ♖c8+ ♔e7 36 c6 ♖c4 37 ♖c7+ ♔f8 ½-½

Game 12
Topalov-Anand
Wijk aan Zee 2003

---

1 e4 e5 2 ♘f3 ♘f6 3 ♘xe5 d6 4 ♘f3 ♘xe4 5 d4 d5 6 ♗d3 ♘c6 7 0-0 ♗e7 8 c4 ♘f6 9 h3 ♘b4

9...0-0 is also reasonable: 10 ♘c3 dxc4 (10...♘b4 11 ♗e2 dxc4 12 ♗xc4 transposes to the main game) 11 ♗xc4 ♘a5 12 ♗d3 ♗e6 13 ♖e1 ♘c6 (13...c5 liquidates the centre but following 14 dxc5 ♗xc5 15 ♗g5 White's superior activity is still annoying) 14 a3 a6 15 ♗f4 ♖e8 (15...♕d7?! exposes the queen to a series of tactics: 16 ♘e5 ♘xe5 17 dxe5 ♘d5 18 ♘xd5 ♗xd5 19 ♕c2 g6 20 ♖ad1 c6 21 ♗h6 ♖fd8 22 e6! fxe6 23 ♗xg6! and White is much better, Kasparov-Karpov, World Championship [Game 48], Moscow 1985) 16 ♖c1 ♘d5 17 ♘xd5 ♗xd5 and Black has comfortable equality.

10 ♗e2 dxc4 11 ♗xc4 0-0 12 ♘c3 c6

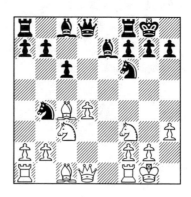

13 ♖e1

13 a3 is a logical alternative, for example 13...♘bd5 14 ♖e1 ♗e6 15 ♗d3 h6 16 ♗d2 ♖e8 (it is best to avoid all the ♖xe6 ideas with 16...♕c8!; after 17 ♕c2 ♖e8 18 ♘e2 ♗d6 19 ♘e5 a complicated struggle lies

ahead) 17 ⨖xe6!? (White sacrifices the exchange to weaken the light squares around Black's king) 17...fxe6 18 ⨗g6 ⨖f8 19 ⨕e2 ⨘c7 20 ⨖e1 ⨗d6 21 ⨗b1 ⨖e8 (In Bologan-Rozentalis, Belfort 1998 Black tried 21...⨕e7?! but after 22 ⨘e5 ⨗xe5 23 dxe5 ⨘fd5 24 ⨘xd5 ⨘xd5 25 ⨕e4 g5 26 ⨕g6+ ⨕g7 27 ⨖xe6+ ⨔h8 28 h4 White had a dangerous attack) 22 ⨘e5 c5 23 ⨘e4 cxd4 24 ⨘xf6+ ⨕xf6 25 ⨘g4 and here Bologan states that White has good compensation for the material deficit.

13...⨘bd5 14 ⨕b3

The other try is 14 ⨗g5 ⨗e6 15 ⨕b3 and now:

a) 15...⨕b6 is far too obliging. White easily achieves a preferable structure after 16 ⨘xd5 cxd5 17 ⨕xb6 axb6. Following 18 ⨗b3 h6 19 ⨗f4 ⨖fc8 20 ⨘e5 g5 21 ⨗h2 ⨗b4 22 ⨖e2 ⨘e4 23 ⨘d3 ⨗f8 24 ⨖ae1 ⨗g7 (not 24...⨘d6?! 25 ⨗xd6 ⨗xd6 26 ⨖xe6! fxe6 27 ⨖xe6 when White will win far too many pawns) 25 ⨗e5 ⨗xe5 26 ⨘xe5 ⨔g7 27 ⨘d3 White had an enduring edge in Leko-Adams, Dortmund 2002.

b) 15...⨖b8 16 ⨖ad1 ⨖e8 17 ⨗h4 h6 18 ⨗g3 ⨗d6 19 ⨗e5 ⨘xc3 20 bxc3 ⨗xc4 (another convincing equaliser is 20...⨘d5!? 21 ⨕c2 b5 22 ⨗d3 a6) 21 ⨕xc4 ⨘d5 22 ⨕b3 b5 23 c4 bxc4 24 ⨕xc4 ⨖e6 25 ⨖c1 ⨖b6 26 ⨗xd6 ⨖xd6 with a balanced position, Lutz-Dautov, Bundesliga 2004.

14...⨘b6 15 ⨗d3 ⨗e6 16 ⨕c2 h6

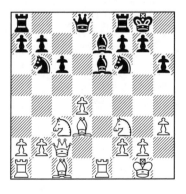

17 ⨖xe6!?

Boldly sacrificing the exchange is the thematic continuation. The safe liner is 17 a3 ⨘bd5 18 ⨘a4 (18 ⨗d2 led nowhere in Gelfand-Yusupov, Istanbul 2000: after 18...⨖c8 19 ⨘a4 ⨘c7 20 ⨖e2 ⨗d6 21 ⨖ae1 ⨘h5 22 ⨗h7+ ⨔h8 23 ⨗f5 ⨘hf4 24 ⨗xf4 ⨘xf4 25 ⨖e3 ⨘d5 26 ⨖3e2 ⨘f4 27 ⨖e3 a draw was agreed) 18...⨘d7 19 ⨗d2 ⨖e8 (Bologan-Kasimdzhanov, Pamplona 2002). Here Bologan suggests 20 ⨖e2!? ⨕c7 21 ⨖ae1 ⨘f4 22 ⨗xf4 ⨕xf4 23 ⨘c3 ⨕c7 24 d5 cxd5 25 ⨘d4 with an edge for White. Instead, 23...⨔f8 allows 24 ⨖xe6! fxe6 25 ⨗g6 ⨖ed8 26 ⨖xe6 with a big advantage.

17...fxe6 18 ⨕e2 ⨕d7 19 ⨗d2 ⨗d6

If 19...⨖ad8 20 ⨖e1 ⨗d6 21 ⨘e4 ⨘bd5 White can claim an edge.

20 ⨘e4 ⨘bd5 21 ⨘xd6 ⨕xd6 22 ⨖e1 ⨖ad8 23 a3 ⨖fe8 24 ⨗b1 c5 25 ⨘e5 cxd4 26 ⨕d3 ⨘e3

After 26...⨕b6 Anand suggests 27 b4 ⨘e7 28 ⨗a2 to keep up the pressure.

27 ⨘f3 ⨘ed5

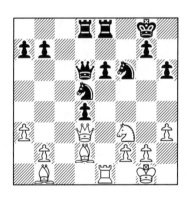

27...⨘f5!? is a solid option, but after 28 ⨗a2 ⨘d5 29 ⨖e4 Topalov still claims compensation.

28 ⨗xh6! ⨘f4

The bishop cannot be taken: 28...gxh6?? 29 ⨕g6+ ⨔f8 30 ⨕xh6+ ⨔g8 31 ⨖e5 and White wins.

29 ⨗xf4 ⨕xf4 30 ⨗a2 ⨖d6 31 h4

A good alternative is 31 ⨕c4!? ⨘d5 32

♘xd4 ♖f8 33 ♘f3 with perfectly adequate compensation.

31...♕h6 32 ♗c4 ♕h7 33 ♕b3 d3 34 ♖d1

Topalov starts to lose his way – it was probably time for 34 ♖xe6. Following 34...♖dxe6 35 ♗xe6+ ♔h8 36 ♘e5 ♕h5 the position is unclear, one possible continuation being 37 ♘f7+ ♕xf7 38 ♗xf7 ♖e1+ 39 ♔h2 d2 40 ♕xb7 d1♕ 41 ♕c8+ ♔h7 42 ♕f5+ with a draw by perpetual check.

34...d2

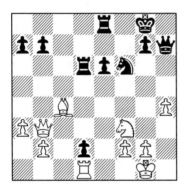

35 ♕b4?!

The d-pawn had to be taken, even though Black is a bit better after 35 ♖xd2 ♖xd2 36 ♘xd2 ♕xh4 37 ♗xe6+ ♔h8.

35...♖ed8 36 ♘g5

Now it is too late for 36 ♖xd2?!. After 36...♕b1+ 37 ♔h2 ♖xd2 38 ♘xd2 ♕e1 the pin is deadly.

36...♕c2 37 ♗b3

Or 37 ♕b3 ♕xb3 38 ♗xb3 ♖b6 39 ♗xe6+ ♖xe6 40 ♘xe6 ♖e8 41 ♖xd2 ♖xe6 and Black should win.

37...♕c6 38 g3 ♕b6 39 ♘xe6 ♕xb4 40 axb4 ♖c8

Since the discovered check is harmless, it is clear that Black is winning.

41 ♔f1

41 ♘c5+ does not help: 41...♔h8 42 ♘xb7 ♖b6.

41...♔h8 42 ♘g5 ♖d4 43 ♘f7+ ♔h7 44 ♘g5+ ♔h6 45 ♘f7+ ♔g6 46 ♘e5+ ♔h7 47 ♘f3 ♖xb4 48 ♘xd2 ♖d8 49 ♗c2+ ♔h8 50 b3 ♖bd4 51 ♔e1 b5

52 ♘b1

The queenside pawns are also decisive after 52 ♘f3 ♖e8+ 53 ♔f1 ♖xd1+ 54 ♗xd1 a5.

52...♖e8+ 53 ♔f1 ♖xd1+ 54 ♗xd1 ♘e4 55 ♗c2 a5 56 ♘a3 ♘d2+ 57 ♔g2 ♖b8 58 g4 b4 59 ♘b1 ♘xb1 60 ♗xb1 ♖c8 61 ♗f5 ♖c3 0-1

Summary

The line 6...♗e7 7 0-0 ♘c6 8 c4 has been enduringly studied, but it is still very popular. Strategic understanding of the variation is the key to success – there is no real need to memorise the details.

Although 8...♘f6 looks quite reasonable, at the moment all the attention is on 8...♘b4. White should really retreat his bishop to e2 – Games 9-10 show that 9 cxd5 does not lead to success against accurate black defence. After 9 ♗e2 the bishop fianchetto to b7 (Game 7) may well not equalise (see the note to White's 18th move). In the case of 10...♗e6 11 ♘e5 neither a counterattack in the centre with 11...c5, nor ousting the centralised knight with 11...f6 shakes off all Black's opening problems. Mobilisation on the queenside with 11 ♗e3 seems to give less chances for an advantage after both 11...f5 and 11...♗f5.

With the knight on b4 it is logical to develop the bishop to f5 as soon as possible. After 9 ♗e2 0-0 10 ♘c3 ♗f5 11 ♘e5, 11...c5 is quite effective, while in the event of 11 a3 ♘xc3 12 bxc3 ♘c6 the complicated, strategic play has not revealed any appreciable advantage for White so far.

1 e4 e5 2 ♘f3 ♘f6 3 ♘xe5 d6 4 ♘f3 ♘xe4 5 d4 d5 6 ♗d3 ♗e7 7 0-0 Nc6 8 c4 ♘b4

8...♘f6

9 ♘c3 – *Game 11;* 9 h3 – *Game 12*

9 ♗e2

9 cxd5 ♘xd3 10 ♕xd3 ♕xd5 11 ♖e1 ♗f5 (D)

12 g4 – *Game 9;* 12 ♘e5 – *Game 10*

9...0-0

9...dxc4 – *Game 8*

10 ♘c3 ♗f5

10...b6 – *Game 7*

10...♗e6 (D)

11 ♘e5

11...c5 – *Game 3;* 11...f6 – *Game 4*

11 ♗e3 ♗f5

12 ♕b3 – *Game 5;* 12 ♖c1 – *Game 6*

11 a3 ♘xc3 12 bxc3 ♘c6 13 ♖e1 ♖e8 (D) 14 cxd5 – *Game 1*

14 ♗f4 – *Game 2*

11...♗f5

10...♗e6

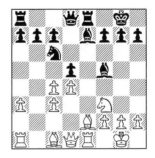

13...♖e8

CHAPTER TWO

3 ♘xe5: The Main Line with 8 ♖e1

1 e4 e5 2 ♘f3 ♘f6 3 ♘xe5 d6 4 ♘f3 ♘xe4 5 d4 d5 6 ♗d3 ♗e7 7 0-0 ♘c6 8 ♖e1

After 1 e4 e5 2 ♘f3 ♘f6 3 ♘xe5 d6 4 ♘f3 ♘xe4 5 d4 d5 6 ♗d3 ♗e7 7 0-0 ♘c6, it's true that the immediate attack on the d5-pawn with 8 c4, as covered in the previous chapter, is in the foreground of modern practice. However, 8 ♖e1, developing the rook and attacking the knight on e4, is a serious alternative. Even Bilguer considered the 'pawn sacrifice' 8...♗g4 to be the best reply, and he indicated that it was unfavourable for White to grab and hold on to the pawn: 9 ♗xe4 dxe4 10 ♖xe4 ♗xf3 11 gxf3?! (11 ♕xf3 ♘xd4 12 ♕d3 maintains equality) 11...f5 12 ♖f4 0-0. Instead White should advance his c-pawn with the aggressive 9 c4 (Games 13-15) or the modern 9 c3 (Games 16-18).

The intensive attack on the centre with 9 c4 virtually forces Black to defend the d5-pawn with 9...♘f6. If White retains pressure in the centre with 10 ♘c3 (Game 13), the d4-pawn falls and Black equalises with either 10...♘xd4 or 10...♗xf3 11 ♕xf3 ♘xd4. This is the reason White often releases the tension in the centre with 10 cxd5 (Games 14-15). Pillsbury introduced 10...♕xd5, but after 11 ♘c3 neither the retreat 11...♕h5 nor the queen swap 11...♗xf3 12 ♘xd5 ♗xd1 leads

to equality (the latter in view of 13 ♘xc7 ♔d7 14 ♗f4!). Black can take on d5 with his queen without harm if he precedes this with 10...♗xf3 11 ♕xf3 (Game 14), while in Game 15 Black takes the strategic decision to occupy the square in front of the isolated pawn with 10...♘xd5.

While 9 c4 looks aggressive, 9 c3 appears distinctly restrained. However, comparing the consequences of the lines leads to unexpected results. 9 c4 leads to the quick reduction of tension in the centre with approximately equal chances, while the consequences after 9 c3 are unproven. White strengthens his d4-pawn and resumes his threat to capture on e4. Moreover, after c2-c3 White's queen has a clear way to b3 and after 9...f5 it is likely to take this road. 10 h3 has not become popular, although it looks logical to force the bishop on g4 to make a decision before the queen leaves for the flank. 10 c4?!, trying to take advantage of the weakening of the a2-g8 diagonal at the cost of a tempo, is unjustified: 10...dxc4! 11 ♗xc4 ♕d6! and ...0-0-0 (Mikhalchishin). 10 ♘bd2 ♕d6!? 11 c4!? (Game 16) makes some sense because ...d5xc4 does not work, while the manoeuvre ♘d2-f1 deserves consideration after 10 ♘bd2 0-0. However, this plan is less appealing after 10 ♘bd2 ♕d6 in view of

Black's possibility of castling long.

An early ♕b3, attacking b7 and d5, is covered in Games 17-18. A comparatively rare plan after 10 ♕b3 is 10...♕d6, preparing queenside castling. This gives White both the typical possibility of 11 ♘bd2, 12 ♕c2 followed by the lunge with the b-pawn, and a paradoxical idea of 11 ♘fd2!? followed by f2-f3. In the main line with 10 ♕b3 0-0 11 ♘bd2 Black has two main options: the king's removal from the dangerous a2-g8 diagonal a2-g8 with 11...♔h8 (Game 17) offers a sacrifice of the b-pawn, while Botvinnik proposed protecting b7 with 11...♘a5 (Game 18).

Game 13
Shirov-Yusupov
European Team Ch., Batumi 1999

---

1 e4 e5 2 ♘f3 ♘f6 3 ♘xe5 d6 4 ♘f3 ♘xe4 5 d4 d5 6 ♗d3 ♘c6 7 0-0 ♗e7 8 ♖e1 ♗g4 9 c4 ♘f6

Trying to win a pawn immediately is a mistake: 9...♗xf3?! 10 ♕xf3 ♘xd4 11 ♕e3 ♘f5 12 ♕h3! ♘fd6 13 cxd5 ♘f6 14 ♗g5 ♘xd5 15 ♘c3 ♔f8 16 ♖xe7! ♘xe7 17 ♘d5 ♘xd5 (this gives up material and admits that it has all gone wrong; if Black tries 17...f6 then 18 ♘xf6! gxf6 19 ♗xf6 ♔f7 20 ♕f3 is far too strong) 18 ♗xd8 ♖xd8 19 ♕h4 ♘f6 20 ♕d4 and White was much better in Lobron-Handoko, Jakarta 1983.

10 ♘c3

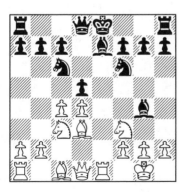

10 cxd5 is the subject of Game 14.

10...♗xf3

Now this capture on f3 is safer. 10...dxc4 is less accurate after 11 ♗xc4 0-0 12 d5 ♘a5 13 ♗d3 c6 14 h3 ♗h5 15 ♗g5!? cxd5 16 ♖e5 ♗xf3 (not 16...d4? 17 ♗xf6 ♗xf3 18 ♕xf3 ♗xf6 19 ♖d5 dxc3 20 ♖xd8 ♖fxd8 21 bxc3 with a big advantage for White, J.Polgar-Kamsky, Las Palmas 1994) 17 ♕xf3 ♘c6 18 ♗xf6 ♗xf6 19 ♖xd5, when White's pieces are sufficiently active to force an advantage even in this symmetrical position.

However, Black should seriously consider 10...♘xd4 here: 11 cxd5 ♗xf3 (11...c5?! is inaccurate: 12 ♗b5+ ♔f8 13 ♗e2 and White has a useful lead in development) 12 gxf3 c5!? 13 dxc6 ♘xc6 14 ♗b5 0-0 15 ♕xd8 ♖xd8 16 ♗xc6 bxc6 17 ♗e3 ♗b6 18 ♖ad1 ♖fd8 and the game was completely level in J.Polgar-Karpov, Hoogeveen 1999.

11 ♕xf3 ♘xd4 12 ♕d1

White can also try 12 ♕g3, when 12...♘e6 is a little better for White after 13 ♗f5 0-0 14 cxd5 ♘xd5 15 ♕h3 ♘f6 16 ♗e3. However, Black is okay after 12...dxc4 13 ♗xc4 (Karpov pointed out the losing blunder 13 ♕xg7? ♘f3+! 14 ♔h1 ♖g8 15 ♕xf6 ♘xe1) 13...0-0 14 ♗g5 ♗d6 15 ♕h4 h6 16 ♗xf6 ♕xf6 17 ♕xf6 gxf6, Lobron-Karpov, Hanover 1983.

12...♘e6 13 ♗f5

After 13 cxd5 Black defends successfully: 13...♘xd5 14 ♗b5+ c6 15 ♘xd5 cxb5 16 ♗f4 ♘xf4 17 ♖xe7+ (not 17 ♘xe7?! ♘e6 18

♘f5 0-0 and Black keeps a useful extra pawn) 17...♔f8 18 ♖e5 ♕d6 19 ♖f5 ♖d8 20 ♘e3 ♕xd1+ 21 ♖xd1 ♖xd1+ 22 ♘xd1 ♘e6 23 ♖xb5 b6 24 ♘c3 ♔e7 and unsurprisingly a draw was agreed in Kasimdzhanov-Yusupov, Essen 2001.

13...dxc4

Much riskier is 13...d4 14 ♗xe6!? (this is more dangerous than 14 ♘e2 d3 15 ♘f4 ♘d4 16 ♗xd3 0-0 17 ♗e3 ♗b4 18 ♖f1 c5 19 ♘e2 ♘g4, which was unclear in J.Polgar-Shirov, Prague 1999) 14...dxc3 (or 14...fxe6 15 ♘b5 e5 16 ♖xe5 a6 17 ♘xd4 c5 18 ♗h6! and White has a vicious attack) 15 ♕xd8+ ♖xd8 16 ♗f5 cxb2 17 ♗xb2. White has good compensation: the bishop pair, a lead in development, and the annoying pin on the e-file.

14 ♕a4+

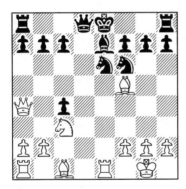

14...c6

14...♕d7?! sees the queen stepping into trouble: 15 ♕xc4 ♖d8 16 ♗g5 and White has a dangerous initiative. For example, 16...h6 17 ♗xe6 fxe6 18 ♗xf6 ♗xf6 19 ♖ad1 ♕c8 20 ♖xe6+ ♔f8 21 ♖xd8+ ♕xd8 22 ♘d5 and White's attack crashes through.

15 ♗xe6 fxe6 16 ♕xc4 ♘d5

Black's simplest plan is 16...0-0 17 ♕xe6+ ♖f7 18 ♗g5 ♕d6 19 ♕xd6 ♗xd6 with easy equality.

17 ♖xe6 0-0

There is no time for 17...♘xc3? because of 18 ♗g5 ♘d5 19 ♗xe7 ♘xe7 20 ♖ae1 ♖f8

21 ♖xe7+ ♕xe7 22 ♖xe7+ ♔xe7 23 ♕b4+ ♔f6 24 ♕xb7 ♖fc8 and White has good winning chances.

18 ♗e3

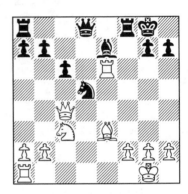

18...♗f6

Another option is 18...♔h8, for example 19 ♘xd5 cxd5 20 ♕d3 ♗f6 21 ♖d1 ♕a5 (or 21...♗xb2 22 ♕xd5 ♖xd5 23 ♖xd5 b6 24 ♖e7 ♔g8 25 g3 and White's activity gives him a small endgame advantage, Magem-Lalic, Seville 2000) 22 ♕b3 ♖ad8 23 ♗d2 ♕c7 24 ♗b4 ♖fe8 and White again has a tiny edge, this time due to his better structure.

19 ♗c5 ♖f7 20 ♖ae1

This is more controlled than 20 ♖d6. For example, 20...♕c7 21 ♖e1 ♗xc3 22 bxc3 ♖e7 23 ♖d8+ ♖xd8 24 ♖xe7 b5 25 ♕b3 (after 25 ♖xc7 bxc4 26 ♖xc6 ♘b4! 27 ♖d6 ♖xd6 28 ♗xd6 ♘xa2 Black's dangerous a-pawn gives him the edge) 25...♕f4 and Black had serious counterplay in Magem-Illescas, France 2000.

20...♗xc3 21 bxc3 h6 22 ♗xa7!?

This trick gains White a small advantage.

22...♘c7! 23 ♖e7 ♕d5 24 ♕xd5 ♘xd5

After 24...cxd5 25 ♖xf7 ♔xf7 26 ♗d4 ♖xa2 27 ♖b1 ♘b5 28 ♗e5 Yusupov still believes White is a bit better.

25 ♖e8+ ♖f8 26 ♖xf8+ ♔xf8 27 ♗c5+ ♔g8 28 c4 ♘f4! 29 ♗d6

After this Black equalises. White could keep pressing with 29 ♗e3! ♘d3 30 ♖e2 ♘b4 31 f3 ♖xa2 32 ♖xa2 ♘xa2 33 ♗d2 ♔f7

34 ♔f2 ♔e6 35 ♔e3 ♔d6 36 ♔d4 (Yusupov).

29...♘d3 30 ♖e2 ♖d8 31 ♗c7 ♖d4 32 g3 ½-½

Game 14
Sax-Yusupov
Thessaloniki Olympiad 1984

1 e4 e5 2 ♘f3 ♘f6 3 ♘xe5 d6 4 ♘f3 ♘xe4 5 d4 d5 6 ♗d3 ♘c6 7 0-0 ♗e7 8 ♖e1 ♗g4 9 c4 ♘f6 10 cxd5

10...♗xf3

This is much safer than 10...♕xd5 11 ♘c3 ♗xf3 (if 11...♕h5 12 ♗b5 ♗xf3 13 gxf3 ♔f8 14 ♗xc6 bxc6 15 ♗f4 White's easier development is worth a slight advantage) 12 ♘xd5 ♗xd1 13 ♘xc7+ ♔d7 14 ♗f4! ♗g4 (Kavalek analysed 14...♘h5 15 ♗f5+ ♔d8 16 ♗e5 ♘xe5 17 ♘xa8 ♘c6 18 ♖axd1 ♗d6 19 ♖e5! as winning for White) 15 d5 ♘d4 16 ♘xa8 ♖xa8 17 ♗e5! ♗f5 (or 17...♗c5 18 ♖ec1 ♗b6 19 ♖c4 and White still has a clear advantage) 18 ♗f1 ♘c2 19 ♗b5+ ♔d8 20 d6 ♘xe1 21 ♖xe1 ♗e6 22 dxe7+ ♔xe7 23 ♗d4 b6 24 a4 (Kavalek-Toth, Haifa 1976), when the tactics have burned out but White's bishop pair still ensures a small advantage.

10...♘xd5 is studied in Game 15.

11 ♕xf3 ♕xd5 12 ♕g3

White has two other moves:

a) 12 ♕h3 ♘xd4 (also playable is 12...♕xd4 13 ♘c3 ♖d8 14 ♗b5 0-0 15 ♗xc6 bxc6 16 ♗g5 ♖fe8 with an unclear position) 13 ♘c3 ♕d7 14 ♕xd7+ ♔xd7 15 ♗e3 ♘e6 16 ♖ad1 ♗d6 17 ♗f5 ♔e7 18 ♘b5 ♖hd8 19 ♘xd6 cxd6 20 h3 (White has obvious compensation for the pawn) 20...b6 21 g4 h6 22 ♗d4 ♖ac8 23 ♗c3 g6 24 ♗c2 h5 25 f3 ½-½ Kasparov-Karpov, World Championship (Game 28), Moscow 1984.

b) 12 ♕xd5 should not be dangerous: 12...♘xd5 13 ♘c3 0-0-0 (Black is well advised not to chase material with 13...♘db4 14 ♗e4 ♘xd4 because after 15 ♗e3 ♖d8 16 ♗xd4 ♖xd4 17 a3 ♘c6 18 ♘b5 White will win back the pawn and force an advantage) 14 ♗e4 ♗b4! 15 ♗d2 ♘f6 16 ♗xc6 bxc6 17 ♗e3 ♘d5 18 a3 (Kamsky-Karpov, Linares 1994 continued 18 ♖ac1 ♘xe3 19 fxe3 c5 20 ♖f1 f6 21 ♖f5 ♖he8 and Black had an edge, which grew considerably after 22 dxc5? ♖xe3) 18...♗xc3 19 bxc3 ♘xc3 20 ♖ac1 ♘b5 21 ♖xc6 ♘xd4 22 ♖c4. Despite Black's extra pawn Karpov assesses the position as equal.

12...♕xd4 13 ♘c3

After 13 ♕xc7 one of Black's options is to force equality with 13...♘g4!? 14 ♕f4 ♕xd3 15 ♕xg4 0-0.

13...0-0 14 ♘b5 ♕g4

Black has a sound alternative in 14...♕b4!? 15 ♗g5 ♖fd8 16 ♕h3 g6 17 ♘xc7 ♖ac8 18 ♗xf6 ♗xf6 19 ♘d5 ♕d6 20 ♘xf6+ ♕xf6, achieving easy equality.

15 ♕xg4

15 ♘xc7 ♖ad8 16 ♕xg4 ♘xg4 17 ♗e2 ♘ge5 18 ♗f4 ♗f6 is also level.

15...♘xg4 16 ♗f5?!

This is inaccurate; 16 ♗e2 ♘f6 17 ♘xc7 ♖ac8 18 ♘b5 ♗b4 is simply equal.

16...♘f6 17 ♘xc7 ♖ad8 18 ♗e3 a6!

A later game, Kamsky-Khalifman, FIDE World Championship, Las Vegas 1999, continued 18...♗b4 19 ♖ed1 g6 20 ♗h3 a6 (or 20...♗d6 21 ♘b5 ♗e5 22 ♘xa7 ♘xa7 23 ♗xa7 ♖xd1+ 24 ♖xd1 ♖a8 25 ♗c5 ♗xb2, again with equality) 21 ♗h6 ♖xd1+ 22 ♖xd1 ♖d8 23 ♖xd8+ ♘xd8 24 ♗g5 ♗e7 with a level position.

19 ♖ac1

Perhaps White should try 19 ♖ed1 ♗d6 20 ♗b6 ♗e5 21 ♖ab1 (after 21 ♖xd8 ♖xd8 White has some problems since 22 ♘xa6? fails to 22...♖d5) 21...♖xd1+ 22 ♖xd1 ♗xb2, when White's activity is enough to hold the balance.

19...♗b4! 20 ♖f1 ♘d4!

This keeps up the pressure. 20...♗d2?! allows White to complicate matters with 21 ♖xc6! bxc6 22 ♗c5.

21 ♖c4?!

Now Black's advantage is serious. After 21 ♗xd4 ♖xd4 22 ♖fd1 ♖fd8 23 ♖xd4 ♖xd4 24 ♔f1 ♗d6 Black has very little.

21...♘xf5 22 ♖xb4 ♖d7! 23 ♖c1

Black's advantage is confirmed by the fact that White cannot grab on b7: 23 ♖xb7? loses to 23...♘xe3 24 fxe3 ♖c8 25 ♖c1 ♘e8, while the line 23 ♗f4? ♖c8 24 ♖xb7 ♘d4! is also hopeless.

23...♖c8 24 ♖bc4 ♖cd8 25 h3 ♘xe3 26 fxe3 ♔f8 27 e4 ♔e7

28 ♖b4

If 28 e5 then 28...♘d5 29 ♘xd5+ ♖xd5 30 ♖g4 g6 and Black has good chances of winning the rook ending.

28...♖d1+ 29 ♖xd1 ♖xd1+ 30 ♔f2 ♔d6 31 e5+?

Now it is all over. Also hopeless is 31 ♖xb7 ♔c6 32 ♖a7 ♔b6, but White can put up more resistance with 31 ♔e2 ♖a1 32 ♘d5

♘xd5 33 exd5 b5.

31...♔xe5 32 ♘a8 b5 33 a4 ♘d5 34 ♖b3 bxa4 35 ♖b7 ♖b1 36 ♔f3 a3 0-1

Game 15
Psakhis-Cooper
Port Erin 2003

---

1 e4 e5 2 ♘f3 ♘f6 3 ♘xe5 d6 4 ♘f3 ♘xe4 5 d4 d5 6 ♗d3 ♘c6 7 0-0 ♗e7 8 ♖e1 ♗g4 9 c4 ♘f6 10 cxd5 ♘xd5 11 ♘c3 0-0 12 h3

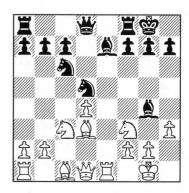

Twenty years earlier Psakhis had tried 12 ♗e4 ♗e6 (after 12...♘f6 Zak assessed 13 d5 ♘b4 14 a3 ♘xe4 15 ♖xe4 ♗xf3 16 ♕xf3 ♘a6 17 b4 as clearly better for White) 13 ♕d3 h6 14 ♗h7+ (if 14 ♕b5 Black draws with 14...♘cb4!? 15 ♕xb7 ♖b8 16 ♕xa7 ♖a8) 14...♔h8 15 ♗f5 ♘cb4 16 ♕b1 ♗xf5 17 ♕xf5 ♘f6 18 ♗f4 ♘bd5 19 ♗e5 c6 with an equal position, Psakhis-Schussler, Tallinn 1983.

12...♗e6

This is the solid option, but two others moves are worth mentioning:

a) 12...♗h5? is just a blunder: 13 ♗xh7+! ♔xh7 14 ♘g5+ ♗xg5 15 ♕xh5+ ♔g8 16 ♗xg5 ♘f6 17 ♗xf6 ♕xf6 18 ♘d5 ♕xd4 19 ♖ad1 g6 20 ♖xd4 gxh5 21 ♖h4 and White had a huge advantage in Yemelin-Kazakov, St Petersburg 1996.

b) More serious is 12...♗xf3, although White should have a slight edge. For example, 13 ♕xf3 ♘db4 14 ♗b1 ♖e8 15 d5 ♗d6 16 ♖xe8+ ♕xe8 17 ♗e3 ♘e5 18 ♕e4 ♘g6 19 a3 ♘a6 20 ♗c2, Dolmatov-Yusupov, Frunze 1981.

13 a3 ♘xc3

Black has also tried the immediate 13...♗f6, for example 14 ♘e4 ♗f5 15 ♕b3 ♘b6 16 d5 ♗xe4 17 ♗xe4 ♘e7 18 ♗e3 ♘ec8 (the greedy 18...♘exd5 does not work: 19 ♗xb6 ♘xb6 20 ♗xb7 ♖b8 21 ♖ad1 ♘d7 22 ♕b5 ♖e8 23 ♖xd7 ♖xe1+ 24 ♘xe1 ♕e8 25 ♘f3 ♖xb7 26 ♕xb7 ♕xd7 27 ♕xa7 and White has good winning chances) 19 ♖ac1 ♘d6 20 ♗b1 ♕d7 (Shirov-I.Sokolov, FIDE World Championship, Las Vegas 1999). Now Ivan Sokolov suggests that 21 ♗g5!? ♗xg5 22 ♘xg5 g6 23 ♕g3 gives an edge to White.

14 bxc3 ♗f6

15 ♖b1

This is natural, but playing 15 ♕c2 g6 and only then 16 ♖b1 is also sensible. Now if Black plays as in the game with 16...b6?!, White has 17 ♗xg6! hxg6 18 ♖xe6 fxe6 19 ♕xg6+ ♔h8 20 ♖b5 with a crushing attack. Instead Vasiukov-B.Vladimirov, USSR 1981 continued 16...♗d5 17 ♘d2 b6 18 ♘c4 ♘e7 19 ♘e5 ♗g7 20 c4 ♗b7 21 ♗b2 and White had a pleasant advantage.

15...b6 16 ♗f4

White could also try 16 ♕c2 h6 17 ♗f4 ♗d5 18 ♗h7+ ♔h8 19 ♗e4 with a promising position.

16...♔h8?!

Black could have limited his disadvantage with 16...♘e7 17 ♘e5 ♘d5 18 ♗d2.

17 ♗e4 ♗d7 18 ♘e5

Now Black has to make a concession.

18...♗xe5 19 dxe5 ♕e8 20 ♗g5 ♕e6

After 20...h6 White does not need to retreat: 21 ♗f6! ♖b8 22 ♕h5 ♔g8 23 ♖e3 and the attack is devastating.

21 ♕h5 h6 22 ♗f6! ♔g8 23 ♖e3 ♘e7 24 ♖g3 ♘g6 25 ♖xg6 fxg6 26 ♕xg6 1-0

Game 16
Leko-Yusupov
Dortmund 1998

---

1 e4 e5 2 ♘f3 ♘f6 3 ♘xe5 d6 4 ♘f3 ♘xe4 5 d4 d5 6 ♗d3 ♗e7 7 0-0 ♘c6 8 ♖e1 ♗g4 9 c3 f5

This is more aggressive than 9...♘f6 10 ♗g5 ♕d7?! (Black should play 10...0-0 but White's position is preferable after 11 ♘bd2 ♗h5 12 ♕b3 ♘a5 13 ♕c2 ♗g6 14 ♘e5) 11 ♘bd2 (White could also choose to shatter Black's kingside with 11 ♗xf6: White is better after 11...gxf6 12 ♘bd2 0-0-0 13 ♗b5) 11...0-0-0 12 ♕a4 h6 13 ♗h4 g5 14 ♗g3 ♗xf3 (or 14...♗d6 15 ♗b5 and Black is still in trouble because 15...♔b8? loses to 16 ♘e5 ♗xe5 17 ♗xe5) 15 ♘xf3 g4 16 ♘e5! ♘xe5 17 ♗f5! ♕xf5 18 ♖xe5 ♕d3 (18...♕d7 19 ♕xa7 ♕d6 20 ♖e3 is also winning) 19 ♖xe7 ♖d7 20 ♖e3 ♕a6 21 ♕xa6 bxa6 22 ♗e5 1-0, Keres-Alexander, Hastings 1954/55.

10 ♘bd2

10 h3 ♗xf3!? offers a promising pawn sacrifice: 11 gxf3 (if White declines the offer with 11 ♕xf3 0-0 12 ♗f4 ♗d6 the game is unclear) 11...♘f6 12 ♗xf5 0-0 13 ♕d3 ♗d6 14 ♗g5 ♘e7 15 ♗e6+ ♔h8 16 ♘d2 ♘g6 17 ♗f5?! (this lets Black take control; White had to try 17 ♘b3 even though Black has compensation after 17...♗f4 18 ♕f5 ♗xg5 19 ♕xg5 ♕d6) 17...♗f4! 18 ♗xf6 (or 18 ♗xg6 ♗xg5 19 ♗f5 ♘h5 and Black's occupation of f4 will be very threatening) 18...♕xf6 19

♗xg6 ♗xd2 20 ♖e2 ♗f4 21 ♗xh7 ♕g5+ 22 ♔h1 ♕h5 0-1 Enklaar-Dvoretsky, Wijk aan Zee 1975.

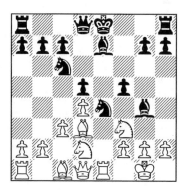

10...♕d6

Possibly preparing to castle long. Instead 10...0-0 is also reasonable, with the following:

a) 11 ♕b3 transposes to Game 17.

b) 11 ♘f1 with a further split:

b1) 11...♗d6 is tricky but probably inaccurate after 12 ♘g3 (not 12 ♘e3? ♗xh2+!, when 13 ♔xh2? is impossible because of 13...♘xf2 14 ♕c2 ♘d3 15 ♕xd3 ♗xf3 winning for Black – the problem with 16 gxf3 is 16...♕h4+, winning the rook) 12...♕f6 13 ♕b3 and White is a bit better.

b2) 11...♗h4 12 g3 ♗g5 13 ♗xg5 ♘xg5 14 ♗e2 ♘h3+ 15 ♔g2 f4 16 ♘3d2 ♗xe2 17 ♕xe2 ♘g5 18 ♕g4 fxg3 19 hxg3 ♕f6 with an unclear position, Ljubojevic-Hjartarsson, Belgrade 1989.

11 c4!?

The other option is 11 ♘f1. For example, 11...0-0-0!? 12 ♘e3 h5!? 13 h3 g6! 14 hxg4 (instead 14 ♗e2 ♗xf3 15 ♗xf3 ♗h4 16 ♖e2 ♘e7 17 ♘f1 ♗f6 18 ♖c2 ♔b8 19 a4 ♖h7 20 a5 g5 was unclear in Adams-Makarychev, Oviedo 1992) 14...hxg4 15 ♗xe4 (White must avoid 15 ♘d2? because of 15...♕h2+ 16 ♔f1 ♘xf2! 17 ♔xf2 ♗h4+ 18 ♔e2 ♖de8 with an immense attack) 15...dxe4 16 ♘c4 ♕f6 and Black has good compensation – 17 ♗g5? loses to 17...♕g7 18 ♗xe7 ♕h6 19 ♘h4 ♘xe7 20 g3 g5.

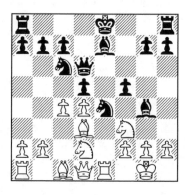

11...0-0?!

Now castling short is a mistake – Black has two better moves:

a) 11...♘xd2 12 ♗xd2 dxc4 (not 12...♘xd4? 13 ♘xd4! ♗xd1 14 ♘xf5 ♕c5 15 b4, when White will have a decisive material advantage) 13 ♗xc4 0-0-0 14 ♗c3 ♗f6 with an unclear position.

b) 11...0-0-0!? leads to sharp play: 12 cxd5 ♘xd2! (once again 12...♘xd4? is a mistake: 13 ♘xd4! ♗xd1 14 ♘xf5 ♕e5 15 ♘xe7+ ♕xe7 16 ♗xe4 and White's extra material ensures a clear advantage) 13 dxc6 ♘xf3+ 14 gxf3 ♗h3 15 cxb7+ ♔b8 16 ♗f1 ♗xf1 17 ♖xf1 ♗f6 with a very messy position (Leko).

12 cxd5 ♘xd4

White a bit better after 12...♘xd2 13 dxc6 ♘xf3+ 14 gxf3 ♗h5 15 cxb7 ♖ab8 16 ♗c4+ ♗f7 17 ♕b3.

13 ♗xe4! fxe4 14 ♘xe4

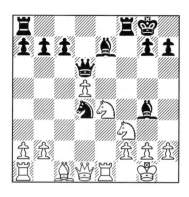

14...♗xf3

Leko assessed 14...♘xf3+ 15 gxf3 ♗xf3 16 ♘xd6 ♗xd1 17 ♘xb7 ♖ab8 18 ♖xe7 ♖xb7 19 d6 as clearly better for White.

15 ♕xd4 ♕b4 16 ♕xb4 ♗xb4 17 ♖e3 ♗h5 18 ♖b3 ♗a5

White also has a clear plus after 18...a5 19 a3 ♗g6 20 f3 ♗xe4 21 fxe4 ♗d6 22 ♗d2.

19 ♗e3 ♗f7 20 ♘g5

Or 20 ♖xb7 ♗xd5 21 ♖b5 ♗xe4 22 ♖xa5 a6 23 ♖c1 and, despite the opposite-coloured bishops, White has an obvious advantage.

20...♗b6 21 ♘xf7 ♖xf7 22 ♗xb6 axb6 23 d6! cxd6 24 ♖xb6 ♖c7 25 ♔f1 ♖a6 26 ♖b4

The direct 26 ♖xa6 should also win. For example, 26...bxa6 27 b4 ♖c2 28 a4 ♖b2 29 b5 axb5 30 a5 ♖c2 31 a6 ♖c8 32 a7 ♖a8 33 ♔e2 etc.

26...♔f7 27 a3 d5 28 ♖d1 ♔e6 29 ♖b5 ♖d6 30 ♔e2 ♔e5 31 ♔d3 ♖dc6

32 ♔e3

Or 32 ♖e1+ ♔d6 33 ♖e8 ♖c5 34 ♖xc5 ♖xc5 35 ♖b8 and White's advantage is evident.

32...♖c5 33 ♖xc5 ♖xc5 34 ♔d3 ♖c4 35 ♖e1+ ♔d6 36 ♖e8 ♖f4 37 f3 ♖h4 38 h3 b6 39 ♖b8 ♔c5 40 ♖c8+ ♔d6 41 ♖f8 g5 42 ♖f6+ ♔c5 43 b4+ ♔b5 44 ♖f5 ♔a4 45 ♖xg5 ♔xa3 46 ♖xd5

46 b5 ♔b4 47 ♖xd5 is even more straight-forward.

46...♖xb4 47 ♖h5 ♖b3+ 48 ♔e4 ♖b4+

49 ♔e3 ♖b3+ 50 ♔f4 ♖b4+ 51 ♔g3

White prefers to avoid the pawn ending 51 ♔g5 ♖b5+ 52 ♔h6 ♖xh5+ 53 ♔xh5 even though he wins neatly after 53...b5 54 f4 b4 55 f5 b3 56 f6 b2 57 f7 b1♕ 58 f8♕+ ♔a2 59 ♕a8+.

51...b5 52 h4 ♖b1 53 ♖xh7 b4 54 ♖a7+ ♔b2 55 ♔f4 ♖h1 56 ♔g5 b3 57 h5 ♔c3 58 ♖c7+ ♔d4 59 ♖b7 ♔c3 60 h6 b2 61 g4 b1♕ 62 ♖xb1 ♖xb1 63 h7 ♖b8 64 ♔f6 ♖b6+ 65 ♔g7 ♖b7+ 66 ♔h6 ♖b6+ 67 ♔h5 ♖b8 68 g5 1-0

Game 17
Ivanchuk-Shirov
Dortmund 1998

---

1 e4 e5 2 ♘f3 ♘f6 3 d4 ♘xe4 4 ♘xe5 d6 5 ♘f3 d5 6 ♗d3 ♘c6 7 0-0 ♗e7 8 ♖e1 ♗g4 9 c3 f5 10 ♘bd2 0-0 11 ♕b3

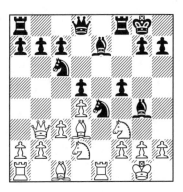

11...♔h8

Sacrificing a pawn. 11...♘a5 will be studied in the next game.

12 ♕xb7

White can opt to include 12 h3 ♗h5 before playing 13 ♕xb7. For example, 13...♖f6 14 ♕b3 ♖g6 (or 14...g5!? 15 ♘f1 ♖b8 16 ♕c2 with a murky position) 15 ♗e2 ♗d6 (15...♗h4?! is the wrong way to build up the attack: 16 ♖f1 ♗xf3 17 ♘xf3 and White is a safe pawn up because 17...♗xf2+?! fails to 18 ♖xf2 ♘xf2 19 ♔xf2 ♕d6 20 ♘g5! ♖f8 21 ♕a3 ♕d8 22 ♗f4 h6 23 ♘f3 ♖e8 24 ♗d3,

---

Karpov-Korchnoi, 6th matchgame, Moscow 1974) 16 ♘e5 ♘xe5 17 ♗xh5 ♖xg2+! 18 ♔xg2 ♕g5+ 19 ♔f1 ♕h4 20 ♘xe4 (not 20 ♖xe4? ♕xh3+ 21 ♔g1 ♘g4! and Black wins) 20...♕xh3+ 21 ♔g1 ♘f3+ 22 ♗xf3 ♗h2+ and Black has a perpetual check (O'Kelly).

12...♖f6

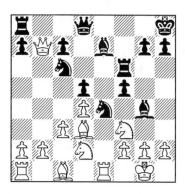

13 ♕b5

The other retreat 13 ♕b3 also allows Black counterplay: 13...♖g6 (13...♖b8 14 ♕a4 simply transposes to the game) and now:

a) 14 ♗b5 ♘xd2 15 ♘xd2 ♗d6 16 g3 (or 16 ♗xc6 ♗xh2+! 17 ♔xh2 ♕h4+ 18 ♔g1 ♖h6 19 f3 ♕xe1+ 20 ♘f1 ♖h1+! 21 ♔xh1 ♕xf1+ 22 ♔h2 ♗xf3 and now White should accept that Black has a perpetual check because if 23 ♕c2? ♗e4 24 ♕d2 ♖d8 Black has a deadly attack) 16...♘e7 17 ♗d3 h5 18 ♘f1 h4 and Black has a dangerous initiative, Peshkov-Raetsky, correspondence 1985.

b) 14 g3!? ♖b8?! 15 ♕c2 ♗d6 16 b4! (Movsesian pointed out that the imprecise 16 ♗f1 ♕f6 17 ♗g2 ♖f8 would allow Black undeserved compensation) 16...♕f6 17 b5 ♘e7 18 ♘e5 ♗xe5 19 dxe5 and White was clearly better in Movsesian-Kroeze, Netherlands 2001. More accurate is 14...♕d6 15 ♗b5 ♖b8, when Black has some compensation.

13...♖b8 14 ♕a4 ♗d6 15 h3

Or 15 ♗b5 ♘xd2 16 ♗xd2 ♗xf3 (16...♘e7?! is too passive: 17 ♘e5 a6 18 ♗f1 ♖xb2 19 ♗g5 ♗h5 20 ♗xf6 gxf6 21 ♕d7 is much better for White, Gagunashvili-

Bayramov, Batumi 2001) 17 ♗xc6 ♖g6 18 g3 ♗e4 and Black's kingside play provides obvious play for the pawn.

15...♗h5 16 ♗e2 ♖g6

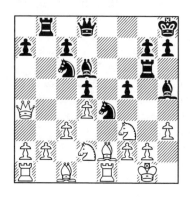

17 ♔f1!?

Trying to escape the pressure along the g-file. In this complex position White has two other main options:

a) 17 ♘xe4 leads to very unclear play after 17...fxe4 18 ♘g5 ♖xg5 19 ♗xg5 ♕xg5 20 ♗xh5 ♘e7! 21 ♕d1 g6 22 ♗g4 h5 23 ♗d7 ♖d8 24 ♗b5 ♘f5.

b) Curiously, 17 ♘e5 allows Black a choice of forced draws: 17...♘xe5 18 dxe5 ♗xe2 19 exd6 ♖xg2+! 20 ♔xg2 ♕g5+ 21 ♔h1 ♘xf2+ 22 ♔h2 f4! 23 ♘f1 ♘g4+ 24 hxg4 ♕h4+ 25 ♔g2 ♕xg4+ with a perpetual check, or 18...♕g5 19 ♗f1 ♘xf2! 20 exd6 ♘xh3+ 21 ♔h1 ♘f2+ (Ivanchuk).

17...♗f4 18 ♘b3 ♗xc1 19 ♖axc1 ♕d6 20 ♖c2

The ambitious 20 ♗b5?! backfires after 20...♖xg2! 21 ♔xg2 ♕g6+ 22 ♔h2 ♗xf3 23 ♖g1 ♕d6+ 24 ♖g3 ♘e7 25 ♖f1 h5, after which Black's attack is very strong.

Ivanchuk analysed 20 ♘h4 as leading to a draw: 20...♕f4 21 ♘xg6+ hxg6 22 f3 ♘e5! 23 ♕xa7! ♘xf3! 24 ♕xb8+ ♔h7 25 ♗xf3 ♗xf3 26 ♖xe4 ♗xe4+ 27 ♔e2 ♕g3 28 ♖g1 ♕d3+ 29 ♔f2 f4 when to avoid mate White must play 30 ♘c5 and allow perpetual check.

20...♕f4 21 ♗d1 ♖e8 22 ♘bd2

It is vital to support f3. If 22 ♘c5?! then

22...♗xf3 23 ♗xf3 ♕h2 24 g3 ♖xg3! 25 ♗xe4 ♕xh3+ 26 ♔e2 ♖g6 and Black's attack is venomous.

22...♖ge6 23 ♘xe4 fxe4 24 g3! ♕f5 25 ♘g1 ♗xd1 26 ♖xd1 e3?!

This is the wrong approach. 26...h5 leads to an unclear position after 27 c4 e3 28 cxd5 ♕xd5 29 ♕c4 ♘e7. However, the best line is the simple 26...♖f6 27 ♖e2 ♖ef8 when Black has a definite edge.

27 ♔g2 ♕e4+?!

One slip follows another... After 27...♖f8 28 f3 ♘e7 29 ♖e2 White would have been only slightly better.

28 f3 ♕f5 29 ♖e2 ♖g6 30 ♖de1 ♕f4 31 g4 h5 32 ♕b5! hxg4

A better try is 32...♖ee6!? when Ivanchuk analysed 33 ♕xd5 hxg4 34 hxg4 ♖xg4+ 35 fxg4 ♕xg4+ 36 ♔h1 ♖h6+ 37 ♖h2 ♖xh2+ 38 ♔xh2 ♕h4+ 39 ♘h3 ♕xe1 40 ♕h5+! ♔g8

41 ♕e8+ ♔h7 42 ♕xc6 ♕d2+ 43 ♕g2 e2 44 ♘g5+ ♕xg5 45 ♕xg5 e1♕ 46 ♕h5+, with White having reasonable winning chances.

33 hxg4

After 33 fxg4? Black can draw with 33...♕e4+ 34 ♘f3 ♖xg4+! 35 hxg4 ♕xg4+ 36 ♔h1 ♕xf3+ 37 ♖g2 e2 38 ♔g1 ♕e3+ 39 ♔h1 ♕f3.

33...♖h6 34 ♕xd5 ♘e7 35 ♕e5

White had a faster win with 35 ♕d7! ♖b8 36 ♕xe7 ♖xb2 37 ♖xb2 ♖h2+ 38 ♔f1 ♖xb2 39 ♖xe3.

35...♕xe5 36 dxe5 ♘d5 37 ♔g3 ♖c6 38 ♘h3 ♖xe5 39 ♘f4 ♘xf4 40 ♔xf4 ♖a5 41 a3 ♖b5 42 ♔xe3 ♖cb6 43 b4 ♖a6 44 ♖a1 c5 45 ♖b2 cxb4 46 ♖xb4 ♖ba5 47 a4 ♖c5 48 ♖a3 1-0

Game 18
Anand-Gelfand
Moscow 2004

---

1 e4 e5 2 ♘f3 ♘f6 3 ♘xe5 d6 4 ♘f3 ♘xe4 5 d4 d5 6 ♗d3 ♗e7 7 0-0 ♘c6 8 ♖e1 ♗g4 9 c3 f5 10 ♕b3 0-0

A major alternative here is 10...♕d6 with the idea of castling queenside. White has three main answers:

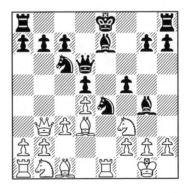

a) Taking the pawn with 11 ♕xb7 should certainly be analysed, but Black has good play after 11...♖b8 12 ♕a6 ♗xf3 13 gxf3 0-0!? 14 fxe4 (not 14 ♗b5?! ♖b6 15 ♕a4 ♗h4 with a dangerous initiative; for example, 16 fxe4?

allows a winning attack after 16...♗xf2+! 17 ♔xf2 ♕xh2+) 14...fxe4 15 ♗f1 ♗h4.

b) 11 ♘fd2!? is interesting but also potentially risky: 11...0-0-0 12 f3 ♗h4 (the tricky 12...♘e5?! fails to 13 ♗xe4 dxe4 14 fxg4 ♘xg4 15 ♘f1 and White is clearly better – Timman) 13 ♖f1 and now:

b1) The creative 13...♗h3?! is refuted by accurate defence: 14 ♕c2 ♕g6 15 ♘b3 ♖hf8 16 ♘a3 ♖de8 17 ♗f4! (but not 17 ♔h1?? ♘f2+! 18 ♖xf2 ♗xg2+! 0-1 Ivanchuk-Anand, Reggio Emilia 1989) 17...♖e6 18 ♘b5 and White has a clear advantage.

b2) 13...♗f2+!? 14 ♖xf2 ♘xf2 15 ♔xf2 ♕xh2 16 ♘f1 ♕h1!? 17 fxg4 fxg4 and the situation is impossible to assess with any confidence: White has a large material advantage but a dangerously exposed king.

c) 11 ♘bd2 is the safest option. 11...0-0-0 12 ♕c2 (12 ♗b5 is less clear, for example 12...♗f6 13 ♕a4 ♖he8!? 14 ♗xc6 bxc6 15 ♘xe4 ♖xe4 16 ♖xe4 fxe4 17 ♘e5 ♗xe5 18 dxe5 ♘c5 19 ♗e3 ♕b5 with an unbalanced position) 12...♔b8 13 b4 ♗f6 14 b5 ♘e7 15 ♘e5 ♗xe5 16 dxe5 ♕g6 17 ♘b3 ♘g5 18 f4 ♘e4 19 ♗e3 and White had an edge in Szelag-Naumann, Rostock 2002.

11 ♘bd2 ♘a5

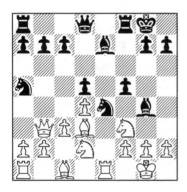

12 ♕c2

12 ♕a4 is a very important alternative. Play continues 12...♘c6 13 ♗b5 and now:

a) White has an easy time after 13...♘xd2?! 14 ♘xd2 ♕d6 15 h3 ♗h5 16 ♘b3 ♗h4 17

♘c5 ♗xf2+ (White is also clearly better after the alternatives 17...f4 18 ♖e6 ♕d8 19 ♘d3 f3 20 g3 and 17...♘d8 18 ♗f1 b6 19 ♘d3 ♘e6 20 ♕b4! – Anand) 18 ♔xf2 ♕h2 19 ♗xc6 bxc6 20 ♕xc6 f4 21 ♖xd5+ ♔h8 22 ♕xh5 f3 23 ♕xf3! ♖xf3+ 24 ♔xf3 and White has cleverly consolidated his advantage, Anand-Kramnik, Tilburg 1998.

b) 13...♗h4! with a further branch:

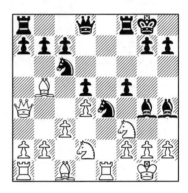

b1) 14 g3 (this is usual) 14...♗f6 15 ♗xc6 bxc6 16 ♕xc6 ♖e8 17 ♘e5 ♗xe5 18 dxe5 ♘g5 19 f4 (Kramnik mentions 19 c4!? d4!? 20 ♕d5+ ♕xd5 21 cxd5 ♖ad8 as still giving compensation) 19...♘h3+! (White has an edge after 19...♖e6?!, for example 20...♘e4?! 21 ♘xe4 dxe4 22 ♗e3 a6 – Shirov-Kramnik, Belgrade 1999 – and now 23 ♖ac1 ♗f3 24 ♖c2 would have clarified White's advantage) 20 ♔g2 ♖b8 21 c4 (21 ♘b3!? ♖b6 22 ♕c5 d4! 23 c4! ♕c8 is messy) 21...dxc4 22 ♘xc4 ♕d3 23 ♘e3 (White has to watch out for mating tricks: 23 ♗d2? ♖ed8 24 ♗c3 ♕c2+ 25 ♔h1 ♕a4!) 23...♖xb2+! 24 ♗xb2 ♕d2+ 25 ♔h1 ♘f2+ 26 ♔g1 ♘h3+ ½-½ Anand-Kramnik, Wijk aan Zee 1999.

b2) 14 ♖f1!? is also worth considering: 14...♘xd2 15 ♘xd2 f4 16 ♗xc6 bxc6 17 ♕xc6 ♕g5 18 c4 (18 g3 allows Black to force a draw with 18...fxg3 19 hxg3 ♗xg3! 20 fxg3 ♕e3+ 21 ♔g2 ♕e2+) 18...♖ad8 19 cxd5 ♖d6 20 ♕c3 ♖g6 21 ♘f3 ♕h5 22 ♘e5 f3 23 ♘xg6 hxg6 24 ♗e3 ♗c8! is totally unclear, Koziak-Motylev, Lvov 1999.

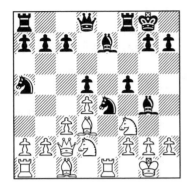

12...♗d6

This is stronger than 12...c5 13 ♘e5 ♗h5 (not 13...cxd4?! 14 ♘xg4 dxc3 15 bxc3 fxg4 16 ♘xe4 dxe4 17 ♗xe4 ♗c5 18 ♗xh7+ ♔h8 19 ♗e3 when White defends easily) 14 f3 cxd4 15 fxe4 fxe4 (15...dxc3 is tricky but White keeps the initiative with 16 exd5!? cxd2 17 ♗xd2 ♕xd5 18 ♗xa5 ♕xa5 19 ♘d7 ♖fe8 20 ♖e5) 16 ♘xe4 dxe4 17 ♗xe4 h6 (Anand-Bologan, Wijk aan Zee 2004) and here White can gain a large advantage with 18 b4! dxc3 19 bxa5 ♕d4+ 20 ♔h1 ♕xe5 21 ♗a3!.

Black has also tried 14...♗h4 but White keeps an edge after 15 g3 ♘xg3 16 hxg3 ♗xg3 17 ♖e2, whereas 15 fxe4 ♗xe1 16 exf5 c4 17 ♗f1 ♗xd2 18 ♗xd2 ♘c6, Morozevich-Adams, Dortmund 2002, is rather unclear.

13 b4

This is reasonable but perhaps White should prefer 13 ♘e5!? ♗xe5 14 dxe5 ♕h4 15 ♖f1 with a pleasant edge.

13...♗xf3! 14 ♘xf3 ♘c4 15 ♗xc4

Or 15 a4 c6 16 ♕b3 b5 17 axb5 cxb5 18 ♖a6 ♖f6 with unclear play.

15...dxc4 16 ♗e3 ♖e8 17 ♖ad1 ♕f6 18 ♘e5 ♗xe5

This is the obvious choice but 18...♖xe5!? is also interesting, 19 dxe5 ♕xe5 20 g3 ♕xc3 leading to a messy position.

19 dxe5 ♕xe5 20 ♗d4 ♕b5 21 a4 ♕d7

White also has compensation for the pawn after Black's two other options: 21...♕a6 22 f3 ♘d6 23 ♗c5 and 21...♕c6 22 f3 ♘d6 23 b5 ♕d7 24 ♗c5 ♖ad8 25 ♕f2.

22 ♗xa7 ♘d6 23 ♖xe8+ ♕xe8 24 ♗c5 ♕xa4 25 ♕xa4 ♖xa4 26 ♗xd6 cxd6 27 ♔f1 ♖a6 28 ♖d4 b5 29 ♖d5 ♖a3 30 ♖xd6 ♖xc3 ½-½

Summary

Nowadays the active continuation 9 c4 does not seem to offer White an advantage in the opening. It can be recommended to fans of the isolated queen's pawn, which arises after 9...♘f6 10 cxd5 ♘xd5. However, we should not forget that 10...♗xf3 11 ♕xf3 ♘xd4 (Game 14) has proven to be a reliable way of equalising.

Despite initial appearances, 9 c3 is one of the sharpest systems in the Petroff Defence. Of course, opposite side castling after 9...f5 10 ♕b3 ♕d6 and ...0-0-0 leads to many complications. After 10...0-0 11 ♘bd2 ♘a5 Black maintains material equality but loses control over the important e5-square, and following 12 ♕c2 ♗d6 (or 12...c5) 13 ♘e5 White's chances are preferable. The line with 11...♔h8 (Game 17) is extremely intricate and every move must be carefully analysed. After 12 ♕xb7 Black's queenside becomes even more vulnerable but the offside position of White's queen exposes his king to danger. Black has ...♖f8-f6-g6 at his disposal increasing his initiative on the kingside, and despite many games it is still impossible to give an exact assessment of this position.

1 e4 e5 2 ♘f3 ♘f6 3 ♘xe5 d6 4 ♘f3 ♘xe4 5 d4 d5 6 ♗d3 ♗e7 7 0-0 ♘c6 8 ♖e1 ♗g4 (D) 9 c4

> 9 c3 f5
>> 10 ♘bd2 – *Game 16*
>> 10 ♕b3 0-0 11 ♘bd2 (D)
>>> 11...♘a5 – *Game 18*
>>> 11...♔h8 – *Game 17*

9...♘f6 (D) 10 cxd5

> 10 ♘c3 – *Game 13*

10...♗xf3 – *Game 14*

> 10...♘xd5 – *Game 15*

8...♗g4

11 ♘bd2

9...♘f6

CHAPTER THREE

3 ♘xe5: Black Plays 6...♗d6

1 e4 e5 2 ♘f3 ♘f6 3 ♘xe5 d6 4 ♘f3 ♘xe4 5 d4 d5 6 ♗d3 ♗d6

The line 1 e4 e5 2 ♘f3 ♘f6 3 ♘xe5 d6 4 ♘f3 ♘xe4 5 d4 d5 6 ♗d3 ♗d6 is sometimes called the symmetrical variation. This is a pretty formal name as the symmetry is ruined quite quickly, and it's actually more accurate to call it the Marshall Variation. At the beginning of the 20th century Marshall often played the gambit 7 0-0 ♗g4?! 8 c4 0-0 9 cxd5 f5, a line that is not quite correct, and eventually White players learned how to dampen Black's dangerous initiative (see Game 19).

The tabiya of the system arises after the moves 7 0-0 0-0 8 c4 c6. Black has strengthened the d5-pawn, which became vulnerable after ....♗d6. 9 ♕c2, attacking the knight on e4, is covered in Games 19-21. Defending the knight with 9...f5, as played in the historic game Williams-Staunton, London 1851 is certainly possible (see the notes to Game 19), but these days most Black players prefer Krauze's suggested pawn sacrifice 9...♘a6!?. Then 10 ♗xe4 dxe4 11 ♕xe4 (Game 19) gives Black active play as compensation for the pawn after either 11...♖e8 or 11...♘b4!? (Raetsky's games are important here). Nowadays, grandmasters, including the elite, prefer to prevent the possibility of ...♘a6-b4 with 10 a3, after which Black continues with 10...♖e8,

10...♗g4 (Game 20) or 10...f5 (Game 21).

Attacking the e4-knight with 9 ♖e1 was unpopular for many years, but it has become quite fashionable recently. Defending the knight with 9...♗f5 and the gambit continuation 9...♗g4 are discussed in Game 22, while 9...♖e8 is the subject of Game 23.

Despite the obvious transposition after 9 ♘c3 ♘xc3 10 bxc3 ♗g4 11 cxd5 cxd5 and 9 cxd5 cxd5 10 ♘c3 ♘xc3 11 bxc3 ♗g4, this does not mean that there are no significant differences between 9 ♘c3 and 9 cxd5. After 9 ♘c3 (Games 24-25) Black can proceed with 9...♘xc3 10 bxc3 dxc4 11 ♗xc4 ♗g4, when the sharpest line is 12 ♕d3 ♘d7 13 ♘g5 ♘f6 14 h3 ♗h5 15 f4 h6 16 g4 as played by Capablanca (Game 25).

The theory is very far advanced in the line of 9 cxd5 cxd5 10 ♘c3 ♘xc3 11 bxc3 ♗g4, and here White manages to develop a strong initiative on the kingside. After 12 ♖b1 the game branches: 12...b6 is studied in Game 26, while 12...♘d7 is the subject of Games 27-28.

Game 19
Burkov-Raetsky
Correspondence 1985

1 e4 e5 2 ♘f3 ♘f6 3 ♘xe5 d6 4 ♘f3

♘xe4 5 d4 d5 6 ♗d3 ♗d6 7 0-0

White has a couple of minor alternatives:

a) 7 ♘bd2 f5 8 ♘e5 0-0 9 0-0 c5 10 c4!? (the passive 10 c3 allows Black to create strong counterplay after 10...cxd4 11 cxd4 ♗xe5!? 12 dxe5 ♘c6 13 ♘f3 f4, for example 14 ♗xe4?! dxe4 15 ♕xd8 ♖xd8 16 ♘g5 ♗f5 17 ♗xf4 h6 18 ♘h3 – Shafranska-Raetsky, Budapest 1991 – and here 18...g5 gives Black an edge) 10...cxd4 11 ♘ef3 (not 11 ♘df3? ♕c7 12 ♗f4 g5!, when Black is already almost winning) 11...dxc4 12 ♘xe4 fxe4 13 ♗xe4 d3 and the position is complex.

b) Playing 7 c4 before castling allows Black an additional option: 7...♗b4+ 8 ♘bd2 0-0 9 0-0 ♗xd2 10 ♘xd2 (also possible is 10 ♗xd2 ♗g4 11 ♗e3 ♘c6 12 h3 ♗h5 13 ♖c1 ♖e8 14 a3 dxc4 15 ♗xc4 ♕f6 16 ♗e2 – Short-Adams, Wijk aan Zee 2000 – and here Adams suggests 16...♘g3! 17 fxg3 ♖xe3 18 g4 ♗g6 19 ♕d2 ♖e4! leading to an unclear position) 10...♘xd2 11 ♗xd2 dxc4 12 ♗xc4 ♗e6 (12...♕xd4 13 ♗b4 ♕xd1 14 ♖axd1 ♖e8 15 ♖fe1 ♖xe1+ 16 ♖xe1 ♗e6 17 ♗xe6 fxe6 18 ♖xe6 ♘c6 is also equal) 13 ♗xe6 fxe6 14 ♕g4 ♕d7 15 ♖fe1 ♖f6 16 ♗g5 ♖f5 17 d5! ♖xd5 18 ♖ad1 ♘c6 is level, Tiulin-Raetsky, correspondence 1985.

7...0-0

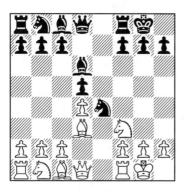

7...♗g4?! is premature after 8 c4 0-0 9 cxd5 f5 10 h3 ♗h5 11 ♘c3 ♘d7 12 ♘xe4 fxe4 13 ♗xe4 ♘f6 14 ♗f5 ♔h8 and now:

a) 15 ♕b3 ♘xd5 (if 15...♗xf3 16 ♕xf3

♘xd5 17 ♕h5 ♘f6 18 ♕h4 White is much better – Cordel. 16 ♗g5 ♗e7 17 ♗xe7 ♘xe7 18 ♗e4 ♗xf3 19 ♗xf3 ♘f5 20 ♕xb7 ♖b8 21 ♕xa7 ♘xd4 22 ♗g4 ♖xb2 23 ♖ad1 ♖b6 24 ♕a4 and White has small advantage, Bernstein-Marshall, San Sebastian 1911.

b) 15 g4! (this is even stronger) 15...♘xd5 16 ♗e6! ♗f7 17 ♘g5 ♗xe6 18 ♘xe6 ♕f6 19 ♘xf8 ♖xf8 20 ♕d3 and White is much better, Gipslis-Christiansen, Gausdal 1992.

8 c4

This is the critical try, but 8 ♖e1 is also reasonable. Now 8...♗f5 9 c4 c6 transposes to 8 c4 c6 9 ♖e1 ♗f5, while 8...♖e8 9 c4 c6 transposes to 8 c4 c6 9 ♖e1 ♖e8. This leaves 8...♗g4!? as the independent try: 9 ♗xe4 dxe4 10 ♖xe4 f5 11 ♖e1 ♘c6 12 c3 ♔h8 13 ♘bd2 ♕f6 14 h3 ♗h5 15 ♘c4 ♖ae8 16 ♖f1 (Black also has compensation after 16 ♖xe8 ♖xe8 17 ♘xd6 ♕xd6 18 ♗d2 f4) 16...f4 17 ♘xd6 cxd6 (White was a bit better after 17...♕xd6 18 b3 b5 19 ♗b2 ♕d5 20 a4 a6 21 axb5 axb5 22 ♗a3 ♖f6 23 ♗c5 in Kulaots-Rozentalis, Cappelle la Grande 2004) 18 b3 g5! 19 ♗b2 ♖g8 20 g4 (not 20 d5?! ♗xf3 21 ♕xf3 g4! 22 hxg4 ♘e5 23 ♕h3 ♖xg4, when White is in serious trouble) 20...fxg3 21 fxg3 ♖e3 22 g4 ♕f4! 23 ♘e1 ♖xh3!? 24 ♖xf4 gxf4 25 ♔g2 ♖h4 26 ♔f2 ♖gxg4 27 ♘f3 ♖h3 with an unclear position (Kulaots).

8...c6 9 ♕c2 ♘a6

9...f5 is a major alternative here. Play continues 10 ♘c3

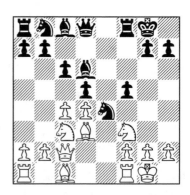

and now:

a) 10...♘a6 11 ♕b3 ♔h8 12 cxd5 cxd5 13 ♘b5 (13 ♗xa6 can lead to a draw after 13...bxa6 14 ♕xd5 ♖b8 15 ♘e5 ♗b7!? 16 ♘f7+ ♖xf7 17 ♕xf7 ♘xc3 18 bxc3 ♗xh2+! 19 ♔xh2 ♕h4+ 20 ♔g1 ♗xg2! 21 ♔xg2 ♕g4+) 13...♗b8 14 ♖e1 ♗e6 15 a3 ♗g8 16 ♘c3 ♗d6 17 ♗f1 g5!? 18 ♕xb7 g4 is unclear, Volchok-Borisov, correspondence 1984.

b) 10...♔h8 11 cxd5 cxd5 12 ♘xd5 ♗xh2+ 13 ♔xh2 ♕xd5 14 ♗c4 ♕d6+ 15 ♘e5 ♘c6 16 ♗f4 ♕f6 (not 16...♘xd4? 17 ♕d3 and White is winning, but perhaps Black should try 16...♘xe5 17 ♗xe5 ♕h6+ 18 ♔g1 ♗e6 19 d5 ♗g8 with unclear play) 17 ♘xc6 bxc6 18 ♗e5 ♕h6+ 19 ♔g1 ♘d2 (19...♘g5?! allows White a strong advantage after 20 f4 ♘e4 21 ♗d3, Macieja-Meijers, Istanbul Olympiad 2000) 20 ♖fe1 (Macieja pointed out 20 ♕c1?! ♘f3+! 21 gxf3 f4 22 ♖e1 ♗h3, when White is in trouble) 20...♘xc4 21 ♕xc4 and White has an edge.

10 ♗xe4

10 a3 is studied in Game 20.

10...dxe4 11 ♕xe4 ♘b4

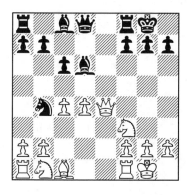

This is strong but Black has a good alternative in 11...♖e8 12 ♕d3 (or 12 ♕c2 ♘b4 13 ♕b3 ♗f5 14 ♘a3 a5 and Black has excellent compensation) 12...♗g4 13 ♗g5 ♕d7 14 ♘bd2 h6 15 ♗e3 (White should probably prefer 15 ♗h4, but Black still has good play after 15...♘c5 16 ♕c2 ♗f5 17 ♕c3 ♘d3)

15...f5 16 ♘b3 ♗xf3 17 gxf3 ♕f7 18 f4 ♘b4 19 ♕c3 ♕h5 with a dangerous attack, Kruppa-Rozentalis, Lvov 1985.

12 ♘g5

White's two other possible options also allow Black good counterplay: 12 ♘c3 ♖e8 13 ♕b1 g6 14 ♘e4 ♗g4, or 12 ♖e1 g6 13 ♗h6 ♗f5 14 ♕e2 ♖e8 15 ♖xe8+ ♕xe8 16 ♖xe8+ ♖xe8 17 ♘c3 ♘d3.

12...f5 13 ♕e2 f4 14 ♘e4

White wants to avoid the nasty pin that arises after 14 ♘f3 ♗g4. For example, 15 a3 ♗xf3 16 gxf3 ♕h4 17 ♕e6+ ♔h8 18 ♕g4 (other tries lose by force: 18 ♕xd6 ♘c2 19 ♖a2 ♕h3! 20 ♗xf4 ♖ad8, and 18 axb4 ♖f6 19 ♕d7 ♖g6+ 20 ♔h1 ♖d8 21 ♕f5 ♖g5 22 ♕e6 ♕h5! 23 ♖a3 ♖g6 24 ♕e4 ♕g5) 18...♕xg4+ 19 fxg4 ♘c2 20 ♖a2 ♘xd4 and Black was slightly better in Kuznetsov-Raetsky, correspondence 1985; or 15 ♘a3 ♕f6 16 c5 ♗c7 17 ♕c4+ ♘d5 and Black's position is preferable.

14...f3! 15 gxf3 ♗h3 16 ♖e1 ♕c7

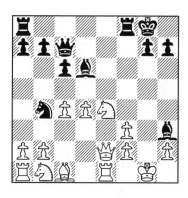

17 a3

Black is also much better after other tries:

a) 17 ♘xd6 ♕xd6 18 ♔h1 ♕xd4.

b) 17 ♘g3 ♖ae8 18 ♗e3 (Black has as strong attack after 18 ♕xe8 ♖xe8 19 ♖xe8+ ♗f8 20 ♘a3 ♕f7 21 ♗e3 h5) 18...♕f7! 19 ♘a3 ♕d3! 20 ♖eb1 ♘f4 21 ♕d2 ♘g2! and White is in terrible trouble.

17...♗xh2+ 18 ♔h1 ♘a6 19 ♘g5 ♗f5 20 ♘c3

20 ♘e6? leads to a quick loss following 20...♕f7 21 ♘xh2 ♖ae8 22 d5 ♕h5+ 23 ♔g1 ♕g6+ 24 ♔h2 ♗xe6 25 dxe6 ♖f5.

20...h6

Black can also try 20...♗f4!? 21 ♘e6 ♗xe6 22 ♕xe6+ ♔h8, when his attack continues.

21 ♘ge4

Playing to block the e-file. After 21 ♘e6 ♕f7 22 ♘xg7 ♔xg7 23 ♔xh2 ♖ae8 Black has excellent play.

21...♖ae8

Also promising is 21...♗g6!? 22 ♗e3 ♖f5 23 ♔g2 ♖af8, when Black has a powerful attack. For example, 24 ♘d2? ♖h5! (instead 24...♗h5 25 ♖h1 ♖xf3?? 26 ♕e1! was suddenly winning for White in Khramov-Raetsky, correspondence 1985) 25 ♖h1 ♗f5 and White has no hope of defending.

22 ♕f1

White could try 22 ♗xh6!? but Black still has compensation after 22...♖e6 23 ♗e3 ♗f4.

22...♕f7 23 ♕g2?

Now White is completely losing. After 23 ♔xh2 ♕h5+ 24 ♔g1 ♗h3 25 ♕e2 ♕g6+ 26 ♗g5 ♘c7! 27 ♕e3 ♘e6 at least White has chances to fend off the attack.

23...♗b8 24 ♗d2

Or 24 f4 ♖e6 25 d5 cxd5 26 cxd5 ♖g6 and the attack is too strong.

24...♕h5+ 25 ♔g1 ♗h3 26 ♘g3 ♗xg3 27 ♕xg3 ♖xe1+ 28 ♖xe1 ♖xf3 29 ♕h2 ♕g6+ 30 ♔h1 ♗g4 31 ♖g1

31 ♕g2 would have allowed a neat finish: 31...♖h3+ 32 ♔g1 ♗f3!.

31...♕f5 32 ♕e5 ♖h3+ 33 ♔g2 ♕f3+ 34 ♔f1 ♖h1 35 ♕g3 ♗h3+ 36 ♔e1 ♕xg3 0-1

Game 20
Kasparov-Shirov
Wijk aan Zee 2001

1 e4 e5 2 ♘f3 ♘f6 3 ♘xe5 d6 4 ♘f3 ♘xe4 5 d4 d5 6 ♗d3 ♗d6 7 0-0 0-0 8 c4 c6 9 ♕c2 ♘a6 10 a3

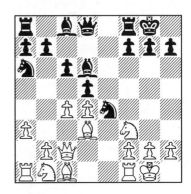

10...♗g4

This and 10...f5 (Game 21) are the usual moves but 10...♖e8 is also reasonable. Play continues 11 ♘c3 and now:

a) 11...♗f5 is a solid line: 12 ♖e1 h6 13 c5 ♗c7 14 ♗d2 ♘a5?! (instead Anand assesses 14...♘xd2 15 ♖xe8+ ♕xe8 16 ♕xd2 ♗xd3 17 ♕xd3 as equal) 15 ♗f4 ♗xc3 16 bxc3 ♘c7 17 h3 ♘e6 18 ♗h2 (Anand-Kasimdzhanov, Hyderabad 2002) and here White is slightly better after 18...♗h7! 19 ♖ab1 b6 20 ♘e5.

b) 11...♗g4 12 ♘xe4 dxe4 13 ♗xe4 ♗xf3 14 ♗xf3 ♕h4 15 g3 ♕xd4 16 ♗g5 ♕e5 17 ♕d2 ♕f5 18 ♗g2 ♘c5 19 ♖ad1 (According to Nataf, 19 ♕xd6 is also equal after 19...♕xg5 20 f4 ♕f5 21 b4 ♘e6 22 ♕d7 ♖ab8 23 ♖ad1 ♖ed8 24 ♕e7 ♖e8 25 ♕h4 ♘f8) 19...♘e6 20 ♗e3 ♖ad8 21 ♕c3 ♗c5 22 b4 ♖xd1 23 ♖xd1 ♗xe3 24 ♕xe3 a5! and

Black had equalised in Nataf-Volzhin, Stockholm 2001.

11 ♘e5

11 c5 ♗b8 12 ♘e5 gives Black more chances: 12...♗xe5 13 dxe5 ♘exc5 (but not 13...♘axc5?! 14 f3 ♘xd3 15 ♕xd3, winning a piece) 14 ♗xh7+ ♔h8 15 b4 ♕h4 16 ♗d3 ♘xd3 17 ♕xd3 ♕h5 18 ♖e1 ♗f5 19 ♕g3 ♘c7 20 ♘d2 ♘e6 21 ♗b2 b6 and Black has strong counterplay, Jobava-Mamedyarov, Plovdiv 2003.

11...♗h5

This is a major decision for Black as the alternatives are very interesting:

a) 11...♗f5 12 ♗e3 ♘ac5 13 dxc5 ♗xe5 14 cxd5 ♕xd5 15 ♘c3 ♗xc3 16 bxc3 ♖ad8 17 ♗d4 ♘xc3! 18 ♗xf5 (after 18 ♕xc3? Motylev assesses 18...♗xd3 19 ♗xg7 ♗xf1 20 ♖xf1 ♖fe8 21 ♗h8 f6 22 ♕xf6 ♖d7 as clearly advantageous for Black) 18...♕xd4 19 ♖ac1 g6 20 ♕xc3 ♕xc3 21 ♖xc3 gxf5 is very drawish, Smirnov-Motylev, Russia 2004.

b) 11...♗xe5 leads to heavily analysed complications after 12 dxe5 ♘ac5

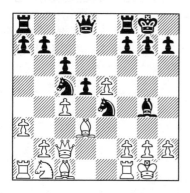

and now:

b1) Black has an easy position after 13 cxd5?! ♕xd5 (less exact is 13...cxd5 14 f3 ♖c8 15 ♗e3 – not 15 fxe4? dxe4! with a clear advantage – 15...d4 16 ♗xe4 ♗e6!? 17 ♗xh7+ ♔h8 with an unclear position) 14 ♗xe4 ♘xe4 15 ♘c3 (if 15 f3 ♘c5 16 ♖d1 ♕b3! Black has tremendous play) 15...♘xc3 16 ♕xc3 ♖fd8.

b2) 13 f3 ♘xd3 14 ♕xd3 ♘c5! 15 ♕d4 ♘b3 16 ♕xg4 ♘xa1 17 ♗h6 g6 (if Black inserts the moves 17...♕b6+ 18 ♔h1 before playing 18...g6 then 19 ♕f4 f6 20 ♗xf8 ♖xf8 21 cxd5 cxd5 22 ♕d2 promises White a strong initiative) 18 ♘c3 (an important choice) 18...♕b6+ 19 ♖f2 ♖fe8 20 ♕f4 ♕c7 (in Shirov-Leko, Linares 2000 White was a bit better after 20...f5 21 cxd5 ♘b3 22 e6 cxd5 23 ♘xd5 ♕xe6 24 ♘c7 ♕c6 25 ♘xe8 ♖xe8 26 g4!) 21 ♖e2 ♖e6, which Shirov assesses as unclear. Instead of 18 ♘c3, 18 cxd5 is very messy after 18...♖e8 19 ♘d2 ♕b6+ 20 ♔h1 ♖xe5! 21 ♖xa1 ♕xb2 22 ♖d1 ♖xd5. Perhaps the best move is 18 ♗xf8 as White has an edge after 18...♕xf8 19 cxd5 ♕c5+ 20 ♔h1 cxd5 21 e6 f5 22 ♕a4.

12 cxd5 cxd5 13 ♘c3

A good, simple developing move. Taking the pawn with 13 ♗xe4 dxe4 14 ♕xe4 allows Black sufficient counterplay: 14...♖e8 15 ♗e3 (or 15 ♗f4 ♗xe5 16 dxe5 ♘c5 17 ♕e3 ♘d3 and Black has excellent compensation) 15...♘c5 16 ♕c2 ♘e6 17 ♕f5 ♕h4!? 18 ♘d2 ♗g6 19 ♕g4 ♕xg4 20 ♘xg4 f5 21 ♘c4 ♗f8 22 d5 fxg4 23 dxe6 ♖xe6 with an equal position, Potkin-Rozentalis, Bad Wiessee 2003.

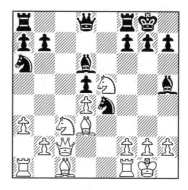

13...♘xc3

This may seem natural, but Black should seriously consider 13...♗xe5. For example, 14 dxe5 ♘ac5 15 ♘xe4 ♘xd3 16 ♕xd3 ♗g6 17 ♕b3 ♗xe4 18 ♕xb7 ♕h4 19 ♕b3 d4 20

♕g3 ♕xg3 21 hxg3 ♖fc8 and Black had sufficient compensation in Leko-Shirov, Linares 2004.

14 bxc3 ♔h8

Black is clearly worse after 14...♗xe5?! 15 ♗xh7+ ♔h8 16 dxe5 g6 17 ♕d2! ♔xh7 18 ♕h6+ ♔g8 19 ♗g5 f6 20 ♗xf6 ♖xf6 21 exf6 ♕xf6 22 f3! (Dokhoian).

15 f4

A natural move but White has a more threatening choice in 15 ♗xh7!?. After 15...g6 the bishop is trapped but 16 ♕d2 ♔xh7 17 ♕h6+ ♔g8 18 ♗g5 ♗e7 19 ♗xe7 ♕xe7 20 ♖ae1 ♕c7 21 ♖e3 creates a dangerous attack.

15...♗xe5?!

Now White's rooks are too strong. Instead 15...f6!? 16 ♘f3 ♕d7 17 ♖b1 ♖ab8 is unclear.

16 fxe5

White would even have a slight advantage after 16 dxe5 ♘c5 17 ♗e3 ♘xd3 18 ♕xd3 b6 19 h3.

16...♗g6 17 a4 ♕d7

Or 17...♗xd3 18 ♕xd3 f6 19 ♗a3 ♖f7 20 ♖f5 ♕d7 21 ♖af1 ♕xa4 22 ♗d6 and the attack continues.

18 ♗a3 ♖fe8 19 ♗xg6 fxg6 20 ♕b3

20...b6

Against 20...♘c7, Dokhoian supplies the neat winning line 21 ♕xb7 ♖eb8 22 e6! ♕d8 23 ♕xa8! ♖xa8 24 e7 ♕g8 25 ♖f8.

21 ♗d6 ♘c7 22 ♖f3 ♖ac8 23 ♖af1 h6

24 ♕c2

24 ♖f7 is also winning for White: 24...♕c6 25 ♕c2 ♘e6 26 ♕xg6 ♕xc3 27 ♗e7! ♕xd4+ 28 ♔h1 ♕xe5 29 ♗f6 ♕e4 30 ♗xg7+ ♔g8 31 ♕g3 h5 32 ♗e5+ ♕g4 33 ♕f2 (Dokhoian).

24...♕g4

There is no way to save the pawn on g6, for example 24...♖e6 25 ♖f7 ♕c6 26 ♖1f6!.

25 ♖g3 ♕h5

The rook ending after 25...♕e4 26 ♕xe4 dxe4 27 ♗xc7 ♖xc7 28 ♖e1 is easily winning for White.

26 ♖h3 ♕g5 27 ♖g3 ♕h5 28 ♗xc7 ♖xc7 29 ♖xg6 ♕h4 30 h3 ♕xd4+ 31 cxd4 ♖xc2 32 ♖f7 ♖g8 33 ♖d6 ♖c4 34 ♖xd5 ♖xa4 35 ♖dd7 ♖a1+ 36 ♔f2 ♖a2+ 37 ♔f3 ♔h7 38 e6 ♔g6 39 d5 ♖c8 40 ♖c7 ♖e8 41 g4 a5 42 ♖xg7+ ♔f6 43 ♖gf7+ ♔e5 44 ♖f5+ ♔d4 45 e7 1-0

Game 21
Grischuk-Gelfand
Wijk aan Zee 2002

1 e4 e5 2 ♘f3 ♘f6 3 ♘xe5 d6 4 ♘f3 ♘xe4 5 d4 d5 6 ♗d3 ♗d6 7 0-0 0-0 8 c4 c6 9 ♕c2 ♘a6 10 a3 f5 11 ♘c3

White has a sound alternative in 11 c5 ♗b8!? (11...♗e7 12 ♘c3 ♘c7 transposes to 11 ♘c3 ♘c7 12 c5 ♗e7) 12 ♘c3 ♘c7 13 ♘e2 (White should try 13 ♗f4!? ♘e6 14 ♗xb8 ♖xb8 15 ♘e2 ♕f6 16 b4 g5 17 ♕b2 with a slight edge) 13...♘e6 14 b4 ♕f6 15 ♗b2 ♗d7 16 ♖ae1 ♗e8 17 ♕c1 ♗h5 18 ♘e5 ♗xe2 (also promising is 18...♘xd4!? 19 ♗xd4 ♗xe2 20 ♘f3 ♗xd3 21 ♗xf6 ♖xf6 with excellent compensation – Piket) 19 ♗xe2 ♘xd4 20 ♘d7 ♘xe2+ (not 20...♕h4?! 21 ♘xb8 ♘xe2+ 22 ♖xe2 ♖axb8 23 f3 ♘f6 24 ♖fe1, when White had plenty of compensation, Morozevich-Piket, Wijk aan Zee 2002) 21 ♖xe2 ♕f7 22 ♘xb8 ♖axb8 23 f3 ♘f6 24 ♕g5 ♖be8 and Black is slightly better (Morozevich).

11...♘c7

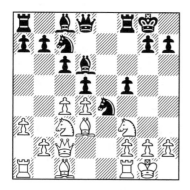

12 ♖e1

White has plenty of alternatives:

a) 12 b4 a5 13 b5 ♗d7 14 ♖b1 (or 14 b6 ♘e6 15 cxd5 cxd5 16 ♘xd5 ♖c8 17 ♕a2 ♔h8 with compensation – Svidler) 14...♔h8 15 c5 ♗e7 16 bxc6 bxc6 17 ♗f4 ♘e6 18 ♗e5 ♗e8 19 ♖b6 ♕c8 20 ♘d2 ♗g5! (White has excellent compensation after 20...♗d8 21 f3 ♗xb6 22 cxb6) 21 ♘b3 ♗h5 22 a4 ♕e8 is unclear, Svidler-Morozevich, Krasnoyarsk 2003.

b) 12 ♘e2 ♘e6 13 b4 ♗d7 14 cxd5 cxd5 15 ♕b3 ♗e8 16 ♘e5 ♗c7 (if 16...♘xd4, A.Sokolov claims an edge for White after 17 ♕xd5+ ♗f7 18 ♕xd4 ♗xe5 19 ♕xe5 ♕xd3 20 ♗b2 ♘f6 21 ♘f4) 17 ♗e3 ♗h5!? (17...♗f7 is inferior: 18 f3 ♗xe5 19 dxe5 d4 20 fxe4 dxe3 21 ♗c4 ♘d4 22 ♕a2! ♘xe2+ 23 ♕xe2 ♕e7 24 ♖xf5 ♗xc4 25 ♕xc4+ ♔h8 26 ♕c3 and White was clearly better in A.Sokolov-Fressinet, Val d'Isere 2002) 18 f3 ♘4g5 19 ♖fd1 f4 20 ♗f2 and White has only a small advantage.

c) 12 c5 ♗e7 13 ♘e2 with a branch:

c1) 13...♗f6!? 14 b4 ♘e6 15 ♗b2 ♕c7 16 ♖ad1 g6 17 ♕b1 ♕g7 18 ♗a1 ♗d7 was unclear in Tseshkovsky-Motylev, Ekaterinburg 2002.

c2) 13...♘e6 is a viable alternative: 14 ♘f4 ♗f6 15 ♘xe6 ♗xe6 16 ♗f4 ♕e8 (less promising is 16...♗f7 17 ♗e5 ♗h5 18 ♗xf6 ♕xf6 19 ♘e5 ♖ad8 20 f3 ♘g5 21 ♖fe1 ♘e6 22 ♕f2 f4 23 b4 ♖fe8 24 ♕b2 ♖e7 25 ♖e2

♖de8 26 ♖ae1 when White had a definite edge in Gipslis-Raetsky, Berlin 1993) 17 ♗e5 ♕h5 18 ♖fe1 ♖ae8 and Black has managed to complicate the game.

12...♔h8 13 b4 ♗d7 14 ♗b2 ♘e6

This is an ambitious move. Black could equalise easily with 14...dxc4 15 ♗xc4 ♘xc3 16 ♗xc3 ♘d5

15 cxd5

This is probably best. White is in trouble after 15 ♘e2 ♘6g5 16 ♘e5 ♗xe5 17 dxe5 f4 18 ♘d4 (or 18 f3 ♘xf3+! 19 gxf3 ♕g5+ 20 ♘g3 fxg3 and Black's attack crashes through) 18...f3, when Black has a dangerous initiative (Gelfand).

15...cxd5 16 ♘xd5 ♖c8 17 ♕d1 ♘6g5!

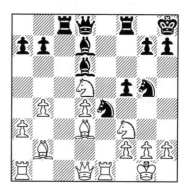

This keeps up the initiative. After 17...♗c6 18 ♘e3 ♘c3!? 19 ♗xc3 ♗xf3 20 ♕xf3 ♖xc3 21 ♘xf5! ♘xd4 22 ♕g4 ♘xf5 23 ♗xf5 White escapes with an edge.

18 ♘e5

After 18 ♘e3 ♘xf3+ 19 ♕xf3 ♕h4! 20 g3 ♕h6 the attack continues (Gelfand).

18...♘h3+ 19 gxh3 ♕g5+ 20 ♔f1

This is forced. 20 ♘g4? loses immediately to 20...♘xf2!.

20...♗xe5

In such a position it is not surprising that Black has more than one possibility: 20...♕h4!? 21 ♖e2 (after 21 ♕e2 ♗xe5 22 dxe5 ♗c6 23 ♗c4 ♕xh3+ 24 ♔g1 ♘d2! 25 ♕xd2 ♕g4+ 26 ♔h1 ♕xc4 Black has a pleasant advantage) 21...♕xh3+ 22 ♔g1 ♗xe5 23

♗xe5 23 dxe5 ♕g4+ 24 ♔f1 ♕h3+ when White should accept a draw (Gelfand).

21 dxe5 ♗c6

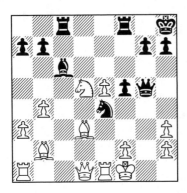

This is promising, but so is 21...♗e6!? 22 ♘e3 ♕f4! 23 ♖e2 ♕xh2 24 ♔e1 ♕h1+ 25 ♘f1 ♘g5 26 ♖c2 ♖cd8 27 f4 ♕xh3 (if Black wishes he can force a draw with 27...♘f3+ 28 ♔f2 ♗d5 29 ♔g3 ♘e1! 30 ♕xe1 ♕f3+ 31 ♔h2 ♕h1+) 28 fxg5 ♖xd3 29 ♕e2 ♖fd8 with excellent compensation (Gelfand).

22 ♗c1!

A superb defensive move. After 22 ♘e3 ♖cd8 23 ♕c2 ♖xd3! 24 ♕xd3 ♕f4 Black has a terrific attack. For example, 25 ♘d1 ♘d2+ 26 ♔g1 ♘f3+ 27 ♔f1 ♕xh2 28 ♔e2 ♕xh3 and Black wins (Gelfand).

22...♕h4 23 ♗xe4 fxe4

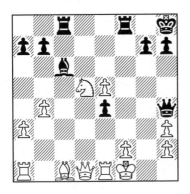

24 ♗e3

White continues to defend stoutly. 24 ♘f4? loses rapidly to 24...♖xf4 25 ♗xf4

♕xh3+ 26 ♔g1 e3, while 24 ♖a2?! e3! 25 ♖xe3 ♕c4+ is not much better.

24...♕xh3+

Now the game must end in a draw. Black could play on with 24...♖f3!? but after 25 b5! ♗xb5+ 26 ♔g1 ♖xh3 27 ♗f4 ♖d3 28 ♗g3 ♕d8 29 ♕g4 ♖xd5 30 ♕xe4 the position is simply unclear.

25 ♔g1 ♗xd5 26 ♕xd5 ♕g4+ 27 ♔f1 ♕h3+ 28 ♔g1 ♕g4+ 29 ♔f1 ½-½

1 e4 e5 2 ♘f3 ♘f6 3 ♘xe5 d6 4 ♘f3 ♘xe4 5 d4 d5 6 ♗d3 ♗d6 7 0-0 0-0 8 c4 c6 9 ♖e1

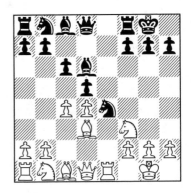

9...♗f5

9...♖e8 is examined in Game 23. Black's two other options make life easier for White:

a) 9...f5 10 ♘c3 ♔h8 11 ♕b3 ♘a6 12 cxd5 cxd5 13 ♘b5 ♗b8 14 ♗d2 ♗e6 15 ♖ac1 ♖f6 (or 15...♘xd2 16 ♘xd2 ♖e8 17 ♘f1 ♗f4 18 ♘e3 and White has a pull) 16 ♗g5 ♘xg5 17 ♘xg5 ♗g8 18 ♘f3 ♗f4 19 ♖c2 ♖b6 20 ♕a3 and White was a bit better in Naiditsch-Meijers, Senden 1999.

b) 9...♗g4 and now:

b1) 10 c5? leads only to trouble: 10...♗xh2+! 11 ♔f1 (or 11 ♔xh2 ♘xf2 and Black is better because 12 ♕e2? loses to 12...♘xd3 13 ♕xd3 ♗xf3) 11...f5 12 ♘c3

♘d7 13 ♘xe4 fxe4 14 ♗xe4 ♗c7 15 ♗g5 ♘f6 16 ♗c2 ♕d7 17 ♕d3 ♘e4 and Black was obviously better in Yemelin-Raetsky, Rostov on Don 1993.

b2) The simple 10 ♗xe4 dxe4 11 ♖xe4 is best. Following 11...f5 White has two options:

b21) 12 ♖e6 gives Black chances after 12...♕d7 13 ♖e1 ♘a6 14 ♕b3 (or 14 ♘c3 ♖ae8 15 ♖xe8 ♖xe8 16 ♗d2 ♗b8 with good attacking possibilities) 14...♗xf3 15 ♕xf3 ♖ae8 16 ♗e3? (White can hang on to equality after 16 ♗d2 ♗b4) 16...♘b4 17 c5? (after 17 ♘a3 ♘d3 18 ♖f1 ♗xa3 19 bxa3 f4 20 ♕d1 ♕f5 21 ♗d2 ♕e4 Black is much better, but there is no forced win) 17...♘c2 18 cxd6 f4 19 ♗d2 ♘xe1 20 ♕b3+ ♔h8 21 ♘a3 f3 0-1 Kosteniuk-Raetsky, Biel 2004.

b22) 12 ♖e1 (again the simple move is the best) 12...♗xf3 13 ♕xf3 ♕h4 14 h3 ♕xd4 15 ♕b3 ♕b6 16 ♕xb6 axb6 17 ♘c3 ♘d7 18 ♖d1 ♖f6 and White had a tiny edge in Ehlvest-Mamedyarov, Moscow 2002.

10 ♕c2

This is probably the best of a wide choice:

a) 10 c5 ♗c7 11 ♘c3 ♖e8 12 ♕c2 ♘d7 13 ♘xe4 dxe4 14 ♗xe4 ♕e7 15 ♘g5 ♘f6 16 f3 (Socko-Skatshkov, Cappelle la Grande 2004) and here Skatshkov suggests that 16...♘xe4 17 fxe4 h6 18 ♕f2 ♗g6 is slightly better for Black.

b) 10 ♕b3 ♘a6 11 cxd5 cxd5 12 ♘c3

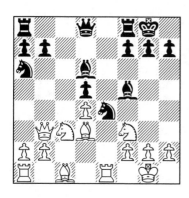

and now:

b1) 12...♗e6 13 a3 ♘c7 14 ♕c2 f5 15 ♘e5 ♖c8 16 ♗f4 g5! 17 ♗d2 (also worth considering is 17 ♗e3 ♘a6 18 f3 ♘xc3 19 bxc3 ♗xe5 20 dxe5 ♘c5 21 ♗d4 with counterplay – Gelfand) 17...♘a6 18 ♕d1 ♗xe5 19 dxe5 ♘ac5 20 ♗c2 ♘xd2 21 ♕xd2 d4 22 ♘a4 ♘b3 23 ♗xb3 ♗xb3 24 e6! was unclear in Fressinet-Gelfand, Cannes 2002.

b2) Also interesting is 12...♗b4 13 ♗b1!? (Black has enough compensation after 13 ♗xe4 dxe4 14 ♗g5 ♕b6 15 ♘xe4 ♗e6 16 ♕d1 ♖ac8) 13...♗e6 14 a3 ♘c6 15 ♕xb7 ♘a5 16 ♕a6 ♘xc3! (not 16...♘b3?! 17 ♘xe4 dxe4 18 ♗xe4 ♘xa1 19 ♗xa8 ♘c2 20 ♖e2 ♘xd4 21 ♘xd4 ♗c5 22 ♗e3 ♗xd4 23 ♖d2 and White was comfortably better in Palac-M.Ivanov, Cannes 2004) 17 bxc3 ♘b3 18 ♗g5! ♗xh2+ 19 ♔h1 ♕c7 20 ♖xe6!? fxe6 21 ♕xe6+ ♕f7! 22 ♕xf7+ ♖xf7 23 ♗a2!? ♘xa1 24 ♗xd5 and after all the complications the position remains unclear.

c) 10 ♘c3 ♘xc3 11 bxc3 ♗xd3 12 ♕xd3 dxc4 13 ♕xc4 ♘d7 with another branch:

c1) 14 ♗g5!? ♕c7 15 ♗e7!? (15 ♕b3 is less enterprising: 15...♖fe8 16 ♖ab1 h6 17 ♗e3 b6 with a dull equality) 15...♘b6 16 ♗xd6 ♕xd6 17 ♕b3 ♖ae8 18 c4 ♕c7 19 a4 ♘d7 20 ♖ab1 b6 21 g3 ♕d8 22 a5 ♕f6 23 axb6 axb6 24 ♔g2 and White had a marginal edge in Ivanchuk-Gelfand, Lvov 2000.

c2) 14 ♕b3 has also been tried: 14...♕c7 15 c4 ♖fe8 16 ♗b2 h6 17 g3 ♖ad8 18 ♘h4 ♗f8 19 ♕c2 (perhaps a better try is 19 ♖ad1 ♕b6 20 ♗c3 with unclear play) 19...♕a5! 20 ♘g2 ♖xe1+ 21 ♖xe1 b5 22 ♗c3 b4 23 ♗a1 ♘b6 24 ♕b3 c5 25 d5 ♕a6 26 ♘e3 ♖e8 27 ♖c1 ♕c8 and Black was a bit better in Adams-Morozevich, Dortmund 2002.

10...♗g6

Solidly defending the bishop. 10...♘d7 is also playable: 11 ♘c3 ♘df6 12 c5 (12 cxd5 cxd5 13 ♕b3 ♖e8 14 ♕xb7 ♖b8 15 ♕xa7 ♖e7 16 ♕a6 ♖e6 17 ♕a7 ♖e7 is simply a draw – Piket) 12...♗c7 13 b4 ♗g6 14 ♗b2 ♘xc3 15 ♕xc3 ♗xd3 16 ♕xd3 ♘e4 17 ♖e2 ♖e8 18 ♖ae1 ♖e6 19 ♘e5 ♕h4 20 ♗c1 (20 f3? loses after 20...♖h6 21 fxe4 ♕xh2+ 22 ♔f1 ♕h1+ 23 ♔f2 ♖f6+ 24 ♘f3 ♗g3+! 25 ♔xg3 ♖g6+ – Haba) 20...f6 21 ♘f3 ♕h5 22 g3 ♖ae8 23 ♔g2 g5 was unclear in Lanka-Haba, Hamburg 2003.

11 c5 ♗c7 12 ♘c3

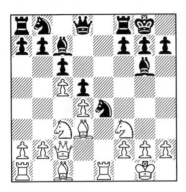

12...♘f6

Alternatives are not so good:

a) 12...♘xc3 13 bxc3 ♘d7 14 ♗xg6 hxg6 15 ♗g5 ♘f6 16 ♘e5 and White has a pleasant initiative – Piket.

b) 12...f5 13 ♕b3!? and now 13...♗f7 allows a trick: 14 ♘g5! b6 (the point is 14...♘xg5? 15 ♗xg5 ♕xg5 16 ♖e8+ ♖f8 17 ♖xf8+ ♔xf8 18 ♕xb7 and White wins) 15 ♗xe4 fxe4 16 ♘xf7 ♗xf7 17 cxb6 axb6 18 ♘e2 ♕f6 19 ♗e3 ♘d7 20 ♖ac1 with a clear advantage, Anand-Morozevich, Monte Carlo (blindfold) 2003. Instead, 13...b6 14 cxb6 axb6 15 ♘xe4 fxe4 16 ♗xe4 ♗xe4 17 ♖xe4 gives White a small advantage.

13 ♗g5 ♘bd7 14 ♘e5 ♗xd3 15 ♕xd3 ♕c8 16 f4

If 16 b4 ♘xe5 17 dxe5 ♘d7 18 f4 f6 19 exf6 ♘xf6 20 g3 ♗d8 Black's stands well.

16...♗a5! 17 ♕g3 ♔h8 18 ♕h4 ♗xc3

Preparing ...♘e4. The immediate 18...♘e4!? is also possible: 19 ♖e3 ♘xe5 20 fxe5 ♗xc3 21 bxc3 f6 22 exf6 gxf6 23 ♗h6 ♖f7 24 c4 ♕e6 25 cxd5 cxd5 26 ♖f1 ♖g8 27 h3 with an unbalanced position – Piket.

19 bxc3 ♘e4 20 ♖e3

White could try 20 ♗e7 ♘xe5 21 fxe5

♖e8 22 ♗d6 ♘xc3 23 ♖e3 ♘e4 24 ♖h3 h6 25 ♖f1 with reasonable play for the pawn.

20...♘xg5 21 ♕xg5 h6

Trying to win a piece with 21...f6? loses to 22 ♘g6+! hxg6 23 ♕xg6 ♘xc5 24 ♖e7.

22 ♕h5 ♘f6 23 ♘xf7+ ♔h7 24 ♘g5+ ♔g8 25 ♕g6 hxg5 26 ♖e7!

Black defends easily after 26 fxg5? ♘e4 27 ♖h3 ♕f5.

26...♘e8 27 ♖ae1 ♕g4

Black would be mated after 27...gxf4? 28 ♖xg7+! ♘xg7 29 ♖e7.

28 fxg5 ♕h4

The safest line is 28...♕f4! 29 h3 ♕g3 30 ♔h1 ♕xc3 31 ♖xe8 ♖axe8 32 ♖xe8 ♕c1+ 33 ♔h2 ♕f4+ with a draw (Piket).

29 g3 ♕h3 30 ♖xb7 ♕f5 31 ♕e6+! ♕xe6 32 ♖xe6 ♖f7?!

32...♖f3!? 33 ♖xc6 ♖xc3 is still unclear. Now Black is in trouble.

33 ♖xf7 ♔xf7 34 ♖xc6 ♖b8 35 ♖a6 ♖b7 36 h4 ♘c7 37 ♖d6 ♘b5 38 g6+ ♔e7 39 ♖xd5 ♘xc3 40 ♖e5+ ♔f6 41 c6! ♖b1+

There is no way to save the game: 41...♖c7 42 h5 ♖xc6 43 g4 ♔e6 44 g5+! ♔e7 45 h6 gxh6 (45...♘e2+ 46 ♖xe2 ♖xe2 47 hxg7 is a beautiful finish) 46 g7 ♖xe5 47 dxe5 ♔f7 48 e6+ ♔xg7 49 gxh6+ and a pawn will queen (Piket).

42 ♔g2 ♖b2+

42...♘b5 doesn't help: 43 ♖d5 ♖b4 44 a3 ♖b2+ 45 ♔h3 ♔e6 46 ♖d7 and White wins.

43 ♔f3 1-0

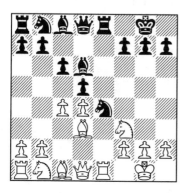

Game 23
Kovalev-Rozentalis
Glogow 2001

1 e4 e5 2 ♘f3 ♘f6 3 ♘xe5 d6 4 ♘f3 ♘xe4 5 d4 d5 6 ♗d3 ♗d6 7 0-0 0-0 8 c4 c6 9 ♖e1 ♖e8

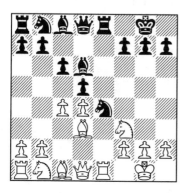

10 ♘c3

This is the most logical of a range of possibilities:

a) 10 ♕c2 ♗g4 11 ♘e5 ♗xe5 12 dxe5 ♘a6 13 ♗xe4 dxe4 14 ♕xe4 f5 15 ♕c2 ♘b4 16 ♕c3 ♘d3 and Black's huge lead in development provides ample compensation for the pawn.

b) 10 ♘bd2 ♗f5 11 c5 (Black equalises easily after 11 ♕c2 ♘xd2 12 ♗xd2 ♗xd3 13 ♕xd3 ♖xe1+ 14 ♖xe1 dxc4 15 ♕xc4 ♘a6 16 ♘g5 ♕d7) 11...♗f8 12 ♕b3 b6! 13 ♘xe4 (or 13 cxb6 axb6 14 ♘f1 ♗d6 with an unclear position) 13...♗xe4 14 ♗xe4 dxe4 15 ♘e5 ♕d5! 16 cxb6 axb6 and Black has equalised. The point is that 17 ♕xb6?! is a mistake after 17...f6 18 ♕b7 (Ulibin-Raetsky, Makhachkala 1993). Black should continue 18...♘a6! 19 ♘d7 ♘b4! 20 ♘xf8 (or 20 ♘b6 ♕b5 21 a4 ♕a6 and Black is clearly better) 20...♘c2! 21 ♗h6!? ♕f7 (of course not 21...gxh6?? 22 ♘xh7 and White wins) 22 ♘d7 ♘xe1 23 ♖xe1 ♖ed8 with a small advantage.

c) 10 cxd5 should not be dangerous: 10...cxd5 11 ♘c3 ♘xc3 12 ♖xe8+ ♕xe8 13

bxc3 ♗g4 14 ♗e3 ♕d8?! (Black should play to exchange White's better bishop; after 14...♕d7 15 h3 ♗f5 16 ♗xf5 ♕xf5 the game is level) 15 ♖b1 ♘d7 16 h3 ♗xf3 (after 16...♗h5 White can simply win a pawn with 17 ♖xb7 ♘b6 18 g4 ♗g6 19 ♗xg6 hxg6 20 ♘g5 ♗e7 21 ♕f3) 17 ♕xf3 (White's bishop pair ensure an edge) 17...♘b6 18 a4 ♖b8 19 a5 ♘a4 20 ♗d2 ♖xa5 21 ♖b5 ♕c7 22 ♖xd5 ♖d8 23 ♖b5 ♘b6 24 h4 a6 25 ♖g5 ♖e8? (White had a promising attack, but this allows a quick kill) 26 ♖xg7+! 1-0 Timofeev-Raetsky, Abu Dhabi 2004 (26...♔xg7 27 ♗h6+! leads to mate).

10...♘xc3 11 bxc3

Also playable is 11 ♖xe8+ ♕xe8 12 bxc3 ♗g4 13 ♗d2 (with the idea of ♕b1 and a double attack) 13...h6 (13...♕d8?! misses the threat: 14 c5 ♗c7 15 ♕b1 ♗xf3 16 ♕xb7 ♘d7 17 gxf3 ♖c8 18 ♖e1 g6 19 h4 and White was much better in Raetsky-Varlamov, correspondence 1985) 14 ♕b3 dxc4 15 ♗xc4 (Black can draw after 15 ♕xb7 cxd3 16 ♖e1 ♕d7 17 ♕xa8 ♗xf3 18 gxf3 ♕h3 as there is no good way to avoid perpetual check) 15...b5 16 ♖e1 ♕f8 17 ♗xf7+! ♕xf7 18 ♖e8+ ♗f8 19 ♘e5 ♕xb3 20 axb3 ♗h5 21 ♖d8 and White has sufficient compensation for the piece: the pins are almost impossible to escape.

11...♗g4 12 ♗g5 ♖xe1+ 13 ♕xe1

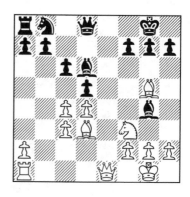

13...♕c8

13...♕d7 is another option: 14 c5! ♗c7 15

♘h4!? h6 16 ♗d2 ♕d8? (now Black is in desperate trouble; instead 16...♘a6 17 ♕b1 ♖e8 18 g3 ♕c8 19 f3 ♗h3 20 ♘f5 is only slightly better for White) 17 f4! ♗c8 18 ♕g3 (surprisingly White is already winning by force) 18...b6 (after 18...♕f8 Anand analyses a beautiful winning line: 19 ♖e1 ♗d8 20 ♘g6! fxg6 21 ♕xg6 ♗e7 22 ♕h7+ ♔f7 23 ♗g6+ ♔f6 24 ♗h5 ♗f5 25 g4! ♗xh7 26 g5+ hxg5 27 fxg5+ ♔f5 28 ♖e5 mate) 19 ♖e1 bxc5 20 dxc5 ♕f8 21 ♗e3 ♘a6 22 ♗d4 g5 23 ♕f2 and Black is defenceless and resigned in Anand-Piket, Wijk aan Zee 2001.

14 ♘h4

This prepares a kingside advance. White has tried two other possibilities:

a) 14 ♗e7 ♗f4! 15 ♗h4 ♘d7 16 ♗g3 ♗xg3 17 hxg3 ♗xf3 18 gxf3 ♘f6 (Black has equalised) 19 ♕e5 dxc4 20 ♗xc4 ♕d7 21 ♕f4 ♖e8 22 ♕d2 h5 23 ♖e1 ♖xe1+ 24 ♕xe1 b5 ½-½ Movsesian-Rozentalis, Neum 2000.

b) Perhaps White's strongest line is 14 c5, for example 14...♗f8 15 ♕b1! h6 (after 15...g6 16 ♘e5 ♗e6 17 f4 ♘d7 18 ♘f3 White has a promising attack – Rozentalis) 16 ♘e5 ♗e6 17 ♗f4 ♘d7 18 a4!? ♗e7 19 a5 ♗d8 20 ♕b4 and White's easier development promises an edge, Degraeve-Rozentalis, Montreal 2002.

14...♘a6

If 14...h6 then 15 ♗e7 ♗c7 16 ♗a3 and White still has pressure.

15 c5 ♗f8 16 h3 ♗e6 17 f4!

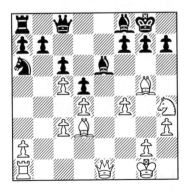

17...h6?!

This is too weakening. Black should play 17...f6, for example 18 f5 fxg5 19 fxe6 ♘xc5 20 dxc5 ♗xc5+ 21 ♔h1 gxh4 22 ♕xh4 g6 23 ♖e1 and White obviously has compensation for the pawn but Black can hope to defend.

18 f5 ♘xc5

Black prefers to sacrifice a piece rather than take one: 18...hxg5 19 fxe6 ♕xe6 (the problem is that 19...gxh4? loses to 20 exf7+ ♔xf7 21 ♕xh4, when the king is doomed) 20 ♕xe6 fxe6 21 ♘f3 ♗e7 22 ♖b1 and White has a clear advantage – Rozentalis.

19 dxc5 hxg5 20 fxe6 ♗xc5+ 21 ♔h1 ♕xe6

If Black tries to recapture the piece White gains a deadly attack: 21...gxh4 22 ♕xh4 g6 23 exf7+ ♔g7 24 ♖e1 ♕d7 25 ♗xg6! ♔xg6 26 ♖e5.

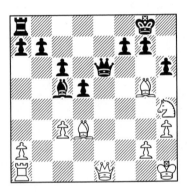

22 ♕xe6 fxe6 23 ♘f3 g4 24 hxg4 ♔f7 25 ♘e5+?!

Now Black's central pawns have a chance to roll. White can keep control with 25 g3 ♔e7 (25...♗d6 26 ♖f1 ♔e7 27 ♘g5 is also unpleasant) 26 ♔g2 ♔d6 27 ♖e1 with good winning chances.

25...♔e7 26 g3 ♔d6 27 ♘f7+

White should probably give up a pawn to blockade Black's centre: 27 ♖e1 ♗f2 28 ♘f7+ ♔e7 29 ♖f1 ♗xg3 30 ♔g2 ♗c7 31 ♘g5 and Black's pawns are not a threat, so White is a bit better.

27...♔e7 28 ♘g5 e5

Now Black has significant counterplay.

29 ♖f1 e4 30 ♖f7+ ♚d6 31 ♗e2

After 31 ♗xe4?! ♗e3! 32 ♖xg7 ♗xg5 Black escapes with a draw.

31...b5 32 ♖xg7 ♗e3 33 ♖g6+ ♚d7 34 ♘f7 ♖e8 35 g5 ♗d2 36 ♖g7 ♗xc3 37 ♖h7 d4 38 ♗g4+ ♚c7 39 g6 d3

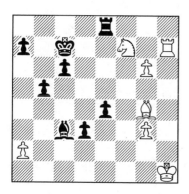

40 g7?

In time trouble White slips up. Instead 40 ♚g2 c5 41 ♘d8+! ♚b6 42 ♖b7+ ♚a6 43 ♖d7 gives good chances.

40...♖g8 41 ♗f5 d2 42 ♗g4 e3?!

Now it is only a draw. 42...♖xg7? 43 ♖xg7 ♗xg7 44 ♘g5, leaving White clearly better, is even worse, but Black could have kept decent winning chances after 42...♗f6! 43 ♚g2 c5.

43 ♘h6 ♖xg7 44 ♖xg7+ ♗xg7 45 ♘f5 ♗e5 46 ♚g2 c5 47 ♘xe3 c4 48 ♗e2 ♚d6 49 g4 ♗f4 50 ♚f3 ♚e5

Of course not 50...♗xe3? 51 ♚xe3 c3 52 ♚d3 b4 53 ♗d1 when White wins as all Black's pawns are worthless.

51 ♘c2 ♗g5 52 ♗d1 ½-½

Game 24
Firman-Bick
Stratton Mountain 2003

---

1 e4 e5 2 ♘f3 ♘f6 3 ♘xe5 d6 4 ♘f3 ♘xe4 5 d4 d5 6 ♗d3 ♗d6 7 0-0 0-0 8 c4 c6 9 ♘c3 ♘xc3 10 bxc3 dxc4

Black can also try the immediate 10...♗g4

and now:

a) 11 c5 (stabilising the space advantage) 11...♗c7 12 ♖e1 ♘d7 13 ♗g5 ♘f6 (or 13...f6 14 ♗h4 ♖f7 15 ♕c2 g5 16 ♗g3 ♗xg3 17 hxg3 – Stellwagen-S.Ernst, Groningen 2002 – and here White can gain an edge with 17...♘f8 18 ♘h2 ♗h5 19 ♘f1) 14 ♕d2!? (14 h3 leads to an unclear position after 14...♗h5 15 g4 ♗g6 16 ♘e5 h6 17 ♗h4 ♗xd3 18 ♕xd3 g5 19 ♗g3 ♘e4) 14...♗xf3 15 gxf3 b6 16 ♖e2 bxc5 17 dxc5 h6 18 ♗xh6! ♘d7 (not 18...gxh6?? 19 ♕xh6 ♖b8 20 ♚h1 and ♖g1+ will lead to mate) 19 ♗g5 f6 20 ♗f4 is messy, Glauser-Raetsky, Lugano 2000.

b) 11 ♖b1 allows 11...dxc4 12 ♗xc4 b5. For example, 13 ♗e2 ♘d7 14 a4 a6 15 c4 bxc4 16 ♕c2 ♗xf3 17 ♗xf3 ♕h4 18 g3 ♕xd4 19 ♖d1 (in Ivanovic-Khalifman, Plovdiv 1986 White now lost the thread with 19 ♗xc6?! ♖ad8 20 ♗g5?! ♕c5 21 ♗xd8?! ♕xc6 22 ♗a5 ♘e5 23 ♖fd1 ♘f3+ 24 ♚f1 ♘xh2+ 25 ♚g1 ♘f3+ 26 ♚f1 ♖e8! and Khalifman had a winning attack) 19...♕f6 20 ♗xc6 ♖ad8 21 ♗xd7 ♖xd7 22 ♗f4 ♖fd8 with a level position (Khalifman).

11 ♗xc4 ♗g4 12 h3

12 ♕d3 is the subject of the next game.

12...♗h5 13 ♖e1 ♘d7

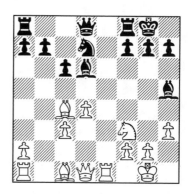

14 g4

White can also play less aggressively with 14 ♗f1. Now 14...♖e8 15 ♖xe8+ ♕xe8 16 ♗e3 b5 17 a4 a6 (17...b4 18 cxb4 ♗xb4 19 ♖c1 ♘b6 is also equal) 18 axb5 axb5 19

♖xa8 ♕xa8 20 d5 cxd5 21 g4 ♗g6 22 ♗xb5 ♕b7 was completely level in Ehlvest-Anand, Linares 1991.

14...♗g6 15 ♗g5 ♕a5 16 ♗e7! ♗xe7 17 ♖xe7 ♘b6

Or 17...♖ad8 18 ♕e1 c5 19 ♘e5 ♘xe5 20 ♖xe5 ♖c8 21 f4 and White's initiative continues.

18 ♗b3 ♖ab8 19 ♕e1

Taking control of the open file. Instead 19 c4 ♖fe8 20 ♕e1 ♕xe1+ 21 ♖axe1 ♖xe7 22 ♖xe7 ♔f8 23 ♖e3 ♖d8 is only equal.

19...♕a3 20 ♕e5 ♘d5

If 20...♕b2 White plays 21 ♖d1 ♕xc3 22 ♘g5, when 23 ♘e6 is a nasty threat.

21 ♗xd5 cxd5 22 ♘g5! ♕xc3 23 ♘e6!

23...♕xa1+?

Taking a rook with check is always tempting, but now Black is lost. Black has to try 23...f6, although White is clearly better after 24 ♖xg7+ ♔h8 25 ♕c7 ♕xc7 26 ♖xc7 ♖fe8 27 ♘c5.

24 ♔h2 f6 25 ♖xg7+ ♔h8 26 ♕c7 1-0

White threatens 27 ♖xh7+ followed by 28 ♕g7 mate, and 26...♖g8 is met by 27 ♕e7 after which f6 cannot be defended.

Game 25
Hamdouchi-Le Roux
Belfort 2003

---

1 e4 e5 2 ♘f3 ♘f6 3 ♘xe5 d6 4 ♘f3 ♘xe4 5 d4 d5 6 ♗d3 ♗d6 7 0-0 0-0 8 c4 c6 9 ♘c3 ♘xc3 10 bxc3 dxc4 11 ♗xc4 ♗g4 12 ♕d3 ♘d7

Sensible development. Black has a solid alternative in 12...♗h5 13 ♘e5 b5 14 ♕h3 bxc4 15 ♕xh5 ♕a5 16 ♗d2 ♕d5 (Black doesn't win a piece with 16...f6?! because of 17 ♕g4 heading for e6; for example, 17...♗xe5 18 dxe5 ♕xe5 19 ♖fe1 and White's lead in development is overwhelming) 17 ♕e2 ♖e8 18 ♗e3 ♗xe5 19 dxe5 ♕xe5 20 ♕xc4 ♕e4 21 ♕xe4 ♖xe4 22 ♖fd1 ♘a6 23 ♖d7 and White had a solid advantage in Agopov-Solozhenkin, Helsinki 2000. Instead of 13...b5, Black should play the simple 13...♗xe5 14 dxe5 ♕xd3 15 ♗xd3 ♖d8 16 ♗c2 ♗g6 17 ♗xg6 hxg6 18 ♖b1 b6 with equality.

13 ♘g5

Starting a kingside attack. 13 ♖e1 allows a clever trick with 13...b5 14 ♗b3 ♘c5! 15 ♕c2 (the idea is 15 dxc5?! ♗xh2+; now 16 ♘xh2 ♕xd3 17 ♘xg4 ♖ae8 18 ♗e3 ♕xc3 is clearly in Black's favour, Klinger-Fuchs, Oberwart 1993) 15...♘xb3 16 ♘g5 g6 17 axb3 ♗f5 and Black has equalised.

13...♘f6 14 h3 ♗h5

This leads to immense complications. A safe, reliable option is 14...♗d7!? 15 ♗b3 h6 16 ♘f3 ♕a5 with equality.

15 f4 h6 16 g4

This is the critical try. Black has no problems after 16 ♘f3 ♗xf3 17 ♖xf3 (or 17 ♕xf3 ♕c7 18 ♗d2 c5 with good counterplay)

17...♖e8 18 ♗e3 ♗c7 19 ♖af1 ♕d6 20 ♗f2 ♖e4 21 ♗h4 ♖ae8 22 ♗xf6 ♕xf6 23 ♔h1 ♖e1 24 a4 h5 25 g3 a6, Kamsky-Bareev, Linares 1993.

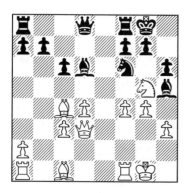

16...b5

It is also possible to take the piece immediately: 16...hxg5 17 fxg5 ♘xg4 18 hxg4 ♕d7 (18...♗xg4? is a mistake: 19 ♕e4 ♕d7 20 g6 ♗e6 21 ♗xe6 fxe6 – Capablanca-Northrop, New York 1909 – and here the simple 22 ♕h4 is winning) 19 ♕h3!? (the independent try; 19 gxh5 ♕g4+ 20 ♔f2 ♖ae8 21 ♖g1 ♕h4+ 22 ♔g2 b5 23 ♗b3 transposes to 16...b5) and now:

a) 19...♕xg4+ is safest: 20 ♕xg4 ♗xg4 21 ♖xf7 b5 22 ♗b3 ♔h7 with equality (Byrne, Mednis).

b) 19...♗xg4 is interesting but also risky: 20 ♕h4 ♗f5 (or 20...♗e6 21 ♗d3 g6 22 ♖f6!? c5 23 ♗e3 and White has a dangerous attack) 21 ♗f4 ♗xf4 22 ♖xf4 b5 23 ♗b3 and White certainly has compensation. Now in the game Morozevich-Ippolito, New York 1997 Black erred with 23...♖ae8?, after which White could have won with 24 ♔f2! ♕e7 25 ♖xf5 ♕e2+ 26 ♔g1 ♖e4 27 ♕h3 (Ippolito).

17 ♗b3 hxg5 18 fxg5 ♘xg4 19 hxg4 ♕d7

Another hugely complicated line is 19...♗xg4 20 g6 (or 20 ♕e4 ♗h3 21 g6 ♗h2+! – not 21...♗xf1? 22 ♕h1! and Black can resign – 22 ♔xh2 ♗xf1 with a very complex position) 20...♗e6 21 ♖xf7!? (Black

takes over the attack after 21 gxf7+ ♗xf7 22 ♖xf7 ♖xf7 23 ♕g6 ♕f6 24 ♗xf7+ ♔xf7 25 ♕xd6 ♖f8) 21...♗xb3 (21...♕e8? allows a neat forced win: 22 ♕h3! ♖xf7 – the trick is 22...♗xh3? 23 ♖f5+! – 23 ♕h7+ ♔f8 24 ♗g5 ♖f6 25 ♗xf6 gxf6 26 g7+ and Black will be mated –Nunn) 22 ♕h3 ♖xf7 23 ♕h7+ ♔f8 24 ♕h8+ ♔e7 25 ♗g5+ ♖f6 26 ♕xg7+ ♔e6 27 ♗xf6 ♕g8 28 axb3 ♕xg7 29 ♗xg7 ♔f5. After all the tactics White has a slight edge in the ending.

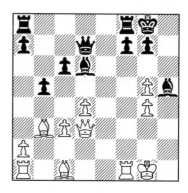

20 ♕f5?!

Now Black has an edge. The correct way to hold equality is 20 gxh5 ♕g4+ 21 ♔f2 ♖ae8 22 ♖g1 ♕h4+ 23 ♔g2 ♕h2+! 24 ♔f1 ♗f4 25 ♕f3 (not 25 ♗xf4? ♕xf4+ 26 ♔g2 ♖e3 and White must give up his queen) 25...♖e1+ 26 ♔xe1 ♕xg1+ 27 ♔e2 ♗xc1 28 ♖xc1 ♕xc1 29 g6 ♖e8+ 30 ♔d3 ♕b1+ (30...♖e7 31 gxf7+ ♔f8 32 ♕h3 ♕b1+ 33 ♗c2 ♕xa2 34 ♕c8+ – Oll – also draws) 31 ♔d2 ♕e1+ 32 ♔d3 ♕b1+ ½-½ A.Sokolov-Oll, Odessa 1989.

20...♗xg4 21 ♕xd7 ♗xd7 22 ♖xf7 ♖xf7 23 g6 ♗e8 24 ♗g5

White is also slightly worse after 24 ♗e3 a5 25 ♗e6 ♔f8 26 gxf7 ♗xf7 27 ♖f1 ♖a7, Nunn-Salov, Brussels 1988

24...a5 25 ♔g2

Black also has an edge after 25 ♖f1 ♖aa7 26 ♖f3 a4 27 ♗e6 ♖ac7 28 ♗d8 ♖b7 29 ♗g5 b4 30 cxb4 ♗xb4.

25...a4 26 ♗e6 ♔f8 27 ♖h1 ♖f6 28

♗xf6 gxf6 29 ♗f5 ♔g8?!

Black fails to make the most of his chances. Better is 29...♖b8 30 ♔f3 (White achieves nothing after 30 ♖h8+ ♔e7 31 ♖h7+ ♔d8) 30...b4 31 cxb4 ♖xb4 with a definite edge for Black.

30 ♖h7

Now the threat of 31 ♗e6+ forces Black to bail out to a drawn ending.

30...♗xg6 31 ♗xg6 ♗f4 32 ♖b7 ♗d2 33 ♗e4 ♖c8 34 ♖b6 ♗xc3 35 ♖xc6 ♖xc6 36 ♗xc6 ½-½

Game 26

V.Gurevich-Meijers

Germany 1999

1 e4 e5 2 ♘f3 ♘f6 3 ♘xe5 d6 4 ♘f3 ♘xe4 5 d4 d5 6 ♗d3 ♗d6 7 0-0 0-0 8 c4 c6 9 cxd5 cxd5 10 ♘c3 ♘xc3

This is the automatic answer to 10 ♘c3, but the rarely played 10...♖e8 is also a consideration. Now 11 ♖e1 transposes to note 'c' to White's 10th move in Game 23, 11 ♗xe4 dxe4 12 ♘g5 ♗f5 13 f3 e3 14 ♘ge4 ♗f4 was unclear in Morozevich-Gelfand, Cannes 2002, while 11 h3 and 11 ♕c2 are also serious possibilities for White.

11 bxc3 ♗g4 12 ♖b1

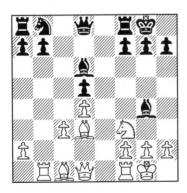

Instead 12 h3 ♗h5 13 ♕b3 is too ambitious: 13...♗xf3 14 ♕xb7 ♘d7 15 gxf3 ♘b6 16 ♖b1 ♕f6 17 ♔g2 ♖ac8 18 ♕xa7? (18 ♖b3 ♖c7 19 ♕a6 ♗f4 20 ♗xf4 ♕xf4 is bet-

ter but Black still has an edge) 18...♖xc3 19 ♖xb6 ♖xd3 20 ♗e3 ♕g6+ 21 ♔h1 ♕f5! (in Capablanca-Marshall, New York 1909 Black missed his chance with 21...♕e6 22 ♔g2 ♕g6+ 23 ♔h1 ♕e6 when a draw was agreed) 22 ♔g2 (if 22 ♖xd6 Black's idea is 22...♕xh3+ 23 ♔g1 ♖xe3! 24 fxe3 ♕g3+ 25 ♔h1 ♕xd6 with a clear advantage because of White's exposed king) 22...♖a3! 23 ♕b7 ♕g6+ 24 ♔h1 ♖xe3! 25 ♖xd6 ♕h5 26 fxe3 ♕xh3+ 27 ♔g1 ♕g3+ 28 ♔h1 ♕xd6 and Black has an obvious advantage.

12...b6

12...♘d7 is studied in Games 27-28.

13 ♖b5 ♗c7

The d-pawn was genuinely threatened. For example, 13...a6? 14 ♖xd5! wins a clear pawn because 14...♗xh2+? 15 ♘xh2 ♗xd1 16 ♖xd8 ♖xd8 17 ♖xd1 is winning for White.

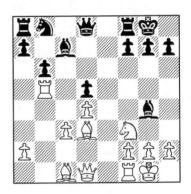

14 h3

14 c4 dxc4! leads to very sharp play after 15 ♗e4 ♘c6 16 ♗g5 (if 16 ♗xc6?! Black's idea is 16...♕d6 17 ♗xa8 ♗xf3 18 ♗f4 ♕xf4 19 g3 ♗xd1 20 gxf4 ♗c2, when the queen-side pawns will be very dangerous) 16...♗xf3 17 ♕xf3 ♕d6 18 ♖g3 (18 g3 eventually peters out to equality after 18...♘xd4 19 ♕e3 ♖fe8 20 ♖d5 ♕xd5 21 ♗xd5 ♖xe3 22 fxe3 ♘e2+ 23 ♔g2 ♖d8 24 ♗xf7+ ♔h8 25 ♗xc4 ♘xc1 26 ♖xc1) 18...♘xd4 19 ♕g4 g6 20 ♗xa8 f5 21 ♕h4 ♖xa8 (the tempting 21...♘e2+? fails to 22 ♔h1 ♘xg3+ 23 hxg3 – White is clearly better because 23...♖xa8?

loses to 24 ♕xc4+ ♔g7 25 ♗f4) 22 ♖h3 h5, Oll-Akopian, Manila 1992.

14...a6 15 hxg4

White has a promising alternative in 15 ♖xd5!?. For example, 15...♕xd5 16 hxg4 ②c6 17 ②g5 h6 18 ♗h7+!? ♔h8 19 ♗e4 ♕d6 20 ②f3 ♖fe8 21 ♗c2 ♕d7 (White has an edge after 21...b5 22 ♕d3 ♕g6 23 ♕xg6 fxg6 24 ♗xg6) 22 g5 ♕g4 (Benjamin-Zamora, Philadelphia 1999). Now Benjamin assesses 23 ♕d3 g6 24 gxh6 ♗f4 25 ♗b3 ♗xc1 26 ♖xc1 as clearly better for White.

15...axb5 16 ♕c2 g6

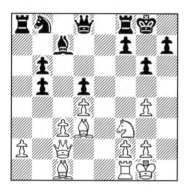

17 ♗h6

This seems the natural try. White has also played 17 ♗xb5 ♕d6 18 g3 ②c6 19 ♔g2 f5 20 ♗f4 ♕d7 21 g5 ♗xf4 22 gxf4 ♕c7 23 ♗xc6 ♕xc6 24 ②e5 ♕d6 (Black should avoid chasing material with 24...♕a4 because after 25 ♕d3 ♕xa2 26 ♖h1 White has a promising attack – Nikcevic) 25 a4 ♖a5 26 ♖b1 ♖b8 with an unclear position, A.Sokolov-Nikcevic, Vrnjacka Banja 1998.

17...♖e8 18 ♗xb5 ♖e4 19 c4 ♖xg4 20 cxd5 ②d7!?

Completing development is logical but 20...♗f4 is also worth considering: 21 ②e5 ♖h4?! (Black has to play 21...♖xg2+ 22 ♔xg2 ♗xh6 with an unclear position) 22 ♗xf4 ♖xf4 23 ♕d2 ♖f6 24 ②g4 ♖d6 (Kotronias-Rozentalis, Debrecen 1992) and here White could have gained a clear advantage with 25 ♖e1 ②d7 26 ♕f4 ②f6 27 ♖e6! (Lepeshkin).

21 ♕c6 ②f6?!

Black overlooks the coming tactic. After 21...②f8 22 ♖e1 ♗f4 23 ②e5 ♖h4 24 ♗xf4 ♖xf4 the position is unclear.

22 ②e5 ♖xd4?

Now Black is lost. Instead 22...♖c8 23 ②xf7!? ♕xd5 24 ♕xd5 ②xd5 25 ♗d7 ♖xd4 26 ♗xc8 ♔xf7 27 ♖e1 is only a little better for White.

23 ②xf7! ♖h4

The obvious point is 23...♔xf7 24 ♕e6 mate!

24 g3 ♕xd5 25 gxh4 ♕xc6 26 ♗xc6 ♖xa2 27 ②g5 ♗f4 28 ♖d1 ♗d2 29 ②xh7! ♗xh6 30 ②xf6+ ♔f7 31 ②g4 ♗d2 32 ♔g2 ♖c2 33 ♗e4 ♖b2 34 ♖a1 1-0

Game 27
Pavlovic-Raetsky
Biel 1999

---

1 e4 e5 2 ②f3 ②f6 3 ②xe5 d6 4 ②f3 ②xe4 5 d4 d5 6 ♗d3 ♗d6 7 0-0 0-0 8 c4 c6 9 cxd5 cxd5 10 ②c3 ②xc3 11 bxc3 ♗g4 12 ♖b1 ②d7

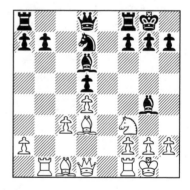

13 h3

Forcing the bishop to the kingside. Instead 13 ♖b5 ②b6 14 h3 gives Black the option of 14...♗d7!?. For example, 15 ♖b1 ♗a4 16 ♕e2 ♖e8 17 ♗e3 ♖c8 18 ②g5 (the game is level after 18 ②e5 ♗xe5 19 dxe5 ♖xe5 20 ♗xb6 ♖xe2 21 ♗xd8 ♖d2) 18...g6

(18...h6 is very risky: 19 ♘xf7!? ♚xf7 20 ♕h5+ ♚g8 21 ♗xh6!? and White has a strong attack) 19 ♘xh7! (instead 19 ♕f3?! ♖c7 was a bit better for Black in Kruszynski-Raetsky, Katowice 1990) 19...♖xc3 (an ambitious attempt to play for a win; after 19...♚xh7 20 ♕h5+ ♚g8 21 ♗xg6 fxg6 22 ♕xg6+ ♚h8 23 ♗g5 ♗e7 White has a perpetual check) 20 ♘g5 ♕f6 with a complex position.

13...♗h5

14 ♖b5

This is probably the most promising of White's options. Alternatives include:

a) 14 ♖xb7 ♘b6 15 ♗d2 ♗g6!? 16 ♗xg6 hxg6 17 ♕e2 (or 17 ♕b3 ♕c8 18 ♖xb6 axb6 19 ♕xd5 ♕c7 with an unbalanced position) 17...♕c8 18 ♕a6 ♖d8 is again unclear. Olivier-Raetsky, Geneva 1999 continued 19 ♘e5 ♗xe5 20 dxe5 ♖d7 21 ♖xb6 axb6 22 ♕xb6 ♖b7 23 ♕d4 ♕c4 24 ♕xc4 dxc4 and here Black is a little better.

b) 14 a4 b6 15 ♖b5 ♘f6 16 ♗g5 ♗e7 17 g4 a6!? 18 ♖b3 ♗g6 19 ♘e5 ♗d6 20 ♘xg6 (an aggressive choice is 20 f4 ♗xd3 21 ♕xd3 ♕c7 22 ♗xf6 gxf6 23 ♘f3 ♗xf4 24 ♘h4 ♖fe8 25 ♘f5, when White has reasonable compensation) 20...fxg6 21 ♗h4 ♗c7 22 ♖e1 g5!? 23 ♗xg5 ♕d6 24 ♖e5 (White must avoid the blunder 24 f4? h6 25 ♗xf6 ♕xf4! 26 ♖b2 ♖xf6) 24...♕c6 and in this level position the players agreed a draw in Semenova-Chetverik, Balatonbereny 1994.

14...♘b6 15 c4

This is the normal move but 15 a4 is also worth considering: 15...a6 (after 15...♗g6 16 ♗xg6 hxg6 17 ♕b3 ♖e8 18 ♗g5 ♕d7 19 a5 ♘c4 20 ♖xb7 ♗c7 21 a6 ♕c6 22 ♕b5 White has a pleasant advantage) 16 ♖xb6!? (the less ambitious 16 ♖b1 leads to an unclear position after 16...♖b8 17 ♗g5 ♕c7 18 a5 ♘c4 19 ♗xc4 ♕xc4) 16...♕xb6 17 ♗xh7+ ♚h8 (if 17...♚xh7 18 ♘g5+ ♚g6 19 g4 White has a strong attack) 18 ♗d3 with an unclear position (Miralles).

15...♗xf3

15...♘xc4 is less accurate because of 16 ♖xd5! (16 ♗xc4 ♗xf3 17 ♕xf3 dxc4 18 ♖xb7 ♕e8 19 ♗e3 ♕e6 20 ♖c1 c3 21 d5 ♕e5 22 g3 ♖ac8, as in Kulaots-Lauk, Tallinn 2000, is only equal) 16...♗h2+ 17 ♘xh2 ♕xd5 18 ♗xc4 ♕xc4 19 ♕xh5 ♕xd4 (19...♕xa2 is even worse: 20 d5 ♖ad8 21 ♖d1 ♖d7 22 d6 and White is much better) 20 ♘f3 ♕c4 21 a3 b6 22 ♗e3 ♖ad8 23 ♖c1 ♕d3 24 a4 and White has an edge, Dvoirys-Vladimirov, Barnaul 1988.

16 ♕xf3 dxc4 17 ♗c2

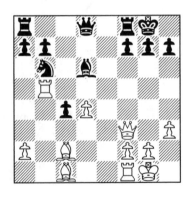

17...♕d7

Black's two other options are probably inferior:

a) 17...a6 allows a dangerous attack: 18 ♗g5! ♕c7 (the queen sacrifice 18...axb5 19 ♗xd8 ♖fxd8 is not sound: 20 ♕h5 g6 21 ♕xb5 ♗c7 22 a4 ♖xd4 23 ♕c5 ♖d7 24 g3 and White was clearly better in Beliavsky-

Petursson, Reykjavik 1988; or 18...f6 19 ♕h5 h6 20 ♗xh6! axb5 21 ♗xg7! f5 22 ♗xf8 ♗xf8 23 ♗xf5 and Black's king is in trouble) 19 ♗f6! g6 (19...axb5? runs into a mating attack after 20 ♗xh7+! ♔xh7 21 ♕h5+ ♔g8 22 ♕g5 g6 23 ♕h6) 20 ♖b2 and White still has a strong initiative.

b) 17...♕c7 18 a4 a6 19 ♖b2 ♖ab8 20 ♗h6! ♕c6 (the point is if 20...gxh6 then 21 ♕f5 ♔g7 22 ♕xh7+ ♔f6 23 ♕xh6+ ♔e7 24 ♖e1+ ♔d7 25 ♗f5+ ♔c6 26 ♗e4+ ♔d7 27 ♖eb1 and the attack breaks through) 21 ♕f5 g6 22 ♕a5 ♘d7 23 ♕c3 ♕d5 24 ♗xf8 ♘xf8 25 ♖e1 and White had an edge in Yandarbiev-Skatchkov, St Petersburg 2001.

18 a4

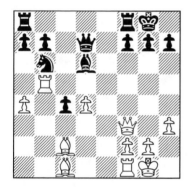

18...♖ab8

Supporting the b-pawn, but this is not the only move:

a) 18...g6 is an important option – see the next game.

b) Black should avoid 18...♗c7?! 19 g3 a6 20 ♖h5 g6 21 ♖c5 ♗d8 22 a5 ♕xd4, as in D. Kaiumov-Chetverik, Harkany 1992. Now White could have built a powerful attack with 23 ♗e3! ♕c3 24 ♖c1! ♖c8 (not 24...♘d7? 25 ♗xg6 ♕xc1+ 26 ♗xc1 ♘xc5 27 ♗f5 and White wins) 25 ♖h5. c) Worth considering, however, is 18...♖fe8!?, for example 19 ♗f5 ♕c7! 20 ♗e4 a6 21 ♖g5 ♖xe4! (the careless 21...h6?? is refuted by 22 ♖xg7+! ♔xg7 23 ♗xh6+!) 22 ♕xe4 ♘xa4 23 ♖e1 g6 24 h4 ♘c3 (also possible is 24...♖d8!? 25 h5 b5

with unclear play) 25 ♕f3 ♘a2 26 ♗a3 ♘b4 27 h5 ♘d3 28 hxg6 hxg6 (Ponomariov-Safin, Yerevan 2001) and here White should force a draw with 29 ♕f6! ♗xa3 30 ♖h5! gxh5 31 ♕g5+.

19 ♗e3

Once again there is a choice:

a) 19 ♗b2 should be equal after 19...♗c7 20 ♖c5 ♖fd8? (this is a fatal slip; 20...♗d6 21 ♖b5 ♗c7 is level) 21 ♖h5 g6 22 d5! ♕d6 23 g3 gxh5 (if 23...f6 then 24 ♖xh7! and the attack crashes through) 24 ♕xh5 and White was winning in Zagrebelny-Chetverik, Gyula 1992.

b) 19 ♗g5!? is a promising alternative to 19 ♗e3. For example, 19...♖fe8 20 ♖fb1 g6 21 ♗e3 ♕c6 22 a5 ♕xf3 23 gxf3 ♘c8 24 ♖xb7 ♖xb7 25 ♖xb7 ♖e7 26 ♖b1 with an edge for White, De Firmian-Kosebay, Copenhagen 1996.

19...♘c8 20 ♖fb1 b6

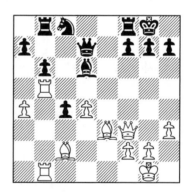

21 ♖h5!?

This is not White's only attacking method. 21 h4 ♘e7 22 h5 h6 23 g4 ♗c7 24 g5 a6 (if 24...hxg5 25 ♖xg5 f6 26 ♖g2 ♔h8 27 ♕e4 f5 28 ♕h4 White has a promising attack) 25 ♖5b4 b5 26 gxh6 f5 27 axb5 axb5 28 ♕g2 ♖f7 with a complex position, Shilov-Raetsky, Lugansk 1989.

21...g6 22 ♗h6 ♖d8 23 ♕f6 ♗f8 24 ♗xf8 ♕xd4

The only move. 24...♖xf8? loses to the clever 25 ♖xh7! ♔xh7 26 ♖b5. For example,

26...♔h6 27 ♖h5+! ♔xh5 28 ♕f4! and mate is unavoidable.

25 ♕xd4

After 25 ♗g7 ♕xf6 26 ♗xf6 ♖d6 27 ♖h4 ♖xf6 28 ♖xc4 ♘d6 Black has won back the piece and keeps a clear extra pawn.

25...♖xd4 26 ♗c5 ♖d2 27 ♖e5 ♖xc2 28 ♖e8+ ♔g7 29 ♗d4+

29 ♗f8+ is less clear: 29...♔f6 30 ♖d1 c3 31 ♖dd8 with an obscure position.

29...f6 30 ♗e3?

This spoils White's advantage. 30 ♖d1 c3 31 ♗e3 ♔f7 32 ♖dd8 ♖a2 33 ♖xc8 ♖xc8 34 ♖xc8 ♖xa4 35 ♖xc3 promises some winning chances.

30...♖c3 31 ♖d1 ♖d3 32 ♖c1 ♖d7 33 ♔f1?

Instead 33 ♗f4 ♖a8 34 ♖xc4 ♘d6 35 ♖c7! holds on to equality.

33...g5 34 ♔e2 ♔f7 35 ♖h8 ♔g7 36 ♖e8 ♖e7 37 ♖d8 ♖c7 38 h4 h6 39 f4?

The final mistake. 39 ♖d4 ♖bb7 40 hxg5 hxg5 41 ♖cxc4 ♘e7 still leaves White some hopes of saving the draw.

39...gxh4 40 f5 ♖bb7 41 ♗f4 ♖c6 42 ♖cd1 a6 43 ♖1d4 h5 44 ♗c1 ♘e7 45 ♖8d7 ♖cc7 46 ♖xc7 ♖xc7 47 ♗f4 ♘xf5 48 ♗xc7 ♘xd4+ 49 ♔e3 ♘f5+ 50 ♔f4 ♘e7 51 ♔e4 b5 52 a5 b4 53 ♔d4 b3 0-1

Game 28

Anand-Shirov

Linares 2000

---

1 e4 e5 2 ♘f3 ♘f6 3 ♘xe5 d6 4 ♘f3 ♘xe4 5 d4 d5 6 ♗d3 ♗d6 7 0-0 0-0 8 c4 c6 9 cxd5 cxd5 10 ♘c3 ♘xc3 11 bxc3 ♗g4 12 ♖b1 ♘d7 13 h3 ♗h5 14 ♖b5 ♘b6 15 c4 ♗xf3 16 ♕xf3 dxc4 17 ♗c2 ♕d7 18 a4 g6 19 ♗e3

White's two other options are less threatening:

a) 19 ♗h6 ♖fe8 20 ♖fb1 ♖ad8 21 ♗g5 ♗e7 22 a5 ♗xg5! (this is more accurate than 22...♘d5 23 ♖xb7 ♕e6 24 ♗d2 ♗f6 25 ♖e1,

which gave White an edge in Svidler-Akopian, Yerevan 1996) 23 axb6 ♗e7! 24 bxa7 b6 25 ♗e4! ♕xa7 26 ♗d5 ♗d6 27 ♖xb6 ♖b8! 28 ♖xb8 ♖xb8 29 ♖xb8+ ♗xb8 30 ♗xc4 ♕a1+ 31 ♗f1 ♕xd4 with a drawn position (Svidler).

b) 19 ♗d2 c3 20 ♗xc3 ♖ac8 21 ♗e4 ♖c4 22 ♖bb1 ♖xa4 (Black has a promising alternative in 22...♖fc8!? 23 ♗a1 ♖xa4 24 ♗xb7 ♖c7 25 ♗e4 ♖a3 with counterplay – Barlov) 23 ♗xb7 ♖a3 24 ♖fc1 (or 24 ♗c6 ♕c7 25 ♖a1 ♖b3 26 ♖fb1 ♖xb1+ 27 ♖xb1 ♖c8 28 d5 ♘xd5 29 ♖b7 ♕xb7 30 ♗xb7 ♖xc3 31 ♕d1 ♗f4! heading for a drawn opposite-coloured bishop ending – Kasparov) 24...♕c7! 25 ♖a1 ♖b8 26 ♗e4 ♖b3 was equal in Kasparov-Shirov, Linares 2000.

19...♖ac8

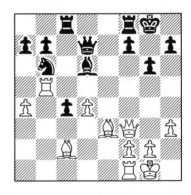

20 ♖fb1

After 20 ♗h6 ♖fe8 White has an unusual way to force a draw: 21 ♗f5! gxf5 22 ♕g4+! fxg4 23 ♖g5+ ♔h8 ½-½ Zaw Win Lay-Paciencia, Surabaya 2002.

20...c3 21 a5 ♘c4 22 ♖xb7

This is promising but 22 ♗h6!? is also interesting: 22...♖fe8 23 ♖xb7 ♕e6 (not 23...♕xb7? 24 ♕xb7 ♖b8 25 a6! and White has a clear advantage) 24 ♖f1! ♖e7 25 ♖xe7 ♗xe7 26 ♖d1 (Greenfeld mentioned the unclear line 26 d5!? ♕e5 27 ♗f4 ♕f6 28 ♕g4 ♖c5 29 ♗h6) 26...♘d2 27 ♕d3 ♗d6 28 a6! ♕c4! and White was a bit better in Alterman-Greenfeld, Haifa 2002.

22...♕e6

More solid than 22...♖c7 23 ♗h6 ♖e8 24 ♖xc7 ♕xc7 25 ♕xc3 when White has a dangerous initiative. For example, 25...♘a3? 26 ♖e1! ♖b8 27 ♕xc7 ♗xc7 28 ♖e7 ♘xc2 29 ♖xc7 ♘xd4 30 ♖xa7 gave White a winning ending in Motylev-Ristic, Novi Sad 2000.

23 ♖a1

Less threatening is 23 ♗b3 ♕f5 24 ♕xf5 gxf5 25 ♖a1 (Grischuk-Shirov, FIDE World Championship, New Delhi 2000) and here Grischuk suggested the equalising 25...♘d2!? 26 g3 ♘xb3 27 ♖xb3 c2 28 ♖c1 ♖c4.

23...♗b8?!

Now Black is in real trouble. 23...♖c7 24 a6 ♘xe3 25 fxe3 ♕e7 26 ♖ab1 is only marginally better for White.

24 ♗b3 ♕d6

If 24...c2 25 ♖c1 ♕d6 26 ♖xc2 ♕h2+ 27 ♔f1 ♘xe3+ 28 fxe3 ♖xc2 29 ♗xc2 White is clearly better (Shirov).

25 g3 ♘xe3 26 ♗xf7+ ♔h8 27 ♕xe3 ♕f6

Pushing the pawn again achieves nothing: 27...c2 28 ♖c1 ♖c7 29 ♖xc7 ♗xc7 30 ♗e6 ♗xa5 31 d5 (Shirov).

28 ♗e6 ♖ce8 29 d5 ♗e5

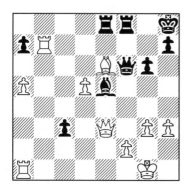

30 ♖a2?

Now White loses control of the position. Even worse is 30 ♕xa7? ♖xe6 31 dxe6 ♗d4 32 ♖xh7+ ♔g8 33 ♕b7 ♕xf2+ 34 ♔h1 c2! 35 ♖f7 ♗xa1 36 ♖xf2 c1♕+ 37 ♔g2 ♖xf2+ 38 ♔xf2 ♗d4+ when Black has decent winning chances. White could have maintained an edge with 30 ♖b4!? ♖b8 31 ♖c4 c2 32 ♖c1 ♖b1 33 ♖4xc2 ♗d4 34 ♕f4 ♖xc1+ 35 ♖xc1 ♗xf2+ 36 ♔g2 (Rogers). However, the best option is Shirov's later suggestion: 30 ♖a4! c2 31 ♖c4 ♗d4 32 ♕f4 ♕xf4 33 gxf4 ♗xf2+ 34 ♔g2 with good winning chances.

30...♗d4 31 ♕e1

31 ♕d3!? ♗xf2+ 32 ♔g2 ♗d4 33 ♖c2 with an unclear position is better.

31...♕f3 32 ♔h2 ♕xd5 33 ♗xd5 ♖xe1

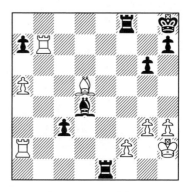

34 ♔g2?

Now White is lost. 34 f4 ♖fe8 35 ♗f3 ♖c1 still leaves White with good drawing chances.

34...♗xf2! 35 ♖f7

The point is 35 ♖xf2 ♖xf2+ 36 ♔xf2 c2 and the pawn queens.

35...♖xf7 36 ♗xf7 ♗c5 37 ♗b3 ♔g7 38 ♖c2 ♗d4 39 a6 ♔f6 40 ♖a2 ♔e5 41 h4 ♔e4 0-1

Summary

The variation 6...♗d6 7 0-0 0-0 8 c4 c6 has become fashionable and is likely to remain popular because of the huge number of complicated, untypical and insufficiently studied positions.

After 9 ♕c2, defending the knight with 9...f5, as in the historic Williams-Staunton game (London 1851) isn't bad because it's not that easy for White to take advantage of the weakened a2-g8 diagonal. After 9 ♕c2 ♘a6 10 a3 Black has a few effective responses: 10...♖e8 11 ♘c3 ♗f5; 11...♗g4; or the immediate 10...♗g4, responding to 11 ♘e5 with 11...♗f5, 11...♗h5 or 11...♗xe5 12 dxe5 ♘ac5. The fashionable 10...f5 appears to give White the better chances after an accurate attack on the queenside with 11 ♘c3 ♘c7 12 ♘e2 ♘e6 13 b4.

In the event of 9 ♖e1, the pawn sacrifice 9...♗g4!? deserves careful consideration. After 10 ♗xe4 dxe4 11 ♖xe4 f5 12 ♖e6 ♕d7 Black has full compensation, while he has prospects of equalising after 12 ♖e1 ♗xf3 13 ♗xf3 ♕h4. In the case of 9...♗f5 White can claim an advantage with 10 ♘c3 ♘xc3 11 bxc3 ♗xd3 12 ♕xd3 dxc4 13 ♕xc4 ♘d7 14 ♗g5!?, while after 9...♖e8 10 ♘c3 ♘xc3 11 bxc3 the position appears to be favourable for White.

To us, the move 9 ♘c3 seems less accurate than 9 cxd5 cxd5 10 ♘c3 because Black can proceed with 9...♘xc3 10 bxc3 dxc4 11 ♗xc4 ♗g4. We can't find any white's advantage in either the calm variations or the sharp 12 ♕d3 ♘d7 13 ♘g5 ♘f6 14 h3 ♗h5 15 f4 h6 16 g4.

Recently 9 cxd5 cxd5 10 ♘c3 ♘xc3 11 bxc3 ♗g4 has not been so popular. White's position seems to be more promising after 12 ♖b1 b6 but, if Black defends accurately, White will not gain an advantage after 12...♘d7. Nowadays there are fewer fans of this complex line, which requires knowledge of variations developed earlier and where every moment is critical.

1 e4 e5 2 ♘f3 ♘f6 3 ♘xe5 d6 4 ♘f3 ♘xe4 5 d4 d5 6 ♗d3 ♗d6 7 0-0 0-0 8 c4 c6
(D) **9 cxd5**

> 9 ♕c2 ♘a6
>> 10 ♗xe4 – *Game 19*; 10 a3 ♗g4 – *Game 20*; 10...f5 – *Game 21*
>
> 9 ♖e1
>> 9...♗f5 – *Game 22*; 9...♖e8 – *Game 23*
>
> 9 ♘c3 ♘xc3 10 bxc3 dxc4 11 ♗xc4 ♗g4 (D): 12 h3 – *Game 24*; 12 ♕d3 – *Game 25*

9...cxd5 10 ♘c3 ♘xc3 11 bxc3 ♗g4 12 ♖b1 (D) **♘d7**

> 12...b6 – *Game 26*

13 h3 ♗h5 14 ♖b5 ♘b6 15 c4 ♗xf3 16 ♕xf3 dxc4 17 ♗c2 ♕d7 18 a4

> 18...♖ab8 – *Game 27*; 18...g6 – *Game 28*

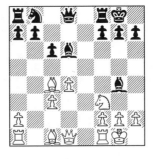
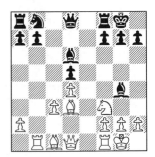

| *8...c6* | *11...♗g4* | *12 ♖b1* |

CHAPTER FOUR

3 ♘xe5: Deviations from the Main Line

1 e4 e5 2 ♘f3 ♘f6 3 ♘xe5 d6 4 ♘f3 ♘xe4 5 d4

After 1 e4 e5 2 ♘f3 ♘f6 3 ♘xe5 d6 4 ♘f3 ♘xe4 5 d4 we've already identified two principal trends: 5...d5 6 ♗d3 ♗e7 7 0-0 ♘c6 (Chapters 1-2) and 6...♗d6 (Chapter 3). It is reasonable to devote a separate chapter to deviations from these lines. Black rarely declines to play the main continuation 5...d5 in favour of the passive 5...♗e7 (Game 32). After 6 ♗d3 the knight retreats to f6 rather than to g5 (in view of 7 ♘xg5 ♗xg5 8 ♕e2+). Then White normally proceeds with 7 h3 in order to restrict the c8-bishop.

After 5 d4 d5 6 ♗d3 Marshall suggested 6...♗g4, which failed the test of time in view of 7 ♕e2+! ♕e7 8 0-0 ♘c6 9 ♗b5, when it is difficult for Black to complete his development. In Game 31 we discuss Marshall's idea of an early ...♗g4 improved by the insertion of the moves 6...♘c6 7 0-0. The two critical lines are 6...♘c6 7 0-0 ♗g4 8 c4 ♘f6 9 cxd5 ♗xf3 10 ♕xf3 ♕xd5 11 ♕xd5 (or 11 ♕e2+; 11 ♖e1+ ♗e7 reaches a tabiya from Chapter 2) and 9 ♘c3 ♗xf3 10 ♕xf3 ♘xd4 11 ♕e3+ (or 11 ♕h3; again 11 ♖e1+ ♗e7 reaches Chapter 2). It should be said, however, that in modern practice Black usually avoids giving his opponent a variety of possibilities and often develops his bishop to e7 early on.

After 5...d5 6 ♗d3 ♗e7 7 0-0 the idea 7...♘d6 is played very seldom, with Bilguer declaring this move a 'motiveless retreat'. In fact, there are some motives, i.e. a countermeasure to c2-c4 and a preparation of ...♗f5. However, after 8 ♗f4! Black fails to develop his bishop to f5 and is forced into passive defence.

If Blacks wishes to move his bishop to f5, he should do so immediately after 5...d5 6 ♗d3 ♗e7 7 0-0 ♗f5. Then 8 c4 can be met by 8...dxc4 since the rook is not yet attacking the knight on e4, and the arising position with an isolated pawn gives approximately equal chances. 8 ♖e1 ♘c6 (Games 29-30) is more common, after which the position branches. Game 29 reviews the fashionable 9 ♘bd2 as well as 9 ♘c3 and the pin 9 ♗b5, taking control of the e5-square; Game 30 is devoted to the more fundamental 9 c4.

Game 29
Kasparov-Karpov
Moscow 1981

---

1 e4 e5 2 ♘f3 ♘f6 3 ♘xe5 d6 4 ♘f3 ♘xe4 5 d4 ♗e7 6 ♗d3 d5 7 0-0 ♗f5

Retreating voluntarily with 7...♘d6 makes White's task easier: 8 ♗f4 0-0 9 ♖e1 ♗e6 (or 9...♗g4 10 h3 ♗h5 11 ♖e5!? ♗xf3 12 ♕xf3 c6 13 c3 ♘d7 14 ♖e2 ♘f6 15 ♘d2 with a clear advantage, Lau-Mathe, Munich 1992) 10 c3 ♘d7 11 ♕c2 h6 (this is forced as 11...g6?! allows the standard tactic 12 ♗h6 ♖e8 13 ♖xe6! fxe6 14 ♗xg6, when White is much better) 12 ♘bd2 ♖e8 13 ♘f1 ♘f8 14 ♘g3 ♗g5 15 ♕d2 f6 16 h4!? ♗xf4 17 ♕xf4 ♕d7 18 ♘h2!? ♕f7 19 ♘g4 and White had a promising initiative in Timman-Skembris, Corfu 1993.

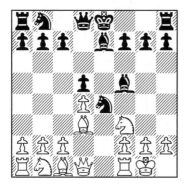

8 ♖e1

This is more promising than the alternatives:

a) 8 ♘e5 ♘d7 9 ♕f3 ♘xe5 10 dxe5 ♕d7 11 ♘c3 ♗g4 12 e6! (a neat trick but Black has a defence) 12...♗xe6 (not 12...♕xe6?! 13 ♘xd5! ♕xd5 14 ♕xg4 ♘f6 15 ♕a4+ ♕d7 16 ♕xd7+ ♘xd7 17 ♖e1 – Ro. Perez – when the bishop pair and especially the nasty pin give White a clear advantage) 13 ♘xe4 dxe4 14 ♗xe4 c6 15 ♖d1 ♕c8 16 ♖e1 0-0 17 ♕h5 f5! 18 ♗d3 ♗f6 19 c3 ♖e8 and Black had equalised in Sutovsky-Ro.Perez, Istanbul Olympiad 2000.

b) 8 c4 has the obvious drawback of losing time with White's king's bishop. 8...dxc4 9 ♗xc4 0-0 10 ♘c3 ♘c6 and now:

b1) If 11 ♗d3 the correct answer is 11...♘xc3 12 bxc3 ♕d7 13 ♖e1 ♗d6 14 ♖b1 b6 15 ♖b5 ♗xd3 16 ♕xd3 ♖fe8, when Black has no problems (but not 11...♘d6 12 ♗xf5 ♘xf5 13 d5 ♘b4 14 a3 ♘a6 15 ♕c2 ♘h4 16 ♘xh4 ♗xh4 17 ♖d1, when White has an

edge, Zhang Pengxiang-Delchev, Linares 2002).

b2) 11 ♖e1 ♘d6 12 ♗d3 ♗f6 13 d5 ♗xd3 14 ♕xd3 ♘b4 15 ♕d1 a5 (a sharper option is 15...♘f5 16 g4 ♘d6 17 a3 ♘a6 18 ♗f4 ♕d7 19 h3 with an unclear position according to Tal) 16 a3 ♘a6 17 ♗e3 ♖e8 18 ♕a4 ♘b8!? 19 ♗d4 (Korneev-Ro.Perez, Collado Villalba 2000) and here Perez now suggests the correct route to equality is 19...♘d7!? 20 ♖xe8+ ♘xe8.

8...♘c6 9 ♘bd2

This is the best of White's alternatives (the main move 9 c4 is discussed in the next game). Other options include:

a) 9 ♗b5 ♗f6 10 ♘bd2 0-0 11 ♘f1 ♘e7 12 c3 ♘g6 13 ♗d3 ♘d6 14 ♗xf5 ♘xf5 15 ♕b3 b6 16 ♕b5 a6 17 ♕d3 ♕d7 18 ♘g3 ♘xg3 19 hxg3 a5 20 ♗g5 ♗xg5 21 ♘xg5 ♖fe8 and Black has easy equality, Karpov-Korchnoi, World Championship (Game 4), Merano 1981.

b) 9 ♘c3 ♘xc3 10 bxc3 ♗xd3 11 cxd3 (11 ♕xd3 also gives nothing after 11...0-0 12 c4 dxc4 13 ♕xc4 ♗f6 14 c3 ♖e8) 11...0-0 12 ♕b3 ♖b8 13 ♖e2 b5 14 ♗d2 ♕d7 15 ♖ae1 ♖fe8 and Black had equalised in A.Ivanov-Pierrot, Buenos Aires 2003.

9...♘xd2 10 ♕xd2 ♗xd3 11 ♕xd3 0-0

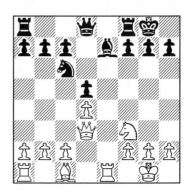

12 c3

Kasparov quietly defends d4 before starting active play. 12 ♗f4 is also possible: 12...♗d6 13 ♘g5 g6 14 ♕h3 h5 15 ♗xd6 (15

♗e3 illustrates the potential weakness of d4: 15...♘xd4! 16 ♘xf7 ♘f3+! 17 ♕xf3 ♖xf7 18 ♕h3 ♖f5 and Black has equalised) 15...cxd6 16 ♘f3 ♕b6 17 ♖ab1 ♘xd4 18 ♘xd4 ♕xd4 19 ♕d7 and White's activity certainly compensates for the missing pawn but is probably not enough to force an advantage.

12...♕d7 13 ♗f4 a6 14 ♖e3 ♖ae8 15 ♖ae1

White is more active but Black is very solid and simplifying exchanges seem likely.

15...♗d8 16 h3

Safeguarding the back rank and keeping the tension. 16 ♘e5 eases Black's task after 16...♘xe5 17 dxe5 ♕b5 18 b3 ♕xd3 19 ♖xd3 c6 20 c4 ♗a5 21 ♖b1 dxc4 22 bxc4 ♖d8 23 ♖a3 (Kavalek-Smyslov, Amsterdam 1981) and here the simplest path to equality is 23...♗d2 24 ♗xd2 ♖xd2.

16...♖xe3 17 ♖xe3

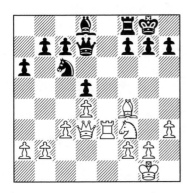

17...f6

Avoiding a nasty back rank trick: 17...♖e8?! 18 ♕f5! ♖e6 19 h4 g6 20 ♕h3 ♕e8 21 ♖xe6 ♕xe6 22 ♕xe6 fxe6 23 ♘g5! and White has a clear advantage (Kasparov).

18 ♖e2

This simply improves coordination while awaiting developments. In a later game 18 ♘d2 was tried and following 18...♘e7 19 ♘b3 ♕f5! 20 ♕xf5 ♘xf5 21 ♖e2 b6 22 ♘c1 ♔f7 23 ♘d3 a5 24 g4 ♘e7 a draw was agreed in Leko-Kramnik, Dortmund 1999.

18...♖f7 19 ♘d2 ♗e7

Playing directly for exchanges with 19...♖e7 leads to some difficulty: 20 ♘b3 ♖xe2 21 ♕xe2 ♗e7 22 ♕g4! ♕xg4 23 hxg4 ♗d6 24 ♗xd6 cxd6 25 f4 and Black's doubled d-pawns ensure White of a slight edge in the ending.

20 ♘f1 ♗f8 21 ♕f3 ♖e7 22 ♘e3

The assessment is typical of this variation: White has a nagging pull.

22...♘d8 23 ♗xc7!?

An interesting way to unbalance the play.

23...♕xc7 24 ♘xd5

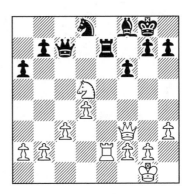

24...♕d6?!

Black should prefer 24...♖xe2!? 25 ♘xc7 ♖e1+ 26 ♔h2 ♗d6+ 27 g3 ♗xc7 28 ♕d5+ ♔f8 29 ♔g2 with unclear play: Black has plenty of material for the queen but regaining coordination without losing more pawns will be very difficult.

25 ♘xe7+ ♗xe7 26 ♕e4 ♗f8 27 ♕e8

Kasparov suggested that 27 c4 b6 28 d5 gains a clear advantage.

27...g6 28 a4

Now Black manages to untangle. 28 h4!? ♔g7 29 h5 keeps an edge.

28...♔g7 29 b4 ♕c7 30 ♖e3 ♘f7 31 ♕e6 ♕d8 32 a5 h5 33 ♕e4 ♕d7 34 ♕e6 ♕d8 35 ♔f1 ♘h6 36 g4 hxg4 37 hxg4 ♘f7 38 ♔e2

Or 38 f4 ♕c7 39 ♖f3 ♗d6 40 ♕e4 ♕c8 and Black still holds on to equality.

38...♘g5 39 ♕b6 ♕d7 40 ♔d3 ♗d6 41 ♔c2 ½-½

Game 30
Herrera-Ro.Perez
Varadero 2000

1 e4 e5 2 ♘f3 ♘f6 3 ♘xe5 d6 4 ♘f3 ♘xe4 5 d4 d5 6 ♗d3 ♗e7 7 0-0 ♗f5 8 ♖e1 ♘c6 9 c4

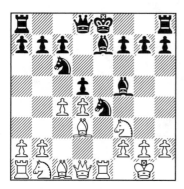

9...♘b4

Provoking a tactical sequence while fighting for control of d5.

Instead 9...0-0 makes it much easier for White to fight for the advantage:

a) 10 cxd5 ♕xd5 11 ♘c3 (the tactics favour Black, who is clearly better after 11 ♕c2? ♘b4 12 ♗xe4 ♘xc2 13 ♗xd5 ♖ae8! 14 ♗xb7 ♗b4 15 ♖xe8 ♖xe8 16 ♗c6 ♖b8, Shirov-Ivanchuk, Monaco [rapid] 2002) 11...♘xc3 12 bxc3 ♖fe8 (Black can try to blockade with 12...b5 but after 13 ♗xf5 ♕xf5 14 ♘e5 ♘a5 15 a4 b4 16 ♗d2 White has a strong initiative) 13 ♗f4 ♗xd3 14 ♕xd3 ♕d7 15 ♖e3 ♗f6 16 ♖ae1 ♖e7 17 ♗g5 ♖xe3 18 fxe3 ♗xg5 19 ♘xg5 g6 20 e4 and White's impressive centre gave him good chances in Yagupov-Sorokin, St Petersburg 2001.

b) Also good is 10 ♘c3 ♘xc3 11 bxc3 ♗xd3 12 ♕xd3 dxc4 13 ♕xc4 with a further branch:

b1) 13...♕d7 14 ♖b1 b6 15 d5 ♘a5 16 ♕d3 ♖fe8 (or 16...c6 17 c4 cxd5 18 cxd5 ♖ad8 19 ♗g5! and White keeps the initiative)

17 ♗f4 ♖ad8 18 ♖bd1 and White has a slight edge. Now the game Bruzon-Ro.Perez, Santa Clara 2000 continued 18...♗f6 19 h3 ♖xe1+ 20 ♖xe1 b5?! 21 ♗g5 ♘c4 (Nogueiras gives 21...♗xg5 22 ♘xg5 f5 23 d6! ♕xd6 24 ♕xf5 with a winning advantage for White) 22 ♗xf6 gxf6 23 ♖e4! and White has a clear plus.

b2) 13...♗d6 14 ♕b5 ♕f6 15 ♖b1 (15 ♕xb7?! grabs a poisoned pawn and Black has tricks based on a later ....♗xh2+, i.e. 15...♖ab8 16 ♕a6 ♘xd4! 17 ♕d3 ♘xf3+ 18 ♕xf3 ♕xf3 19 gxf3 a6 and Black's stronger pawn structure gives him an edge) 15...a6 16 ♕d3 b5 17 a4!? ♕g6 (or 17...bxa4 18 ♖a1 ♖fe8 19 ♖xe8+ ♖xe8 20 ♖xa4 a5 21 ♗d2 ♖b8 22 ♖a1 and White is a bit better) 18 ♕xg6 hxg6 19 axb5 ♖fb8 20 c4 axb5 21 c5 ♗f8 22 ♗f4 ♖a4! and despite Black's enterprising play White still has an edge, Abreu-Ro.Perez, Cuba 2003.

10 cxd5!?

Now the play becomes very complicated. The simple 10 ♗f1 also allows White to try for an edge, for example:

a) 10...dxc4 leads to very sharp play after 11 ♘c3 (or 11 ♗xc4?! 0-0 12 a3 ♘d6! 13 ♗xf7+!? ♖xf7 14 axb4 ♗g4 15 ♘bd2 ♗g5!? and Black has superb compensation for the pawn) 11...♘f6 12 ♗xc4 0-0 13 a3 ♘c6 (trying to win material with 13...♘c2?! fails to 14 ♘h4 ♗e4 15 ♘xe4 ♘xa1 16 ♘f5, when White has a large advantage – the knight on a1 has no chance of escaping) 14 d5 ♘a5 15 ♗a2 c5 16 ♗g5 ♖e8 17 ♕a4! ♗d7 18 ♕c2 h6 19 ♗h4 and White had a strong initiative in Karpov-Portisch, Tilburg 1982.

b) 10...0-0 11 a3 ♘c6 12 cxd5 (12 ♘c3 ♘xc3 13 bxc3 dxc4 14 ♗xc4 transposes to 7...♘c6 8 c4 ♘b4 9 ♗e2 0-0 10 ♘c3 ♗f5 11 a3 ♘xc3 12 bxc3 ♘c6 13 ♖e1 dxc4 14 ♗xc4 – see Game 2) 12...♕xd5 13 ♘c3 ♘xc3 14 bxc3 ♗f6 15 ♗f4 ♕d7 16 ♖a2!? ♖ae8 17 ♖ae2 ♖xe2 18 ♕xe2 ♘a5 19 ♘e5 ♕a4 20 g4!? (White's advantage is his activity rather than his structure, so it is vital to continue aggressively) 20...♗e6 (or 20...♗xe5 21 ♘xe5 ♗d7 22 ♗xc7 ♖e8 23 ♕d2 ♖xa3 24 ♖xe8+ ♗xe8 25 ♕g5! and White keeps an edge) 21 g5 ♗d8 and White was a bit better in Korneev-Ro.Perez, Albacete 2000.

10...♘xf2!?

This is the critical try. 10...♘xd3 11 ♕xd3 ♕xd5 transposes to 7...♘c6 8 c4 ♘b4 9 cxd5 ♘xd3 10 ♕xd3 ♕xd5 11 ♖e1 ♗f5 (see Games 9-10).

11 ♕a4+

The only good move. If 11 ♗b5+?! c6 12 ♕a4 0-0 13 dxc6 bxc6 14 ♗xc6 ♘fd3 Black has a clear advantage. 12 dxc6? is even worse: 12...♘xd1 13 c7+ ♕d7 14 ♗xd7+ ♗xd7 15 ♘a3 ♘f2! and Black is winning.

11...♗d7

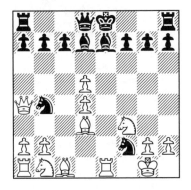

12 ♗b5

Again White has no choice. After 12 ♕xb4? ♘xd3 13 ♖e7+ ♕xe7 14 ♕xb7 0-0 15 ♗d2 ♕e2 Black wins easily.

12...♘fd3

Advancing further into White's position with 12...♘bd3?! leads only to trouble: 13 ♖e2 a6 (or 13...♘xc1 14 ♖xf2 ♘d3 15 ♖d2 ♘f4 16 ♘e5 ♗xb5 17 ♕xb5+ ♔f8 18 ♖f2 and White is much better) 14 ♗xd7+ ♕xd7 15 ♕xd7+ ♔xd7 16 ♖xf2 ♘xf2 17 ♔xf2 ♗d6 18 ♘c3 and White's material advantage is almost decisive.

13 ♖e3 0-0

13...♗xb5 is no improvement: 14 ♕xb5+ ♔f8 15 ♖xd3 ♘c2 16 ♕c4 ♘xa1 17 b3 and

the wayward knight will soon be collected.

14 ♗xd7 ♘xc1 15 ♘c3

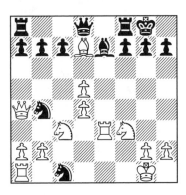

15...♘cd3

Black can also try 15...♘cxa2, after which White's best is 16 ♖xa2!? ♘xa2 17 ♘xa2 a6 18 ♗f5 with an edge. Instead after 16 ♘xa2 ♘xd5 Black hits e3 and threatens ...♘b6, 17 ♖ae1 ♘xe3 18 ♖xe3 ♗d6 leading to an unclear position.

16 a3 ♘c5

Ro.Perez assesses 16...♘xb2 17 ♕b3 ♘c4 18 ♖xe7 ♕xe7 19 axb4 as a bit better for White.

17 dxc5

This allows White to keep some control. Instead 17 ♕xb4 a5 18 ♕b5 ♘xd7 19 ♖ae1 ♗d6 20 ♕xb7 ♖b8 21 ♕a7 ♖xb2 22 ♕xa5 ♘b6 is very messy.

17...♗xc5 18 axb4 ♗xe3+ 19 ♔h1

White's two minor pieces are preferable to Black's rook and pawn.

19...♕f6

19...a6 20 ♖e1 ♗b6 21 ♗f5 is also marginally in White's favour.

20 ♗b5 ♖ad8 21 ♕c2 ♕f4 22 ♗d3 g6

The other way to cover h7 is 22...h6, but White keeps the attack going with 23 b5 ♖fe8 24 ♖f1.

23 b5 ♖fe8 24 ♖f1 f5 25 ♕b3 ♕d6 26 ♕c4 26...♕c5?

Overlooking a nasty trick. 26...♔h8 27 ♗c2 ♖d7 28 ♘d4 limits White to just an edge.

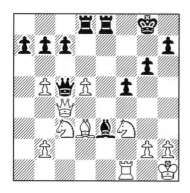

27 ♕xc5?!

White misses it as well: 27 d6+! ♔g7 28 dxc7 ♖d7 29 b6 is effectively winning.

27...♗xc5 28 ♗c4 h6?!

This allows White a second chance for the same tactic. Instead 28...♗d6 29 ♘g5 ♖e5 30 ♘e6 ♖c8 31 g3 is very unpleasant, but at least Black can play on.

29 d6+ ♔g7 30 dxc7 ♖d7 31 b6! a6 32 ♗e6 1-0

Game 31
Kupreichik-Yusupov
Minsk 1987

---

1 e4 e5 2 ♘f3 ♘f6 3 ♘xe5 d6 4 ♘f3 ♘xe4 5 d4 d5 6 ♗d3 ♗g4

Or 6...♘c6 7 0-0 ♗g4.

7 0-0

Also interesting is the simple 7 ♕e2 ♕e7 (instead 7...f5?! allows an instructive trick: 8 h3 ♗h5 9 g4! fxg4 10 ♘e5 ♗f7 11 hxg4 and White is clearly better) 8 0-0 ♘c6 9 ♗b5 and White has an edge, which will grow considerably if Black plays too directly with 9...a6 10 ♗xc6+ bxc6 11 ♖e1 ♕e6 12 ♘bd2.

7...♘c6 8 c4

Immediately undermining the e4-knight but 8 ♖e1 is also possible. Now 8...♗e7 transposes to Chapter 2, while 8...f5 is another possibility: 9 c4!? ♗d6?! (Black must play 9...♗b4, which leads to very unclear play after 10 ♖e3 0-0 11 a3 ♗a5 12 cxd5 ♕xd5)

10 cxd5 ♗xf3 11 ♕xf3 ♘xd4 12 ♕e3 (this is simplest but 12 ♕d1!? also works: 12...♗xh2+ 13 ♔f1 ♕xd5 14 ♘c3 and White is much better) 12...♕f6 13 ♗xe4 fxe4 14 ♘d2! (less ambitious is 14 ♕xe4+ ♔f7 15 ♗g5 ♕xg5 16 ♕xd4 ♖he8 17 ♘c3 when White was only a little better in Capablanca-Marshall, New York 1910) 14...♘f5 15 ♕xe4+ ♘e7 16 ♘f3 h6 17 ♕a4+ ♔d8 18 ♕b5 ♔c8 19 ♗e3 when White's extra pawn and safer king ensures a huge advantage.

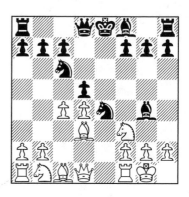

8...♘f6

Trying to grab material with 8...♗xf3 9 ♕xf3 ♘xd4?! backfires after 10 ♕e3 ♘f5 11 ♕f4 ♕d7 12 ♗xe4 dxe4 13 ♕xe4+ ♗e7 14 ♕xb7 0-0 15 ♘c3 when White is clearly better.

9 ♘c3

Developing and increasing the pressure is the correct approach. The simple 9 cxd5 leads nowhere after 9...♗xf3 (9...♘xd5 10 ♘c3 ♗e7 transposes to 6...♗e7 7 0-0 ♘c6 8 c4 ♘f6 9 ♘c3 ♗g4 10 cxd5 ♘xd5 – see Game 11) 10 ♕xf3 ♕xd5 11 ♕e2+ (11 ♕xd5 ♘xd5 12 ♘c3 0-0-0 13 ♗c4 ♘ce7 14 ♗d2 g6 15 ♖fe1 ♗g7 16 ♗g5 ♖d7 17 ♗xe7 ♘xe7 18 ♗xf7 ♔b8 19 ♖e2 ♘c8 20 ♗b3 ♖xd4 21 g3 a5, as in Adams-Piket, Dortmund 2000, is also equal) 11...♗e7 12 ♗b5 ♕d6 13 ♘c3 0-0 14 ♗xc6 bxc6 15 ♖d1 ♖fe8 16 ♕f3 ♘d5 17 ♘xd5 ♕xd5 18 ♕xd5 cxd5 19 ♗f4 c6 20 ♖ac1 ♖ac8 and White had no more than equality in Short-H.Olafsson,

Reykjavik 1987.

9...♗xf3

9...♗e7 transposes to 6...♗e7 7 0-0 ♘c6 8 c4 ♘f6 9 ♘c3 ♗g4 (see Game 11).

10 ♕xf3 ♘xd4 11 ♕h3

This is probably the most dangerous option but 11 ♕e3+ is also worth considering: 11...♘e6 12 cxd5 ♘xd5 13 ♘xd5 ♕xd5 14 ♗e4 ♕b5 15 a4 ♕a6 16 ♖d1 ♗e7 (the seemingly more active 16...♗c5 simply helps White to open lines: 17 ♕f3 c6 18 b4!? ♗xb4 19 ♖b1 ♗c5 20 ♖xb7 and White has the initiative) 17 b4! 0-0 (17...♗xb4 is too greedy: 18 ♗b2 0-0 19 ♕h3 ♘g5 20 ♕g4 ♗e7 21 h4 and White has a strong attack) 18 ♕h3 g6 19 ♕c3 (keeping Black's queen out of the game; instead 19 ♗b2 allows 19...♕c4! 20 ♖d7 ♖ae8 21 ♗d5 ♕xb4 22 ♗c3 ♘f4 23 ♗xb4 ♘xh3+ 24 gxh3 ♗xb4 25 ♖xc7 b6 26 ♖xa7 ♔g7 when Black has cleverly equalised, Kasparov-Karpov, World Championship [Game 6], London/Leningrad 1986) 19...♘g5 20 ♗xg5 (20 ♗b2 may seem more natural but 20...♗f6 21 ♕xf6 ♕xf6 22 ♗xf6 ♘xe4 23 ♗e7 ♖fe8 24 ♖d7 ♘c3! equalises according to Kasparov) 20...♗xg5 21 ♕xc7 ♖ad8 22 ♖xd8 ♖xd8 23 ♗xb7 ♕e2 24 ♗f3 ♕b2 25 ♖f1 ♕xb4 26 ♕xa7 (Bauer-Koch, Belfort 2002). Clearly White's extra pawn makes his position preferable, but the opposite-coloured bishops will make any winning attempt very difficult.

11...dxc4 12 ♗xc4 ♗e7 13 ♗g5 0-0

This is certainly the natural move but Black should seriously consider 13...♕c8. For example, 14 ♕e3!? ♘e6 (14...♕c2 is too greedy: 15 ♕e2 ♕g4 – 15...♘xa1? is refuted by 16 ♗xf6 gxf6 17 ♘d5 – 16 ♕xg4 ♘xg4 17 ♗xe7 ♔xe7 18 ♘d5+ ♔f8 19 ♖ac1 ♘d4 20 ♘xc7 ♖d8 21 ♖fe1 and Black's awkward king delays his development, giving White a pleasant edge) 15 ♗xf6 ♗xf6 16 ♘d5 ♕d8 17 ♕b3 ♗d4 18 ♕xb7 0-0 19 ♖ab1 ♖b8 20 ♕a6 c6 21 ♕xc6 ♗xb2 and Black has escaped to equality, Bologan-Koch, Belfort 2002.

14 ♖ad1 c5

If 14...h6 White should play calmly with 15 ♗f4 c5 16 ♘b5 when his initiative is very threatening. 15 ♗xh6?! is premature: 15...gxh6 16 ♖d3 ♔h7 17 ♖g3 ♘g8! and Black defends successfully.

15 ♖fe1

White's lead in development and the various potential pins constitute good compensation for the pawn.

15...h6 16 ♗xh6!

This is even stronger than the tempting 16 ♖xe7!? hxg5 (Black can give up the queen with 16...♕xe7 17 ♘d5 ♘xd5 18 ♗xe7 ♘xe7, but after 19 b4 b6 20 bxc5 bxc5 21 ♕h5 White still has an edge) 17 ♖xb7 ♖b8 18 ♖xb8 ♕xb8 19 b3 ♕e5 when the position is unclear according to Yusupov.

16...gxh6 17 ♕xh6 ♘h7

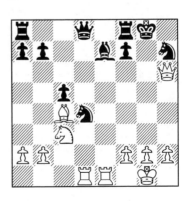

18 ♖d3

This is the right rook. After 18 ♖e3?! ♗g5 19 ♖g3 ♔h8 20 ♕h5 f5 Yusupov again gives the verdict 'unclear'.

18...♗g5 19 ♕h5

19 ♖g3 allows Black some additional defensive resources: 19...♘f5 20 ♕g6+ ♘g7 21 ♘e4 (not 21 h4? ♗f6 22 ♘d5 ♔h8 and Black refutes the attack) 21...♔h8 22 ♗xf7 ♕e7 with a position that is very difficult to assess accurately. For example, 23 ♕xh7+ ♔xh7 24 ♘xg5+ ♕xg5 25 ♖xg5 ♖xf7 26 ♖xc5 ♖d8 and Black's extra knight will have an interesting battle against the three pawns.

19...♕f6 20 ♖g3

A strong alternative is 20 ♖h3!? ♕g7 21 f4 ♗xf4 22 ♘d5 ♗g5 23 ♘e7+ ♗xe7 24 ♖xe7 ♘c6 25 ♖ee3 with a dangerous attack.

20...♖ae8

Also possible is 20...♘f5 21 ♖h3 ♕g7 22 f4 ♖ae8 23 ♖e2 when White's attack continues although there is no clear win. However, after 22 ♖e5? (!! – Kupreichik) 22...♘f6 23 ♕f3 ♘h4 24 ♕g3 ♗f4! Black successfully defends.

21 ♘e4

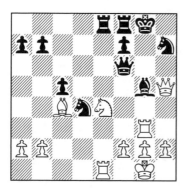

21...♔h8?

Black cracks under the pressure. 21...♔g7 is essential, when the fight continues. Following 22 ♘xf6 (Black has counterplay after 22 h4 ♕g6 23 ♕xg6+ fxg6 24 hxg5 ♖f4 – Yusupov) 22...♖xe1+ 23 ♗f1 ♔xf6 24 f4! ♗xf4 25 ♖f3 ♘xf3+ 26 ♕xf3 the position is still unclear.

22 h4!

By freeing his back rank, White threatens the queen. Now White has a large advantage.

22...♖xe4

If 22...♕h6 Kupreichik suggests 23 ♖xg5! ♕xh5 24 ♖xh5 f5 25 ♖xh7+! ♔xh7 26 ♘f6+, when White is much better.

23 ♖xe4 ♗f4 24 ♖g4 ♗h6

Or 24...♗d6 25 ♖xd4! cxd4 26 ♗d3 and Black must resign.

25 ♕xc5 ♘c6 26 ♕h5 ♕d6 27 ♗xf7 ♕d1+ 28 ♔h2 ♕d6+ 29 f4 ♕c7 30 ♗b3 ♕d6 31 ♖e8 ♗xf4+ 32 g3 ♗xg3+ 33 ♔h3 1-0

Mate is inevitable.

Game 32

Tukmakov-Bronstein
Moscow 1971

---

1 e4 e5 2 ♘f3 ♘f6 3 ♘xe5 d6 4 ♘f3 ♘xe4 5 d4 ♗e7

Of course 5...d5 is the more popular and reliable move.

6 ♗d3 ♘f6

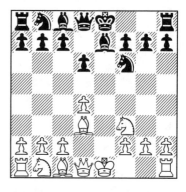

Trying to equalise by seeking exchanges with 6...♘g5 just falls short: 7 ♘xg5 ♗xg5 8 ♕e2+ ♔f8 (or 8...♗e7 9 0-0 0-0 10 ♘c3 ♘c6 11 ♘d5 ♖e8 12 ♗e3 and White also has a slight edge, while after 8...♗e6 9 f4 ♗h4+ 10 g3 ♗e7 11 f5 ♗d5 12 0-0 0-0 13 ♘c3 ♗c6 14 d5 ♗d7 15 ♘e4 White has a dangerous initiative) 9 0-0 ♗xc1 10 ♖xc1 ♘c6 11 c3 g6

12 ♘d2 ♔g7 13 ♖e1 ♗d7 14 f4 ♖e8 15 ♕f3 ♕h4 16 g3 ♕g4 17 ♕f2 and White was a bit better in Palac-Murey, Pula 2002.

7 h3

White plays to dominate his opponent's queen bishop. 7 0-0 is a sensible alternative, for example 7...♗g4 8 ♘bd2 0-0 9 ♖e1 c5 10 h3 ♗h5 11 ♘f1 ♘c6 and now:

a) Breaking the pin with 12 g4 is weakening: 12...♗g6 13 ♘g3 d5!? (White has a small advantage after 13...♖e8 14 c3 ♕c7 15 ♘f5 ♗f8 16 ♖xe8 ♖xe8 17 ♗f4 cxd4 18 ♘3xd4 a6 19 ♕a4 ♘d5 20 ♗g3 ♘b6 21 ♕c2, Stefansson-Kholmov, Pardubice 2001) 14 dxc5 ♗xc5 15 ♗e3 ♗xe3 16 ♖xe3 d4 17 ♖e1 ♕b6 with complicated play.

b) 12 ♘g3 is better: 12...♗xf3 (or 12...♗g6 13 ♗xg6 hxg6 14 d5 ♘b4 15 c4 and White has a pleasant space advantage) 13 ♕xf3 ♘xd4 14 ♕xb7 ♖e8 15 ♘f5 ♘xf5 16 ♗xf5 ♗f8 17 ♖xe8 ♕xe8 18 ♗d2 g6 19 ♗d3 d5 20 c4 and White has a strong initiative, Ljubojevic-Smyslov, London 1984.

7...0-0 8 0-0 ♖e8

Black has alternatives but no path to equality:

a) 8...c5 9 ♘c3 ♘c6 10 ♖e1 a6 (10...♘b4 doesn't solve Black's problems: White has an edge following 11 ♗f4 d5 12 dxc5 ♗xc5 13 ♗e5) 11 d5 ♘a7 (after 11...♘b4 Karpov suggests 12 ♗e4!? as a way to keep the initiative) 12 a4 ♗d7 13 a5 ♖e8 14 ♗f1 h6 15 ♗f4 ♗f8 16 ♖xe8 ♕xe8 17 ♗h2 ♕d8 18 ♘d2 ♕c7 19 ♘de4 ♘xe4 20 ♘xe4 and White was a bit better in Karpov-Smyslov, Moscow 1972.

b) 8...♘c6 9 c3 ♖e8 10 ♖e1 ♗d7 11 ♘bd2 ♗f8 12 ♘e4 d5 (exchanging with 12...♘xe4 still leaves White with an edge after 13 ♗xe4 h6 14 ♕c2 ♕f6 15 ♗e3) ♘g3 ♗d6 14 ♖xe8+ ♕xe8 15 ♕c2 h6 16 ♗d2 ♕f8 17 ♘f5 ♗xf5 18 ♗xf5 ♖e8 19 ♗d3 ♘d8 20 c4 and White had an initiative in Bronstein-Smyslov, Leningrad 1971.

9 c4 c6

The alternative is 9...♘bd7 10 ♘c3 and:

a) 10...♘f8 11 ♖e1 ♘g6 (White has a clear plus after 11...d5 12 ♘e5 c6 13 cxd5 ♘xd5 14 ♘xd5 cxd5 15 ♗b5) 12 ♕c2 ♗d7 13 ♗g5 ♗c6 14 d5 ♗d7 15 ♖ad1 a6 16 ♘e2 ♘h5 17 ♗c1 ♕c8 18 ♘ed4 c5 19 dxc6 bxc6 20 ♘f5 ♗xf5 21 ♗xf5 ♕c7 22 ♕a4 ♘f6 23 ♘d4 c5 24 ♘c6 and White was much better in Luther-Bellin, Catalan Bay 2003.

b) 10...c6 11 ♖e1 ♘f8 12 ♗f4 a6 13 ♕b3?! (this allows counterplay; 13 d5!? ♘g6 14 ♗h2 c5 15 ♕d2, with a slight edge, is better, while also promising is 13 b4!? ♘e6 14 ♗h2 a5 15 b5) 13...♘e6 14 ♗h2 ♗f8 (Fischer assessed 14...b5!? 15 a4 bxc4 16 ♗xc4 d5 17 ♗f1 c5 as unclear) 15 ♖e2 b5 16 ♕c2 ♗b7 17 ♖ae1 g6 with a complex position, Fischer-Petrosian, 5th matchgame, Buenos Aires 1971.

10 ♘c3 a6 11 b4 ♘bd7 12 ♗e3 ♘f8 13 a4

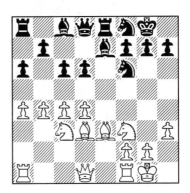

13...a5

White's initiative continues after 13...d5 14 c5 ♘e6 15 ♕c2 ♗f8 16 b5.

14 b5 ♘g6 15 ♖e1 ♘h5 16 ♕d2 ♗d7 17 ♖ab1 ♕c8 18 ♗f1

18 d5!? c5 19 ♘e4 with promising play is also interesting.

18...♗f5 19 ♖b3

19 g4? would be a naive blunder: 19...♗xg4! 20 hxg4 ♕xg4+ and Black has a clear plus.

19...h6 20 ♔h2 ♘f6 21 ♕b2 d5 22 bxc6 bxc6 23 cxd5 ♗b4

If 23...cxd5 then 24 ♖c1 ♕d8 25 ♗b5 and White keeps an edge.

24 ♖c1 cxd5 25 ♘b5 ♕b8+ 26 ♔g1 ♖e7?!

This allows White's advantage to grow. Black can limit the damage with 26...♖c8 27 ♘e1 ♖xc1 28 ♕xc1 ♕d8 29 ♘d3, when White is only a bit better.

27 ♘e5! ♗d7

The tactical justification is seen after 27...♘xe5 28 dxe5 ♕xe5 29 ♗d4 ♕e4 30 ♗d3 ♕f4 31 ♗xf5 ♕xf5 32 ♖f3 ♕e6 33 ♗xf6 gxf6 34 ♖g3+ ♔f8 35 ♕c2, when Black's weakened kingside causes terrible trouble.

28 ♘d3 ♗xb5 29 axb5 ♗d6 30 ♘c5!

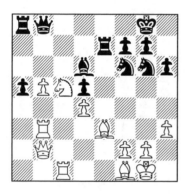

After 30 b6 a4 31 ♖b5 a3 32 ♕a2 ♖b7 33 ♖cb1 White's advantage, if any, is very small indeed.

30...♕b6 31 ♘a4 ♕d8 32 b6 ♖b8 33 ♘c5 ♖e8 34 ♖a1 ♘h4 35 ♖xa5 ♘f5 36 ♖a7

36 ♗d2!? ♘e4 37 ♘xe4 ♖xe4 38 ♗c3 with a clear advantage is a good alternative.

36...♘xe3 37 fxe3 ♗g3 38 e4

This is a good move but White could also cash in immediately with 38 ♘a6 ♘e4 39 ♘xb8 ♕xb8 40 ♗d3.

38...♕d6 39 e5?!

This allows Black to complicate. 39 ♘b7?! ♖xb7 40 ♖xb7 ♘xe4 with unclear play is also unconvincing, but the simple solution is to prepare e4-e5 by supporting the knight with 39 ♕c3 – White wins easily after 39...♗h2+ 40 ♔h1 ♕f4 41 e5.

39...♗xe5 40 dxe5 ♕xc5+ 41 ♔h1?!

Now White's advantage disappears entirely. 41 ♔h2 ♘e4 42 ♖c7 ♕a5 43 ♗b5 maintains a slight edge.

41...♘e4 42 ♔h2 ♖e6 43 ♖c7 ♕a5

43...♖c6 44 ♖xc6 ♕xc6 45 ♗d3 ♕g6 is also good enough for equality.

44 ♗d3

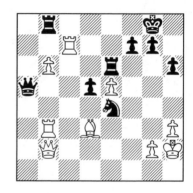

44...♖g6

The b-pawn is poisoned due to a back rank trick: If 44...♖exb6? then 45 ♖xb6 ♖xb6 46 ♕f2! wins, while after 44...♖bxb6? 45 ♕f2! White has a clear advantage.

45 ♗xe4 dxe4 46 ♕d4 e3 47 ♖xe3 ♕xb6 48 ♕xb6 ♖bxb6 ½-½

Summary

Firstly, the passive continuations covered in this chapter (5...♗e7 and a quick ...♘d6 after 5...d5) are not of great interest. The key position of the chapter is the one arising after 5...d5 6 ♗d3 ♗e7 7 0-0 ♗f5 8 ♖e1 ♘c6 9 c4. In response to 9...0-0, White successfully develops his knight to c3 either immediately or after 10 cxd5 ♕xd5. In the case of 9...♘b4 White maintains an opening initiative by retreating with 10 ♗f1, but 10 cxd5 also appears to be a good response – the tactical blow 10...♘xf2!? is not a refutation. Probably Black should transpose to the line 6...♗e7 7 0-0 ♘c6 8 c4 ♘b4 9 cxd5 ♘xd3 10 ♕xd3 ♕xd5 11 ♖e1 ♗f5 (see Chapter 2) by means of 10...♘xd3 11 ♕xd3 ♕xd5.

1 e4 e5 2 ♘f3 ♘f6 3 ♘xe5 d6 4 ♘f3 ♘xe4 5 d4 (D) d5

     5...♗e7 – *Game 32*

6 ♗d3 (D) ♗e7

     6...♗g4 – *Game 31*

7 0-0 ♗f5 8 ♖e1 ♘c6 (D) 9 c4 – *Game 30*

     9 ♘bd2 – *Game 29*

5 d4

6 ♗d3

8...♘c6

CHAPTER FIVE

3 ♘xe5: Fourth and Fifth Move Alternatives

1 e4 e5 2 ♘f3 ♘f6 3 ♘xe5 d6 4 ♘f3 ♘xe4

After 1 e4 e5 2 ♘f3 ♘f6 3 ♘xe5 d6 4 ♘f3 ♘xe4 White sometimes declines to play 5 d4 in favour of the other continuations, and these fifth move alternatives are the subject of the first part of this chapter.

5 ♘c3 (Games 33-34) was played as far back as the 19th century, while later on Nimzowitsch focused on it.

5 ♕e2 (Games 35-36) was introduced by a 13-year old Paul Morphy against Löwenthal (New Orleans, 1850), and the line found worthy adherents in the form of Emanuel Lasker and Jose Raul Capablanca. Owing to the success of such celebrities (see, for example, Game 35) 5 ♕e2 was considered to be nearly a refutation of the Petroff Defence, but now we know several ways for Black to equalise.

Kaufmann, a chess player from Vienna, suggested 5 c4 (Game 37) as a way to prevent Black from supporting the e4-knight with ...d6-d5. In principle it's still possible to play 5...d5, but an attack on Black's centralised forces with 6 ♘c3 gives White the better chances. Instead Black should continue his development with either 5...♘c6 or 5...♗e7 to avoid any problems.

5 ♗d3 (Game 38) is a comparatively new

idea. In the event of 5...♘c5 White retreats his bishop to e2 and makes up for lost time by attacking the knight with d2-d4. After 5...d5 White continues the attack on the e4-knight with 6 ♕e2, while if 5...♘f6 White clears the way for the d-pawn by means of c2-c3 and ♗d3-c2.

5 d3 (Game 39) is the most modest of White's 5th move options. White offers Black the opportunity to transpose to the Exchange Variation of the French Defence after 5...♘f6 6 d4 d5 where, as it is known, an extra tempo in this symmetrical line promises White just a microscopic advantage. However, Black can equalise after 6...♗e7 followed up by ...c7-c5.

Moving onto 4th move alternatives, besides 4 ♘f3 White has two interesting options.

The first major game to witness 4 ♘c4 was L.Paulsen-Schallopp, Frankfurt 1887. The idea to transfer the knight to e3 is not particularly impressive. In particular, Black's attack on f2 after 4...♘e4 5 d4 d5 6 ♘e3 ♕f6 (Game 40) deserves serious consideration for Black.

The Cochrane Gambit 4 ♘xf7!? (Games 41-42), originated by John Cochrane in the 1840s, stands in total contrast to the other lines in the Petroff Defence. Staunton also analysed this knight-for-two-pawns sacrifice in his *Chess Praxis* (1860). Curiously enough, both Cochrane and the famous maestro concentrated on 4...♔xf7 5 ♗c4+?!, which is poor in view of 5...d5!. It might be appropriate to rename the Cochrane Gambit to the Bronstein Gambit (he was the one who breathed new life into the sacrifice by indicating the possibility of 5 d4!) or the Vitolinsh Gambit (the Latvian IM played a number of brilliant attacks with 4 ♘xf7). After the piece sacrifice Black's king gets stuck in the centre and White's initiative can be lasting and dangerous.

Finally, Game 43 studies a couple of rare 3rd move options for Black. Strictly speaking, 3...♘xe4 was the move studied at the very beginning of the Petroff Defence theory, Damiano considering it as far back as 1512! After 4 ♕e2 ♕e7 Black gives up his knight but immediately wins it back due to the pin on the e-file, and he is left a pawn down with the hope of active play for his pieces. Black's only other option is 3...♕e7, but hereWhite has more than one way to obtain a clear plus.

Game 33
Alekhine-A.Rabinovich
Moscow 1918

---

1 e4 e5 2 ♘f3 ♘f6 3 ♘xe5 d6 4 ♘f3 ♘xe4 5 ♘c3

5...d5?!

This is not a particularly good pawn sacrifice, but the alternatives covered here are also not great. The best move, 5...♘xc3, is considered in the next game.

a) 5...♗f5?? 6 ♘xe4?? ♗xe4 7 d3 ♗g6 8 ♗g5 ♗e7 9 ♗xe7 ♕xe7+ 10 ♗e2 ♘c6 11 0-0 0 was a comedy of errors that led to equal chances in Miles-Christiansen, San Francisco 1987. After the infinitely stronger 6 ♕e2! Black immediately resigned in Zapata-Anand, Biel 1987.

b) 5...♘f6 doesn't promise full equality: 6 d4 ♗e7 7 ♗d3 0-0 and now:

b1) 8 ♘e2 with a further branch:

b11) 8...♖e8 9 0-0 ♘c6 10 c3 ♗f8 11 ♘g3 d5 12 ♕c2 h6 13 ♘h4 ♔h8 14 b4 ♘g8 15 ♘hf5 ♘ce7 16 ♘e3 ♘f6 17 a4 ♘eg8 18 b5 ♘g4 19 ♘xg4 (19 c4 allows 19...♖xe3! 20 fxe3 ♕h4 21 h3 ♕xg3 22 hxg4 ♗d6 23 ♗a3 ♕h2+ 24 ♔f2 ♕g3+ with a draw, Ulibin-Akopian, Tbilisi 1989) 19...♗xg4 20 ♘f5 and White has a bit of pressure.

b12) 8...c5 9 h3 ♘c6 10 c3 ♖e8 11 0-0 b6 12 ♕c2 ♗b7 13 dxc5 bxc5 (probably 13...♘e5!? is stronger: 14 ♘xe5 dxe5 15 ♖d1 ♕c7 16 cxb6 ♕c6 17 f3 ♕xb6+ 18 ♔h1 ♖ad8 gives Black play for the pawn, while 15 cxb6 ♗c5 16 ♔h2 ♕xb6 also seems to give Black decent counterplay) 14 ♘g5! g6 (14...h6? lead to a fabulous end in the following game: 15 ♗h7+ ♔f8 16 ♘xf7! ♔xf7 17 ♕g6+ ♔f8 18 ♗xh6! gxh6 19 ♘f4 ♕d7 20 ♕xh6+ ♔f7 21 ♕g6+ ♔f8 22 ♘h5 ♖eb8 23 ♖ae1 ♘xh7 24 ♕xh7 ♘e5 25 f4 ♗f6 26 ♕h6+ ♗g7 27 fxe5+ ♔g8 28 ♘f6+ 1-0 L.Dominguez-Ro.Perez, Cuba 2003) 15 ♕b3 ♘e5 16 ♘xf7! ♗d5 17 ♘xd8 ♗xb3 18 axb3 ♘xd3 19 ♘e6 ♗d8 20 ♘6f4 ♘xc1 21 ♘xc1 g5 22 ♘fd3 and White retains some advantage (L.Dominguez).

b2) 8 h3 is also good, for example 8...♘c6 9 a3 ♖e8 10 0-0 h6 11 ♖e1 ♗f8 12 ♖xe8 ♕xe8 13 ♘b5 ♕d8 14 c4 a6 15 ♘c3 ♘e7 (15...d5 16 c5 ♗e6 17 b4 also looks better for White) 16 d5 ♗f5 17 ♗e2 ♗h7 18 b3 ♕d7

19 ♗b2 and White's chances were preferable in Acs-Haba, Bled 2002.

6 ♕e2 ♗e7 7 ♘xe4 dxe4 8 ♕xe4 0-0 9 ♗c4

Black obtains good play after 9 ♗d3 g6 10 0-0 ♘c6 11 ♗b5 ♗f5 12 ♕e2 ♖e8 13 ♗xc6 bxc6 14 d4 ♗b8, when the bishops and the development compensate for the pawn deficit.

9...♗d6 10 0-0

White is aiming for rapid development. Alekhine gave the following line: 10 d4 ♖e8 11 ♘e5 ♗xe5 12 dxe5 ♘c6 13 ♗f4 ♕h4 14 0-0-0 ♖xe5 15 ♖d8+! ♕xd8 16 ♗xe5 ♕e7 17 ♖e1 ♘xe5 18 ♕xe5 ♕xe5 19 ♖xe5 ♔f8, when the draw is near.

10...♖e8 11 ♕d3 ♘c6 12 b3!

White needs to get his dark-squared bishop into play. After something like 12 ♕c3 ♗g4 13 ♗d5 ♗xf3 14 ♗xf3 ♘d4! Black would have good play for the pawn.

12...♕f6 13 ♗b2!!

The master of attack strikes again! Instead of clinging onto his pawn, White launches a strong counterattack.

13...♕xb2 14 ♘g5 ♗e6

After 14...g6 White has 15 ♗xf7+ ♔g7 16 ♗xe8 ♕e5 17 ♕c3 ♘d4 18 f4 and a very nice position (Alekhine); 14...♘d8 15 ♕xh7+ ♔f8 16 ♖ae1 ♗e6 17 c3 also looks very promising for White.

15 ♗xe6 fxe6 16 ♕xh7+ ♔f8 17 ♖ae1?!

This natural looking move allows Black to bring the queen home. 17 c3! is stronger: 17...♕xd2 18 ♕h8+ ♔e7 19 ♕xg7+ ♔d8 20 ♖ad1 ♕f4 21 g3 ♕f8 22 ♘xe6+ and White wins (Alekhine); or 17...♗e5 18 ♕h5 ♔g8 19 ♕f7+ ♔h8 20 ♕g6! ♔g8 21 d4 ♗f6 22 ♕h7+ ♔f8 23 ♘xe6+ and White has a very large plus.

17...♕f6 18 ♕h5

18 ♕h8+?! is weaker: after 18...♔e7 19 ♖xe6+ ♔d7 20 ♖xf6 ♖xh8 21 ♖f7+ ♘e7 22 h3 g6 Black's chances in the endgame are preferable.

18...♔g8 19 ♖e3 ♗f4?

Now I know we should not talk badly of the dead, and Rabinovich was truly one of the great fathers of Russian Chess, but here his defence was not particularly good. White is also very happy after 19...♘d4?! 20 ♖h3 g6 21 ♕h7+ ♔f8 22 ♕d7 ♖e7 (22...♔g8? 23 ♖h8+! would be an unpleasant surprise) 23 ♘h7+ ♔g7 24 ♘xf6 ♖xd7 25 ♘xd7 ♖d8 26 ♖d3 ♘e2+ 27 ♔h1 ♖xd7 28 g3 (Alekhine). However, Black can play 19...♘e5! 20 ♕h7+ ♔f8 21 f4 ♘f7 22 ♕h5 ♔g8, probably keeping the position level.

20 ♕h7+ ♔f8 21 ♕h8+ ♔e7

22 ♖xe6+!

This is probably what Rabinovich missed.

22...♕xe6

Or 22...♔d7 23 ♖xf6 ♖xh8 24 ♖xf4 with a winning endgame.

23 ♕xg7+ ♔d6 24 ♘xe6 ♖xe6 25 d4 ♖ae8 26 c4 ♖8e7 27 ♕f8 ♖e4 28 ♕f5!

♖xd4

28...♖7e6 29 ♕c5+ ♔d7 30 d5 also wins for White.

29 c5 mate (1-0)

> ## Game 34
> ## Khalifman-Atalik
> *Halkidiki 2002*

1 e4 e5 2 ♘f3 ♘f6 3 ♘xe5 d6 4 ♘f3 ♘xe4 5 ♘c3 ♘xc3

The best move.

6 dxc3

Also possible is 6 bxc3, when the game could continue 6...♗e7 7 d4 0-0 8 ♗d3 ♗g4 9 0-0 ♘d7 10 ♖b1 ♘b6 11 c4 ♗f6 (or 11...c5 12 h3 ♗h5 13 dxc5 dxc5 14 a4 ♕c7 with an unclear position) 12 ♗e3 ♖b8 13 c3 ♕d7 14 ♖b5 a6 15 ♖a5 d5 16 cxd5 ♘xd5 17 ♗d2 c6 18 h3 ♗e6 and Black is okay, Upton-Dutreeuw, Batumi 1999.

6...♗e7

7 ♗f4

White has tried two other means of development:

a) 7 ♗d3 ♘c6 8 ♗e3 ♗g4 9 ♗e4 doesn't look particularly appealing, even though this worked well in the following example: 9...♕d7 10 ♕d2 0-0-0 11 0-0-0 ♖he8 12 ♘d4 d5 (12...♗xd1? 13 ♘xc6 bxc6? 14 ♕d3 and White wins) 13 ♘xc6 ♕xc6 14 ♗xd5 ♕a6 15 ♕d3 ♗xd1 (this is necessary; 15...♕a5 16 f3 c6 17 ♕c4 ♖xd5 was played

in Nimzowitsch-Marshall, San Sebastian 1911, when 18 ♕xg4+ f5 19 ♕c4 looks like a clear extra pawn to us) 16 ♕xa6 bxa6 17 ♖xd1 and White has fine compensation for the exchange.

b) 7 ♗e3 ♘c6 8 ♕d2 looks more sensible: 8...0-0 9 0-0-0 ♘e5 10 ♘d4 c5 (10...a6 11 f4 ♘g4 12 ♗d3 c5 13 ♘f5 ♖e8 14 ♖he1 ♗f8 15 h3 ♘xe3 16 ♘xe3 gives a position where the control over the light squares favours White) 11 ♘b5 ♕a5 (or 11...♗e6!? 12 ♘xd6 ♕b6 13 b4 ♗xd6 14 ♕xd6 ♕xd6 15 ♖xd6 cxb4 16 cxb4 ♗xa2 17 ♗f4 f6 when Black has equalised, Nunn-Zsu.Polgar, Brussels 1985) 12 a3 a6 13 ♘xd6 ♖d8 14 ♘xc8! ♖axc8 (but not 14...♖xd2? 15 ♘xe7+ ♔f8 16 ♖xd2 ♔xe7 17 ♖d5 ♘d7 18 ♗e2! when Black has too many problems: 18...b6 19 ♗f3 ♘f8 – 19...♖a7 20 ♖e1 ♔f8 21 ♗f4 – 20 ♖e5+ 1-0 Van Der Wiel-Van Der Sterren, Wijk aan Zee 1984) 15 ♕e2 b5 16 ♖xd8+ ♖xd8 17 ♗d2 ♘g6 18 ♔b1 b4 19 cxb4 cxb4 20 axb4 ♗xb4 21 ♗c1 ♗e7 and Black has fine compensation for the pawn, Volokitin-Kozakov, Lvov 2001.

7...♘d7

7...♘c6 also looks sensible, for example 8 ♕d2 ♗g4 9 ♗e2 ♕d7 10 h3 ♗f5 11 0-0-0 0-0-0, avoiding the danger of opposite side castling. Now after 12 ♖he1 ♖he8 13 g4 ♗g6 14 ♗b5 a6 15 ♗a4 b5 16 ♗b3 ♘a5 17 c4 ♘xc4 18 ♗xc4 bxc4 19 ♕d5 ♕b5 20 ♕a8+ ♕b8 21 ♕xa6+ ♕b7 22 ♕xb7+ ♔xb7 Black has equal chances in the ending. In this line 17...♘xb3+ is weaker: 18 axb3 ♕c6 19 ♘d4 ♕b7 20 cxb5 axb5 21 ♕a5 with an attack for White, Boricsev-Raetsky, Fribourg 2000.

8 ♕d2

8...♘c5

Black needs to get in ...♗g4 to have a chance of equalising. After 8...0-0 9 0-0-0 ♘c5 10 h3 ♖e8 11 g4 White develops some pressure: 11...♘e4 12 ♕e1 ♗f6 13 ♗e3 c6 14 ♗d3 ♕a5 15 ♗xe4! ♖xe4 16 ♗b6! ♗g5+ (Black also suffers after 16...♕a4 17 ♖d4! ♕xd4 18 ♗xd4 ♖xe1+ 19 ♖xe1 ♗e6 20 ♗xf6 gxf6 21 ♘d4) 17 ♘xg5 ♕xg5+ 18 ♗e3 ♕g6 19 ♕d2 d5 20 f3 ♖e8 21 h4 gave Black serious problems in the form of an advancing attack in Tseshkovsky-I.Zaitsev, USSR 1975.

9 0-0-0 ♗g4 10 ♗e2 0-0 11 h3 ♗h5

11...♗e6 12 ♘d4 ♕d7 13 b3 looks better for White.

12 g4 ♗g6 13 h4 ♖e8

13...♗e4!? 14 h5 ♘e6 15 ♗e3 c5, immediately establishing counterplay in the centre, also looks good.

14 h5 ♗e4 15 ♖hg1 ♘e6 16 ♗e3 c5 17 g5 d5 18 g6!

White has no reason to wait.

18...hxg6

Forced. After 18...♗f6 19 gxh7+ ♔xh7 20 ♘g5+ ♘xg5 21 ♗xg5 d4 22 f3 ♗f5 23 ♗d3 White has a raging attack.

19 hxg6 fxg6

19...♗xg6? is bad on account of 20 ♘e5 ♗f5 21 ♗b5 ♖f8 22 ♘d7, when White has a clear advantage. Now Black loses after 22...♖e8 23 ♕xd5, so he is forced to play 22...d4, which is hardly ideal.

20 ♘e5 ♗f6 21 ♘g4

21...d4?!

A natural push, but it's tactical suspect. Black can improve with 21...♕a5!?, when after 22 ♔b1 the push is stronger: 22...d4 23 ♗c4 b5 (the difference; 23...dxe3? 24 ♘xf6+ gxf6 25 ♕xe3 still does not work, though) 24 ♗xe6+ ♖xe6 25 cxd4 ♕xd2 26 ♖xd2 cxd4 27 ♗xd4 ♖d8 28 ♘xf6+ gxf6 with a likely draw.

22 ♗c4

22 ♘xf6+ is also good for White: 22...♕xf6 23 cxd4 cxd4 (23...♖ed8? 24 ♗c4 b5 25 ♗g5! and White wins) 24 ♗xd4 ♘xd4 25 ♕xd4 ♕xd4 26 ♖xd4 ♖ad8 27 ♖gd1 ♖xd4 28 ♖xd4 ♗f5 with a slight pull in the endgame (Atalik).

22...dxc3?

A very risky move, even if there were no forced win. 22...dxe3? 23 ♕xe3 ♗g5 24 f4 would also not work for Black, but after 22...b5 23 ♗xe6+ ♖xe6 24 cxd4 ♕d5 25 ♘xf6+ gxf6 26 ♕a5 his position is still defendable.

23 ♕e2! ♕b6

Or 23...cxb2+ 24 ♔b1 ♕c7 (24...♕e7 25 ♗xc5! wins) 25 ♘xf6+ gxf6 26 ♕g4 ♕e5 27 ♖d5! and White wins (Atalik).

24 ♘xf6+ gxf6 25 bxc3 ♕c7 26 ♕g4! ♕e5

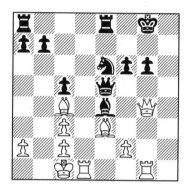

27 ♖d5!! ♕xc3

White wins in all lines: 27...♗f5 28 ♕xf5 or 27...♗xd5 28 ♕xg6+ ♔f8 29 ♗xc5+! when Black will get mated.

28 ♕xe4 ♕a1+ 29 ♔d2 ♕xg1 30 ♖d7! 1-0

Game 35
Em.Lasker-Marshall
St Petersburg 1912

---

1 e4 e5 2 ♘f3 ♘f6 3 ♘xe5 d6 4 ♘f3 ♘xe4 5 ♕e2

This line is usually played with the hope of a draw. However, many White players have found that achieving the draw from an even ending is not always so easy.

5...♕e7 6 d3

The score from this position in our database is actually 51% for White and 49% for Black, which suggests complete equality. However, it also shows that people play on from here...

6...♘f6

The most common move, but not the only one. For example, 6...♘c5 7 ♘c3 ♗g4 8 ♗e3 (8 ♘d5 ♗xf3!? 9 ♕xe7+ ♗xe7 10 ♘xc7+ ♔d7 11 ♘xa8 ♗c6 is not clear, but should be fine for Black) 8...c6 9 h3 ♗h5 10 g4 ♗g6 11 ♗g2 ♘bd7 12 ♘d4 ♘e6 13 f4 ♘xd4 14 ♗xd4 f5 15 0-0-0 ♕xe2 16 ♘xe2

gave White the chance to irritate Black in Hodgson-Barua, London 1986.

7 ♗g5

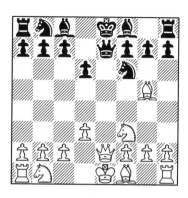

7...♗e6

For some reason Black insists on keeping the queens on, which is not necessary because the endgame promises Black good chances. 7...♕xe2+ is studied in the next game, while 7...♘bd7 8 ♘c3 ♕xe2+ (8...h6?! 9 ♗e3 ♘b6 10 0-0-0 ♗d7 11 ♕d2 0-0-0 12 ♖e1 is a tad uncomfortable for Black) 9 ♗xe2 transposes to 7...♕xe2+ 8 ♗xe2 ♘bd7 9 ♘c3 (see the notes to the next game).

8 ♘c3 ♘bd7

8...♘c6 is answered by the natural 9 ♘e4 0-0-0 10 ♘xf6 gxf6 11 ♗e3 d5 12 d4 ♗g4 13 0-0-0 when White's position is preferable.

8...h6 looks dubious after 9 ♗xf6 ♕xf6 10 d4 ♗e7 11 ♕b5+ ♘d7 12 ♗d3 (12 ♕xb7 0-0 13 ♕xc7 ♘b6 appears very risky for White) 12...g5 13 h3 (or 13 ♘e4 ♕g7 14 h3 with a slight edge – Keres) 13...0-0 14 ♕xb7 ♖ab8 15 ♕e4 ♕g7 16 b3 (we think White is better here) 16...c5? (16...♘c5 17 ♕e3 ♗f6 18 0-0 ♖fe8 19 ♕d2 g4 – Tarrasch – with a messy position is necessary) 17 0-0 cxd4 18 ♘d5 ♗d8 19 ♗c4 ♘c5 20 ♕xd4 ♕xd4 21 ♘xd4 ♗xd5 22 ♗xd5 ♗f6 23 ♖ad1 and White enjoyed a large plus in Capablanca-Marshall, St Petersburg 1914.

9 0-0-0

9 d4 leads to equality after 9...h6 10 ♗h4 g5 11 ♗g3 ♘d5 12 ♘xd5 ♗xd5 13 0-0-0

♕xe2 14 ♗xe2 ♗g7. More interesting is 9
♘b5!? ♘b6 10 ♗xf6 gxf6 11 g3 d5 12 0-0-0
♗h6+ 13 ♔b1 with an unbalanced position,
something that no one would have thought
possible just a few moves ago.

9...h6 10 ♗h4 g5

10...0-0-0 seems to be more accurate. After 11 d4 g5 12 ♗g3 ♘b6 13 ♕b5 a6 14 ♕a5
♗g7 the position is unclear.

11 ♗g3 ♘h5

This looks like a loss of time, but Black
does not have it easy. 11...♗g7 12 ♘d4 0-0
13 h4 g4 14 ♘f5 ♕d8 15 ♘xg7 ♔xg7 16 h5
is not a serious alternative.

12 d4 ♘xg3 13 hxg3 g4?!

This move deprives the bishop of the f5-
square, which proves to be a problem in the
later tactics. 13...0-0-0 14 ♕e3!? with a slight
edge for White was better.

14 ♘h4 d5 15 ♕b5! 0-0-0

15...♕b4? loses to the pretty 16 ♘xd5!.

16 ♕a5

White should avoid 16 ♘xd5? ♗xd5 17
♕xd5 ♕g5+ 18 ♕xg5 hxg5, winning a piece.

16...a6 17 ♗xa6! bxa6

Or 17...♕b4 18 ♕xb4 ♗xb4 19 ♗d3
♗xc3 20 bxc3 when White is simply just a
pawn up (Kasparov).

18 ♕xa6+ ♔b8 19 ♘b5 ♘b6 20 ♖d3

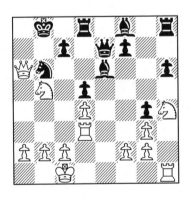

20...♕g5+

After this we cannot find a defence for
Black. The last chance for was given by Kasparov in his series of books *My Great Predeces-*

sors. 20...♘c4 is the only move, although after
21 ♖b3! ♕g5+ 22 ♔b1 (also strong is 22 f4!?
gxf3+ 23 ♔b1 ♘d2+ 24 ♔a1 ♘xb3+ 25 cxb3
♕xg3 26 ♘xf3 ♗d6 27 ♖c1 ♗f4 28 ♘e5!
♗xe5 29 ♕a7+! ♔c8 30 dxe5 ♔d7 31 ♘xc7
with a clear plus for White) 22...♘d2+ 23
♔a1 ♘xb3+ 24 cxb3 ♗d6 25 ♕a7+ ♔c8 26
♘xd6+ ♖xd6 (26...cxd6 27 f4! gxf3 28 ♘xf3
♕e3 29 ♖e1 and Black can no longer prevent
the deadly ♖c1+) 27 ♕a8+ ♔d7 28 ♕xh8
White has every chance of winning even if
Black can put up some resistance.

21 ♔b1 ♗d6

Black also loses after 21...♕e7 22 ♖b3
♖d6 23 a4 ♖c6 24 a5, when White's attack is
conclusive.

22 ♖b3

Or 22 ♖c3!? ♘c4 23 ♕a7+ ♔c8 24
♘xd6+ cxd6 25 ♔a1! ♖de8 26 ♖b3 and
Black is busted.

22...♖he8 23 a4! ♗f5

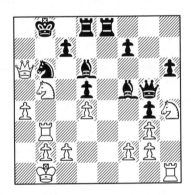

24 ♘a7

Or 24 a5 ♗xc2+ 25 ♔xc2 ♖e2+ 26 ♔b1
and it is all over.

**24...♗d7 25 a5 ♕d2 26 axb6 ♖e1+
27 ♔a2 c6 28 ♘b5 cxb5 29 ♕a7+ 1-0**

Game 36
Aronian-Akopian
Ohrid 2001

**1 e4 e5 2 ♘f3 ♘f6 3 ♘xe5 d6 4 ♘f3
♘xe4 5 ♕e2 ♕e7 6 d3 ♘f6 7 ♗g5**

♕xe2+

This is definitely the solid choice.

8 ♗xe2

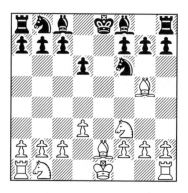

8...♗e7

8...♘bd7 is equally good after 9 ♘c3 h6 and now:

a) 10 ♗h4 g5 11 ♗g3 ♘h5 12 ♘d4 (12 ♘d5 ♔d8 13 d4 ♘b6 is totally level too) 12...♘xg3 13 hxg3 ♘f6 14 0-0-0 ♗d7 15 ♖de1 0-0-0 16 ♘d1 c5 17 ♘f3 ♗g7 18 ♘e3 ♗e6 with equal chances, Apicella-Nikcevic, France 2000.

b) 10 ♗d2 g6 (10...♘b6 11 ♘b5!? ♘bd5 – 11...♔d8!? – 12 c4 ♗d7 13 a4 c6 14 ♘bd4 ♘c7 15 0-0 ♗e7 16 b4 lead to a white advantage in Spassky-Yusupov, Moscow 1981) 11 0-0-0 (11 ♘b5 ♔d8 12 c4 ♗g7 13 0-0 ♖e8 14 ♖fe1 a6 15 ♘c3 ♘c5 16 b4 ♘e6 17 d4 a5 18 b5 g5 is another example of Black obtaining equal play) 11...♗g7 12 d4 ♘b6 13 h3 0-0 14 ♗d3 ♗e6 15 ♖he1 ♖fe8 16 b3 a6 17 ♘e4 ♘xe4 18 ♗xe4 ♗d5 19 ♗xd5 ♘xd5 20 c4 ♘f6 with complete equality, Westerinen-Raetsky, Hafnarfjordur 1999.

9 ♘c3

Or 9 c4 h6 10 ♗f4 ♘c6 11 ♘c3 ♗f5 12 0-0-0 0-0-0 13 ♖he1 g5 14 ♗e3 ♘g4 15 ♘d5 ♘xe3 16 ♘xe7+ ♘xe7 17 fxe3 ♖de8 with a level position, Spassky-Karpov, Hamburg 1982.

9...h6

Another option is 9...c6 and now:

a) 10 0-0-0 ♘a6 11 ♖he1 ♘c7 12 ♘e4

♘xe4 13 dxe4 ♗xg5+ 14 ♘xg5 ♔e7 15 f4 ♘e6 16 ♘h3 ♘c5 17 ♘f2 (17 f5 ♖b8 18 ♖d4 b6 19 ♖ed1 ♖d8 20 c4 a5 also looks level) 17...♖d8 18 ♗f3 f6 19 h4 ♗e6 20 g4 a5 21 a3 h6 22 h5 ♖d7 23 ♘h1 ♖e8 24 ♘g3 ♔d8 ½-½ Spassky-Hort, Reykjavik 1977.

b) 10 0-0 ♘a6 11 ♖fe1 ♘c7 12 d4 d5 13 ♗d3 ♘e6 14 ♗e3 0-0 15 ♖ad1 ♗d6 16 ♘e5 ♘e8!? (White is better after the risky 16...c5 17 ♘b5 ♗b8 18 c3 a6 19 ♘a3 – Yusupov) 17 ♘e2 f6 18 ♘f3 ♘8c7 19 b3 ♗d7 with full equality, Spassky-Yusupov, Toluka 1982.

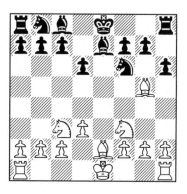

10 ♗h4

10 ♗f4 does not look very dangerous either: what exactly is the bishop meant to be doing here? Anyway, one game continued 10...♘c6 11 0-0-0 ♗e6 12 d4 ♘b4 13 a3 ♘bd5 14 ♘xd5 ♘xd5 15 ♗d2 0-0-0 16 ♖he1 ♖he8 17 h3 ♘b6 18 b3 ♗d5 19 ♗e3 ♗e4 20 c4 ♘d7 21 g3 c5 22 b4 ♗f6 23 ♘g1 cxb4 24 axb4 ♘b6 25 ♔b2 ♗f5 with chances for both sides, McShane-Mamedyarov, Lausanne 2004.

10...♘bd7

10...♘c6 is also fine, for example 11 0-0-0 ♗d7 12 h3 0-0-0 13 d4 ♖de8 14 ♗c4 ♖hf8 15 ♗g3 ♗d8 16 d5 ♘e7 17 ♗h2 a6 18 a3 ♘g6 19 ♖he1 ♖xe1 20 ♖xe1 ♖e8 21 ♖xe8 ♘xe8 22 ♔d2 ♘h4 23 ♘xh4 ½-½ Short-Anand, Wijk aan Zee 2000.

11 ♘d4 ♘b6 12 a4 a6 13 a5 ♘bd5 14 ♘xd5 ♘xd5 15 ♗xe7 ♘xe7 16 ♗f3 c5 17 ♘e2 ♘c6 18 ♗xc6+ bxc6

Black has equalised.

19 0-0-0 ♗g4 20 f3 ♗e6 21 d4 cxd4

21...c4 22 ♘f4 ♔d7 23 d5 cxd5 24 ♘xd5 would give White a real reason to play for a win, even though the disturbance of the balance is very minor indeed.

22 ♖xd4 ♔e7 23 ♖hd1 ♖hd8 24 ♘f4 ♖ab8 25 b4 ♖b5 26 ♘d3 ♖db8 27 c4 ♖xb4!? 28 ♘xb4 ♖xb4 29 h4

29 ♖xd6 ♖xc4+ 30 ♔b1 ♖b4+ also leads to a draw.

29...g5 30 hxg5 hxg5 31 ♖xd6 ♖xc4+ 32 ♔b2 ♖c5 33 ♖6d3 ♖b5+ 34 ♔c3 ♖xa5 35 ♔d4 ♔d6 36 ♔e3+ ♔e5 37 ♖h1 c5 38 ♖h5 ♔f6 39 ♖h6+ ♔g7 40 ♖h1 c4 41 ♖c3 ♖a2 42 ♖hc1 ♖xg2 43 ♖a1 g4 44 fxg4 ♖g3+ 45 ♔d2 ♖xg4 46 ♖xa6 ♔f6 47 ♖a5 ♖g6 ½-½

Game 37
Areshchenko-Mista
Cappelle la Grande 2003

---

1 e4 e5 2 ♘f3 ♘f6 3 ♘xe5 d6 4 ♘f3 ♘xe4 5 c4 ♗e7

Black has a couple of serious alternatives to this very natural move.

5...d5 seems a bit risky:. 6 ♘c3 ♗e6 (6...♘f6?! leads to an French Defence, Exchange Variation with the loss of a tempo! White should be able to organise a real advantage here: 7 d4 ♗e7 8 cxd5 ♘xd5 9 ♗c4 ♘xc3 10 bxc3 0-0 11 0-0 ♘d7 12 ♖e1 ♘b6

13 ♗d3 ♗e6 14 ♕c2 g6 15 a4 is one example) 7 ♕c2!? ♘xc3 8 dxc3 dxc4 9 ♘d4 ♗d5 10 ♗e3 ♘c6 11 0-0-0 and White has good compensation for the pawn in the shape of rapid development.

However, 5...♘c6 seems to be a strong alternative. Now we have:

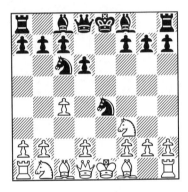

a) 6 ♘c3 will most likely transpose to the main game (see the note to Black's 7th move).

b) 6 d4 d5 7 ♘c3 ♗b4 8 ♕b3?! (8 ♗d2 0-0 with equality is preferable) 8...♕e7! (an improvement over 8...♗e6 9 c5!? ♘xc5 10 dxc5 d4 11 ♗c4 dxc3 12 0-0 ♘xc4 13 ♕xc4 cxb2 14 ♗xb2 0-0 15 a3 ♗a5 16 ♖ad1 ♕e7 17 ♖d5 ♖ad8 18 ♖g5 g6 19 h4 when White had good compensation for the pawn in Velicka-Raetsky, Cappelle la Grande 1996) 9 ♗e3 ♘a5 10 ♕c2 dxc4 11 ♗e2 ♗f5 and Black has emerged from the opening with an advantage.

c) 6 ♗e2 ♗e7 7 0-0 0-0 8 d4 ♗f6 9 d5 ♘e7 10 ♘a3 ♖e8 11 ♘c2 with a further branch:

c1) 11...h6 12 ♖e1 a5 13 ♖b1 ♗f5 14 ♗e3 ♗h7 (an improvement over 14...♕d7 15 ♘fd4 ♗h7 16 ♗g4 ♕d8 17 ♕e2 c6 18 dxc6 bxc6 19 f3 ♘c5 20 ♖bd1 ♕b6 21 b3, which is slightly preferable for White, Kholmov-Raetsky, Voronezh 1988) 15 ♘fd4 ♘f5 16 ♘xf5 ♗xf5 17 ♗d3 ♕d7 and Black is equal.

c2) Also strong is 11...♘f5 12 ♖b1 h6 13 ♖e1 ♗d7 14 ♗d3 ♘c5 15 ♗f1 (15 ♖xe8+

♕xe8 16 ♘e3 ♘xd3 17 ♕xd3 with an equal position is better) 15...♖xe1 16 ♕xe1 ♕e8 17 ♕d1?! ♕e4 18 b3 a5 19 ♗b2 ♗xb2 20 ♖xb2 ♖e8 21 ♘ce1 and here, with Black slightly better, the players agreed a draw, Brodsky-Raetsky, Cappelle la Grande 2000.

6 ♘c3

6 d4 is also interesting, for example:

a) 6...0-0 7 ♗d3 ♘g5!? leads to wild play after 8 ♘xg5 ♗xg5 9 ♕h5 ♖e8+ 10 ♔d1 ♗xc1 11 ♕xh7+ ♔f8 12 ♕h8+ ♔e7 13 ♕h4+ ♔f8 14 ♕xd8 ♖xd8 15 ♔xc1 d5 and we end up in an endgame where Black has enough counterplay for the pawn, Slobodjan-Van Der Sterren, Bundesliga 1999.

b) 6...d5 7 cxd5 (7 ♘c3 ♘xc3 8 bxc3 0-0 9 cxd5 ♕xd5 transposes to 7 cxd5) 7...♕xd5 8 ♘c3 ♘xc3 9 bxc3 0-0 10 ♗d3 c5 11 0-0 cxd4 12 ♖e1 ♗f6 13 ♖b1 ♘c6 14 ♗e4 ♕xa2 15 ♕d3 h6 16 cxd4 ♗g4!? (or 16...♖d8 17 ♗a3 ♗e6 18 ♖b2 ♕c4 with an unclear position) 17 ♗a3 ♗xf3 18 gxf3 ♘xd4 19 ♗xf8 ♖xf8 20 ♖xb7 ♕a5 21 ♕f1 ♗e5 22 ♖eb1 f5 23 ♕c4+ ♔h7 24 ♗d5 ♕d2 and Black had good play for the exchange in Gajewsky-Mista, Poland 2003.

6...♘xc3

6...♘g5 is worse: 7 ♗e2 0-0 8 0-0 ♘c6 9 d4 ♖e8 10 ♘d5 ♘xf3+ 11 ♗xf3 ♗f6 12 ♗e3 ♗f5 13 b4 a6 14 a4 h6 15 ♕d2 and White was better in Nisipeanu-Motylev, Bucharest 2001.

7 dxc3

7...0-0

We consider ...♘d7-c5 to be the most reliable way to develop, but there are other options: 7...♘c6 8 ♗d3 ♘e5 9 ♘xe5 dxe5 10 ♕c2 ♗g5 11 0-0 ♗e6 12 ♖e1 ♗xc1 13 ♖axc1 ♕g5 14 ♖e3 0-0-0 15 ♖ce1 f6 16 b4 ♖d7 and Black has solved his problems. Maróczy-Marshall, San Sebastian 1911.

8 ♗d3 ♘d7 9 ♕c2 g6

9...h6 seems to be less harmonious. After 10 ♗e3 ♗f6 11 0-0-0 (the unambitious 11 0-0 ♖e8 12 ♖ad1 ♘e5 13 ♘xe5 ♗xe5 14 ♖fe1 ♕h4 15 g3 ♕h5 gives equal chances) 11...♘e5 12 ♘xe5 ♗xe5 13 f4 ♗f6 14 ♕f2 ♖e8 15 h3 ♗d7 16 ♖he1 a6 17 ♗e2 b5 18 c5 White was a bit better in Velimirovic-Motylev, Novi Sad 2000.

10 ♗e3

10 ♗h6 ♖e8 11 0-0 looks less aggressive: 11...♘c5 12 ♖fe1 ♗g4 13 ♘d4 ♗f8 14 ♗e3 (14 ♗xf8 ♖xe1+ 15 ♖xe1 ♕xf8 16 ♘b5 ♕d8 is simply level) 14...♘xd3 15 ♕xd3 ♗g7 16 h3 ♗d7 17 ♕d2 ♕h4 18 ♗g5 ♕h5 19 ♘e2 h6 20 ♗e3 ♗c6 21 ♘f4 ♕f5 22 ♗d4 a6 23 ♗xg7 ♔xg7 24 ♘d5 ♗xd5 25 cxd5 and a draw was agreed in G.Kuzmin-Murdzia, Cappelle la Grande 2003.

10...♘c5 11 0-0-0

11 ♗xc5 dxc5 12 0-0-0 is interesting: following 12...♗d6 13 h4 ♗g4 14 h5!? ♗xh5 15 ♖xh5!? gxh5 16 ♗xh7+ ♔g7 the position is highly unclear.

11...♘xd3+ 12 ♕xd3 ♗f5 13 ♕d2 c5

13...♗e6!? 14 b3 a5 with counterplay is also logical.

14 ♗g5 ♗xg5 15 ♘xg5 ♕a5 16 b3 b5!?

Energetically played. White has an edge after 16...♕a3+ 17 ♕b2 ♕xb2+ 18 ♔xb2 ♖ae8 19 ♖d2.

17 cxb5 c4

The most precise. After 17...a6 18 b6 ♖ab8 19 ♔b2 ♖xb6 20 ♕f4 White enjoys a slight plus because Black has no easy way to weaken White's king's position.

18 ♔b2 ♖ab8 19 b4

19 ♕xd6?! is very risky. After cxb3 20

axb3 ♕xb5 21 b4 a5 Black's attack has every chance of being successful.

19...♖xb5

19...♕xb5 is another attractive option. Following 20 ♕d5 ♕xd5 (20...♕a4!?) 21 ♖xd5 ♖fe8 22 ♖d2 the endgame is probably equal, though not necessarily drawn.

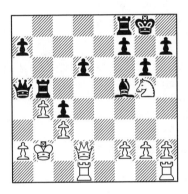

20 ♘f3

After 20 ♕xd6 ♕a4 21 ♔a1 ♕a3 22 ♖c1 ♖b6 23 ♕e7 ♖a6 24 ♕e2 ♗d3 25 ♕b2 ♕a4 Black has good play for the pawn.

20...♖fb8 21 ♘d4 ♖xb4+! 22 cxb4 ♖xb4+ 23 ♘b3

The only move. If 23 ♔a1? then 23...♖b1+! wins.

23...♕b5!?

Black can keep the game alive with 23...cxb3 24 a3 ♕e5+ 25 ♕c3, when it's still very complicated.

24 ♕xd6 cxb3 25 ♖d4 ♖xd4 ½-½

26 ♕xd4 bxa2+ 27 ♔xa2 ♕a6+ is equal.

Game 38
Naiditsch-Timman
Dortmund 2002

1 e4 e5 2 ♘f3 ♘f6 3 ♘xe5 d6 4 ♘f3 ♘xe4 5 ♗d3

This somewhat anti-positional move has found some popularity over the last few years. However, it shouldn't seriously threaten Black.

5...♘f6

Black has also tried:

a) 5...♘c5 6 ♗e2 and now:

a1) 6...♗e7 7 0-0 0-0 8 d4 ♘e4 (8...♘e6 seems inferior: 9 ♖e1 ♖e8 10 ♗d3 ♘d7 11 h3 ♘f6 12 c4 gives White a slight edge, and now Black should play 12...d5 instead of 12...c5?! 13 d5 ♘f8 14 ♘c3 ♘g6 15 ♕c2 ♗d7 16 ♗d2 a6 17 a4 after which White is very happy, Safin-S.Ernst, Dieren 2002) 9 c4 c6 10 ♕c2 d5 11 ♗d3 ♗e6 with a complex struggle ahead.

a2) 6...d5 7 d4 ♘e4 8 0-0 ♗d6 9 c4 c6 10 ♘c3 (10 ♖e1 0-0 11 ♗d3 transposes to 5 d4 d5 6 ♗d3 ♗d6 7 0-0 0-0 8 c4 c6 9 ♖e1) 10...0-0 11 ♕b3 ♘xc3 12 bxc3 dxc4 13 ♗xc4 h6 14 ♖e1 ♘d7 15 ♕c2 ♘b6 16 ♗d3 c5 was level in Constantini-Raetsky, Biel 2001.

b) 5...d5 6 ♕e2 ♕e7 7 0-0 with another branch:

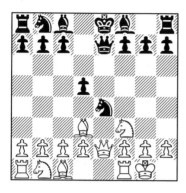

b1) 7...♘d6 8 ♕d1!? (8 ♖e1 ♕xe2 9 ♖xe2+ ♗e7 10 ♘c3 ♗e6 11 ♘d4 ♔d7 12 ♘xe6 fxe6 13 ♘b5 ♗xb5 14 ♗xb5+ c6 15 ♗d3 ♗f6 16 c3 c5 lead to a drawish ending in Leko-Kramnik, Linares 1999) 8...♕d8 (this seems best; 8...g6 9 ♖e1 ♗e6 10 ♗f1 ♗g7 11 d4 0-0 12 ♗f4 ♘c6 13 c3 ♕d7 14 ♘bd2 gave White a slight plus in Morozevich-Shirov, Astana 2001) 9 ♘c3 c6 10 ♖e1+ ♗e7 11 ♕e2 ♗g4 (11...♘d7 12 b4!? ♘f8 13 b5 ♘e6, as suggested by Romero, looks a bit better for White) 12 b3 ♘d7 13 ♗b2 ♘c5 14 ♘a4 ♗xf3 15 ♕xf3 ♘xd3 16 ♕xd3 ½-½ Morozevich-Kramnik, Wijk aan Zee 2000. Black has no problems at all in the final position.

b2) 7...♘c5 is less reliable: 8 ♖e1 ♗e6 9 ♗b5+ c6 10 d4 cxb5 11 dxc5 ♘c6 (11...♕xc5?! 12 ♘g5 ♕c4 13 ♘xe6 ♕xe2 14 ♖xe2 fxe6 15 ♖xe6+ ♔f7 16 ♖e5 is awful for Black) 12 ♗e3 a6 13 a4 b4 14 c3 a5 15 cxb4 axb4 16 ♘bd2 and White enjoys a plus, Morozevich-Shirov, Sarajevo 2000.

6 h3 ♗e7 7 0-0 0-0 8 c3 ♘c6

Alternatively:

a) 8...d5 9 ♗c2 ♖e8 10 d4 ♗d6 11 ♗g5 ♘bd7 12 ♘bd2 h6 (12...♘f8 13 ♖e1 ♖xe1+ 14 ♕xe1 h6 15 ♗h4 ♘g6 16 ♗g3 ♗xg3 17 fxg3 ♘f8 18 g4 was better for White in Shirov-Anand, Leon 2001 – Black's pieces cannot really get into the game) 13 ♗h4 ♘b6 14 a4 a5 and Black has nothing to fear.

b) 8...c5 9 ♗c2 ♘c6 10 d4 ♗e6 11 ♖e1 h6

12 ♗e3 ♖e8 13 ♘bd2 ♗f8 14 ♘e4 ♘d5 15 dxc5 ♘xe3 16 ♖xe3 dxc5 17 ♕e2 ♕c7 18 ♖e1 ♖ad8 with complete equality, Morozevich-Topalov, Dortmund 2001. 14 ♗b3 ♘d5 15 ♗xd5 ♗xd5 16 c4 ♗xf3 17 ♘xf3 ♕f6 provides more imbalance, but it's not clear who if anyone gains from this.

9 ♗c2 ♘e5

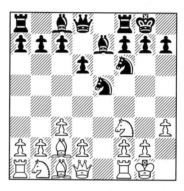

White's position looks preferable after 9...d5 10 d4 ♘e4 11 ♖e1 f5 12 ♗f4.

10 d4 ♘xf3+ 11 ♕xf3 c6 12 ♗f4

White gained nothing after 12 ♖e1 ♗e6 13 ♘d2 ♕d7 14 ♘f1 ♖ae8 15 ♘g3 ♗d8 16 ♗g5 ♘d5 17 ♕d3 f5 18 ♗d2 g6 19 ♗h6 ♖f7 20 ♕f3, Lalic-Nikcevic, Paris 2000. In fact, the players agreed a draw in this position.

12...♗e6

Here we recommend that Black should deviate with 12...♕b6!? 13 b3 d5 14 ♘d2 ♗e6 leading to a position with equal chances.

13 ♘d2 ♕d7 14 ♖fe1 ♖fe8 15 ♗h2

We suggest 15 ♖e2, for example 15...♗f5 16 ♗xf5 ♕xf5 17 ♖ae1 ♗f8 18 ♘e4 ♘xe4 19 ♖xe4 and White's control of the e-file annoys Black; or 15...c5 16 dxc5 dxc5 17 ♖ae1 and White has a slight plus.

15...g6 16 c4 d5 17 c5 ♘h5

17...♘e4 leads to trouble after 18 ♘xe4 dxe4 19 ♖xe4 ♗d5 20 ♗b3!, when the attack against f7 leads to a position with an extra pawn for White.

18 ♕b3 f6 19 ♘f1 ♗f8 20 ♘e3 ♗h6

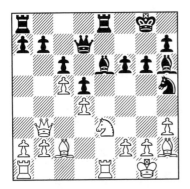

Alternatively 20...f5 21 ♘f1 ♗g7 22 ♕c3 ♗h6 23 f3 ♗f7 with even chances.

21 ♘g4?!

This spells trouble. White should play 21 ♗d6 ♗f4 22 ♗xf4 ♘xf4 23 ♘f1 b6, when nothing is decided yet.

21...♗xg4

21...♗g5 is weaker, as after 22 ♕f3 f5 23 ♘e5 ♕g7 24 ♖e2 ♖e7 25 ♖ae1 White's position looks a good deal preferable.

22 hxg4 ♕xg4

22...♘f4 only leads to equality after 23 ♕f3 ♘e6 24 ♕c3 ♘f4.

23 ♕xb7 ♗f4! 24 ♕xc6

24 g3 would be strongly met by 24...♘xg3! 25 fxg3 ♗xg3 26 ♗xg3 ♕xg3+ 27 ♔f1 ♕f4+ with an advantage for Black.

24...♗xh2+

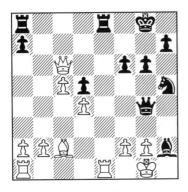

25 ♔f1

After 25 ♔xh2 ♘f4! White cannot defend

himself. The main line runs 26 ♖xe8+ ♖xe8 27 ♕xe8+ ♔g7 28 ♕e7+ ♔h6 29 ♗e4 dxe4 30 ♕xe4 ♕h4+ 31 ♔g1 ♘h3+!, winning.

25...♖ed8 26 ♗d1 ♕f5

Also possible is 26...♕xd4 27 ♗xh5 gxh5 28 g3 h4 and Black should be winning.

27 ♗xh5 gxh5 28 ♕e6+ ♕xe6 29 ♖xe6 ♔f7 30 ♖a6 ♗f4?!

A much better choice is 30...♖db8 31 b3 h4, when Black has every chance to win.

31 g3 ♗h6 32 b4 ♖d7 33 b5 ♖b8 34 a4 ♗g7 35 ♖b1 f5 36 ♖b4 f4 37 a5 fxg3 38 fxg3

38 b6 axb6 39 axb6 ♖e7! 40 c6 ♖e1+ 41 ♔g2 gxf2 42 ♔xf2 ♖be8 43 ♖a7+ ♔g6 44 ♖xg7+ ♔xg7 45 b7 ♖c1 46 b8♕ ♖xb8 47 ♖xb8 ♖xc6 48 ♖d8 ♖f6+ 49 ♔g3 ♖f5 gives Black winning chances. In this line 43 ♖a2 ♗f6 is probably bad for White, although these complications are really difficult to assess.

38...♖c7 39 ♖d6

39 b6 also leads to a draw after 39...axb6 40 axb6 ♖c6 41 ♖a7+ ♔g6 42 ♖d7 ♗xd4 43 ♖xd4 ♖xc5.

39...♗xd4 40 ♖xd4 ♖xb5 41 ♖4xd5 ½-½

Game 39
Dolmatov-Raetsky
Podolsk Voronezh 1992

---

1 e4 e5 2 ♘f3 ♘f6 3 ♘xe5 d6 4 ♘f3 ♘xe4 5 d3

This can lead to symmetrical play and is rather harmless.

5...♘f6 6 d4 ♗e7

Or:

a) 6...d5 transposes to the Exchange French, which is outside the scope of this book

b) 6...g6 7 ♗d3 ♕e7+ (the most precise; 7...♗g7 8 0-0 0-0 9 h3 ♘c6 10 a3 ♘e7 11 c4 ♗f5 12 ♘c3 ♖e8 13 ♖e1 ♗xd3 14 ♕xd3 ♕d7 15 ♗g5 gave White a small plus in Nikolenko-Donchenko, Moscow 2000) 8 ♕e2

♕xe2+ 9 ♔xe2 ♗g7 10 ♘c3 ♘c6 11 ♘b5 ♔d8 and the endgame should of course end in a draw.

7 ♗d3 ♗g4

7...0-0 allows 8 h3 when White may be able to gain a slight pull: 8...c5!? 9 0-0 ♘c6 10 ♖e1 h6 11 ♘c3 ♗e6 12 ♗b5 ♘d5 13 ♘xd5 ♗xd5 14 dxc5 (this is better than 14 c3 a6 15 ♗xc6 ♗xc6 16 dxc5 dxc5 17 ♕xd8 ♗xd8 18 ♗e3, Kveinys-Schandorff, Germany 2001; here Black can play 18...♗xf3 19 gxf3 b6 with a slightly more comfortable position, even though it is probably not enough for an advantage) 14...dxc5 15 ♗f4 ♗f6 16 ♘e5 and as so often in the Petroff the position is more or less level but Black is a bit passive.

8 0-0

8 ♘bd2 isn't intimidating: 8...0-0 9 ♘f1 c5!? 10 ♘e3 ♗h5 11 0-0 ♘c6 12 ♘f5 ♖e8 13 dxc5 (13 c3 cxd4 14 cxd4 ♗f8 15 ♗g5 h6 16 ♗e3 ♘d5 17 ♘g3 ♗g4 18 h3 ♗e6 equalised fully in Strzelecki-Raetsky, Katowice 1990) 13...dxc5 14 ♖e1 ♗f8 15 ♖xe8 ♕xe8 16 ♗g5 ♘e5 and Black has enough counterplay.

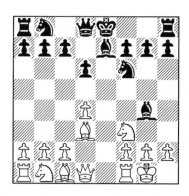

8...0-0 9 ♖e1

9 ♗f4 should be met by 9...♘d5 (9...♘c6 10 c3 ♖e8 11 ♘bd2 and White is a bit better – Keres) 10 ♗d2 ♗f6 11 h3 ♗h5 12 c3 c6 with level chances.

9...c5!? 10 h3 ♗h5 11 dxc5

This is not particularly ambitious. After 11 d5 ♘bd7 (11...♘xd5?? loses to 12 g4) 12 ♘c3 ♘e5 13 ♗e2 ♗xf3 14 ♗xf3 ♘e8!? 15 ♗e2 f5 16 f4 ♘d7 17 ♗d3 ♘c7 18 ♕f3 ♗f6 19 ♘d1 b5 20 c3 g6 21 ♗d2 ♘b6 22 ♘e3 ♕d7 both sides have chances, Shtyrenkov-Raetsky, Voronezh 1989. Instead of 12 ♘c3, 12 g4 ♗g6 13 ♗xg6 hxg6 14 ♘c3 ♘h7!? 15 a4 ♘g5 is interesting – maybe White is a bit better here

11...dxc5 12 g4 ♗g6 13 ♗xg6 hxg6 14 ♕xd8 ♖xd8 15 ♗f4 ♖a5!

Accurate play. After 15...♘bd7? 16 g5 ♘h5 17 ♗d6 ♗a5 18 ♖e7! White has gained a serious advantage.

16 c3

Or 16 ♖d1 ♘a6 17 ♘a3 ♗c7 18 ♗xc7 ♘xc7 19 ♖d2 ♖fd8 20 ♖ad1 ♖xd2 21 ♖xd2 (Panchenko-Tolstikh, Cheliabinsk 1993). Now Black is no worse after 21...♘e6 22 ♘b5 b6.

16...♖d8

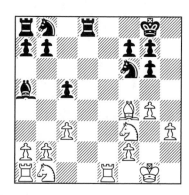

16...♘bd7?! is imprecise. After 17 ♘a3 ♘d5 18 ♗d6 ♖fe8 19 ♘c4 ♗b6 20 ♖ad1 the problems are mounting up for Black.

17 ♘bd2 ♘c6 18 ♘e4

White also has nothing after 18 ♘c4 ♘d5 19 ♘xa5 (19 ♗d6 ♗xc3! 20 bxc3 b5 21 ♗xc5 bxc4 and Black is no worse) 19...♘xa5 20 ♗g3 f6 21 ♖ad1 ♔f7.

18...♘xe4 19 ♖xe4 ♖d5

Black has neutralised whatever pull White ever had.

20 ♖ae1 f6 21 h4 ♖ad8 22 ♔g2 ♔f7 23 ♖1e2 ♖8d7 24 ♗e3 ♗b6 25 a3 ♖d3 26 ♘d2 ½-½

Game 40
Smagin-Makarychev
Moscow 1987

1 e4 e5 2 ♘f3 ♘f6 3 ♘xe5 d6 4 ♘c4

Fortunately for our understanding of the game, the eccentric 4 ♘d3?! has not lead great practical results. 4...♘xe4 5 ♕e2 ♕e7 6 b3 ♘c6 7 ♗b2 ♗f5 8 ♘a3 0-0-0 9 0-0-0 d5 10 f3 ♘c5 11 ♕xe7 ♗xe7 12 ♘xc5 ♗xc5 13 d4 ♗d6 14 ♔b1 ♘b4 15 ♗c3 a6 gave Black a healthier position in Yandemirov-Raetsky, Voronezh 1988.

4...♘xe4 5 d4

Or:

a) 5 ♕e2 ♕e7 6 ♘e3 ♘f6 7 b3 ♘c6 8 ♗b2 ♗e6 9 g3 0-0-0 10 ♗g2 d5 11 d4 (11 0-0 h5 12 h4 ♕d7 and Black has good counterplay on the kingside) 11...♕d7 12 ♘d2 g6 13 h3 ♗h6 14 0-0-0 ♖he8 with even chances, Murey-Harikrishna, Pardubice 2002.

b) 5 ♘c3 shouldn't lead to an advantage:

b1) 5...♘xc3 6 bxc3 (6 dxc3 is not very dangerous: 6...♗e7 7 ♗f4 0-0 8 ♕d2 ♘c6 9 0-0-0 ♗e6 10 ♗d3 ♗f6 and Black can't be worse) 6...g6 (also fine is 6...♘d7 7 d4 d5 8 ♘e3 ♘f6 9 ♗d3 ♗d6 10 0-0 0-0 11 ♕f3 ♖e8 12 ♖b1 c6 13 c4 dxc4 14 ♗xc4 ♕c7 15 h3 b5 16 ♗d3 ♗e6 17 c4 bxc4 18 ♗xc4 ♖ad8 and Black has equalised, Gallagher-Delchev, Batumi 1999) 7 d4 ♗g7 8 ♗d3 0-0 9 0-0 ♘d7 10 f4 ♘b6 11 ♘xb6 axb6 12 f5 ♖a5! and the inclusion of the queenside rook into the struggle guarantees Black decent chances in this complicated position. 11 ♘e3?! is weaker after 11...♘a4! 12 ♗d2 c5! (12...♘b2?! 13 ♕f3 ♘xd3 14 cxd3 f5 and White had a slight edge in Ovetchkin-Motylev, Russia 2004) 13 dxc5 ♘xc3 14 ♕f3 dxc5, when we think Black has the better chances.

b2) Even 5...♘f6 is possible: 6 d4 ♗e7 7 ♗d3 ♘c6 8 d5 ♘e5 9 ♘xe5 dxe5 10 0-0 0-0 11 ♖e1 ♘d7 12 ♗f5 ♘b6 13 ♗xc8 ♖xc8 14 ♖xe5 ♗f6 15 ♖e3 ♖e8 16 ♖d3 ♗xc3 17

bxc3 ♖e5 with equal chances, Khairullin-Bezgodov, Cheliabinsk 2004. In this line 11...♗c5 is not so good after 12 ♗g5 ♗g4 13 ♕d2 (13 ♗xf6?! ♗xf2+! 14 ♔f1 ♗xd1 – 14...♕xf6 15 ♕xg4 ♗xe1+ 16 ♔xe1 ♕b6 with unclear play is also possible – 15 ♗xd8 ♗xe1 16 ♔xe1 ♗xc2 17 ♗xc2 ♖axd8 with an endgame that is hard to assess) 13...♗d6 and Black is only a bit worse, but still, why choose to be so?

5...d5 6 ♘e3 ♕f6!

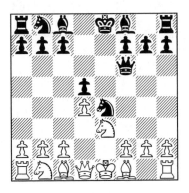

This move seems to be the strongest – Black develops quickly and annoys White in the process. Alternatively:

a) After 6...c5?! White gains a plus with 7 ♗b5+ ♘c6 8 0-0 a6 (8...♗e7 was met by 9 c4! dxc4 10 d5 ♘d6 11 ♗a4 b5 12 dxc6 bxa4 13 ♘d5 with some advantage in Jansa-Miralles, Paris 1989) 9 ♗xc6+ bxc6 10 c4! ♗e6 11 cxd5 cxd5 12 ♘c3 ♘f6 (12...♘xc3 13 bxc3 ♗d6 14 ♗a3 leads to a rigid structure with better chances for White) 13 f4 cxd4 14 ♕xd4 ♖c8 15 ♘a4 ♗e7 16 b3 0-0 17 ♗b2 ♕a5 18 ♖ad1, Sanakoev-Raetsky, Voronezh 1987.

b) 6...c6 7 ♘d2 ♗d6 should be playable too, but Black was unlucky in the following game: 8 ♗d3 f5 9 0-0 0-0 10 f4 (10 c4 f4 11 ♘c2 ♘xd2 12 ♗xd2 f3 13 g3 dxc4 14 ♗xc4+ ♔h8 is completely unclear, but probably more unpleasant for White than for Black) 10...♗e6 11 g3 c5 12 c4!? ♘xd2 (a reasonable alternative is 12...cxd4 13 ♘xd5

♘c5 14 ♘f3 ♘xd3 15 ♕xd3 ♘c6 with a complex position offering level chances) 13 ♗xd2 dxc4 14 ♗xc4 ♗xc4 15 ♘xc4 ♗e7?! (15...cxd4 was necessary, although 16 ♕f3 ♖f7 17 ♕d5 would have been a little uncomfortable) 16 ♕b3 ♕d5 (maybe this is also not the best, but Black completely missed White's next move) 17 ♘b6!! ♕xb3 18 axb3 with a clear edge, Lukjanenko-Raetsky, Voronezh 2000.

7 ♗b5+!?

A very ambitious, but not necessarily foolish, piece sacrifice. 7 ♕e2 is less adventurous; following 7...♗e6 8 c3 ♘c6 9 ♘d2 0-0-0 10 g3 (10 ♘xd5 ♗xd5 11 ♘e4 ♕g6 12 ♘g3 ♗d6 gives Black excellent compensation for his pawn) 10...♕g6 (an improvement over 10...♘xd2 11 ♗xd2 h5 12 ♗g2 ♕g6 13 0-0-0 ♘e7 14 ♗f3 with a slight edge for White, Smagin-Makarychev, Moscow 1990) 11 ♗g2 f5 12 ♘f3 ♗d6 13 0-0 ♕f7 Black has good counterchances.

7...c6 8 0-0!?

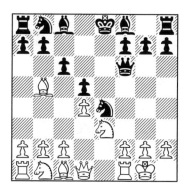

8...cxb5

Accepting the sacrifice is not the only possibility:

a) 8...♗d6 9 ♘xd5!? ♕g6 leads to a very complex position, though 10 f3 ♕h5 11 ♘f4 ♗xf4 12 ♗xf4 ♕xb5 13 ♕e1!? (13 fxe4 ♕xb2 14 ♕d2 ♕xa1 15 c4 0-0 16 ♘c3 ♕xf1+ 17 ♔xf1 is not that clear) 13...0-0 14 fxe4 ♕xb2 15 ♘c3 seems to favour White.

b) 8...♗e6 is perfectly possible. After 9 f3

♗d6 10 ♗a4 ♘d7 Black's chances are no worse.

9 ♘xd5 ♕d8 10 ♖e1 ♕xd5 11 ♘c3 ♕d8 12 ♖xe4+

12 ♗g5 is inferior. White's main idea is to reach a murky position after 12...♕xg5 13 ♘xe4 ♕g6 14 ♘f6+ ♔d8 15 ♖e8+ ♔c7 16 ♘d5+ ♔d7 17 ♕e2 ♘c6 18 ♖e1 (here Black is mated after 18...b6?? 19 ♖d8+!). Instead Black can play 12...♗e7 13 ♗xe7 ♔xe7 14 ♖xe4+ ♔f8 when, according to Makarychev and Smagin, the compensation is insufficient and Black has slightly better chances.

12...♗e7 13 ♕e2

13 ♗g5 ♘c6 14 ♕e2 f6 15 d5 ♘e5 doesn't seem to cause Black the same kind of problems.

13...♘c6

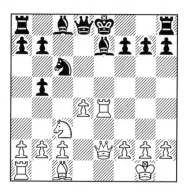

An interesting alternative is 13...♗f5!? 14 ♕xb5+ ♕d7 15 ♖e2 ♕xb5 16 ♘xb5 ♔d7 17 ♘c7!? ♔xc7 18 ♖xe7+ ♔b6 when the endgame is very difficult to assess. However, it's hard to believe that White should be worse here.

14 ♗g5 ♗f5

Black is also all right after 14...♗e6, for example 15 ♗xe7 ♘xe7 16 d5 (otherwise the initiative disappears) 16...♘xd5 17 ♖d1 0-0 18 ♘xd5 ♗xd5 19 ♖e5! ♗c4! 20 ♖xd8 ♗xe2 21 ♖xa8 ♖xa8 22 ♖xe2 with a drawn position. On the other hand, 14...b4 15 ♗xe7 ♘xe7 16 ♕b5+ ♗d7 17 ♕xb4 promises White plenty of compensation.

15 ♗xe7 ♘xe7 16 ♖e5 0-0

16...♔f8 17 ♕xb5 ♕d7 18 ♖ae1 would ensure White an initiative.

17 ♖xe7 ½-½

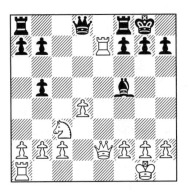

After 17...b4 18 ♘d1 ♕xd4 19 c3 bxc3 20 ♘xc3 ♗g4! (Makarychev/Smagin) the position is level.

Game 41
Vitolinsh-Anikaev
Riga 1982

---

1 e4 e5 2 ♘f3 ♘f6 3 ♘xe5 d6 4 ♘xf7

The Cochrane Gambit is probably not entirely correct, but it is also not that easy to refute. Vitolinsh was a great expert on this line.

4...♔xf7

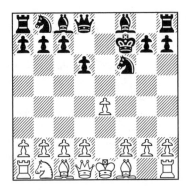

5 d4

Or:

a) 5 ♗c4+?! was the original idea, but it is considered more or less refuted these days: 5...d5! (this is stronger than 5...♗e6 6 ♗xe6+ ♔xe6 7 0-0 ♔d7 8 d4 ♔c8 9 c4 ♘bd7 10 ♘c3 – White has compensation here as Black has no easy way to coordinate his forces – 10...♔b8 11 f4 a6 12 a4 ♔a7 13 b4 ♖c8 14 ♗e3 with a continued attack, Cochrane-Mohishunder, Calcutta 1848) 6 ♗b3 (6 exd5 ♗d6 7 0-0 ♖f8 8 d4 ♔g8 and Black is close to winning – Bisguier) 6...♗e6 7 e5 ♘e4 8 d4 c5 9 ♕f3+ ♔e8 and Black has a large advantage, as stated in *Schachzeitung* as far back as 1861!

b) 5 ♘c3 is more inventive: 5...c5!? (5...♕e8 6 d4 transposes to 5 d4 ♕e8 6 ♘c3) 6 ♗c4+ ♗e6 7 ♗xe6+ ♔xe6 8 d4 ♔f7 9 dxc5 ♘c6 10 ♕e2 ♕d7 11 ♗e3 dxc5 12 f4 ♖e8 13 e5 ♘g4 (13...♘d4 14 ♕c4+ ♕e6 15 ♕xe6+ ♖xe6 16 0-0-0 is unclear) 14 ♖d1 ♕f5 15 0-0 h5 16 ♗c1 ♘d4 17 ♕c4+ ♔g6 and the advantage was probably with Black in Topalov-Kramnik, Linares 1999.

5...g6

The most important alternative, 5...c5, can be seen in the next game. Other tries include:

a) 5...♘xe4? is bad because of 6 ♕h5+ g6 7 ♕d5+ ♔g7 8 ♕xe4 ♘c6 9 d5 ♗f5 10 ♕a4 ♘e5 11 ♗e2 ♗e7 12 0-0 when White's position is preferable.

b) 5...♗e7 6 ♘c3 ♖e8 is a very natural way to develop, although after 7 ♗c4+ ♗e6 8 ♗xe6+ ♔xe6 9 f4 ♔f7 10 e5 dxe5 11 fxe5 White has a genuine attack. Now Black should play 11...♘c6!, for example 12 0-0 (12 exf6?! ♗b4+ 13 ♔f2 ♕xf6+ does not work, while the slow 12 ♗e3?! ♔g8 13 ♗f2 ♘d5 14 ♘e4 ♗h4 15 0-0 ♗xf2+ 16 ♖xf2 ♖f8 gave Black a clear edge for Black in Petrik-Kujovic, Slovakia 2000) 12...♕xd4+ 13 ♕xd4 ♘xd4 14 exf6 ♗xf6 15 ♗g5 ♘xc2 16 ♖ad1 ♘e3 17 ♗xe3 ♖xe3 18 ♖d7+ ♖e7 19 ♖xe7+ ♔xe7 20 ♘d5+ ♔f7 21 ♘xc7 ♖d8 and White has some practical problems holding this endgame.

c) 5...♕e8, taking prophylactic measures

against ♗c4+, is a very recent idea: 6 ♘c3 (6 ♗d3 is punished by 6...c5! 7 dxc5 d5! 8 ♘c3 dxe4 9 ♘xe4 ♗f5 10 f3 ♗xc5 11 ♕e2 ♗xe4 12 ♗xe4 ♕a4, when Black is clearly better) 6...d5 (6...c5 also looks fine) 7 e5 ♗b4

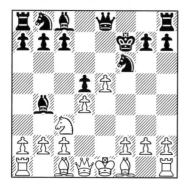

and now:

c1) 8 ♗e2 ♘e4 9 0-0 ♗xc3 10 bxc3 ♘xc3 (10...♕c6 11 c4!? also gives White play) 11 ♗h5+ g6 12 ♕f3+ ♔g8 13 ♕xc3 gxh5 14 ♖b1 and the position was a complete mess in Fernandez Romero-Andres, Seville 1999.

c2) 8 ♕f3 ♔g8 9 ♗d3 ♘e4!? 10 0-0 (this is stronger than 10 ♗xe4 dxe4 11 ♕xe4 ♕c6! with an advantage for Black – Reinderman) 10...♗xc3 11 bxc3 ♘c6 12 ♗xe4 dxe4 13 ♕xe4 ♕g6 with a complex position, Bergez-Grimberg, Clichy 1998.

6 ♘c3 ♕e8

Alternatively:

a) 6...♗g7 7 f4 ♕e8 8 e5 looks very dangerous for Black, for example 8...dxe5 9 fxe5 ♗b4 10 ♗c4!? ♗xc3+ 11 bxc3 with the idea 11...♗g4? 12 0-0!! ♗xd1 13 exf6+ ♔f8 14 ♗h6 mate!

b) 6...♗g7 7 ♗c4+ ♗e6 8 ♗xe6+ ♔xe6 9 f4 ♔f7 10 e5 ♖e8 11 0-0 was played in Vitolinsh-Anikaev, Frunze 1979. Now after 11...♘fd7 12 f5 dxe5 13 fxg6+ ♔g8 14 ♕f3 White would have a strong attack.

7 ♗c4+

7 ♗d3!? is another possibility, for example 7...♗g7 8 0-0 ♖f8 9 e5 ♘g4 (the pawn-grabbing 9...dxe5? leads to a disaster after 10

dxe5 ♕xe5 11 ♖e1 ♕c5 12 ♗e3 ♕b4 13 a3 ♕g4 14 f3) 10 h3 ♘h6 11 exd6 ♔g8 (White wins after 11...cxd6? 12 ♖e1 ♕c6 13 ♗e4) 12 dxc7 (12 ♘d5!? cxd6 13 ♘c7 ♕c6 14 ♘xa8 b6 15 ♘xb6 axb6 16 c3 with a slight edge is also possible) 12...♘c6 13 d5 ♘e5 (Vitolinsh-Domuls, Riga 1983). Now after 14 ♗xh6!? ♗xh6 15 d6 ♕f7 16 ♗e4 we're leaning towards giving White a clear edge. This of course is not all due to 7 ♗d3, but it does confirm that it's a viable option for White.

7...♗e6 8 d5 ♗c8

Here we assess 8...♗d7!? 9 0-0 b5 10 ♗d3 ♗g7 as a bit better for Black.

9 0-0 ♗g7 10 ♖e1 ♖f8

11 e5

11 f4 regains the piece but then the attack dissipates after 11...♔g8 12 e5 dxe5 13 fxe5 ♘g4 14 d6+ ♔h8 15 e6 ♘e5 16 d7 (16 e7 ♘xc4 17 exf8♕+ ♕xf8 18 dxc7 ♘c6 is very unclear play but we do not think Black should fear this) 16...♘bxd7 17 exd7 ♕xd7 18 ♕xd7 ♗xd7 with a drawish endgame, Popov-Grodzensky, correspondence 1983.

11...dxe5 12 d6+ ♗e6 13 ♖xe5 ♗xc4 14 ♖xe8 ♖xe8 15 dxc7 ♘a6

After 15...♘c6 16 ♗g5 ♖ac8 17 ♕f3 ♖xc7 18 ♕f4 ♘e5 19 ♘e4 ♖c6 20 ♖d1 White manages to generate threats.

16 ♗f4 ♖ec8?!

A sad decision – Anikaev was probably afraid of ghosts such as ♘b5-d6. It would have been better to leave a rook on e8, e.g.

16...♖ac8 17 ♕d4 b5 18 ♕xa7 ♘xc7 19 ♗xc7 ♖e7 20 ♕a5 ♖exc7 with an unclear endgame.

17 b3

17 ♕d4! is simple and strong. After 17...b5? 18 b3 ♘d5 19 ♗e5 Black's position collapses.

17...♗e6 18 ♘b5 ♘e8

18...♘d5 is a weak move: 19 ♘d6+ ♔g8 20 ♘xc8 ♖xc8 21 ♗e5! ♗xe5 22 ♕e1 and White has a huge advantage.

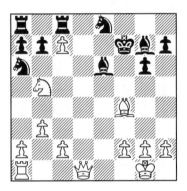

19 ♕f3?!

After the stronger 19 ♖c1 ♔g8 20 ♕f3 ♘axc7 21 ♘xc7 ♘xc7 22 c4 Black's uncoordinated forces promise White some kind of edge.

19...♗xa1 20 ♗e5+ ♔g8 21 ♗xa1 ♘axc7 22 ♘d4

Vitolinsh could have offered better resistance with 22 ♕c3!? ♘xb5 23 ♕h8+ ♔f7 24 ♕xh7+ ♔f8 25 ♕xg6. Here Kaerner and Petkevich give the line 25...♗f7 26 ♕h6+ ♔e7 27 ♕g5+ with a draw, but after the stronger 25...♘bc7 26 ♗b2 ♖d8 we still believe Black can play for a win.

22...♗d5 23 ♕g3 ♘g7 24 c4 ♗f7 25 h4 ♘ce8 26 ♕e5 h5

Also strong is 26...b6!? 27 h5 ♖c5 28 ♕e4 ♖ac8 29 h6 ♘f6 30 ♕f3 ♘ge8 with clear advantage for Black.

27 g4!? hxg4 28 h5 ♘xh5

28...gxh5?? 29 ♘f5 would reverse the trend!

29 ♘f5 ♘ef6 30 ♘e7+ ♔f8 31 ♘xc8 ♖xc8 32 ♕d6+ ♔g7 33 ♗d4 ♖e8 34 ♔f1 g5 35 ♗xa7 ♔g6 36 ♕c7 ♗e6 37 ♕xb7 ♗f5 38 ♗e3 g3 39 ♔g1

After 39 ♕b6 gxf2 40 ♗xf2 ♗d3+ 41 ♔g1 ♖e2 Black has excellent attacking chances.

39...♘g4 40 a4 ♘hf6 41 ♕f3 0-1

Game 42
Novozhilov-Raetsky
Correspondence 1983

1 e4 e5 2 ♘f3 ♘f6 3 ♘xe5 d6 4 ♘xf7 ♔xf7 5 d4 c5

Time has proven this to be the most testing response to the Cochrane Gambit.

6 dxc5

This is the most commonly played move, but 6 ♗c4+ is worth considering: 6...d5 7 exd5 ♗d6 8 0-0 ♖e8 9 ♘c3 ♗g4 (maybe 9...cxd4 10 ♕xd4 ♗e5 11 ♕d3 ♔g8, when we prefer Black — we think!) 10 f3 ♗f5 11 dxc5 ♗xc5+ 12 ♔h1 ♗d6 13 ♘b5 ♔g8 14 ♗g5 a6 15 ♘d4 ♗d7 16 ♘e6 ♗xe6 17 dxe6 ♕c7 with a typically messy position, Stellwagen-I.Smirnov, Heraklio 2002.

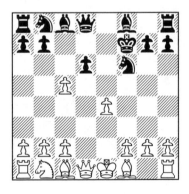

6...♕a5+

After 6...♘c6 7 ♗c4+ we have two possibilities:

a) 7...d5 8 ♗xd5+ ♗e6 (not the only option; 8...♘xd5!? 9 exd5 ♘b4 looks very strong for Black) 9 ♗xe6+ ♔xe6 10 ♕e2

♕a5+ 11 ♘c3 ♗xc5 12 0-0 (12 ♕c4+ ♔e7 13 0-0 ♖ad8 is unclear) 12...♔f7 13 ♕c4+

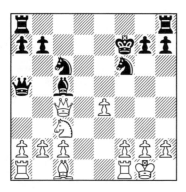

and now:

a1) 13...♔g6?! 14 ♘d5 ♗d6 15 ♗f4 ♖ad8 16 ♖ad1 ♕c5 17 ♕b3 ♘xe4? (a mistake, although Black was already in trouble) 18 ♗e3 ♕a5 19 ♕xb7 ♖c8 20 b4!? (20 ♕d7! also wins) 20...♘xb4 21 ♘f4+ ♗xf4 22 ♕xe4+ ♕f5 23 ♕xb4 and White was winning, Vitolinsh-Raetsky, Naberezhnye Chelny 1988.

a2) 13...♔f8 14 ♘d5 ♘e5 15 ♕b3 ♘xe4 16 ♕xb7 ♖e8 and nothing has been decided.

b) 7...♗e6 8 ♗xe6+ ♔xe6 9 0-0 with:

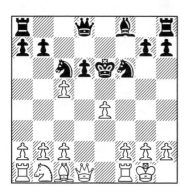

b1) 9...♔f7 10 ♕e2 ♕e8 11 ♖e1 d5 (11...♕e6!?) 12 e5 ♘e4 13 ♘c3 ♘xc3 14 bxc3?! (14 ♕f3+ ♔g8 15 ♕xc3 ♕e6 is stronger, but Black still looks pretty solid here) 14...♕e6 15 ♖b1 ♖b8 16 ♗e3 ♗e7 17 f4 ♖hf8 18 ♗d4 ♔g8 19 ♖f1 g5 and White

was close to losing in Short-Shirov, Dubai (rapid) 2002.

b2) 9...d5 is also interesting:

b21) 10 e5?! ♘e4 11 ♕g4+ ♔f7 12 ♕f5+ ♔e8 and we do not think there is enough compensation, for example 13 ♘c3 ♘d4 14 ♕h3 ♕d7 15 e6 ♕xe6 16 ♕d3 ♘xc3 17 bxc3 ♘e2+ 18 ♔h1 ♘xc1 19 ♖axc1 ♔f7 20 ♖ce1 ♕c6 with a clear edge for Black, Vitolinsh-Dautov, Minsk 1988.

b22) 10 ♘c3!? d4 11 ♘a4 (11 ♕e2?! is awarded a '!' by Forintos and Haag, but after 11...dxc3! 12 ♕c4+ ♔e7 13 e5 ♕d4! 14 exf6+ ♔xf6 White has no compensation) 11...♔f7 with chances for both sides.

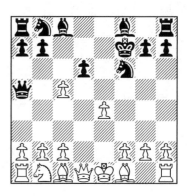

7 ♘c3 ♕xc5 8 ♗e3 ♕a5

8...♕c7!? 9 ♘b5 ♕a5+ 10 c3 ♘c6 is a possible recommendation– White seems to have difficulties generating an initiative.

9 ♗c4+ ♗e6 10 ♗xe6+ ♔xe6

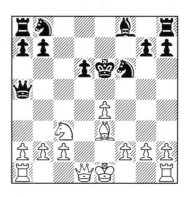

11 0-0

11 ♕e2 has also been played: 11...♗e7 12 g4 ♖c8 (this and Black's next move are not strictly necessary) 13 0-0 ♖xc3!? 14 bxc3 ♘c6 with a very unclear position, Zelinsky-Volchok, correspondence 1988.

11...♘c6 12 f4 ♖d8

12...♗e7 13 ♕e2 ♕a6 14 ♘b5 ♔f7 is also pretty messy. If push came to shove, we would probably choose to be Black.

13 g4?!

This is too risky and is met by a strong counter in the centre. 13 a3 ♔f7 14 b4 ♕c7 15 ♘d5 gives White the initiative, even though the position is probably still okay for Black. However, perhaps 13...♕h5!? gives Black the better chances.

13...d5

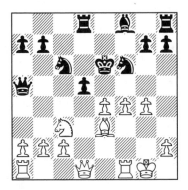

14 f5+?!

This eliminates White's chances to invade

with his queen. The stronger option is 14 g5!? and now:

a) 14...♘xe4 15 ♕g4+ ♔f7 (15...♔e7!? 16 ♖ae1 is also unclear) 16 ♕f5+ ♔e8 17 ♘xe4 dxe4 18 ♕xe4+ ♗e7 19 f5 and the position continues to be very difficult to assess.

b) 14...dxe4 is not so good: 15 ♕e2 ♘d5 16 f5+ ♔f7 (16...♔e7! may well be an improvement) 17 ♕h5+ ♔g8 18 f6 gxf6 19 ♖f5 (Bielak-Borys, Poland 1992). Now after 19...♘ce7 (what else?) 20 gxf6 ♘xf5 21 f7+ ♔g7 22 ♕g5+ ♔xf7 23 ♕xf5+ ♔e8 24 ♕e5+ ♔d7 25 ♘xd5 White has serious attacking chances.

14...♔f7 15 g5 ♗c5 16 gxf6 ♗xe3+ 17 ♔h1 d4

Stronger than 17...dxe4 18 fxg7 ♔xg7 19 ♕g4+ ♔f8, when Black's king is extremely insecure.

18 fxg7 ♖hg8!

18...♔xg7?! is inferior. After 19 f6+ ♔f7 20 ♖f5 ♕xf5 21 exf5 dxc3 22 ♕g4 ♔xf6 23 bxc3 Black's superiority is not as clear as it should be.

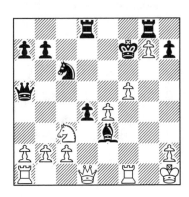

19 f6

This leads nowhere. White can struggle on a while with 19 ♘d5 ♖xd5 20 exd5 ♕xd5+ 21 ♕f3 ♕xf3+ 22 ♖xf3 ♖xg7, or 19 ♕h5+ ♔xg7 20 f6+ ♔h8. Although Black is clearly better, the game is not totally decided.

19...dxc3 20 ♕e2 ♕c5

Also strong is 20...cxb2 21 ♖ae1 ♕c5 22 ♕xe3 ♕xe3 23 ♖xe3 ♖d6! 24 e5 ♖e6 25

♖b3 b6, when Black is a knight up for nothing.

21 ♖f5 cxb2 22 ♖af1 ♕b4 23 ♕h5+ ♔e6 24 ♕h3 ♕xe4+ 25 ♖5f3+ ♔d6 26 ♕g2 ♘d4 27 ♖xe3 ♕xe3 28 ♕xb7 ♖b8 29 f7 ♕f3+ 0-1

White resigned because of 30 ♖f3 b1♕ 31 ♕b1 ♖b1 32 ♔g2 ♖g7.

Game 43
Kholmov-Belousov
Gorky 1974

1 e4 e5 2 ♘f3 ♘f6 3 ♘xe5 ♘xe4?!

This gambit/beginner's move is simply bad.

3...♕e7?! is also poor: 4 d4 (a decent alternative is 4 ♘f3!? ♘xe4 5 ♗e2 d5 6 0-0 ♗e6 7 ♖e1 ♕f6 8 d3 ♘c5 9 ♘g5 ♗d6 10 ♗f3 when White has a clear advantage) 4...d6 (after 4...♘xe4 5 ♗d3 d5 6 0-0 ♕f6 7 ♗xe4 dxe4 8 ♘c3 ♗f5 9 ♖e1 White ends up a pawn ahead) 5 ♘f3 ♕xe4+ (5...♘xe4 6 ♗e2 ♗g4 7 0-0 d5 8 ♖e1 ♘c6 9 c3 0-0-0 10 ♘g5 ♗xe2 11 ♖xe2 also gives Black a serious headache) 6 ♗e2 ♗e7 (or 6...♗f5 7 c4 ♕c2 8 ♕xc2 ♗xc2 9 ♘a3 ♗e4 10 ♘b5 ♘a6 11 ♗g5 with an advantage for White – all Black's pieces are passive) 7 0-0 0-0 8 c4 ♖e8 9 ♘c3 ♕f5 10 ♗d3 ♕h5 11 h3 c6 12 ♖e1 ♘a6 13 ♗g5 (White has emerged from the opening with a decent plus) 13...♘b4 14 ♗xf6 gxf6 15 ♘e4 ♗e6 16 ♘g3 ♕a5? 17

♕d2 ♕b6 18 ♕h6 1-0 Timofeev-Phoobalan, Goa 2002.

4 ♕e2 ♕e7 5 ♕xe4 d6 6 d4 dxe5 7 dxe5

7 ♕xe5?! is a weaker choice: 7...♕xe5+ 8 dxe5 ♗f5 9 c3 (9 ♘c3!? ♗xc2 10 ♘d5 ♔d7 11 ♗f4 ♘c6 12 ♗b5 ♖d8 13 ♖c1 is still probably better for White) 9...♘d7 10 f4 (10 ♗f4 0-0-0 11 ♘d2 ♘xe5 12 ♗xe5 ♖e8 and Black is at least equal – Yusupov) 10...0-0-0 11 ♗e3 f6!? 12 ♘d2 (12 ♗xa7 fxe5 13 fxe5 ♘xe5 14 ♗d4 ♖e8 15 ♔d2 g6 gives Black serious threats) 12...fxe5 13 fxe5 ♘xe5 14 0-0-0 ♘d3+ 15 ♗xd3 ♖xd3 and Black's position is preferable, Kos-Potapov, Ceske Budejovice 1995.

7...♘c6

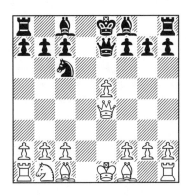

8 ♗b5

We think this is a good decision. Alternatively:

a) 8 ♗f4 g5!? 9 ♗b5 (9 ♗g3?? f5! 10 ♕e2 f4 and Black wins!) 9...♗d7 10 ♘d2 ♗g7 11 ♘c3 0-0-0 12 0-0-0 ♗xe5 and Black has certainly survived the opening.

b) 8 ♘c3!? is interesting: 8...♘xe5 9 ♕xe5+ ♘xe5 10 ♗f4 (10 ♘b5 ♗b4+ 11 c3 ♗a5 12 ♗f4 f6 and Black holds his own) 10...♗d6 11 ♗g3 ♗d7 12 0-0-0 0-0-0 13 ♘e4 ♗c6 14 ♘xd6+ cxd6 15 f3 ♖he8 16 ♖d4!? ♔c7 17 a4 and White had the advantage in the endgame, Vasiukov-Chekhov, Moscow 1975.

8...♗d7 9 ♘c3 0-0-0

After 9...♕b4?! 10 ♗c4 ♘a5 11 ♗d3

White is a pawn up for nothing.

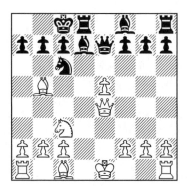

10 0-0

A simpler way to play is 10 &f4 g5 11 &g3 (11 e6 fxe6 12 &e3 &g7 is unclear) 11...&g7 12 0-0-0 h5 13 h4! with a clear advantage.

10...&xe5

10...a6 11 &c4 &xe5 12 &d5 ♕e6 13 &g5 f6 14 &f4 gives White good attacking chances, while 11 &xc6 &xc6 12 ♕f5+ ♕d7 13 ♕f4 should be better for White too.

11 &e3

11 &xd7+ &xd7 12 ♕a4 a6 13 &d5 ♕e5 14 ♕a5 also provides White with an edge.

11...&xb5

Or 11...a6 12 &d5 (12 &xa6 &c6 13 ♕f5+ &d7 14 ♕e4 &c6 with a repetition – Kholmov) 12...♕e6 13 &f4 ♕e8 14 &xd7+ &xd7 15 ♕f5 and White retains the initiative.

12 &xb5 &c6?!

Missing a chance. After 12...a6 13 &d4 g6 14 &fe1 &g7 15 &ad1 &he8 Black would be all right.

13 &xa7+!?

This tempting sacrifice is not strictly necessary. After 13 ♕f4 &b8 14 &ad1 White has a big advantage. Still, it is very difficult to defend against such a sacrifice. This, along with the aesthetic beauty of the idea, encouraged Kholmov take the risk.

13...&xa7 14 ♕a4 &c6 15 ♕a8+ &d7 16 &ad1+ &e8 17 ♕xb7 ♕e6 18 &de1 &e7

18...&b8 loses to 19 ♕xc7 &c8 20 ♕g3 ♕g6 21 &c5+ &e7 22 ♕a3 ♕g5 23 &e3 followed by &fe1.

19 &c5 &b8

19...♕d7? is met with by elegant 20 ♕xc6! ♕xc6 21 &xe7+ &f8 22 &xc7+, winning.

20 ♕a6 ♕d5?!

This loses by force. After 20...♕f6 21 ♕a4 &f8 22 &xe7 &xe7 23 &e1 White has every chance of winning, but the game is still on.

21 ♕a3 ♕g5 22 &e3 &f8 23 &xe7+ &xe7 24 f4 ♕f6 25 &fe1 &e8

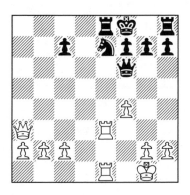

26 &xe7!

Forcing a winning endgame.

26...♕xe7 27 &xe7 &xe7 28 g4 f5 29 ♕c5 g6 30 gxf5 gxf5 31 ♕xf5+ &f7 32 ♕c5+ &g8 33 &g2 h5 34 &f3 &h6 35 ♕g5+ &h7 36 a4 1-0

Summary

5 ♘c3 has been underestimated by theory, and Black should act carefully here. In Game 33 Alekhine played fantastically to defeat Rabinovich, but the pawn sacrifice with 5...d5 is dubious. 5...♘f6 is quite passive, but Black appears to be on the verge of equalising here. The more popular and sharper 5...♘xc3 6 dxc3 ♗e7 normally results in opposite side castling and a fight with mutual chances.

The easiest way for Black to equalise against 5 ♕e2 is with 5...♕e7 6 d3 ♘f6 7 ♗g5 ♕xe2+ 8 ♗xe2 ♘bd7 and 9...h6, preparing the simple ...g7-g6 or the extended fianchetto (...g7-g5). The continuation 5 c4 is more challenging than 5 d3, but Black's play in Game 37 demonstrates that it's also fairly harmless. The modern 5 ♗d3 is pretty safe for Black. However, the positions are quite untypical and have not been studied very much.

The sacrifice 3 ♘xe5 d6 4 ♘xf7 deserves consideration because it has been shown that it is not easy for Black despite the extra piece. 5 d4 ♕e8, in conjunction with either ...g7-g6 or ...d6-d5, seems to be promising for Black, while 5...c5 and in particular 6 dxc5 ♘c6 7 ♗c4 ♗e6 8 ♗xe6+ ♔xe6 has not lost its favourable reputation. Of course, the presence of the black king in the centre puts higher demands on Black but, objectively speaking, Black's chances are preferable in the Cochrane Gambit.

After 3...♘xe4 4 ♕e2 ♕e7 5 ♕xe4 d6 6 d4 dxe5 7 dxe5 ♘c6 White has better prospects. He has a pleasant choice between 8 ♘c3 and 8 ♗b5.

1 e4 e5 2 ♘f3 ♘f6 3 ♘xe5 d6

  3...♘xe4 – *Game 43*

4 ♘f3

  4 ♘c4 – *Game 40*

  4 ♘xf7 ♔xf7 5 d4 (D)

    5...c5 – *Game 42*; 5...g6 – *Game 41*

5...♘xe4 5 ♘c3 (D)

  5 d3 – *Game 39*; 5 ♗d3 – *Game 38*; 5 c4 – *Game 37*

  5 ♕e2 ♕e7 6 d3 ♘f6 7 ♗g5 (D)

    7...♗e6 – *Game 35*; 7...♕xe2+ – *Game 36*

5...♘xc3 – *Game 34*

  5...d5 – *Game 33*

| *5 d4* | *5 ♘c3* | *7 ♗g5* |

CHAPTER SIX

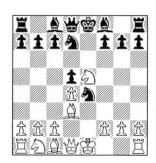

3 d4: The Main Line

1 e4 e5 2 ♘f3 ♘f6 3 d4 ♘xe4 4 ♗d3 d5 5 ♘xe5 ♘d7

In this chapter we begin our study of 3 d4, the Steinitz system. 1 e4 e5 2 ♘f3 ♘f6 3 d4 ♘xe4 4 ♗d3 d5 5 ♘xe5 is one of the key lines in the Petroff Defence. Having placed his knight on e5, White obtains a symmetrical position with an extra tempo. In this chapter we look at Black's main choice, 5...♘d7

The authors have special feelings towards the line with 5...♘d7. In 1990 in Voronezh a small book (40 pages) was published in Russian under the title *A Fashionable Variation in the Petroff Defence*. It was our first serious joint work...

In his first correspondence theme tournament devoted to the Petroff Defence (1982-1983), Alexander Raetsky faced the following problem: how to initiate a complicated fight after 3 d4 ♘xe4 4 ♗d3 d5 5 ♘xe5. At that time the main continuations were 5...♗d6 and 5...♗e7. However, in both lines Black only dreamed of 'beating off' White's attack and attaining a draw. But Alexander had a burning desire for something 'sharp' and 'interesting'.

In search of the active weapon let's refer to Bilguer. The omniscient *Handbuch* informs us: 'after 5...♘d7, which was played in the Barry-Showalter match (1896), White easily

develops by means of 6 ♕e2 ♕e7 7 ♗f4 followed by 0-0 and ♖e1.' The Black Army leader could hardly expect that many years later his idea would rise like a phoenix from its ashes.

Up to the 1980s, 5...♘d7 had been a dead branch on the spreading tree of the Petroff Defence. However, the year 1980 proved to be a crucial moment in the history of the variation. In the Tilburg super-GM tournament, Larsen sacrificed a pawn for counterplay and the bishop pair against Karpov, the world champion at the time, with 6 ♕e2 ♘xe5! 7 ♗xe4 dxe4 8 ♕xe4 ♗e6 9 ♕xe5 ♕d7 (following the game Unzicker-Rogoff from Amsterdam earlier in the year). The Danish GM could hardly have hoped for better publicity than he received after this impressive win. Players started to employ 5...♘d7 at major tournaments and now this is Black's main weapon against the Steinitz system – 3 d4. At present almost all the chess elite, players such as Kramnik, Anand, Morozevich, Ivanchuk, Ponomariov and Kasimdzhanov, are advocates of 5...♘d7.

The main continuation is 6 ♘xd7 ♗xd7 7 0-0 (Games 44-55). Black has a wide choice between the modest 7...♗e7 (Game 55), the queen lunges 7...♕f6 (Game 54) or 7...♕h4 (Games 49-53), and the fashionable 7...♗d6

(Games 44-48).

At the end of the 20th century, the sharpest line 7...♕h4 8 c4 0-0-0 9 c5 g5!? (Games 49-52) had been hotly debated for almost two decades – amazing for such a quiet opening! Even the representatives of the chess beau monde like Kasparov, Anand, Ivanchuk, Judit Polgar participated in these interesting discussions. Despite the statistics being in White's favour, we believe that there are possibilities to improve Black's play in all the main lines (10 ♗e3, 10 f3, 10 ♘c3).

At the beginning of the 21st century 7...♗d6!? is in the limelight. (It is surprising how the theory is developing: in the above-mentioned book of 1990 we gave only one reference out of 78 to the 'third-rate' move 7...♗d6) After the pretty typical 8 c4 c6 9 cxd5 cxd5 White is at the crossroads: he can play either 10 ♘c3 ♘xc3 11 bxc3 0-0 12 ♕h5 (Games 44-45) or the immediate 10 ♕h5 (Games 46-47). In both cases Black has reasonable play.

Nowadays Black is not afraid of the tactical move 6 ♕e2 (Game 56), intending to use the pin along the e-file; in fact, Black even looks forward to it. Extensive practice has proven that the pawn sacrifice after 6...♘xe5!? 7 ♗xe4 dxe4 8 ♕xe4 ♗e6 9 ♕xe5 ♕d7 is correct; easy development, two bishops in the open, and awkward position of the white queen create enough compensation for Black.

The practical continuation 6 ♘c3 (Game 57) opposes the knight on e4. But once all four knights have been exchanged (6...♘xc3 7 bxc3 ♘xe5 8 dxe5) White is unlikely to have an advantage, due to his broken pawn structure. On the other hand, grabbing material with 6...♗b4 7 0-0 ♘xc3 8 bxc3 ♗xc3 9 ♖b1 provides White with a dangerous initiative. Also in Game 57 is the unimpressive 6 0-0, which was often played in the earliest days of 5...♘d7. Black has easy play after 6...♘xe5 7 dxe5 ♘c5.

Finally, the unexpected sacrifice 6 ♘xf7!?

(Game 58) is one of the numerous discoveries by Igor Zaitsev, one of the most creative grandmasters in the world. This novelty led to a quick and amusing draw by perpetual check in Zaitsev-Karpov, Leningrad 1966 after 6...♕e7 7 ♘xh8 ♘c3 8 ♔d2 ♘xd1 9 ♖e1 ♘xf2 10 ♗xh7 ♘e4 11 ♖xe4 dxe4 12 ♗g6 ♔d8 13 ♘f7. Six years later, Gurgenidze routed Bellin by employing 7 ♕e2!? ♔xf7? 8 ♕h5 ♔f6 9 0-0 ♕f7 10 ♕h4 g5 11 ♗xg5! ♘xg5 12 f4 with a mating attack. But this is too good to be true, and Game 58 demonstrates Black's superior options.

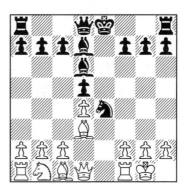

Game 44
Svidler-Ponomariov
Moscow 2001

1 e4 e5 2 ♘f3 ♘f6 3 d4 ♘xe4 4 ♗d3 d5 5 ♘xe5 ♘d7 6 ♘xd7

Sixth move alternatives for White will be considered in Games 56-58.

6...♗xd7 7 0-0 ♗d6

This is the solid alternative to 7...♕h4, which is discussed in Games 50-53. Less common options for Black are studied in Games 54-55.

8 c4

8 ♘c3 features in Game 48.

8...c6

8...♕h4 transposes to 7...♕h4 8 c4 ♗d6 – see the notes to Game 49, while 8...0-0 9 cxd5 ♖e8 10 ♘c3 ♕h4 11 g3 ♘xc3 12 bxc3

♕h3 13 ♖b1 favours White – Black has no easy way to get his pawn back.

9 cxd5

Another option is 9 ♘c3 and now:

a) 9...0-0 10 ♕h5 ♘f6 11 ♕h4 dxc4 12 ♗xc4 ♖e8 13 ♗g5 h6 14 ♗xf6 ♕xf6 15 ♕xf6 gxf6 is fine for Black. After 16 ♖fe1 ♗e6 17 ♘e4 ♗e7 18 ♗xe6 fxe6 19 ♘c5 ♗xc5 20 dxc5 ♖ad8 21 ♖ad1 ♔f7 the players agreed a draw in Sveshnikov-Mikhalchishin, Kuibyshev 1986.

b) 9...♘xc3 10 bxc3 dxc4?! (Black could still transpose to the main game with 10...0-0) 11 ♖e1+ ♗e7 12 ♗a3 ♗e6 13 ♗xe7 ♕xe7 14 ♗xc4 0-0 15 ♖e5 ♕a3 16 ♗xe6 fxe6 17 ♕e1 and White had some pressure, Short-Hübner, Wijk aan Zee 1986.

9...cxd5 10 ♘c3

The main alternative is 10 ♕h5 – see Games 46-47.

10...♘xc3 11 bxc3 0-0 12 ♕h5 f5

This is the most solid move. The pawn sacrifice with 12...g6 is considered in the next game.

13 ♖e1

Alternatively:

a) 13 ♕f3 ♔h8! is fine for Black, for example 14 ♗f4 ♕c7 15 ♗xd6 ♕xd6 16 ♗c2 ♖fe8 17 ♖fe1 ♖ac8 18 h4 g6 19 h5 ♔g7 20 g3 ♕c6 21 ♖xe8 ♖xe8 22 ♔g2 ♕d6 23 ♖h1 ♗b5 24 ♗b3 ♖e4 with equal chances, Galkin-Macieja, Istanbul 2003.

b) More interesting is 13 c4 ♕f6 (13...dxc4 14 ♗xc4+ ♔h8 15 ♗g5 ♕e8 16 ♕h4 looks a bit better for White) 14 ♖b1!? ♕xd4 15 ♖xb7 dxc4 16 ♗xc4+ ♕xc4. Here the players agreed a draw in Velicka-Rabiega, Berlin, 1999. After 17 ♖xd7 ♕c6 White is forced to play the adventurous 18 ♖xg7+! ♔xg7 19 ♗b2+ ♗e5 (19...♔g8 20 ♕g5+ ♔f7 21 ♕f6+ ♔e8 22 ♕e6+ ♔d8 23 ♖d1 looks very dangerous for Black) 20 ♗xe5+ ♔g8 21 ♖d1 when he has substantial compensation for the exchange.

13...♕c7 14 ♗d2 ♖ae8

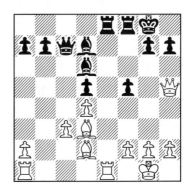

15 ♗c2

Maybe White has a brighter future after 15 g3, for instance:

a) 15...♖xe1+ 16 ♖xe1 ♕a5 17 ♕f3 ♕xa2 18 ♗f4 ♗xf4 19 ♖e7 ♕f7 20 ♖xf7 ♕a1+ 21 ♔g2 ♔xf7 22 ♕xf4 when White has considerable activity for his pawn, and Black needs to defend precisely to survive.

b) 15...g6 16 ♕f3 ♖e4!? (this compelling idea crops up more than once) 17 ♖ec1 b5 18 a4 a6 19 ♗h6 ♖c8 20 ♗xe4 dxe4 (20...fxe4?! 21 ♕f6 ♗f8 22 ♗xf8 ♖xf8 23 ♕xa6 bxa4 24 c4 and there is no compensation for the exchange) 21 ♕e3 ♕c4 22 axb5 ♗xb5 23 ♗f4 ♗f8 24 ♗e5 and it looks like White has a slight edge, Ponomariov-Morozevich, Moscow (rapid) 2002.

15...g6 16 ♕f3 ♖e4! 17 g3

17 ♗xe4? fxe4 18 ♕e2 ♗xh2+ 19 ♔h1 ♖f5 (Golubev) gives Black a strong attack.

17...♗b5 18 ♗f4

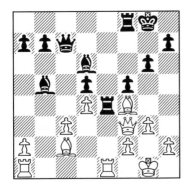

18 ♗xe4 fxe4 19 ♕g4 ♗d7 offers Black compensation, while 18 ♗h6 ♖f7 19 ♖ab1 ♕c6 is equally unclear.

18...♗xf4 19 gxf4 ♕d6

19...♕xf4 20 ♗xe4 fxe4 21 ♕xf4 ♖xf4 is also fine for Black, but probably just a draw.

20 ♗xe4

White no longer has a choice. Even though objectively the position is probably equal, White's game is harder to play.

20...fxe4 21 ♕g3 ♖xf4 22 ♖ab1 ♗d7 23 f3

23 h3 b6 24 c4 ♕f6 25 cxd5 ♖f5 26 ♕b8+ ♔g7 27 ♖b3 ♕xd4 28 ♖be3 (Baklan) is an interesting possibility for White, who has some counterplay of his own.

23...b6

A weaker option is 23...exf3?! 24 ♔f2 b6 25 ♖e3 ♗f5 26 ♖e5 ♕a3 27 ♕xf4 ♕xa2+, when Black has not completely equalised.

24 ♖e3 ♕f6 25 ♖f1?

25 ♖b2 ♕f8 26 ♖f2 ♕h6 is equal according to Golubev.

25...♗g4!

This 'sacrifice' destroys White's position.

26 ♕xg4

26 h3 ♗xf3 27 ♔h2 ♖f5 28 a4 ♖g5 29 ♕b8+ ♔g7 30 ♖f2 ♔h6 is also discouraging for White.

26...♖xg4+ 27 fxg4 ♕g5 28 ♖g3 b5 29 ♖f2 ♔g7 30 ♔g2 a5 31 ♖b2 b4 32 cxb4 axb4 33 h3 ♕c1 34 ♖gb3 ♔h6 35 ♖xb4 ♕d1 36 ♔f2?!

36 ♖4b3 ♕xd4 37 ♖e2 ♔g5 is probably better, though Black has all the chances.

36...♔g5 37 ♖e2 ♔f4 38 ♖b3 ♕xd4+ 39 ♔g2 ♕c4 40 ♖f2+

Or 40 ♖be3 ♕c1 41 ♔f2 ♕h1 and Black wins.

40...♔g5 41 ♖f7 d4 42 h4+ ♔xh4 43 ♖xh7+ ♔xg4 44 ♖g3+ ♔f5 0-1

Game 45
Rublevsky-Vallejo
Ohrid 2001

1 e4 e5 2 ♘f3 ♘f6 3 d4 ♘xe4 4 ♗d3 d5 5 ♘xe5 ♘d7 6 ♘xd7 ♗xd7 7 0-0 ♗d6 8 c4 c6 9 cxd5 cxd5 10 ♘c3 ♘xc3 11 bxc3 0-0 12 ♕h5 g6!? 13 ♕xd5 ♕c7

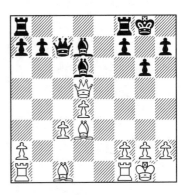

14 ♕f3

It seems that the text move is the most dangerous for Black, although it's not the only attractive option. In fact, White has tried a few other moves here:

a) 14 h3 does not appear to be dangerous for Black: 14...♗e6 15 ♕f3 ♕xc3 16 ♖b1 (after 16 ♗h6 Black plays 16...♖fd8 17 ♗g5 ♖e8 18 ♗f6 ♗f5 19 ♗xf5 ♕xf5 20 gxf3 gxf5 with equal chances) 16...♕xd4 (16...♗xa2 17 ♖xb7 ♕xd4 18 ♗b2 ♕f4 19 ♕xf4 ♗xf4 20 ♖a1 ♖fd8 21 ♗f1 ♗e6 22 ♖axa7 ♖ac8 is level according to Belikov) 17 ♗e4 ♕e5 18 g3 ♗xh3 19 ♗b2 ♕e7 20 ♖fe1 ♖ae8 21 ♗c2 (or 21 ♗xb7 ♕xe1+ 22 ♖xe1 ♖xe1+ 23 ♔h2 ♗f5 24 ♕c3 ♖e5 25 f4 ♖e2+ 26 ♗g2 ♗e5 27 fxe5 ♗e4 28 e6 ♖xg2+ 29 ♔h3 ♖xb2 30 exf7+ ♖xf7 31 ♕xb2 with a draw – Belikov) 21...♕g5 22 ♗b3 (G.Guseinov-Belikov, Alushta 2001). Now Belikov gives the following line as the most natural way to end the game: 22...♕f5! 23 ♕c3 ♗e5 24 ♖xe5 ♕xb1+ 25 ♔h2 ♕f1 26 ♗xf7+! ♔xf7 27 ♖f5+! ♔e6!! 28 ♖e5+ ♔f7! 29 ♖f5+! with perpetual check – a very attractive variation.

b) 14 h4 ♗e6 15 ♕f3 ♕xc3 16 ♗h6 ♖fd8!? 17 ♗g5 (17 ♕f6?! ♗f8 18 ♗xf8 ♕xd4! and Black is better) 17...♖d7 18 ♖fd1 ♗f8 (18...♕xd4 19 ♗e4 ♕e5 20 g3 ♖c8 also seems fine) 19 ♖ac1 ♕a5 20 ♗f6 a6 21 ♗e4 ♗d5 22 ♕g4 ♗e6 23 ♕f4 ♗d5 24 ♖c5 ♕xa2 25 ♗e5 with compensation for the pawn, Nedev-Urban, Elista 1998.

c) 14 ♗h6 ♖fe8

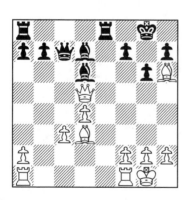

with a further branch:

c1) 15 ♖ac1 ♗xh2+ 16 ♔h1 and now

strongest is 16...♗e5! 17 f4 (17 dxe5? ♖xe5 18 ♗f4 ♖xd5 19 ♗xc7 ♖xd3 favours Black slightly) 17...♗c6 18 ♕c4 b5 19 ♕b3 ♕d7!? 20 f5!? ♗g3 21 ♔g1 with complex play, Lepelletier-Marciano, Auxerre 1996.

c2) 15 h4 ♗e6 16 ♕f3 ♕xc3 17 ♕f6 ♗f8 18 ♗xf8 ♖xf8 with a final split:

c21) 19 ♗e4 19...♖ad8 20 ♖fd1 ♗d5 21 ♖ac1 ♕a3 22 h5 ♕d6 23 ♕xd6 ♖xd6 24 ♗xd5 ♖xd5 25 ♖c7 ♖xh5 26 d5 ♖d8 27 ♖xb7 ♖hxd5 with a draw in Sutovsky-Fridman, Medellin 1996.

c22) 19 ♖fd1 ♕a5 (19...♖ad8!? should be fine; maybe White continues with 20 ♗e4, as 20 ♗xg6!? hxg6 21 h5 leads to a draw after 21...gxh5 22 ♕g5+ ♔h7 23 ♕xh5+ ♔g7 24 ♕g5+ ♔h7 25 ♖ac1 ♕b4) 20 ♗e4 ♕d8 21 ♕xd8 ♖axd8 22 d5 (White should have a pull here) 22...♗f5 23 ♗xf5 gxf5 24 d6 ♖d7 25 ♖d5 ♖fd8 26 ♖ad1 ♔g7 27 ♖1d3 f6 28 ♖g3+ ½-½ Tiviakov-Yusupov, Groningen 1994.

14...♗xh2+

14...♕xc3 15 ♗h6 ♖fe8 16 ♕f6 ♗f8 17 ♗xf8 ♖xf8 18 ♗e4 is preferable for White as Black cannot free himself easily. Black has compensation for the exchange after 15...♕xd4!? 16 ♗xf8 ♗c6 17 ♕h3 ♖xf8 but he still has much to prove.

15 ♔h1 ♗d6 16 c4

16 ♗h6 ♕d8!? 17 g3 ♖e8 18 ♖fe1 ♖c8 is less dangerous for Black.

16...♖fe8

Maybe 16...♕d8!? 17 g3 ♗c6 18 d5 ♗d7 19 ♗b2 ♖c8 is better. Most players would prefer White, but is there really an advantage? **17 c5 ♗f8 18 ♗e4 ♗c6 19 d5 ♗b5 20 d6! ♕xc5 21 ♗d5 ♗g7 22 ♖a3 ♕c3**

After 22...♕d4 23 ♗xf7+ ♔h8 24 ♗xe8 ♖xe8 25 ♖ad1 ♕h4+ 26 ♔g1 ♗xf1 27 ♖xf1 White's strong passed pawn promises him great prospects.

23 ♗xf7+ ♔h8 24 ♕xc3 ♗xc3 25 ♗xe8 ♗xf1 26 ♖c1 ♖xe8 27 ♖xc3

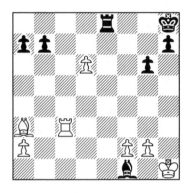

This endgame is deeply unpleasant for Black.

27...♖d8 28 ♖c7 ♔g8 29 ♖xb7 ♗c4 30 ♖e7 a6

30...♗xa2? 31 d7 ♗f7 32 ♗b4 wins in an instant.

31 ♗b4 ♗b5 32 ♔h2 ♖d7 33 ♖e5 ♔f7 34 ♔g3 ♗c4 35 a3 ♖b7 36 ♔f4 ♗e6 37 ♖a5 ♖b6 38 ♔e4 ♖c6 39 ♗c5 ♔e8 40 ♔e5 ♔d7 41 ♔f6 ♗f5 42 f3 h5 43 ♗b4 ♖c2 44 ♖xa6 ♖xg2 45 ♖a7+ ♔c8 46 ♖c7+ ♔b8 47 ♗c5 ♖g3 48 f4 ♖f3 49 ♔e5 ♖d3 50 a4 h4 51 a5 h3 52 ♖h7 ♗c8 53 ♗a7+

53 ♖h8 h2 54 a6 is a simple win.

53...♔a8 54 ♗d4 ♖a3 55 ♗b6 ♖d3 56 ♗c5?

56 a6, intending 56...♗xa6 57 d7, would have won.

56...♖c3 57 ♗b4 ♖c4 58 ♗d2 ♖c5+ 59 ♔f6?!

59 ♔e4 ♖h5 60 ♖xh5 gxh5 61 ♔f3 would

still give real chances of winning.

59...♖h5 60 d7 ♗xd7 61 ♖xd7 h2 62 ♖d8+ ♔b7 63 a6+ ♔xa6 64 ♖a8+ ♔b7 65 ♖a1 h1♕ 66 ♖xh1 ♖xh1 ½-½

Game 46
Svidler-Yusupov
Bad Homburg 1998

---

1 e4 e5 2 ♘f3 ♘f6 3 d4 ♘xe4 4 ♗d3 d5 5 ♘xe5 ♘d7 6 ♘xd7 ♗xd7 7 0-0 ♗d6 8 c4 c6 9 cxd5 cxd5 10 ♕h5

This alternative to 10 ♘c3 is perhaps more dangerous for Black.

10...0-0

Black has alternatives, but they all appear to give White the edge.

a) 10...♘f6 11 ♖e1+ ♔f8 (11...♗e6? 12 ♖xe6+ ♔f8 13 ♖xf6 and White wins) 12 ♕h4 gives White a slight pull. Now a fantasy line runs 12...♕b6 13 ♘c3 ♘g4 14 ♗f4!? ♗xf4 15 ♕e7+ ♔g8 16 ♕xd7 ♗xh2+ 17 ♔h1 ♘f6 18 ♘xd5! ♘xd7 19 ♘xb6 ♘xb6 20 ♔xh2 and the endgame is wonderful for White.

b) 10...♕f6 was suggested by Igor Zaitsev.

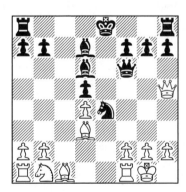

Now White has the following options:

b1) 11 ♕xd5 ♗c6 12 ♗b5 0-0-0 13 ♕b3 (13 ♕c4? ♗xh2+! 14 ♔xh2 ♘d6 gives Black the advantage) 13...♗xb5 14 ♕xb5 ♕xd4 and it is White who has to prove equality.

b2) 11 ♗e3 ♕g6 12 ♕xd5 ♗c6 looks like enough compensation for the pawn to us.

After 13 ♕a5 b6 14 ♕a6 Black is of course fine, but now the simplest solution is 14...♘c5! 15 ♗xg6 hxg6 16 ♗f4!? (otherwise it's perpetual check) 16...♘xa6 17 ♗xd6 0-0-0 18 ♗g3 ♖xd4.

c) 11 ♘c3 (the most challenging) 11...♕xd4 12 ♕xd5 ♕xd5 13 ♘xd5 ♘c5 (after 13...f5 14 ♗f4 ♗xf4 15 ♘xf4 0-0-0 16 ♖fe1 ♗c6 17 ♖ad1 g6 18 f3 ♘f6 Black was close to being level in Konguvel-Barua, Sangli 2000) 14 ♖e1+ ♘e6 15 ♗g5 0-0 (Black is not much worse after 15...h6 16 ♗e3 ♗c6 17 ♘f4 ♔e7) 16 ♗e7 ♖xe7 17 ♘xe7+ ♔h8 18 ♖ad1 ♖ad8 19 ♗e4 with a plus for White, Sveshnikov-I. Zaitsev, Moscow 1991.

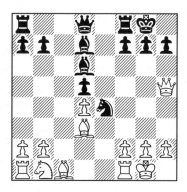

11 ♕xd5

11 ♘c3 leads to a draw after 11...g6 12 ♕xd5 ♗c6 13 ♕b3 ♘xc3 14 bxc3 ♗xh2+ 15 ♔xh2 ♕h4+ 16 ♔g1 ♗xg2 (Ivanchuk).

11...♗c6 12 ♕h5 g6

12...♕f6?! 13 ♘c3 ♕xd4 14 ♗xe4 ♗xe4 15 ♖d1 ♗d3 16 ♕h3 ♖fd8 17 ♖xd3 ♕xd3 18 ♕xd3 ♗xh2+ 19 ♔xh2 ♖xd3 20 ♗e3 gives White good winning chances, while 13...g6 14 ♕h6 ♖fe8 15 d5! (Yusupov) is also good for White. However, 12...♗b4 is playable, 13 ♗e3 ♖e8 14 a3 g6 15 ♕h3 transposing to the main game.

13 ♕h3

This move reaches the most critical position in the 7...♗d6 line.

13 ♕h6 ♖e8 14 ♗e3 ♗f8 is an improvement for Black: 15 ♕h3 ♗d7 (15...h5!? 16

♗c4 ♘d6 17 ♘d2 ♘xc4 18 ♘xc4 ♕c8 with some compensation) 16 ♕f3 ♗c6 17 ♗c4 (here White should consider 17 ♗xe4!? ♖xe4 18 ♕d1 ♗d6 19 ♘c3 ♕h4 20 h3 ♖xe3 21 fxe3 ♗g2! 22 ♕g4 ♕xg4 23 hxg4 ♗xf1 24 ♖xf1 with an edge – Y.Gonzalez) 17...♘d6 18 ♗d5 ♗xd5 19 ♕xd5 ♕b6 20 ♘d2 ♕xb2 21 ♖ab1 ♕c2 22 ♖fc1 ♕d3 23 ♘f3 ♖ac8 and a draw was agreed in De la Paz-Y. Gonzalez, Santa Clara 2004.

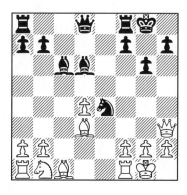

13...♗b4

Apart from 13...♘g5 (see the next game) Black has a couple of enticing alternatives:

a) 13...♖c8?! is punished by 14 ♗xe4! (less strong is 14 ♗h6 ♖e8 15 ♘d2 ♗d7 16 ♕f3 ♕h4 17 g3 ♘xd2 18 ♗xd2 ♕xd4 19 ♗c3 ♕g4 20 ♕xg4?! [20 ♕f6 ♖xc3 21 ♕xc3 ♗c6 22 f3! could give White a slight edge; it is not easy to tell, but not too relevant either] 20...♗xg4 with a draw, Ivanchuk-Yusupov, Linares 1993) 14...♗xe4 15 ♘c3 ♖e8 (or 15...♗f5 16 ♕f3 ♕h4 17 g3 ♕xd4 18 ♖d1 ♕c5 19 ♗e3 ♕c6 20 ♘d5 with some advantage) 16 ♗e3 (also strong is 16 ♗g5!? ♖xc3 17 ♕h4! ♖h3 18 ♗xd8 ♗xh2+ 19 ♔h1 ♖xh4 20 ♗xh4 ♗d6 21 ♗g5 with good winning chances) 16...♗f5 17 ♕f3 ♗b8 18 ♖fe1 b5 19 g4 (Timman-Yusupov, Linares 1993) and now following 19...b4 20 gxf5 bxc3 21 bxc3 ♖xc3 22 ♖ac1 ♖xc1 23 ♖xc1 White simply has an extra pawn.

b) 13...♕b6?! is probably not particularly good: 14 ♘c3 ♕xd4 15 ♗xe4 ♗xe4 16 ♕h4 f5 17 ♗h6 ♖fe8?! (17...♖f7, with a slightly worse position, is a better option) 18 ♖ad1 (18 ♘b5!? might offer a slight edge) 18...♕c5 19 ♘xe4 ♖xe4 20 ♕f6 ♗e5. Now the game Palac-Marciano, Cannes 1998 continued 21 ♕e6+? ♔h8 22 ♕d7 and here Black is fine after 22...♕c6 23 b3 ♖e8. However, 21 ♖d8+ ♖xd8 22 ♕xd8+ ♔f7 23 ♕d7+ ♕e7 24 ♕d5+ ♕e6 25 ♕xb7+ ♕e7 26 ♕d5+ ♕e6 27 ♕a8 would have given Palac a large advantage.

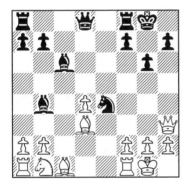

14 ♗e3 ♖e8 15 a3 ♗a5

15...♕a5?? is punished by 16 axb4 ♕xa1 17 b5 ♗d5 18 ♘c3, when Black must resign.

16 ♖c1 ♖c8

16...h5?! is weaker: 17 ♘c3 ♗d7 18 ♕f3 ♗g4 19 ♕f4 ♗xc3 (Svidler-Anand, Dortmund 1998) and here White can play 20 bxc3 g5 21 ♕xe4 ♖xe4 22 ♗xe4 f5 23 ♗xb7 ♖b8 24 ♖ab1 f4 25 ♗d2 with an edge (Anand).

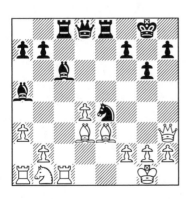

17 ♕h6

17 ♗xe4 ♗xe4 18 ♘c3 ♗xc3 19 ♖xc3 ♖xc3 20 bxc3 ♕c8 21 ♕xc8 ♖xc8 22 ♗d2 ♗d5 was not particularly testing in Sadvakasov-Kasimdzhanov, Lausanne 1999.

17...♗b6 18 ♘c3 ♗xf2!

This seems to be the best option. Yusupov does not believe in Black's position after 18...♗xd4?! 19 ♗xe4 ♗xe4 20 ♖d1 ♗xe3 21 ♕xe3 ♕b6 22 ♕xb6 axb6 23 ♖d4, and we follow our guru all the way here.

19 ♗xf2 ♗xd4 20 ♖d1

The strongest move. After 20 ♘d1?? ♖e1+ 21 ♗f1 ♗b5 22 ♘c3 ♗xf2+ 23 ♔xf2 ♕f6+! Black has a decisive attack, while 20 ♕h3?! ♗xf2+ 21 ♔xf2 ♕d4+ 22 ♔f1 ♗d7 23 ♕f3 ♖e3 is also unappealing.

20...♗xf2+ 21 ♔xf2 ♕b6+ 22 ♔f1

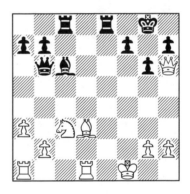

22...♕xb2

22...♖e6!? is another attractive possibility: 23 ♕h4 ♖f6+ 24 ♕xf6 (24 ♔e1 is met by the convincing 24...♗a4! when White is in trouble, e.g. 25 ♘xa4? ♕g1+ 26 ♔d2 ♕xg2+ 27 ♗e2 ♖d6+ with mate to follow) 24...♗xg2+ 25 ♔xg2 ♕xf6 26 ♗e4 with a murky position.

23 ♕d2

Possible is 23 ♘e2 ♖cd8!? (23...♗xg2+ 24 ♔xg2 ♖xe2+ 25 ♔h1 ♖e7 26 ♗c4 favours White) 24 ♖ab1 ♕e5 25 ♕h3 ♕f6+ 26 ♔g1 ♕e5 when it's unclear whether Black is worse here – for one thing ...♖xd3 is a threat.

23...♕xc3 ½-½

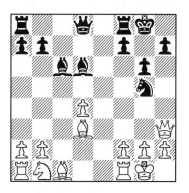

Game 47
Macieja-Rozentalis
Reno 1999

1 e4 e5 2 ♘f3 ♘f6 3 d4 ♘xe4 4 ♗d3 d5
5 ♘xe5 ♘d7 6 ♘xd7 ♗xd7 7 0-0 ♗d6 8
c4 c6 9 cxd5 cxd5 10 ♕h5 0-0 11 ♕xd5
♗c6 12 ♕h5 g6 13 ♕h3 ♘g5!

Time has shown that this is Black's best
path, after which he seems to be able to
count on equality.

14 ♗xg5

Alternatively:

a) 14 ♕h6 ♗e7 15 ♗e3 ♘e6 16 ♘c3 ♗f6
17 ♖ad1 ♗xd4 18 ♗xd4 ♘xd4 19 ♘e4
♗xe4 20 ♗xe4 ♕b6 21 ♖d2 ♖ad8 22 ♖fd1
♖d7 is equal, Mikhalchishin-Pavasovic, Celje
2003. More critical is 18 ♗e4!? ♗xe3 19
♕xe3 ♕b6 20 ♗xc6 bxc6; this could be a
tiny advantage for White.

b) 14 ♕g4 is White's main alternative. After 14...♘e6 there are three options:

b1) 15 ♗e3 h5 16 ♕h3 ♗d7 17 ♕f3 ♗c6
(Black has equalised but now White goes
crazy) 18 ♕d1? ♕h4 19 h3? (although 19 g3
♕h3 20 f3 h4 is great for Black anyway)
19...♘g5 20 d5 ♘xh3+! 21 gxh3 ♕xh3 22
♖e1 ♗h2+ 23 ♔h1 ♗d5+ 24 f3 ♗f4+ 25
♔g1 ♗xf3 0-1 Lautier-Gelfand, FIDE
World Championship, Las Vegas 1999.

b2) 15 ♘c3 h5 16 ♕h3 ♘xd4 looks fine
for Black, for example 17 ♘e4 ♘e2+ 18

♗xe2 ♗xe4 19 ♗h6 ♖e8 20 ♗b5 ♖e5 21
♗d3 ♗c6 22 ♖ae1 ♖xe1 23 ♖xe1 ♕f6 with
equal chances, Blehm-Ribshtein, Patras 1999.

b3) 15 ♗h6

with a further branch:

b31) 15...♗f4!? is an interesting option.
Black's point is that after 16 ♗xf8 ♕xd4 17
♕h3 ♘g5 (17...♕xb2 18 ♘a3 ♖xf8 19 ♗c4
♘g5 20 ♕g4 ♕e5 is unclear) 18 ♕h4 ♕xd3
19 ♕xf4 ♗xg2 20 ♔xg2 ♕h3+ 21 ♔g1
♘f3+ 22 ♕xf3 ♕xf3 White has some problems. Instead Holzke-Schandorff, Bundesliga
2001 continued 16 ♗xf4 ♕xd4 17 ♘c3
♕xf4 18 ♕xf4 ♘xf4 ½-½.

b32) 15...♖e8 16 ♘c3 with a final split:

b321) 16...♘xd4 17 ♖ad1 ♗e5 18 f4 f5 19
♕h3 (19 ♗xf5?! ♕b6 20 ♗xg6 ♘f5+ 21 ♖f2
♘xh6 22 ♕g5 ♗f6! 23 ♕xh6 hxg6 24 ♕xg6+
♗g7 and White has nowhere near enough for
the piece – Van der Sterren) 19...♗f6 20 ♗g5
♗xg5 21 ♗c4+ ♔h8 22 fxg5 ♕b6 23 ♔h1
♕xb2 24 ♖xd4 ♖e3! 25 ♘d1 ♕xd4 26 ♘xe3
♖e8 27 ♕h6! ♕xe3 28 ♗xf5! with an equal
position, Nijboer-Van der Sterren, Rotterdam
1999. The main point is 28...♕c1+ 29 ♖f1
♕xc4 30 ♖f8+ ♖xf8 31 ♕xf8+ ♕g8 32
♕f6+ ♕g7 33 ♕d8+ with a draw.

b322) Black can also try 16...♗f4 17 ♗xf4
♕xd4 18 ♗e4 f5 (or 18...♘xf4 19 ♕xf4 ♗xe4
20 ♖fe1 ♗b1! 21 ♕c1 ♗f5 22 ♕d1 ♕xd1 23
♖exd1 ♖ad8 24 f3 ♔g7 ½-½ Bologan-
Onischuk, Biel 1999) 19 ♕d1 (19 ♗xf5 leads
to a draw after 19...♘xf4 20 ♖ad1 ♕e5 21 g3

♕xf5 22 ♕xf5 gxf5 23 gxf4 ♔f7 – Kasparov)
19...♕xd1 20 ♖fxd1 fxe4 21 ♗e3 ♔f7 22 b4
b6 23 a4 and White has a bit of pressure, Kas-
parov-Piket, Wijk aan Zee 1999.

14...♕xg5 15 ♘c3 ♖ae8

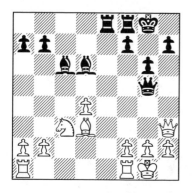

Black has a reasonable alternative in
15...♖fe8, after which 16 ♖ad1 is probably
best. 16 d5!? has been played a few times, for
example 16...♗xd5 17 f4 ♕d8 (17...♕f6!? 18
♘xd5 ♕d4+ 19 ♔h1 ♕xd5 20 ♖ad1 ♕xa2
21 f5!? is very unclear – Van der Wiel) 18
♘xd5 ♗c5+ 19 ♔h1 ♕xd5 20 ♖ac1 (Shirov-
Kramnik, 4th matchgame, Cazorla 1998) and
here Black equalises after 20...♖e3 21 ♗c4
♕d4. The point is that following 22 ♗xf7+?!
♔g7 23 ♖f3?! ♔xf7 24 ♖xe3 ♕xe3 25
♕xh7+ ♔f6 Black should win.

**16 ♖ad1 ♖e7 17 d5 ♗d7 18 ♘e4 ♖xe4
19 ♕xd7 ♖d8**

Another plan is 19...♕e7 20 ♕xe7 ♖xe7
21 g3 ♖d8 with an ending that should be
drawn, Luther-Delchev, Nova Gorica 2000.

20 ♕xb7

Black is fine after 20 ♕xd8+ ♕xd8 21
♗xe4 ♕h4! 22 f4 ♗xf4 23 ♖xf4 ♕xf4 24 d6
♕g4! 25 ♗f3 ♕d7 26 ♔h1 ♔f8 27 ♗xb7
♔e8 – the king acts as a blockader of the
passed d-pawn. Instead of 21...♕h4, the game
Luther-Alterman, Recklinghausen 1998 continued 21...♕f6 22 g3 ♕xb2 23 ♖b1 ♕d4 24
♗f3 b6 25 ♖bc1 ♗c5 when we prefer White,
even though the players agreed a draw.

20...♗xh2+

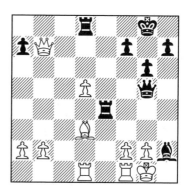

This sacrifice leads to a draw. Or at least it
should...

21 ♔xh2 ♖h4+ 22 ♔g1 ♕h6 23 g3

23 f3 ♕e3+ 24 ♔f2 ♕h6 25 ♔f1 ♕e3 26
♔g1 is quite a cute draw.

23...♖h1+ 24 ♔g2 ♖h2+ 25 ♔f3!?

White wants to win, but maybe this is not
in the cards. Safer is 25 ♔g1 ♖h1+ with a
draw by perpetual check.

25...♖e8!

Cutting off the king.

26 ♕d7?

After this mistake Black wins with a sensa-
tional attack. White should play 26 ♗e4! f5
27 ♔e2! ♕h5+ 28 ♔d2 fxe4 29 ♔c1 ♕f5! 30
g4! (30 d6? ♖c8+ 31 ♔b1 e3+ 32 ♔a1 e2 is
winning for Black) 30...♕f4+! 31 ♔b1 ♖b8
32 ♕e7 e3! with a very complicated position
(Macieja/Rozentalis).

26...♕h5+ 27 ♕g4 ♖xf2+!

Macieja must have either missed or mis-evaluated this sacrifice.

28 ☖xf2 ♕xd5+ 29 ☗f4 ♕d4+ 30 ☗g5

30 ☗f3 ☖e3+ is winning for Black.

30...♕xf2!

No perpetual – Black is winning!

31 ♕f4

White cannot escape, for example 31 ☗h4 ☖e5 32 ♕c8+ ☗g7 33 ♕c3 f6 34 ♕c7+ ☗h6 and there is no defence; or 31 ☗h6 ♕f6 32 ♕f4 ☖e5!!, winning instantly.

31...♕c5+ 32 ♗f5 ♕e7+ 33 ☗h6

Or 33 ☗g4 ♕e2+ and Black wins.

33...f6 34 ♗xg6 ♕g7+ 0-1

Game 48
Shirov-Kramnik
Belgrade 1997

---

1 e4 e5 2 ♘f3 ♘f6 3 d4 ♘xe4 4 ♗d3 d5 5 ♘xe5 ♘d7 6 ♘xd7 ♗xd7 7 0-0 ♗d6 8 ♘c3!?

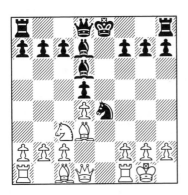

This move has been popularised by Shirov. 8 ♕h5 has also been tested:

a) 8...c6 9 ☖e1 0-0 10 ♗xe4 dxe4 11 ☖xe4 ☖e8 12 ☖xe8+ (not 12 ♘d2?! ♕f6 13 ♕e2 c5 14 c3 cxd4 15 cxd4 ☖ac8 when Black's development ensures him of an initiative) 12...♕xe8 13 ♗e3 ♕e4 14 ♕d1 ♗g4 15 ♕c1 ♗f5 16 c4 ♕h4 17 g3 ♕h5 and Black has good compensation for the pawn, Xie Jun-Karpov, Buenos Aires 2001.

b) 8...♘f6 and now:

b1) 9 ♕h4 ♗e6 (or 9...♘e4 10 ♕xd8+ ☖xd8 11 f3 – 11 ☖e1 0-0 12 ♗xe4 dxe4 13 ☖xe4 ☖fe8 14 ☖xe8+ ☖xe8 15 ♗e3 ♗f4 is equal – 11...♘f6 12 ♗g5 c6 13 ♘c3 ♗f8 14 ☖ae1 h6 15 ♗xf6 gxf6 16 ♘d1 ♗g7 and it is not clear whether White has any advantage at all, Tiviakov-P.Nielsen, Bergen 2000) 10 ♘c3 ♗e7 11 ☖e1 (11 ♕g3 0-0 12 ♘b5 ♘e8 13 ♗f4 c6 14 ♘c7 ♘xc7 15 ♗xc7 ♕d7 is level – Tiviakov) 11...♕d7 12 ♗f1 a6 13 f3 ♘e4 14 ♕h5 g6 15 ♕h6 ♗f8 16 ♕h4 ♗e7 17 ♕h6 ♗f8 ½-½ Tiviakov-Leko, Wijk aan Zee 2001.

b2) 9 ☖e1+ is a worthy alternative.

9...♗f8 10 ♕e2 (10 ♕h4 is harmless due to 10...♘g4! 11 ♕xd8+ ☖xd8 with equality: 12 h3 ♘f6 13 ♘d2 g6 14 ♘f3 ♗g7 15 ♘e5 ♗c8 16 ♗g5 h6 17 ♗f4 g5 18 ♗h2 ☖he8 19 ☖e2 ♘g8 20 ☖ae1 f6 21 ♘f3 ½-½ Movsesian-Akopian, FIDE World Championship, Las Vegas 1999) 10...c6 11 ♘d2 ♕c7 12 ♘f3 ♗g4 13 ♕e3 ♗xf3 14 ♕xf3 ♗xh2+ 15 ☗f1 ♗d6 16 ♗g5 ♕d8 17 ☖e2 (an improvement over 17 ☖e3?! ♘e4! 18 ♗xe4 ♕xg5 19 ♗d3 g6 20 ☖ae1 ☗g7 21 ♕h3 ☖ad8 22 c3 h5 and White didn't have quite enough for his pawn, Sutovsky-David, Istanbul 2003) 17...h6 18 ♗h4 g5 19 ♗g3 with chances for both sides. However, we cannot see how Black can ever be worse here.

8...♘xc3

8...♕h4 has also been tried, e.g. 9 g3 ♘xc3 10 bxc3 ♕g4 (10...♕h3 11 ☖e1+ ☗f8 12 ♕f3 c6 13 ♗f4 ♗e7 14 ♖ab1 b6 15 c4 favours White) 11 ♖e1+ ♔d8 (11...♔f8 12 ♗e2 ♕f5 13 ♖b1 ♖b8 14 c4 dxc4 15 ♗xc4 h5 16 h4 is also a bit better for White) 12 ♗e2 ♕f5 13 ♖b1 b6 14 c4 dxc4 15 ♗xc4 ♖e8 16 ♗e3 ♗c6 17 d5 ♗d7 18 ♗f1 h6 19 c4 with a slight plus for White, Kamsky-Karpov, FIDE World Championship (Game 6), Elista 1996.

9 bxc3 0-0

A recent game in this line continued 9...♗e6 10 ♖b1 ♖b8 11 ♕h5 c6 (11...g6 12 ♕h6 ♔d7 13 ♗g5 ♕f8 14 ♕h4 h6 15 ♗f6 ♗e7 16 ♖fe1 looks slightly better for White) 12 ♗g5 ♗e7 13 ♗xe7 ♕xe7 14 f4 ♕f6 15 ♖be1 ♔d8 16 g4 g6 17 ♕h6

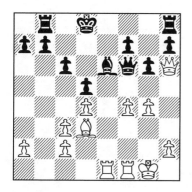

and now:

a) 17...♔c7?! 18 f5 ♗d7 19 fxg6 ♕d6 20 ♖xf7 hxg6 21 ♕f4 ♕xf4 22 ♖xf4 and White eventually converted his pawn in Shirov-Bologan, Sarajevo 2004.

b) Shirov described the position after 17 ♕h6 as the most fascinating he had ever analysed. The following variation is a summery of several page of his analysis: 17...♗xg4 18 f5! ♔d7 19 h3 ♗h5 20 fxg6 ♗f3! 21 ♖e5! hxg6 22 ♕f5! ♕xf5 23 ♗xf5+ gxf5 24 ♕f6 ♖bg8+ 25 ♔f2 ♗e4 26 ♕xf7+ ♔c8 27 ♕e6+ ♔c7 28 ♕e7+ ♔c8 29 h4 and White is a bit better.

10 ♕h5 f5 11 ♖b1

11 ♖e1 is interesting: 11...♕f6 12 ♕f3 ♔h8 13 ♖b1 b6 14 ♗f4 (or 14 ♕xd5 ♗c6 15

♕b3 ♖ad8 16 ♗d2 ♕g6 with compensation – Mikhalchishin) 14...♖ae8 15 ♖xe8 ♗xe8 16 ♖e1 ♗h5 17 ♕g3 (17 ♕xh5 ♗xf4 18 ♕xf5 ♕xf5 19 ♗xf5 ♗d2 is drawing) 17...♖e8 18 ♖xe8+ ♗xe8 19 ♗xd6 cxd6 20 ♕f3 g6 21 ♕xd5 ♕e7 and Black has play for the pawn, Pavlovic-Mikhalchishin, Lenk 1999.

11...b6

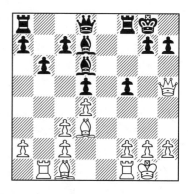

12 ♕f3

Again White has other options:

a) 12 c4 dxc4 13 ♗xc4+ ♔h8 14 ♗g5 ♕e8 15 ♕h4 ♕g6 16 ♗d3 ♖ae8 17 c4 h6 18 ♗e3 ♕f7 was level in Palac-Fridman, Pula 1997.

b) 12 ♖e1 c6 (this is even better than 12...♕f6 13 ♕f3 c6 14 ♗f4 b5 15 ♕g3 ♗xf4 16 ♕xf4 ♖f7 17 ♔f1 ♖af8 18 ♖e2 ♕d8 19 ♖be1 ♕b8 when Black is close to equality, Shirov-Anand, Groningen 1997) 13 ♗g5 ♕c7 14 c4 ♗e8 15 ♕h3 dxc4 16 ♗xc4+ (16 ♗xf5 ♗xh2+ 17 ♔h1 ♖xf5 18 ♕xf5 ♗d6 gives Black sufficient compensation – Salov) 16...♗f7 17 ♗e6 ♗xe6 18 ♖xe6 ♖ae8 with level prospects, Shirov-Kramnik, 2nd match-game, Cazorla 1998.

12...c6 13 ♗f4 ♕c7 14 ♗xd6 ♕xd6 15 ♖fe1 ♖ae8

Black has completely equalised. In fact, it is White who should be careful. For example, 16 c4 ♖xe1+ 17 ♖xe1 ♕b4 and White is already starting to encounter problems.

16 ♖xe8 ♖xe8 17 c4 ♕a3! 18 h4?!

After this move Black is probably slightly

better. Possibly stronger is 18 ♕f4 ♕xa2 19 ♕c1 ♕a5 20 c3 b5 21 ♖a1 ♕c7 22 cxd5 cxd5 23 ♕c2 g6 24 ♕b3 ♗c6 25 ♕b4 when White has good compensation for the pawn.

18...♕xa2 19 ♖f1 dxc4 20 ♗xf5 ♗xf5 21 ♕xf5 c3

21...a5 22 ♕d7 ♖f8 23 ♖e1 gives White enough compensation. One point is that after 23...♕xc2 24 ♕e6+ Black must acquiesce to a draw as 24...♔h8?? 25 ♕f7! ♖g8 26 ♖e8 wins for White.

22 ♕d3 ♕d5 23 ♕xc3 ♖e4 24 ♕g3 ♖xd4 25 ♕b8+ ♕d8 26 ♕xa7 h6

26...♖xh4 27 ♕b7 ♕d6 28 ♕c8+ ♔f7 29 ♕f5+ is also a draw, but Kramnik could have continued playing for a win with 26...♖c4 27 ♕b7 h5 28 ♖a1 ♔h7. Note, however, that 27...♖xc2?? is out of the question due to 28 ♖a1.

27 ♕a2+ ♔h8 28 g3 b5 29 ♕e6 ♕d5 30 ♕xd5 ♖xd5 31 ♖a1 ♖c5 32 ♖a2 ♔h7 33 ♔f1 ½-½

Game 49
Anand-Ivanchuk
Linares 1993

---

1 e4 e5 2 ♘f3 ♘f6 3 d4 ♘xe4 4 ♗d3 d5 5 ♘xe5 ♘d7 6 ♘xd7 ♗xd7 7 0-0 ♕h4

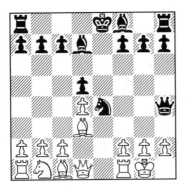

This is the 'active' main line.

8 c4

This is the principal move. The alternatives fail to impress:

a) 8 ♘d2 ♘xd2 9 ♕xd2 ♗d6 (not 9...♕xd4?! 10 ♖e1+ ♗e7 11 ♕a5!? b6 12 ♕a6 with compensation – Yusupov) 10 ♕e2+ (after 10 ♖e1+? ♔f8! Black wins a pawn, 11 f4? losing to 11...♗xf4!) 10...♗e6 11 f4 0-0 12 g3 ♕f6 13 f5 ♗d7 14 ♗e3 ♖fe8 and Black is no worse.

b) 8 ♘c3 is also not very strong: 8...♘xc3 9 bxc3 0-0-0 10 ♕f3 ♗e6 11 ♗f4 (what else?) 11...♗g4 12 ♕e3 ♗d6 13 ♗xd6 ♖xd6 14 ♖ae1 ♗d7 15 ♕f3 ♕f6 16 ♕g3 (or 16 ♕xf6 ♖xf6 17 c4 dxc4 18 ♗xc4 ♗f5 19 ♗b3 ♖d8 20 d5 c6 with a likely draw) 16...♖c6 17 ♖e5!? ♖xc3 18 ♖xd5 ♗e6 19 ♖g5 g6 20 d5 ♗d7 21 ♕e3 ♖a3 with unclear play, Klovans-Raetsky, Apolda, 1994.

c) 8 g3

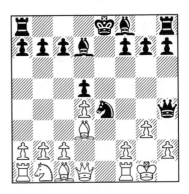

and now:

c1) 8...♕h3? looks natural but White can play 9 f3 ♘d6 (9...♘f6?! is even worse after 10 ♖e1+ ♗e6 11 ♖e5! g5 12 ♗f5 g4 13 ♗g5 ♗e7 14 ♘c3!, when Black is in trouble, Pavlovic-Konguvel, Benasque 1998) 10 ♖e1+ ♗e7 11 ♖e5 ♗c6 12 g4 ♕h4 13 ♗g5, winning the queen for insufficient compensation.

c2) 8...♕f6! 9 ♘xe4 dxe4 10 ♘c3 ♕g6 11 ♘xe4 0-0-0 12 ♖e1 h5 and the weakening of the light squares guarantees Black compensation for the pawn.

8...0-0-0

Other moves are weaker:

a) 8...♗d6 9 g3 ♕h3 10 ♘c3 ♘xc3 11

---

bxc3 dxc4 12 ♖e1+ ♔f8 13 ♗xc4 ♗g4 14 ♕d3 should favour White.

b) 8...♘f6 can be met by 9 ♘d2!?, for example 9...♕xd4 10 ♘f3 ♕b6 11 cxd5 ♗e7 (11...♘xd5 12 ♘g5! h6 13 ♘xf7 ♔xf7 14 ♕h5+ ♔g8 15 ♕xd5+ ♗e6 16 ♕e4 is great for White) 12 ♖e1 ♕d6 (12...♘xd5 13 ♗c4 c6 14 ♗g5 gives White a very strong attack) 13 ♗g5 h6 14 ♗h4 ♕xd5 15 ♖c1 ♗c6 16 ♕e2 ♕d8? (Z.Almasi-Cs.Horvath, Hungary 1997) and now 17 ♖xc6! bxc6 18 ♗xf6 gxf6 19 ♘d4 is a nice win. 16...♕e6 is stronger, but Black's position is still unenviable.

9 c5

9 cxd5 is less critical. Black continues 9...♗d6 10 g3 (10 h3? ♗xh3! is simply too dangerous!) 10...♘xg3! 11 fxg3 ♗xg3 12 ♕c2 ♕xd4+ 13 ♔g2 ♗xh2 14 ♔xh2 ♕h4+ 15 ♔g1 ♕g3+ 16 ♕g2 ♕xd3 with great counterplay for the piece.

9 ♘c3 is also not to be feared.

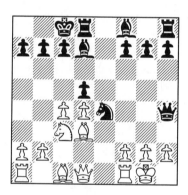

Black can play the following:

a) 9...♘f6 10 c5 ♗e7 11 ♗e3 ♘g4 12 ♗f4 looks good for White.

b) 9...♗d6 10 g3 ♘xg3!? 11 fxg3 ♗xg3 12 ♕d2 ♕xd4+ 13 ♕e3 ♗xh2+ 14 ♔xh2 ♕h4+ 15 ♔g1 ♕g4+ 16 ♔f2 d4 17 ♕g3 dxc3 18 bxc3 ♗e6 is equal according to Yusupov and Hübner, but 10 f4 may be better for White.

c) 9...♘xc3 (the easiest) 10 bxc3 dxc4 11 ♗xc4 ♗d6 12 f4 f6 13 ♗d5 c6 14 g3 ♕g4 15 ♗f3 ♕g6!? (but not 15...♕e6 16 ♕a4 a6 17 ♖b1 h5 18 ♗d2 ♕f5 19 ♖b2 and White had

the attack in Rublevsky-Nguen Anh Dung, Moscow 2001) 16 ♖f2 h5 17 ♖b2 h4 with reasonable counterplay.

9...g5 10 ♘c3

Other options will be discussed in Games 51-52.

10...♗g7

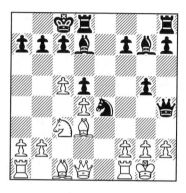

The best reply. The alternatives have not been successful:

a) 10...♘f6?! 11 g3!? ♕h3 (11...♕xd4?! 12 c6! is a well-known trick) 12 ♕f3 ♘g4 13 ♕g2 ♕xg2+ 14 ♔xg2 h6 15 f4! ♗g7 (or 15...♖e8 16 fxg5 hxg5 17 h3 ♘e3+ 18 ♗xe3 ♖xe3 19 ♗f5 with a clear edge) 16 h3 ♘f6 17 fxg5 hxg5 18 g4 and White has a clear advantage, Tseshkovsky-Gagloshvili, Krasnodar 1997.

b) 10...f5?! 11 ♘xd5 and now:

b1) 11...♗xf2!? 12 ♖xf2 ♕xd4 13 ♗xg5 (we think that White should play 13 c6!? ♕xd5 14 cxd7+ ♖xd7 15 ♖d2 ♗b4 16 ♗c4 ♕c5+ 17 ♔h1 ♗xd2 18 ♗e6 with a clear edge) 13...♗xc5 14 ♘e3 (14 ♕f3!? ♗c6 15 ♗xd8 ♖xd8 16 ♗xf5+ ♔b8 17 ♖d1 ♕xf2+ 18 ♕xf2 ♗xf2+ 19 ♔xf2 ♗xd5 20 ♗xh7 looks great for White) 14...f4 15 ♗xf4 ♖hf8 16 ♕f1 ♗xe3 17 ♗xe3 ♗xe3 18 ♕e2 ♗xf2+ 19 ♔h1 ♖de8 20 ♕c2 and White had decent chances to win the endgame, Wedberg-Schneider, Torshavn, 1987. Even so, White should punish Black further with deviations on move 13 or 14.

b2) 11...♗e6 also does not work after 12

♘c3 ♖xd4 (or 12...♗g7 13 g3 ♕h6 14 ♘xe4 fxe4 15 ♗xe4 ♖xd4 16 ♕f3 and Black is in trouble) 13 ♗e3 ♖d8 14 ♕c2 ♘xc5 15 ♗xf5 ♗d6 16 g3 ♕c4 17 ♗xg5 ♖df8 18 ♗xe6+ ♘xe6 19 ♗e3 and Black is simply a pawn down, Glek-Raetsky, Zell am Ziller 1993.

11 g3

This is the most critical line for Black. Other options are featured in the next game.

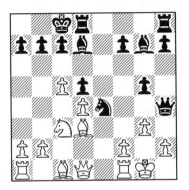

11...♕h3

Another possibility is 11...♕h6!? 12 ♘xe4 (12 ♘xd5?! ♖he8 13 ♘c3 ♘xf2! 14 ♖xf2 ♗xd4 with a clear edge for Black – Yusupov) 12...dxe4 13 ♗xe4

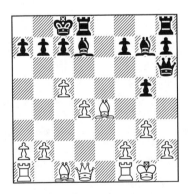

and here Black has two choices:

a) 13...♗h3 14 ♕f3!? ♗xf1 15 ♗xb7+ ♔b8 16 ♗xg5!? (16 ♔xf1 ♗xd4 17 h4 ♕e6 18 ♗xg5 f6 19 ♗f4 is very messy) 16...♕xg5 17 ♕b3 ♗c4 18 ♕b4 a5 19 ♕xa5 c6 (19...♔xb7 20 c6+ ♔b8 21 ♕xg5 ♗xd4 also

unclear) 20 ♕b6 ♕e7 21 ♗a6+ ♔a8 22 ♕xc6+ ♔b8 23 ♕b6+ ♔a8 and now taking the draw by perpetual check with 24 ♕c6+ might make sense as after 24 ♗xc4 24...♕b7 the game could go either way.

b) 13...f5 14 ♗g2 with a further branch:

b1) 14...♗c6 15 ♗xc6 (15 d5 ♗xd5 16 ♗xd5 c6 17 ♕a4 ♖xd5 18 ♕xa7 f4 is unclear according to Vladimirov – White has problems developing) 15...♕xc6 16 ♗xg5 ♖xd4 17 ♕c2 ♖d5 18 ♗e3 gave White some advantage in Macieja-Stefanova, Krynica 1998.

b2) 14...f4 15 d5 (after 15 gxf4 gxf4 16 ♕f3 ♗c6 17 ♕g4+ ♔b8 18 d5 – 18 ♗xf4? ♖xd4! would be a nasty surprise – 18...♗xd5 19 ♗xf4 ♕f6 Black has excellent compensation for the pawn) 15...♖hf8 16 ♖e1 ♔b8 17 d6 cxd6 (Arencibia-Vladimirov, Leon 1991) and now after 18 ♕xd6+ ♕xd6 19 cxd6 ♗d4 20 gxf4 gxf4 21 ♖e4 ♖de8 Black can be happy with his counterplay.

12 ♘xe4

The older line is 12 ♘xd5 ♖he8 (12...♗g4? 13 ♗xe4! ♗xd1 14 ♗f5+! and White wins – H.Olafsson) 13 ♕f3 (13 ♗xe4? ♖xe4 14 ♗xg5 ♗c6! 15 ♗xd8 ♗xd5 16 f3 ♖xd4 17 ♕c1 ♖d3 gives Black a decisive attack) 13...♗f5 14 ♘e3 (14 ♘c3?! ♖xd4 15 ♖e1 – or 15 ♗xe4?! ♖dxe4 16 ♗xg5 ♗xc3 17 bxc3 ♖e2 and Black has all the threats – 15...♗g4! 16 ♕xf7 ♖f8 17 ♕xf8+ ♗xf8 18 ♗f1 ♕h5 19 ♘xe4 ♗f5 and Black's material gains give him the advantage) 14...♗g6

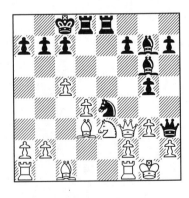

and now:

a) 15 c6 is risky: 15...♖xd4 16 ♗e2 h5 17 cxb7+ ♔b8 18 ♖e1 ♕d7 19 ♘f1 g4 20 ♕g2 ♘c5 21 ♗e3 ♗e4 22 f3 ♗xb7 and it was Black who had the attack, Smagin-H.Olafsson, Sochi 1988.

b) 15 d5 ♘d2 (also good is 15...♘xc5!? 16 ♗f5+ ♗xf5 17 ♘xf5 ♗f6, with chances for both sides) 16 ♗xd2 ♗xd3 17 ♕xf7 ♗xb2 (17...♗xf1? 18 ♕xg7 ♖xe3 19 ♖xf1 ♖d3 20 ♗xg5 is better for White) 18 d6 ♕d7 19 ♕b3 ♕b5 with unclear play, Ioseliani-Howell, Spijknisse 1989.

12...dxe4 13 ♗xe4 ♗b5 14 ♗g2!

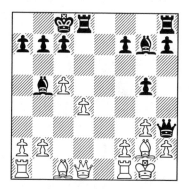

Anand's improvement over a previous game against Ivanchuk, albeit with colours reversed. With 14 ♗g2 White obvious does not worry about losing the exchange; the attack is much more important, and Black has no way to force exchanges.

The alternative is 14 ♗xg5 ♖xd4 and now:

a) 15 ♕b3 ♖xe4 16 ♕xb5 h6 17 ♗e3 ♖h4! 18 ♖fd1 ♕xh2+ 19 ♔f1 ♕h3+ 20 ♔e1 ♖e4 (20...♖h5 21 ♕a4 a6 22 c6 ♔b8 is unclear) 21 c6 ♖xe3+ 22 fxe3 ♕xg3+ 23 ♔e2 ♕g2+ 24 ♔e1 ♕g3+ ½-½ Dolmatov-Akopian 1988.

b) 15 ♗g2 ♕f5 (or 15...♕e6 16 ♕f3 ♗c6 17 ♕b3 ♗xg2 18 ♔xg2 ♕d5+ 19 ♕xd5 ♖xd5 20 ♗e3 ♗xb2 21 ♖ab1 ♗g7 and Black is only very slightly worse) 16 ♕b3 c6 17 ♗e3 ♗xf1 18 ♖xf1 (18 ♗xd4 ♗xd4 19 ♖xf1

♗xc5 is equal – Howell) and here Black must make a choice:

b1) The dubious 18...♖d7?! is met by 19 ♕a4:

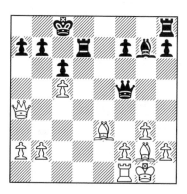

b11) 19...♔b8 20 b4 ♕d3 21 ♗f4+ ♔a8 22 ♗d6 (this looks great for White so Black's reaction is understandable) 22...♖xd6 23 cxd6 ♕xd6 24 b5 cxb5? (24...c5 25 ♕c4 ♕c7 26 ♖c1 with a clear edge – Howell) 25 ♕xb5 ♖b8 26 ♖b1 ♕c7 27 a4 ♗c3 28 ♖c1 ♕e5 29 ♕b3 ♗d4 30 ♗xb7+! 1-0 Geller-J.Howell, Reykjavik 1990.

b12) 19...a6 20 ♗xc6! bxc6 21 ♕xc6+ ♔d8 (21...♗b8?! 22 ♕b6+ ♖b7 23 ♕d6+ ♔c8 24 ♕xa6 ♔b8 25 c6 and White wins; 21...♖c7?! 22 ♕xa6+ ♔b8 23 c6 ♖e8 24 ♖d1 ♕c2 25 ♖d3 ♖xc6 26 ♕a7+ ♔c8 27 ♕d7+ 1-0 Hracek-Haba, Czech Republic 1998) 22 ♖e1 ♕f6 23 ♕a4 ♕xb2 24 c6 ♗c3 25 cxd7 ♗xe1 26 ♕c6 ♗xf2+ 27 ♔xf2 ♕b1+ 28 ♔g2 ♕b2 29 ♔f3 with a clear plus for White – Hracek.

b2) 18...♖hd8! 19 h4 (or 19 ♕a3 ♖d1 20 ♕xa7 ♖xf1+ 21 ♗xf1 ♗e5 22 ♕a8+ ♔c7 23 ♕a5+ with a draw – Yusupov) 19...♗e5 20 ♗xd4 ♗xd4 21 ♔h2 ♔c7 22 ♕c4 ♗xc5 23 b4 ♗b6 24 b5 ♖d4 25 ♕b3 ♖d3 26 ♕c4 ♖d4 and Black escaped with a draw, Ivanchuk-Anand, Roquebrune 1992.

14...♕f5 15 ♗e3

15 ♕b3 c6 16 ♖d1 ♖xd4 17 ♖xd4 ♗xd4 18 ♗e3 is equal – Akopian.

15...♗xf1 16 ♗xf1 ♖he8

16...c6 17 ♕a4 looks good for White: 17...h5?! 18 ♕xa7 ♖xd4 19 ♖e1! ♖d7 (19...♖dd8 20 ♗a6! and wins!) 20 b4 ♕g4 21 b5 and White has a very strong attack.

17 ♕a4 ♔b8 18 ♖d1 c6

18...♖e6 19 d5!? ♖xd5 20 ♗h3! ♕e4 21 ♖xd5 ♕xd5 22 ♗xe6 ♕xe6 23 c6 also assures White of an edge.

19 ♖d3 ♕e4 20 ♖a3 a6 21 ♗d3

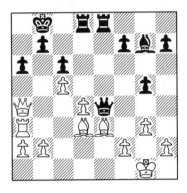

21...♕g4?!

Soon after this game Black's play was repaired to some extent with 21...♕d5 22 ♗xa6 ♗xd4 23 ♗xb7 ♗xc5! 24 ♗xc6 ♕d1+ 25 ♔g2 ♕xa4 26 ♖xa4 ♖xe3 27 fxe3 ♖d2+ 28 ♔f3 ♖xb2 (Hernandez-J.Howell, Matanzas 1993). This position should be within the 'drawing range', although it will take Black some time and technique.

22 ♖b3!

22 ♗xa6?! allows Black back into the

game via 22...♖xd4! 23 ♗xd4 ♕xd4 24 ♕b3 ♖e7 25 ♗f1 ♕xc5, with chances for both sides.

22...♗xd4?

More resilient is 22...♖e7 23 ♖b4!? f5 24 d5 f4 25 d6 ♖ed7 26 ♗xa6, when Black is still just about breathing.

23 ♖xb7+! ♔xb7 24 ♕xa6+ ♔b8 25 ♕b6+ ♔a8 26 ♕xc6+ ♔b8 27 ♕b6+ ♔a8 28 ♗b5 1-0

Game 50

J.Howell-Makarychev

Frunze 1989

1 e4 e5 2 ♘f3 ♘f6 3 d4 ♘xe4 4 ♗d3 d5 5 ♘xe5 ♘d7 6 ♘xd7 ♗xd7 7 0-0 ♕h4 8 c4 0-0-0 9 c5 g5 10 ♘c3 ♗g7 11 ♘e2

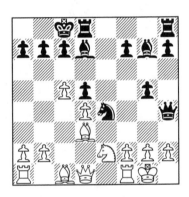

11 ♘xd5 ♗xd4 12 ♗e3 ♗xe3 13 fxe3 does not seem frightening for Black after 13...♗e6 (but not 13...♘xc5?! 14 ♕c2 ♗e6 15 ♘xc7 ♔xc7 16 ♕xc5+ ♔b8 17 ♖ac1 with attacking chances for White) 14 ♘e7+ ♔b8 15 ♘f5 ♗xf5 16 ♖xf5 ♖he8 when Black has good counterplay. 11 ♗e3 allows the trick 11...♘xc5!?, when 12 ♘xd5 ♘xd3 13 ♕xd3 ♔b8 looks equal.

11...♖he8

11...f5 is an attractive alternative. Following 12 f3 Black has a choice:

a) 12...♘f6 13 ♗e3 f4 14 ♗f2 ♕h6 15 ♕d2 ♖he8 16 ♖ac1 ♘g8?! 17 b4 ♘e7 18 b5 (Black has clearly wasted his chance for an attack) 18...♔b8 19 ♘c3 ♘f5 20 c6 ♗c8 21 cxb7 ♔xb7 22 ♗xf5 ♗xf5 23 ♘a4 with a clear plus, Tiviakov-Raetsky, Makhachkala 1987. Instead of 16...♘g8?!, Black needs to act quickly with 16...g4!? 17 ♕xf4 gxf3 18 gxf3 ♗h3 19 ♖fd1 ♘h5 20 ♕xh6 ♗xh6, assuring him of reasonable counterplay.

b) 12...♖hf8

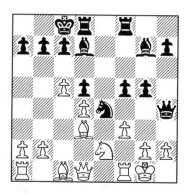

and now it's White who has to make a decision:

b1) 13 fxe4?! (this reckless move hasn't been tried) 13...fxe4 14 ♖xf8 (not 14 ♗c2? ♖xf1+ 15 ♕xf1 ♖f8 and the game is already over) 14...♖xf8 15 ♗e3 exd3 16 ♕xd3 ♖f6 and Black has the advantage.

b2) After 13 ♕e1 Black should exchange with 13...♕xe1. Instead 13...♕h5?! proved futile after 14 fxe4 dxe4 15 ♗c4 f4 16 d5 ♔b8 17 c6 ♗c8 18 cxb7 ♗g4 19 ♘xf4!? gxf4 20 ♗xf4 and White was virtually winning, Mannion-Kobese, Yerevan Olympiad 1996.

b3) 13 a4 ♖de8 with a final split:

b31) 14 g3 ♘xg3!? 15 hxg3 (15 ♘xg3 ♗xd4+ 16 ♔h1 f4 17 ♘e2 ♗h3 gives Black a good attack) 15...♕h3 16 c6! (16 ♖f2?! ♗xd4! 17 ♘xd4 ♕xg3+ 18 ♔f1 f4 is very bad for White) 16...♗xc6 17 ♖f2 ♗xd4 18 ♘xd4 ♕xg3+ 19 ♔f1 ♕h3+ with a draw.

b32) 14 ♕e1 ♕xe1 15 ♖xe1 f4! 16 fxe4 dxe4 17 ♗c4 f3 18 ♗e3 fxe2 19 ♖xe2 c6 20 d5 cxd5 21 ♗xd5 h6 22 ♖d2 ♖d8 with a level ending, Sax-Salov, Brussels 1988.

12 f3 ♘f6 13 ♗d2

13 ♕e1 ♕xe1 14 ♖xe1 h6 15 ♗d2 ♘g8 is equal. Now after 16 ♖ad1?! ♘e7 17 ♗e3 ♘f5 18 ♗f2 ♘e3 19 ♖c1 ♖e7 20 b4 ♖de8 Black was already better in Vidarsson-Raetsky, Hafnarfjordur 1996.

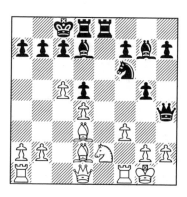

13...♖xe2!

An idea of Akopian's.

14 ♕xe2

14 ♗xe2 is strongly met by 14...♘g4!

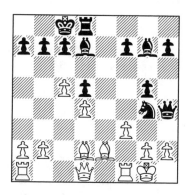

and now:

a) 15 fxg4? ♗xd4+ 16 ♔h1 ♗e5 17 ♗f4 (even worse is 17 h3? ♕g3 18 ♔g1 ♕h2+ 19 ♔f2 ♗g3+! 20 ♔e3 – 20 ♔f3 ♗h4! – 20...♖e8+ 21 ♔d3 ♗b5+ and Black wins) 17...♗xf4 18 ♖xf4 gxf4 19 ♕xd5 ♖e8! 20 ♕d1 ♗c6 21 ♕f1 ♖e3 22 ♖c1 ♕e7 23 ♗f3 ♗xf3 24 gxf3 ♖e2 and Black had an edge in Sherzer-Halasz, Budapest 1990.

b) 15 ♗f4 ♘f2!? 16 ♗g3?! (16 ♗g5 ♘h3+! 17 gxh3 ♕xg5+ 18 ♔h1 ♕f4 with unclear play is stronger) 16...♘xd1 17 ♗xh4 ♗xd4+ 18 ♔h1 ♘e3 (we prefer Black's position after the stronger 18...♘xb2!? 19 ♗xg5 ♖e8) 19 ♗xg5 ♖e8 20 ♗xe3 ♖xe3 21 ♖fe1 ♗xb2 22 ♗f1 ♗d4 with an unclear endgame, Movsesian-Raetsky, Pardubice, 1992.

14...♘h5!?

14...♕xd4+ 15 ♗e3 ♕e5 16 ♕d2 is simply great for White.

15 ♕f2 ♕xf2+ 16 ♔xf2

16 ♖xf2 ♘f4 17 ♗xf4 gxf4 18 c6 ♗e6 19 cxb7+ ♔b8 with unclear play (Yusupov)

is probably a better option.

16...♘f4 17 ♗xf4 gxf4 18 ♖fe1 ♗xd4+ 19 ♔f1 ♗xb2

19...♗xc5 20 ♖e5 ♗e6 21 ♖h5 allows counterplay.

20 ♖ab1 ♗d4

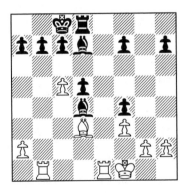

21 ♖e7?!

More resilient is 21 ♖ec1 ♗e3 22 ♖c2

♖e8. Although Black is better, the game is still open.

21...♖f8 22 ♗xh7?!

Now it is all over. 22 c6 bxc6 23 ♖ee1 ♗e6 was the last chance.

22...♗e6 23 ♖e1 ♗e3 24 g4 ♖h8 25 ♗f5 ♔d8 26 ♖xe6 fxe6 27 ♗xe6 ♖xh2 28 ♖d1 ♖h1+ 0-1

White resigned because of 29 ♔e2 ♖xd1 30 ♔xd1 c6 31 g5 ♗xc5.

Game 51
Kasparov-Ivanchuk
Debrecen 1992

---

1 e4 e5 2 ♘f3 ♘f6 3 d4 ♘xe4 4 ♗d3 d5 5 ♘xe5 ♘d7 6 ♘xd7 ♗xd7 7 0-0 ♕h4 8 c4 0-0-0 9 c5 g5

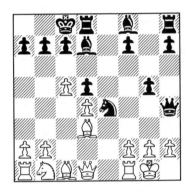

10 ♗e3

White has a couple of alternatives here:

a) 10 g3 ♕h3 11 ♘c3 f5!? 12 ♗e2 ♖g8 13 ♗f3 ♗e8 14 a4 ♕h6 15 ♖a3 ♕f6 16 b4 ♗g7 17 ♘e2 h5 with chances to both sides, Filipovic-Nikcevic, Tivat 1995.

b) 10 ♘d2 ♘xd2 (also possible is 10...♗g7 11 ♘f3 ♕h5 12 ♘e5 ♕xd1 13 ♖xd1 ♗e6 14 ♗c2 f6 15 ♘d3 f5 16 ♘e5 f4 when Black is no worse) 11 ♗xd2 ♖g8 12 ♗c3 (or 12 ♖c1!? ♕xd4 13 ♗c3 ♕h4 14 ♗f6 ♖e8 15 f4 ♗e7 16 c6!? with unclear play, Pinkas-Kuczynski, Wroclaw 1987; one continuation is 16...♗xc6 17 ♗f5+ ♔b8 18 ♖xc6! bxc6 19 ♕b3+ ♔a8 20 ♗d7 ♗c5+ 21

@h1 &b6 22 &xc6+ &b8 23 &xe8 &xe8 with a messy position) 12...g4 13 b4 &b8 14 b5 &f6 15 &d2!? &f5 (15...&xd4 16 &e3 &e5 17 &a4 gives White good compensation) 16 &xf5 &xf5 17 a4 &d3 18 &f4 &xd1 19 &fxd1 &g6 20 a5 &c8 with an complicated struggle, Korneev-Raetsky, Cannes 1994.

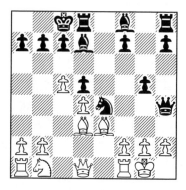

10...&e8

Black should probably look carefully at the alternatives to this:

a) 10...&g7 11 f3 &f6 transposes to 10 f3, while 11...&xc5?! 12 dxc5 &xb2 13 &d2 &xa1 14 &xa1 is fantastic for White.

b) 10...&f6 is certainly a playable alternative: 11 &d2 &g8 (the main point) 12 &f3 &h5 13 &e5 &xd1 14 &axd1 &e6 15 f4 gxf4 16 &xf4 (16 &xf4 &h6 17 &f3 &xe3+ 18 &xe3 &e4 19 &f1, with a slight edge, should be considered) 16...&e4 17 c6 f6 18 cxb7+ &xb7 19 &c4 f5 (I.Gurevich-Barua, Hastings 1993/94). Now White could probably have been slightly better after 20 &e3 &g7 21 &e5 &xe5 22 dxe5 &g5 23 &f4.

c) 10...f5 is also enticing – we see no fault with this move. For example, 11 f3 &f6 (not 11...f4?! 12 fxe4 fxe3 13 g3 &h3 14 e5! h5?! 15 c6! and Black was in deep trouble, Erneste-Goldmane, Riga 1989) 12 &c3 (12 c6 &xc6 13 &xf5+ &d7 14 g3 &h5 15 &xd7+ &xd7 16 &c3 &g7 gives both sides chances) 12...f4 13 &f2

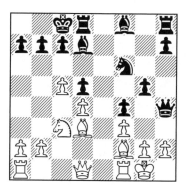

and now:

c1) 13...&h5 14 &b5 &b8 15 &e1!? g4 16 &e5 &xe5 (Black should play 16...&xb5 17 &xh5 &xh5 18 &xb5 gxf3 19 gxf3 &e7 20 &fe1 &f6 with a slightly worse position) 17 dxe5 &h5 18 fxg4 &xg4 (Khait-Raetsky, Lipetsk 1993) and now after 19 c6!? bxc6 20 &d4 &b7 21 &b3 Black's position looks uncomfortable.

c2) 13...&h6!? is stronger: 14 &e1?! g4 (Black now has the initiative) 15 c6 &xc6 16 &f5+ &b8 17 fxg4 &d6 18 &f3 &g7 19 &e2?! (19 &h4 is better, although Black's position remains preferable after 19...&df8 20 g5 &d7) 19...h5 20 gxh5 &xh5 21 &h3 &dh8 22 &f1 &e4 and Black was close to winning in Werner-Raetsky, Cappelle la Grande 1999. Instead of 14 &e1?!, White should play 14 &b5 &b8 15 &d2 g4 16 &a5 &xb5 17 &xb5 (but not 17 &xb5?? gxf3 and Black has a winning attack) 17...c6 18 &a5 &g7 with chances for both sides.

11 &d2 &g7 12 &f3 &h5 13 &xg5

This leads to a slightly dull position, but one that is preferable for Black. 13 &xe4 &xe4 (13...dxe4 14 &xg5 &g6 15 d5 h6 16 c6 is also really messy) 14 &xg5 &g4 15 f4 (15 &f3? &xg2+! 16 &xg2 &h3+ 17 &h1 &g4 and Black wins) 15...h6 16 &f3 &g8 is certainly very unclear.

13...&xd1

13...&g4?! is strongly met by 14 f3 &xg5 15 fxg4 &h6 16 &f5+ &b8 17 &f4 and

White is dominating the board.

14 ♖fxd1 ♘xg5 15 ♗xg5

15...♗g4

15...♗xd4 16 c6 ♗e6 17 cxb7+ ♔xb7 18 ♗b5 ♖eg8 19 ♖xd4 ♖xg5 20 ♖c1 is a bit unpleasant for Black.

16 ♖d2 ♗xd4 17 c6 ♗e5 18 ♗b5 b6 19 ♗h4 ♖hg8

The alternative 19...d4 20 ♗g3 ♗g7 21 ♗a6+ ♔b8 22 a4 would be dangerous for Black (Kasparov).

20 ♗a6+ ♔b8 21 ♗g3 ♗xg3 22 hxg3 ♖d8 23 ♖d4 ♖d6 24 ♖c1 ♗c8 25 ♗d3?!

25 ♗xc8 is a better move: 25...♖xc8 26 b4 a6 27 a4 h5 28 b5 and White has some pressure.

25...♖g4!? 26 ♖xg4 ♗xg4 27 f3

27 ♗xh7 d4 28 ♗d3 ♗e6 29 b3 ♗d5 gives Black sufficient counterplay (Kasparov).

27...♗e6 28 b4 d4 29 a4 a5 30 b5 ♗b3 31 ♖a1 ♔c8 32 ♔f2 h6

32...h5!? is probably stronger: 33 ♔e2 ♔d8 34 ♔d2 ♔e7 35 ♗c2 ♗xc2 36 ♔xc2 ♖g6 37 ♔d3 ♖xg3 38 ♖a2 ♔d6 39 ♔xd4 ♖g5 and Black should be okay.

33 ♔e2 ♔d8 34 ♔d2 ♔e7 35 ♗c2 ♗c4 36 ♖h1 d3?!

In time trouble Ivanchuk pushes his pawn, but he only succeeds in weakening it . 36...♖e6 37 ♗d3 ♗b3 38 ♖h4 ♖d6 39 ♗c2 ♗c4 40 ♖e4+ ♔f8 41 g4 is slightly better for White (Kasparov).

37 ♗d1 ♔f8 38 ♖h4 ♗a2 39 ♖e4 ♖g6 40 g4 h5

Or 40...♖d6 41 ♖e3 ♗b1 42 ♔c3 and White has a great advantage.

41 f4!? hxg4 42 f5 ♖d6 43 ♖xg4 ♗d5 44 ♖h4 ♔g7 45 g3

45...♔f6?!

This loses and should be avoided, though 45...♗a2 46 ♖e4 ♔f8 47 ♖e3 is also nice for White.

46 ♖h8 ♔e5 47 ♖c8 ♔d4 48 ♖xc7 ♖h6 49 ♖d7 ♖h2+ 50 ♔c1 1-0

Game 52
Lastin-Najer
Elista 2000

1 e4 e5 2 ♘f3 ♘f6 3 d4 ♘xe4 4 ♗d3 d5 5 ♘xe5 ♘d7 6 ♘xd7 ♗xd7 7 0-0 ♕h4 8 c4 0-0-0 9 c5 g5 10 f3 ♘f6 11 ♗e3

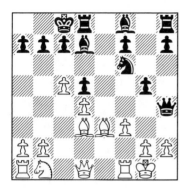

11...♗g7

In this tabiya Black has many interesting opportunities:

a) 11...g4 12 g3 ♕h5 13 f4 ♖e8 14 ♖e1 ♗g7 15 ♘c3 ♖e7 16 ♕d2 ♖he8 17 b4 ♗f5 (17...♘e4 18 ♗xe4 dxe4 19 b5 ♖d8 20 ♕b2 looks very dangerous for Black) 18 c6!? bxc6 19 ♘a4 ♗xd3 20 ♕xd3 ♘e4 21 ♖ac1 with compensation, Matsuura-Kapelari, Sao Paulo 1997.

b) 11...♖g8 12 ♘c3 g4 looks very attractive:

b1) 13 ♕e1?! is strongly met by 13...g3! 14 hxg3 ♖xg3 15 ♘e2 (even worse is 15 ♕d2? ♗xc5 16 dxc5 ♖dg8 17 ♖fd1 d4 18 c6 dxe3 19 cxd7+ ♔d8 0-1 Dolmatov-Makarychev, Palma de Mallorca 1989) 15...♗d6! 16 ♕f2 (16 cxd6? ♖xg2+! and it is all over) 16...♗h3 17 ♘xg3 ♗xg3 18 ♕c2 ♖g8 with a fantastic attack.

b2) 13 g3 ♕h3 14 f4 ♘h5 15 ♕e1 (weaker is 15 ♗f2? ♘xf4! 16 gxf4 g3 17 ♗xg3 ♖xg3+ 18 hxg3 ♕xg3+ 19 ♔h1 ♕h4+ 20 ♔g1 ♗g7 and Black wins, despite being a rook down) 15...♖e8 16 ♕f2 ♘f6 17 ♖ae1 h5 with an unclear game.

c) 11...♖e8 12 ♕d2 (12 ♗f2 ♕h6 13 ♘c3 g4 14 f4 – 14 ♖c1 c6 15 b4 gxf3 16 ♕xf3 ♘g4 also gives Black considerable counterplay – 14...♕xf4 15 ♗h4 ♕xd4+ 16 ♔h1 ♗g7 with unclear play – Makarychev) 12...♗g7 (12...♖xe3? is too optimistic: 13 ♕xe3 ♘h5 14 g3! ♘xg3 15 ♕e5 ♖g8 16

hxg3 ♕h3 17 ♖d1 ♗g7 18 ♗f1 1-0, Tomashevic-Kondali, correspondence 1991) 13 ♗f2 ♕h6 14 ♕a5 ♔b8 15 ♘c3 ♖e6 16 a4 (or 16 ♘b5 ♗xb5 17 ♕xb5 ♘h5 18 g3 ♕f6 19 ♖ae1 c6 20 ♕a5 ♖he8 and Black has decent counterplay) 16...♗c8 17 ♖a3 g4 18 ♘b5 ♖a6 19 ♕b4 gxf3 20 ♘xc7!? ♖xc7 21 ♗xa6 fxg2 22 ♔xg2 ♘h5 with a real mess, Morgado-Gottardi, correspondence 1997.

12 ♘c3

12 g3 is worth considering: 12...♕h5 13 ♘c3 ♖he8 14 ♖e1 g4 15 f4 ♘e4!? 16 ♘xe4 (16 ♕c2 ♘xc5! 17 dxc5 d4 18 ♗f2 dxc3 19 bxc3 ♗c6 gives Black a fine game) 16...dxe4 17 ♗e2 ♕g6 18 ♕b3 (18 d5 ♗c6 19 ♗xg4+ ♔b8 20 f5 ♕f6 21 d6 cxd6 22 cxd6 ♕xb2 isn't clear at all) 18...♗c6 19 ♗c4 ♕f5 20 ♖ed1 (20 ♗xf7 ♖e7 21 d5 ♗xd5 22 ♗xd5 ♕xd5 23 ♕a4 a6 shouldn't be worse for Black) 20...♗d5 21 c6 bxc6 22 ♖ac1 ♖e6 23 ♕a3 ♗xc4 24 ♖xc4 ♕b5 25 ♖dc1 and White had fantastic play for the pawn in Tiviakov-Rozentalis, Groningen 1997.

12...♖he8 13 ♗f2 ♕h6 14 ♕b3

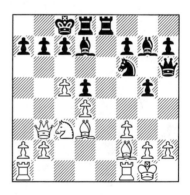

Another try is 14 ♘b5 ♔b8 15 a4 ♘h5 16 ♕d2 a6 17 ♖fc1!? ♘f4 (not 17...axb5? 18 axb5 b6 19 ♕b4 with a winning attack) 18 ♗f1 ♗e6 19 ♕a5 ♖c6 20 ♖a3 ♗c8 21 ♖e1 ♗f6 22 ♕d2 ♕g7 with chances for both sides, Zulfurgarli-Bayramov, Baku 1998.

14...g4 15 ♘b5 ♔b8 16 ♖fe1?!

White should have played 16 ♗g3 ♖c8 17 ♗e5; after 17...g3!? 18 ♗xg3 ♘h5 19 ♗f2

♘f4 Black has good play for his pawn.

16...gxf3 17 ♘d6!?

White is trying to complicate matters; after 17 gxf3 ♘h5 18 ♔h1 ♕d2 Black is in control.

17...cxd6 18 ♗a6 b6?!

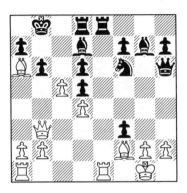

This makes no sense – Black probably overlooked the note to White's 20th move. After 18...♗c6 19 ♗xb7 ♗a4 (even 19...♗xb7 20 c6 ♖xe1+ 21 ♖xe1 ♖d7 22 cxd7 ♘xd7 23 ♕c3 a6 is comfortable for Black) 20 ♕b4 (20 ♕xa4? ♘g4 and Black wins) 20...a5 21 ♕b6 ♘d7 22 ♕xa5 ♖xe1+ 23 ♖xe1 ♔xb7 24 ♕xd8 dxc5 Black has the advantage.

19 cxb6 ♗c6

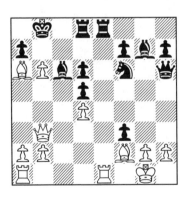

20 bxa7+

Much stronger is 20 ♕c3! ♘g4 21 h4 ♘e5 22 dxe5 dxe5 23 ♖ac1 and Black is under attack.

20...♔xa7

After 20...♔a8? 21 ♕b6! Black cannot defend himself.

21 ♕a3

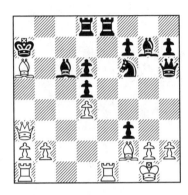

21...♗b7

21...♖a8? would be met by 22 ♕a5! ♗b7 23 ♖ac1!! ♖xe1+ 24 ♗f1+ ♔b8 25 ♕c7+ ♔a7 26 ♖c3 and White wins.

22 ♗xb7+ ♔xb7 23 ♕b4+ ♔a8 24 ♕a5+ ♔b7 25 ♕b5+ ♔a7 26 ♕a5+ ½-½

Game 53

Anand-Hübner

Dortmund 1992

---

1 e4 e5 2 ♘f3 ♘f6 3 d4 ♘xe4 4 ♗d3 d5 5 ♘xe5 ♘d7 6 ♘xd7 ♗xd7 7 0-0 ♕h4 8 c4 0-0-0 9 c5 g6!?

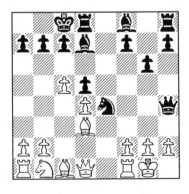

This move keeps the g5-square vacant as a possible retreat square for the knight.

10 ♘c3

10 f3?! ♘g5 11 ♗e3 ♗g7 12 g3 ♕h5 gives Black considerable counterplay.

10...♗g7 11 g3

Or:

a) 11 ♘e2 ♖he8

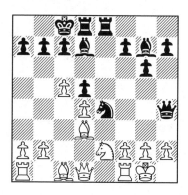

and now:

a1) 12 a4 ♘g5!? 13 ♖a3 h6! 14 ♗c2 (14 ♗e3 ♘e6 15 ♕d2 with unclear play is probably better) 14...♖xe2! 15 ♕xe2 ♘e6 16 ♕d1 ♘xd4 and Black had enormous play for the exchange, Ivanchuk-Rozentalis, Debrecen 1992.

a2) 12 ♗e3 ♗h6 13 ♗xh6 ♕xh6 14 ♕c1 and White might have a very slight edge.

b) 11 ♗e3 ♘xc5 12 g3 ♕h3 13 ♗e2 (13 dxc5 d4 14 ♘d5 dxe3 15 fxe3 – 15 c6? exf2+ 16 ♖xf2 ♗d4 17 cxd7+ ♖xd7 is bad for White – 15...♗e5 16 ♕c2 ♔b8 leads to an unclear position) 13...h5 14 ♘xd5 ♗a4! 15 b3 ♖xd5 16 bxa4 ♖e8 (but not 16...♖hd8?! 17 ♗f3 ♖xd4 18 ♕c2! with a clear edge for White, J.Polgar-Skembris, Moscow 1994) 17 ♕c2 ♘e4 18 ♖fc1 ♕d7 and the position is very complex.

11...♕f6

11...♕h3?! was cleverly refuted by board one of the 2004 Olympiad Champions, Ukraine: 12 ♘xd5 ♗g4 13 ♘e7+! (not 13 ♕b3?! ♗f3 14 ♘f4 ♘g5! and the position is less clear – Ivanchuk) 13...♔b8? (Black should settle for a bad position after 13...♔d7 14 ♕a4+ ♔xe7 15 ♗xe4 ♖xd4 16

♗g5+ ♔f8 17 ♕c2 according to Rozentalis) 14 ♘c6+! (the move Rozentalis overlooked?) 14...♔c8 15 ♘xa7+ ♔b8 16 ♘c6+ ♔c8 17 f3 ♖xd4 18 ♗e3 ♖xd3 19 ♕xd3 ♘xg3 20 ♗f4! 1-0 Ivanchuk-Rozentalis, Debrecen 1992.

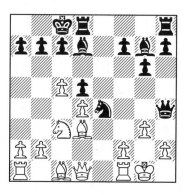

12 ♗e3

White has also tried 12 ♘xe4 dxe4 13 ♗xe4 ♘h3 14 ♕b3 ♕a6 (or 14...c6!? 15 d5 cxd5 16 ♗xd5 ♖xd5 17 ♕xd5 ♖d8 18 ♕b3 ♕c6 19 f3 ♗xf1 20 ♔xf1 ♖d5 with unclear play) 15 ♖e1 ♖xd4 16 ♗f4 ♗e6 17 ♕f3 c6 18 ♗d6 ♖d2 19 ♕f4 ♖d4 and the position was very messy, Sax-Skembris, Burgas 1992.

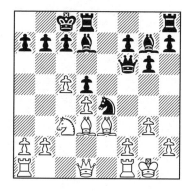

12...♗f5?

12...♘g5 is necessary. Now 13 ♘xd5? ♘h3+ 14 ♔g2 ♗c6 15 ♕g4+ ♔b8 16 ♕xh3 ♖xd5! gives Black a clear advantage for Black (Anand). Instead White plays 13 f4 when Black has the following tries:

a) 13...♕e6?! 14 ♖e1 ♘e4 15 ♗xe4 dxe4

16 d5 ♕a6 17 ♗d4 with a considerable advantage (Yusupov).

b) 13...♕e7?! 14 ♖e1 ♘e6 15 ♗f1! (a nice refutation of Alexander's idea; 15 ♘xd5 ♕e8 gives Black enough counterplay, Sasha's preparation running 16 f5 gxf5 17 ♗xf5 ♗a4 18 ♕g4 ♖xd5 19 ♗xe6+ fxe6 20 ♕xg7 ♖g8) 15...c6 16 ♕a4 ♔b8 17 f5! (another strong move from the strongest player of our little region) 17...gxf5 18 ♗f4+ ♔a8 19 ♗e3! ♘xc5 (19...♕f6 would fail to 20 ♕xa7+!! ♔xa7 21 ♘b5+! cxb5 22 ♖a3 mate) 20 ♖xe7 ♘xa4 21 ♘xa4 ♗xd4+ 22 ♗e3 ♗xe3+ 23 ♖xe3 and White went on to win with his extra piece, Belikov-Raetsky, Voronezh 2004.

c) 13...♘h3+! (the best move) 14 ♔g2 ♖he8 15 ♕d2 (Leko-S.Farago, Budapest 1993). Now after 15...♗g4 16 b4 h5 Black has counterplay, but it's difficult to tell whether it is enough for equality.

13 ♘b5! ♗h3

Black is in a bad way. After 13...a6 14 ♘xc7! ♔xc7 (14...♕c6 15 ♘a8! is horrible too) 15 ♗f4+ ♔d7 16 ♗e5 ♕e6 17 ♗xg7 ♖hg8 18 ♗e5 ♘xc5 19 ♗xf5 ♕xf5 20 g4 ♕e6 21 ♖e1 ♘e4 22 f3 ♘d6 23 ♕b3 White won in Har Zvi-Lev, Tel Aviv 1995.

14 ♘xa7+ ♔b8 15 ♘b5 ♗xf1 16 ♗xf1

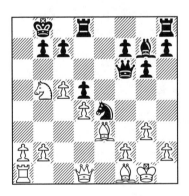

White has a clear edge despite the missing exchange – Black's king is simply too weak.

16...♖he8 17 ♕a4 ♕a6 18 ♕b4 ♕a8

Or 18...♕c6 19 ♗f4 ♖e7 20 ♕a5 and White wins.

19 a4 g5 20 a5

20 f3? would allow 20...♘xg3 21 ♗xg5 ♘xf1 22 ♗xd8 ♖xd8 23 ♔xf1 ♕a6 when Black suddenly has counterplay.

20...c6 21 ♘c3 ♘xc3 22 bxc3 h6 23 a6

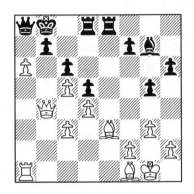

Now White is winning.

23...f5 24 ♗h3 ♖f8 25 a7+ ♔c8 26 ♕b1 g4 27 ♗f1 ♔d7 28 ♗d3 ♔e6 29 ♗f4 ♖f7 30 ♕c2 ♗f8 31 ♕e2+ 1-0

Game 54
Elizarov-Raetsky
Belorechensk 1989

---

1 e4 e5 2 ♘f3 ♘f6 3 d4 ♘xe4 4 ♗d3 d5 5 ♘xe5 ♘d7 6 ♘xd7 ♗xd7 7 0-0 ♕f6!?

This is probably a little bit better for White, but it's still playable.

8 ♗xe4

Probably the critical move, but White has some alternatives:

a) 8 ♗e3!? is also a decent option: 8...♗d6 9 c4 c6 10 cxd5 (10 ♘c3 ♘xc3 11 bxc3 dxc4 12 ♗xc4 0-0 13 ♕h5 ♖fe8 is fine for Black) 10...cxd5 11 ♕b3 ♗c6 12 ♗xe4 dxe4 13 ♘c3 0-0 14 d5 ♗d7 15 ♘xe4 (15 ♕xb7?! ♕e5 16 g3 ♗h3 with an attack on the light squares) 15...♗xh2+ 16 ♔xh2 ♕h4+ 17 ♔g1 ♕xe4 18 ♕xb7 ♗e6 19 ♖fd1 (Macieja-Rowson, Duisburg 1992). Now after 19...♖fb8 20 ♕c6 ♖d8 21 ♖d4 ♗xd5 22 ♖xe4 ♗xc6 23 ♖e7 White might have slightly better chances in this endgame.

b) 8 c4 is very aggressive, but not clear at all. Black plays 8...♕xd4

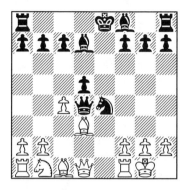

and now:

b1) 9 ♘c3 ♘c5 10 ♖e1+ ♗e6?! (10...♔d8 is necessary; after 11 ♗e2 ♕xd1 12 ♖xd1 dxc4 13 ♗xc4 White has compensation, but nothing more) 11 ♖xe6+! ♘xe6 12 cxd5 ♗c5 13 ♗e3 ♕e5 14 dxe6 ♗xe3 15 ♗b5+ ♔f8 16 ♕f3 ♕xe6 17 fxe3 c6 18 ♗a4 ♖d8 19 ♗b3 ♕e7 20 ♖f1 f6 21 ♘e2 and White had a clear edge in the game Tseshkovsky-Bareev, Kiev, 1986.

b2) 9 cxd5 is probably less dangerous: 9...0-0-0 10 ♕c2?! (10 ♗xe4!? ♕xe4 11 ♘c3 ♕h4 12 ♗e3 ♗d6 13 g3 with unclear play was necessary) 10...♘c5 11 ♗c4 ♗d6 12 ♗e3 ♕e5 13 g3 ♗f5 14 ♕d2 ♕e4 15 ♘a3 ♖he8 16 ♖fd1 ♗h3 17 ♗f1 ♗xf1 18 ♖xf1 ♘d3 and Black dominated events in Chudinovskikh-Raetsky, Briansk 1995.

c) 8 ♘c3 is pretty tame:

c1) 8...♕xd4 9 ♘xe4 dxe4 10 ♗xe4 ♕xd1 11 ♖xd1 0-0-0 12 ♗g5 f6 13 ♗f4 ♗c5 14 ♖d5 ♗b6 15 ♖ad1 g6 16 a3 c6 17 ♖5d3 ♗g4 18 ♖xd8+ ♖xd8 19 ♖xd8+ ♔xd8 ½-½ Kengis-Rozentalis, Vilnius 1984.

c2) 8...♘xc3 9 bxc3 0-0-0 is possible, but White seems to be slightly better: 10 ♕h5 ♕e6 11 ♗d2 g6 12 ♕f3 f6 13 ♖fe1 ♕f7 14 c4 dxc4 15 ♗e4 c6 16 d5 ♗e8?! (16...♗f5 17 ♗xf5+ gxf5 18 ♕xf5+ ♕d7 19 ♕xd7+ ♔xd7 20 ♖ab1 is better for White, but the game would still be undecided) 17 dxc6! ♖xd2 18

♕e3 ♖d6 19 ♕xa7 ♖xc6 20 ♕a8+ ♔c7 21 ♖ab1 ♖b6 22 ♖xb6 ♔xb6 23 ♖b1+ ♔c5 24 ♕a3+ ♔d4 25 ♕e3+ ♔e5 26 ♗xg6+ 1-0 Kotronias-Atalik, Pucarevo 1987.

8...dxe4 9 ♘c3 0-0-0 10 ♘xe4 ♕g6

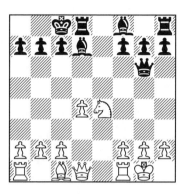

11 f3

The alternative 11 ♘g5 is probably best met by 11...f6, for example 12 ♘f3 ♗h3!? (12...h5 13 c4 h4 14 ♘e1 h3 15 g3 ♗g4 16 f3 ♗c5 17 ♗e3 ♖he8 18 ♗f2 ♗f5 19 d5 ♗d6 20 ♕d2 gives White a slight edge, Sziebert-Raetsky, Cappelle la Grande 1999) 13 ♘e1 ♗c5 14 c3 ♖he8 15 ♗e3 ♗d6 with compensation for the pawn.

11...h5

Black has no path to absolute equality, for example:

a) 11...f5 12 ♘f2 ♗b5 13 ♖e1 ♗d6 14 ♘h3 ♖de8 15 ♗f4 ♖xe1+ 16 ♕xe1 ♖e8 17 ♕g3 ♕xg3 18 hxg3 is a bit better for White.

b) 11...&f5 12 c3 h5 (or 12...&xe4 13 fxe4
Wxe4 14 Xxf7 &d6 15 &g5 Xdf8 16 Xxf8+
Xxf8 17 Wd2 and we prefer White due to the
extra pawn) 13 Wa4 &b8 14 &f4 h4 15 Xae1
h3 16 g4 &d7 (Klovans-Rozentalis, USSR
1985). Now after 17 Wc4 Xc8 18 Dg5 &d6
19 &xd6 Wxg5 20 &e7 &b5 21 &xg5 &xc4
22 Xf2 &xa2 Black is worse but he has good
drawing chances in the endgame.

12 &g5

12 &f4 is also strong after 12...h4 13 Wd3

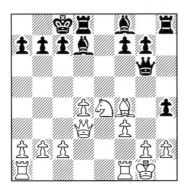

and now:

a) 13...Wb6 14 a4 &e6 15 Xfd1 h3 16 a5
Wc6 17 a6 b6 18 c4 f5 19 Df2 (this is
stronger than 19 d5?! fxe4 20 Wxe4, Raetsky-
Kveinys, correspondence 1987) 19...hxg2 20
d5 Wc5 21 &xg2 and White is clearly better.

b) 13...h3 14 g4 Wb6 15 a4 &e6 16 Xfd1
and here Black must choose between the
following options:

b1) 16...f5 17 a5 Wc6 (or 17...fxe4 18 axb6
exd3 19 bxa7 &d7 20 a8W Xxa8 21 Xxa8
dxc2 22 Xc1 &b3 23 &e5 c5 24 Xa3 c4 25
Xa8 and the advantage is definitely with
White) 18 gxf5 &xf5 19 a6 b6 20 &g3 Wg6
21 Wc4 Xd7 22 d5 &xe4 23 Wxe4 Xh6 24
Xa4 &c5+ 25 &f1 and White was clearly
better in Raetsky-Sivets, correspondence. In
fact, following 25...&e7? 26 d6! it was already
time to resign.

b2) 16...a6?! 17 a5 Wxb2?! (17...Wc6 is better, even though after 18 Wc3 Wxc3 19
Dxc3 &b4 20 De4 Black has no compensa-

tion for the pawn) 18 Dc3 Wb4 19 Xa4 We7
20 d5 g5 21 &g3 f5 22 gxf5 &f7 23 Xc4 with
a close-to-winning advantage for White,
A.Ivanov-Kochiev, Kostroma 1985.

b3) 16...a5!? seems to be necessary, although after 17 Wb5!? Xxd4 18 Wxb6
Xxd1+ 19 Xxd1 cxb6 20 &e5 the endgame is
more pleasant for White.

12...f6 13 &h4 Wh6

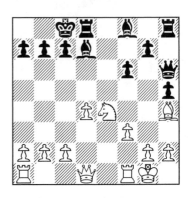

Or 13...Wf7 14 Wd2 g5 15 &f2 h4 16 d5
h3 17 g3 and White is better.

14 c4 g5 15 &f2 f5 16 Dc3 h4 17 d5 g4 18 &d4 &d6

White cannot be allowed to play 19 f4, for
example 18...Xg8 19 f4 &d6 20 Wd2 c5 21
dxc6 &xc6 22 Dd5 and White has all the
chances.

19 fxg4

19 &xh8? We3+ 20 Xf2 g3 21 &d4 gxf2+
22 &f1 Wf4 is bad for White.

19...Xhg8!

Not 19...fxg4 20 &xh8 (20 Xf6!? Wh5 21
c5 &e5 22 c6! is equally strong) 20...Wxh8 21
De4 &xh2+ 22 &xh2 We5+ 23 &g1 Wxe4
24 Wd2 and White the advantage, and a substantial one at that.

20 gxf5?

For some reason White decides to assist
Black's attack with his next two moves. Here
he should play 20 c5! &e5 21 &xe5 We3+ 22
Xf2 Wxe5 23 Wf1 fxg4 24 c6 bxc6 25 Wa6+
&b8 26 dxc6 &c8 and Black is only a bit
worse in this messy position.

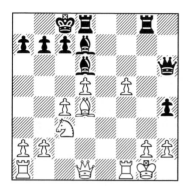

20...c5!

Black grabs his chance instantly. The key idea is 21 ♗f2 ♕f4! 22 ♗g3 ♕g5 23 ♘e4 ♕g3+ and the queen's dance wins a piece. 20...♗xh2+!? 21 ♔xh2 ♕d6+ 22 ♔h1 ♖xg2! leads to a draw as 23 ♗g1?? ♕g3! 24 ♖f3 ♖xg1+ 25 ♕xg1 ♕xf3+ 26 ♔g2 ♕xf5 is clearly better for Black.

21 dxc6?

A terrible mistake, and suddenly Black has a fantastic attack. After 21 ♘e4! cxd4 22 ♕xd4 ♖df8 the game would have remained unclear.

21...♗xc6 22 ♘d5

22...h3!

The right way to attack. After 22...♗xh2+?! 23 ♔xh2 ♖xd5 24 cxd5 ♕d6+ 25 ♔h1 ♖xg2! 26 ♗e5! ♕xe5 27 ♔xg2 ♕g3+ all Black has is a draw.

23 g4

23 g3 is met strongly by 23...♗xg3! 24 hxg3 ♖xg3+ 25 ♔h2 ♖g2+ 26 ♔h1 ♖xd5! 27 cxd5 ♕d6 with mate to come.

23...♕h4 24 ♔h1 ♖xg4

25 ♗f6

After 25 ♗f2 ♕g5 26 ♕f3 ♖xc4 White is finished.

25...♖g1+! 26 ♔xg1

Or 26 ♖xg1 ♕e4+.

26...♗c5+ 27 ♔h1 ♕xc4 0-1

Game 55
Tiviakov-Miles
Linares 1998

---

1 e4 e5 2 ♘f3 ♘f6 3 d4 ♘xe4 4 ♗d3 d5 5 ♘xe5 ♘d7 6 ♘xd7 ♗xd7 7 0-0 ♗e7

This is a bit passive, and so is 7...♘f6, for example:

a) 8 ♗g5 ♗e7 9 c3 c6 10 ♘d2 0-0 11 ♕c2 h6 12 ♗h4 ♘h5 13 ♗xe7 ♕xe7 14 ♖fe1 ♕d6 15 ♘f3 ♘f4 16 ♗h7+ ♔h8 17 ♗f5 ♗xf5 18 ♕xf5 was very slightly better for White in Geller-Smyslov, Moscow 1981, although here the players agreed a draw.

b) 8 ♖e1+ ♗e7 9 ♗f4 (or 9 ♕e2 ♗e6 10 f4 g6 11 ♘c3 ♕d7 12 f5!? gxf5 – 12...♗xf5? 13 ♗xf5 gxf5 14 ♕e5 would of course be bad – 13 ♗f4 ♘e4 14 ♘b5 ♗d8 with unclear play) 9...♗g4 (9...0-0? is met strongly by 10 ♗xc7 ♕xc7 11 ♖xe7 ♕b6 12 ♘c3 ♕xb2 13 ♘xd5 ♘xd5 14 ♖xd7 ♘c3 15 ♕c1 ♕xc1+ 16 ♖xc1 ♘xa2 17 ♖a1 ♘b4 18 ♗e4 and Black is struggling, possibly in vain) 10 ♕d2 0-0 11 ♘c3 c6 12 ♘e2 ♕d7 13 ♘g3 ♘h5 14 ♘xh5 ♗xh5 15 ♗f5 ♕d8 (not 15...♕xf5?! 16 ♖xe7 ♖fe8 17 ♖ae1 ♖xe7 18 ♖xe7 with a clear edge, as 18...b6? 19 ♖e5 ♕g6 20 ♖g5 is winning) 16 ♖e3 ♗g6 17 ♗xg6 fxg6 18 ♖ae1 ♖f7 19 g3 with a slight edge for White, Palac-Zaja, Pula 2000.

8 c4

8 ♖e1 doesn't really work: 8...0-0 (8...♘f6 transposes to 7...♘f6 above) 9 ♗xe4 dxe4 10 ♖xe4 ♗f6 11 ♖e1 ♗c6 12 ♗e3 ♕d5 13 f3 ♖fe8 14 ♘c3 (14 c3?! ♗h4! 15 ♗f2 ♗xf2+ 16 ♔xf2 ♖xe1 17 ♕xe1 ♖e8 18 ♕d1 ♗b5 with a strong initiative) 14...♕d6 15 ♔h1 ♖ad8 16 ♕d2 ♗xd4 17 ♗xd4 ♕xd4 18 ♖xe8+ ♗xe8 19 ♕xd4 ♖xd4 and Black is ever-so-slightly better (Skatchkov).

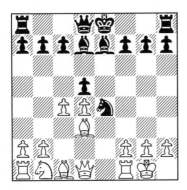

8...♘f6

Or 8...c6 9 cxd5 cxd5 10 ♘c3 ♘f6 (10...♘xc3 11 bxc3 ♕c7 12 ♖e1 is good for white; 12...♕xc3 13 ♗d2 ♕xd3? 14 ♖xe7+! is even winning!) 11 ♗g5 ♗c6 12 ♗c2 (12 ♖e1 0-0 13 ♕f3 looks even stronger) 12...0-0 13 f3 ♖e8 14 ♕d3 g6 15 ♖fe1 ♕d6 16 ♕d2 ♘h5 17 ♗xe7 ♖xe7 18 ♖xe7 ♕xe7 19 ♖e1 ♕f6 20 ♖e5 and White had an edge in Alekseev-Skatchkov, St Petersburg 2002.

9 ♘c3 ♗e6

Zapata-Perdomo, Colombia 1998 continued 9...dxc4 10 ♗xc4 0-0 11 ♖e1 c6 12 ♗g5 h6 13 ♗h4 ♘d5 14 ♗xe7 ♘xe7 15 ♕h5 ♘f5 16 ♖ad1 ♘d6 17 ♗b3 ♕g5 18 ♕xg5

hxg5. Now 19 d5!? should ensure some advantage. Black has to be careful, for example 19...♖fe8 20 ♖xe8+ ♖xe8 21 dxc6 ♗xc6 22 h4! ♘b5 23 ♘xb5 ♗xb5 24 hxg5 with a clear edge for White.

10 c5 0-0 11 ♗f4 c6 12 b4

It's advisable for White to get going here. Svidler-Yusupov, Kazan, 1997 continued more slowly with 12 h3 ♖e8 13 ♖e1 ♘d7 14 ♕d2 (or 14 b4 ♗g5 15 ♗g3 ♕f6 and Black is okay) 14...♗f6 15 ♗c2 ♘f8 16 ♖e2 b6 17 ♖ae1 bxc5 18 dxc5 ♗d7 19 ♖xe8 ♗xe8 20 b4 ♘e6 21 ♗d6 g6 22 f4. Here Svidler gives the line 22...a5! 23 f5 gxf5 24 ♗xf5 ♗g7 25 ♗xe6 fxe6 26 ♖xe6 ♕h4 27 ♘e2 and assesses the position as unclear.

12...♕d7 13 ♕c2 g6

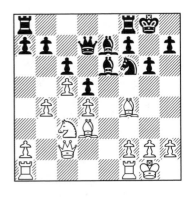

14 ♖fe1

14 b5!? ♖fe8 (14...♘h5 15 ♗h6 ♘g7 16 a4 ♗f6 17 ♘e2 also looks a touch better for

White) 15 a4 ♘h5 16 ♗e3 gives White a slight plus. Now in J.Polgar-Van der Sterren, Wijk aan Zee 1998 Black went astray with 16...♗d8?! 17 a5 a6 18 bxa6 bxa6 19 ♘a4! ♗xa5 20 ♘b6 ♗xb6 21 cxb6 ♗f5 22 ♗xf5 ♕xf5 23 ♖fc1 ♕xc2 24 ♖xc2 a5 25 ♖xc6, giving White a clear plus.

14...♘h5 15 ♗e5

15 ♗h6 ♖fe8 16 b5 ♗f6 17 bxc6 bxc6 18 ♕a4 ♘g7 with the idea of ...♘f5 gives Black sufficient counterplay.

15...f6 16 ♗g3 ♘xg3 17 hxg3 ♗f7 18 b5 ♖fe8

18...f5 19 ♖ab1 ♗f6 20 ♘e2 ♖fe8, with chances for both sides, is probably a better option.

19 a4

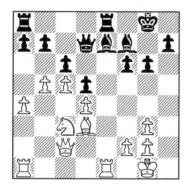

19...♗d8?!

19...f5 is still correct.

20 ♖xe8+ ♕xe8 21 a5 a6 22 bxa6 bxa6 23 ♕d2 f5 24 ♘a4 ♗f6 25 ♖e1 ♕d8 26 ♘b6

Or 26 ♗f1 ♗g7 27 ♖b1 ♕f6 28 ♖b4, when White is more comfortable.

26...♖a7 27 ♗f1 ♔g7 28 ♖b1 h5 29 ♕c3 ♕h8 30 ♖b4 ♔h7

Black should probably play 30...h4!? 31 gxh4 ♕xh4 32 g3 ♕h5, although White does keep an edge.

31 ♕d2 ♕e8 32 ♘a4 ♕d8 33 ♖b6 ♕h8?!

33...♕c8 is a better option, although after 34 ♕b4 White has a strong pressure.

34 ♖xa6

Or 34 ♖xc6 ♗xd4 35 ♖xa6 ♖xa6 36 ♗xa6 ♗e8 37 ♘b6 ♕e5 and the endgame is bad for Black.

34...♖e7 35 ♖xc6 ♗xd4 36 ♘b6 ♗c3 37 ♕g5

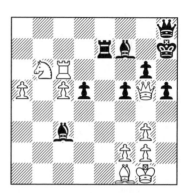

37...♕e5?

37...♖e1 38 ♘xd5 ♗xa5 39 ♘e3 is obviously nice for White, but at least it's not over! Now, though, White strikes a winning blow.

38 ♘xd5! ♖b7

Or 38...♕xd5 39 ♕xe7.

39 ♘xc3 ♕xc3 40 ♕f6 ♕xa5 41 ♖c8 ♗g8 42 ♗c4 1-0

Game 56
Sorokin-Raetsky
Krasnodar 1984

1982, Voronezh State University, Department of Mathematics, 23 years before the publication of *Petroff Defence* by Everyman Chess. Wasting no time during a physics lecture, the future author makes an important discovery on his pocket chess computer (a version of the computer software Fritz 0.03): the Petroff Defence is still alive!

He has just found a beautiful combinational refutation of *ECO's* critical assessment. The bible of that time insists on '14 ♘d2 with a slight edge' as in the game Mortensen-Borik played at the 1980 Chess Olympiad, but his intuition whispers 'it's not that simple' and 'Eureka!'...

We had to wait for two years until my university analysis was included into all books on the Petroff Defence. My 'co-author' was the future GM Sorokin.

1 e4 e5 2 ♘f3 ♘f6 3 d4 ♘xe4 4 ♗d3 d5 5 ♘xe5 ♘d7 6 ♕e2

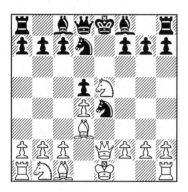

This is not really considered dangerous now.

6...♘xe5

Another option is 6...♕e7 7 ♗xe4 (7 ♘xf7!? transposes to 6 ♘xf7 ♕e7 7 ♕e2) 7...dxe4 8 ♗f4 ♘xe5 9 ♗xe5 and now:

a) 9...f6 is weak: 10 ♗g3 f5 11 ♘c3 c6 12 0-0-0 g6 (even worse is 12...♕g5+?! 13 ♔b1 ♗b4? 14 ♘b5 f4?! – 14...cxb5 15 ♕xb5+ ♔f7 16 ♕xb4 f4 17 h4 is more resilient although White keeps an advantage – 15 ♘c7+ ♔f8 16 ♕xe4 and Black resigned in Dely-Malich, Pecs 1964) 13 ♗e5 ♗h6+ 14 ♔b1 0-0 15 h4 and White clearly has all the fun.

b) 9...♗f5 10 ♘c3 0-0-0 11 0-0-0 ♕e6 12 ♕e3 h5 13 h3 f6 14 ♗h2 g6 15 ♔b1 ♗h6 16 ♕g3 ♖h7 17 ♖he1 ♕b6 18 ♘xe4 ♖xd4 19 ♖xd4 ♕xd4 with level chances, Karpov-Hort, Amsterdam 1980. More energetic is 14 ♗xc7!? ♕xc7 15 d5 ♕e5 16 ♕xa7 ♗d6 17 ♘b5+ ♔d7 (17...♔c8 18 ♖d4 is dangerous) 18 ♕xb7+ ♔e8 19 ♕xg7 ♖h7 20 ♘xd6+ ♕xd6 21 ♕g3 ♕xg3 22 fxg3 with a very difficult endgame for both players.

7 ♗xe4 dxe4

A weaker option is the move 7...♗e6?! 8 dxe5 dxe4

and now:

a) 9 ♘c3!? ♕d4 10 ♕b5+ c6 11 ♕xb7 ♖c8 12 ♗e3 ♕xe5 13 ♕xa7 ♗b4 14 ♕d4 and White was a bit better in Suetin-Radulov, Athens 1984.

b) 9 ♕xe4 is less clear: 9...♗d5 10 ♕g4 h5 11 ♕h3 ♕e7 12 f4 ♕e6 13 ♕xe6+ fxe6 14 ♔f2 (14 0-0 ♗c5+ 15 ♔h1 0-0-0 16 ♘d2 ♖hf8 gives Black excellent play) 14...g5!? 15 fxg5 (15 ♘c3 ♗c5+ 16 ♗e3 ♗xe3+ 17 ♔xe3 ♗xg2 18 ♖hg1 gxf4+ 19 ♔xf4 ♖g8 looks level) 15...♗c5+ 16 ♔g3 (16 ♗e3 0-0+ 17 ♔e2 ♗xe3 18 ♔xe3 ♖f5 19 ♘c3 ♖xe5+ 20 ♔f4 ♖f5+ 21 ♔e3 ♖xg5 and Black is no worse) 16...h4+ 17 ♔h3 ♗e4 and Black has good counterplay.

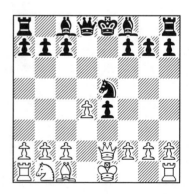

8 ♕xe4 ♗e6

8...♗d6 9 dxe5 ♕e7 10 0-0 0-0 11 ♗f4 ♖e8 12 ♖e1 f6 13 ♘d2 fxe5 14 ♗g3 (or 14 ♗xe5 ♗xe5 15 ♕d5+ ♔h8 16 f4 ♗e6 17

♕xe5 ♕b4 with a slight edge for White) 14...♗d7 15 ♘f3 ♗c6 16 ♕c4+ ♕f7 17 ♕xf7+ ♔xf7 18 ♘xe5+ ♗xe5 19 ♗xe5 and White was a pawn up in Suetin-Bex, Biel 1995.

9 ♕xe5 ♕d7

10 ♗e3

White has two main alternatives here:

a) 10 ♘c3 0-0-0 11 ♗e3 ♗b4 12 0-0 f6 13 ♕g3?! (13 ♕e4 ♗f5 14 ♕f3 ♗xc2 15 ♖ac1 ♕f5, with equal chances, is better) 13...♗xc3 14 bxc3 h5 15 h4 g5 16 f3 (16 hxg5 h4 17 ♕h2 h3 18 g3 fxg5 19 ♗xg5 ♖dg8 20 f4 ♕c6 also gives Black a strong attack) 16...♖dg8 17 ♖f2 ♕c6 18 ♗d2 g4 19 f4 ♗c4 and Black has an attack. The game Karpov-Larsen, Tilburg 1980 continued 20 d5 ♗xd5 21 f5 ♖e8 22 a3 ♖e4 23 ♖e1 ♖he8 24 ♖xe4 ♖xe4 25 ♔h2 ♕c5 and Black was clearly better.

b) 10 0-0 0-0-0 11 ♗e3 ♗b4 12 c3 f6 13 ♕g3 with a further split:

b1) 13...♗d6 14 ♗f4 ♗f8 15 ♕d3 g5 16 ♗e3 h5 17 ♘d2 (we prefer 17 c4!? ♗f5 18 ♕d2 h4 19 d5 g4 20 ♘c3 h3 21 g3 and White is slightly better) 17...h4 18 f3 ♖g8 19 c4 f5 20 f4 gxf4 21 ♖xf4 ♕g7 with an unclear position, Magem Badals-Macieja, Batumi 1999.

b2) 13...♗e7 14 ♘d2 h5 15 f3 h4 16 ♕f2 h3 (16...g5 17 c4 is better for White – Yusupov) 17 g3 ♕b5 18 b3 ♖he8 19 c4 ♕a5 20 a3 ♕c3 21 d5 ♗f5 with chances for both

sides, Krakops-Raetsky, Apolda 1994.

10...♗b4+

10...0-0-0 11 ♕a5

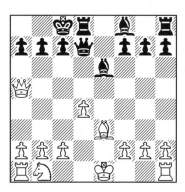

gives Black a wide, but unsatisfactory, choice:

a) 11...♗d5 12 ♘c3 ♗xg2 13 ♖g1 b6 14 ♕xa7 ♗b7 15 0-0-0 ♗d6 16 h4 f6 17 d5 ♖he8 18 ♖d3 h6 19 ♗xb6! cxb6 20 ♘a4 ♗c7 21 d6! ♕xd6 22 ♖xd6 ♖xd6 23 b3 and Black was much worse, Udalov-Raetsky, correspondence 1982.

b) 11...♕c6 12 ♘c3 ♕xg2 (instead of 12...b6 13 ♕a6+ ♔b8 14 ♘b5 ♗c4 15 a4 ♗b4+ 16 c3 ♗d6 17 ♕xa7+ ♔c8 18 0-0-0 ♕xg2 19 d5! ♗xd5 20 ♖hg1 ♕xh2 21 a5 with a raging attack, Hort-Short, Bundesliga 1986) 13 0-0-0 a6 14 d5 ♗h3!? 15 ♗f4 ♖d7 16 ♖he1 ♗e7 17 ♗g3 and White's position looks preferable.

c) 11...♔b8!? is probably best: 12 ♘c3 b6 13 ♕a6 ♗b4 (13...♕c6 14 ♘b5 ♕b7 15 ♕xb7+ ♔xb7 16 0-0-0 is better for White) 14 0-0 ♗xc3 15 bxc3 ♕c6 and Black has some compensation for the pawn.

11 c3 ♗d6 12 ♕a5

White has other options, but none that is comforting:

a) 12 ♕h5 0-0 13 0-0 ♗g4 14 ♕h4 ♖fe8 15 ♘d2 f5 16 h3 ♗e2 17 ♖fe1 ♕b5 18 c4?! ♗xc4 19 b3 ♗d5 20 ♗f4 ♖xe1+ 21 ♖xe1 ♕d3 22 ♗xd6 ♕xd2 23 ♖e5 was agreed drawn, Movsesian-Haba, Pardubice 1998, although of course Black is to be preferred here. Instead White should play 18 b3 ♗d3 19 c4 ♕d7, although Black retains excellent compensation.

b) 12 ♕xg7 0-0-0 13 ♘d2 was played in Oll-Khalifman, Sochi, 1984. Now after 13...♕c6!? 14 f3 ♖hg8 15 ♕xh7 ♖xg2 Black has excellent play for the pawns.

12...♕c6 13 f3

13 0-0?! ♗d5 gives Black a clear edge. One game continued 14 f3? b6 15 ♕a6 ♗c4 16 d5 ♕xd5 (16...♗xh2+ 17 ♔f2 ♗g3+ 18 ♔g1 ♕xd5 19 ♕a4+ b5 20 ♕c2 0-0 also wins for Black) 17 ♕a4+ b5 18 ♕d1 ♕e5 19 ♔f2 ♕xh2 20 f4 ♗xf1 0-1 Klinger-Wolff, Baguio 1987.

13...♗d5 14 ♘d2 0-0 15 0-0

15 ♔f2 b6 16 ♕a6 f5 is also unappetising for White.

15...♖fe8

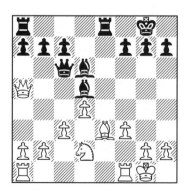

16 ♗g5?

Other moves played here include:

a) 16 ♖fe1 b6 17 ♕a6 ♗xh2+ 18 ♔xh2 ♖xe3 19 ♔g1 ♕e6 20 ♕f1 ♖e8 21 ♖xe3 ♕xe3+ 22 ♕f2 ♕d3 and Black was slightly better, Barcenilla-Ye Rongguang, Beijing 1992.

b) 16 ♗f2 b6 17 ♕a6 ♗xh2+ 18 ♔xh2 ♕h6+ 19 ♔g1 ♕xd2 looks good for Black, based on 20 c4?! ♗xf3! when White is in trouble.

16...♖e2 17 c4

17 ♖fe1 is met by 17...b6 18 ♕a6 ♖xd2 19 ♗xd2 ♗c4 20 d5 ♗xh2+ 21 ♔h1 ♕xd5 and Black will win on the kingside.

17...♗xh2+

18 ♔h1?

The last chance was with 18 ♔xh2 ♕d6+ 19 ♔h1 ♕g3 20 ♖g1 ♕xg5 21 ♕xc7 (not 21 ♘f1 ♕h4+ 22 ♘h2 ♗xf3! 23 ♕xc7 ♗e4 and Black should win) 21...♖xd2 22 cxd5 ♖xd4 23 ♖ge1 ♖d2 24 ♕h2 ♕xd5, although the endgame a pawn down leaves few drawing chances.

18...♕g6 19 ♕xd5 ♗f4 20 g4 ♗xg5 0-1

Game 57
Dolmatov-Mamedyarov
Moscow 2002

---

1 e4 e5 2 ♘f3 ♘f6 3 d4 ♘xe4 4 ♗d3 d5 5 ♘xe5 ♘d7 6 ♘c3

White also has a tame option in 6 0-0 ♘xe5 7 dxe5 ♘c5 8 ♘c3 (8 ♗e2 ♗e7 9 ♗e3

0-0 10 f4 f6!? 11 exf6 ♖xf6 12 c4 ♗e6 13 cxd5 ♕xd5 14 ♘c3 ♕xd1 15 ♖axd1 c6 16 ♖d2 a5 17 b3 ♖ff8 18 ♖fd1 ♖ae8 lead to even chances in Wedberg-Rozentalis, Vasby 2000)

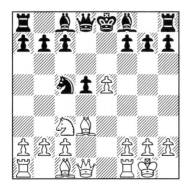

and now:

a) 8...c6 (the solid choice) 9 f4 f5!? 10 ♘e2 (10 exf6?! is weaker: 10...♕xf6 11 f5 – 11 ♖e1+ ♗e7 12 ♕e2 ♘xd3 13 cxd3 ♔f7 and as White has no ♘e5+ coming, Black is better – 11...♘xd3 12 ♕xd3 ♗e7 13 ♘e2 0-0 14 ♘g3 ♕f7 15 ♗e3 b6 and Black was slightly better, Rozentalis-Turov, Montreal 2001) 10...♗e7 11 ♗e3 0-0 with chances for both sides.

b) 8...♘xd3 9 ♕xd3 c6 10 ♘e2 g6 11 ♕g3 ♗g7 12 ♘f4 0-0 (12...♗xe5?! looks risky: 13 ♖e1 f6 14 ♘d3 0-0 15 ♘xe5 fxe5 16 ♖xe5 and Black is weak on the dark squares) 13 ♘h5!? gxh5 14 ♗h6 ♗g4 15 ♗xg7 ♔xg7 16 h3 ♕g5 17 f3 f5 18 exf6+ ♖xf6 19 fxg4 ♖af8 20 ♖xf6 ♖xf6 21 ♖e1 hxg4 22 hxg4 ♖f7 with level prospects, Tiviakov-Van Wely, Leeuwarden 2002.

6...♘xc3

Black has a couple of valid alternatives to this natural move:

a) 6...♗b4 wins a pawn, but is quite dangerous: 7 0-0 ♘xc3 8 bxc3 ♗xc3 and now:

a1) 9 ♗a3?! is too optimistic: 9...♘xe5 (but not 9...♗xa1?! 10 ♘c6!? bxc6 11 ♕e2+ ♘e5 12 ♕xe5+ ♗e6 13 ♖xa1 with an attack) 10 dxe5 ♗xa1 11 ♕xa1 and we feel that

White hasn't quite got the most from his position.

a2) 9 ♖b1 ♗xd4?! (9...♘xe5, transposing to 6...♘xe5, is better) 10 ♘xd7 ♗xd7! 11 ♖xb7 0-0 (11...♗c6? loses to 12 ♗a3! ♗xb7 13 ♖e1+ ♔d7 14 ♗f5+ ♔c6 15 ♕xd4 and mate is imminent) 12 ♗xh7+ ♔xh7 13 ♕xd4 and White has a clear edge.

b) 6...♘xe5 7 dxe5 ♗b4 (7...♕h4?! 8 ♗xe4 dxe4 9 ♘d5 ♕d8 10 ♗g5 ♕d7 11 e6 fxe6 12 ♕h5+ g6 13 ♘f6+ ♔f7 14 ♕h4 gives Black serious problems, while 7...♘c5?! 8 ♘xd5! ♘xd3+ 9 ♕xd3 ♗e6 10 ♘f4 obviously favours White) 8 0-0

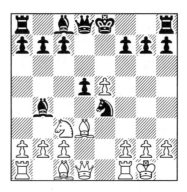

and now:

b1) 8...♗xc3 9 bxc3 ♗e6 with a further branch:

b11) 10 ♕e1!? ♘c5 (10...f5 11 exf6 ♕xf6 12 ♗xe4 dxe4 13 ♕xe4 0-0 14 ♗a3 ♖fe8 15 ♕xb7 ♕xc3 16 ♗b2 ♕c4 and White is only slightly better) 11 ♗b5+ c6 12 ♗a3 ♘d7 13 ♗d3 c5 14 f4 g6 15 c4 ♕c7 16 cxd5 ♗xd5 17 c4 ♗e6 18 ♖b1 with the initiative for White, Reefat-Hossain, Dhaka 2003.

b12) 10 f4 f5 11 exf6 ♕xf6 12 f5!? (12 ♗xe4 dxe4 13 ♕h5+ ♕f7 14 ♕b5+ c6 15 ♕b4 ♗d5 16 a4 b6 was equal in Palac-Arkhipov, Belgrade 1988) 12...♗f7 (not 12...♗xf5?! 13 ♗b5+ c6 14 ♕xd5 ♖f8 15 ♗a3 ♖d8 16 ♕c4 and Black is under serious attack) 13 ♗xe4 dxe4 14 ♗e3 0-0 and Black is probably not worse in this complex position.

b2) 8...♘xc3 9 bxc3 ♗xc3 10 ♖b1 0-0 (10...♕e7 11 ♖b3 ♗xe5? – Sax gives 11...♗b4 12 f4 with unclear play – 12 ♖e1 leaves Black in trouble; Sax-Nunn, Brussels 1985 concluded 12...0-0? 13 ♕h5 f5 14 ♗f4 1-0) 11 ♗xh7+ ♔xh7 12 ♕d3+ ♔g8 13 ♕xc3 d4 14 ♕g3 ♕d7!? 15 c3 d3 16 ♖d1 ♕g4 17 ♕xg4 (17 ♖xd3 ♕xg3 18 ♖xg3 ♗f5 19 ♖a1 ♖fd8 gives Black enough play for the pawn) 17...♗xg4 18 f3 ♗c8 19 ♖b3 c5 is level, Roiz-D.Fridman, Pardubice 2002.

7 bxc3 ♘xe5

7...♗d6 transposes to 5...♗d6 6 0-0 0-0 7 ♘c3 ♘xc3 8 bxc3 ♘d7.

8 dxe5 ♗e7

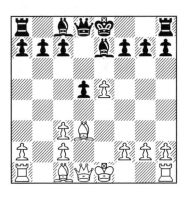

Other moves:

a) 8...♗e6 9 ♖b1 ♕c8 10 ♗g5 h6 11 ♗h4 ♗c5 12 0-0 c6 13 ♔h1 g5 14 ♗g3 ♕d7 15 f4 gxf4 16 ♗h4 ♗e7 17 ♖xf4 0-0-0? (Movsesian-Weglarz, Litomysl 1995) and now 18 ♗a6! would have won after 18...bxa6 19 ♕f1 ♕c7 20 ♕xa6+ ♔d7 21 ♖b7. Instead Black should play 17...♗xh4 18 ♖xh4 ♕e7 with an unclear position.

b) 8...♗c5 9 0-0 ♗e6 (9...♕h4?! loses a pawn to 10 ♗b5+ c6 11 ♕xd5) 10 ♖b1 ♗b6 11 ♕h5 h6 12 ♔h1 ♕e7 13 f4 g6 14 ♕e2 0-0-0 15 a4 ♕c5 16 ♖b5 ♕c6 (or 16...♕xc3 17 ♗d2 ♕c6 18 a5 ♗c5 19 ♖fb1 with an attack) 17 a5!? a6 18 axb6 axb5 19 bxc7 with compensation for the exchange, Reefat-Vakhidov, Dhaka 2003.

9 ♕h5 ♗e6 10 f4

Or 10 ♖b1 ♕d7 11 ♗g5 0-0-0 12 0-0 h6 13 ♗xe7 ♕xe7 14 ♕e2 (14 ♖b3 c5 15 ♖b5 c4 16 ♗f5 ♖he8 with equal) 14...♕c5 15 ♕d2 d4 16 cxd4 ♖xd4 17 ♕e3 ♖hd8 and Black was no worse in Kremenietsky-Pripis, Moscow 1977.

10...g6 11 ♕f3 f5 12 exf6

12 ♖b1 ♕c8 13 ♗e3 0-0 14 0-0 c5 also gives Black decent counterplay.

12...♗xf6 13 0-0 0-0 14 ♗a3

14 ♖b1 c5 15 ♖xb7 ♕c8 16 ♖b1 ♗xc3 offers chances to both sides.

14...♗xc3 15 ♖ad1 ♗d4+ 16 ♔h1 c5 17 c3 ♕a5

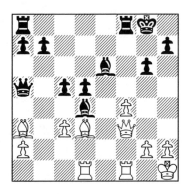

After 17...♗xc3 18 ♗xc5 ♗f6 19 ♗c4 ♕a5 20 ♖xd5 ♗xd5 21 ♕xd5+ ♔h8 22 ♗d4 ♕xd5 23 ♗xf6+ ♗xf6 24 ♗xd5 the game would end in a draw (but not 18...♖f7 19 ♗xg6 hxg6 20 ♕xc3 when Black has vulnerable dark squares).

18 cxd4 ♕xa3 19 ♗f5! ♕a6 20 ♗xe6+ ♕xe6 21 dxc5 ♖ad8 22 ♖fe1 ♕c6 23 ♖e7 ♖d7

23...♖de8 24 ♖xe8 ♖xe8 25 f5 ♕xc5 26 fxg6 hxg6 with unclear play was a more challenging try.

24 ♖xd7 ♕xd7 25 ♖xd5 ♕a4 26 f5 ♕xa2 27 h3 ♖xf5 28 ♖d8+ ♔g7 29 ♕xb7+ ♔h6 30 ♕e4 ♕a1+

Or 30...♖xc5 31 ♕f4+ ♖g5 32 ♕f8+ ♔h5 33 ♕f3+ with perpetual check.

31 ♔h2 ♕e5+ 32 ♕xe5 ♖xe5 33 ♖c8 a5 34 ♔g3 a4 35 ♔f4 ♖e1 36 ♖a8 ♖c1 ½-½

1 e4 e5 2 ♘f3 ♘f6 3 d4 ♘xe4 4 ♗d3 d5 5 ♘xe5 ♘d7 6 ♘xf7

This sacrifice is an attempt to achieve a draw directly from the opening, but Black has enough resources to play on.

6...♔xf7

Also to be considered is 6...♕e7!?, which is a bit risky but playable. Now we have a many of variations to look at!

a) 7 ♘e5 is good for Black: 7...♘xe5 8 dxe5 ♕xe5 9 ♕e2 ♗d6 10 ♘d2 ♘c5 11 ♕xe5+ ♗xe5 12 ♘f3 ♘xd3+ 13 cxd3 ♗f6 with a better endgame due to the two bishops and the stronger pawn structure.

b) 7 ♘xh8 ♘c3+ 8 ♔d2 ♘xd1 9 ♖e1 ♘xf2 10 ♗xh7 (but not 10 ♖xe7+? ♗xe7 11 ♘c3 ♘f6 and Black wins) 10...♘e5!? (10...♘e4+ 11 ♖xe4 dxe4 12 ♗g6+ ♔d8 13 ♘f7+ ♔e8 14 ♘d6+ ½-½, I.Zaitsev-Karpov, Leningrad 1966, is safer) 11 ♖xe5 ♗e6 and now:

b1) 12 ♗g6+?! ♔d7 13 ♗f7 (13 ♗f5? loses to 13...♕g5+ 14 ♔e2 ♕xc1 15 ♗xe6+ ♔c6 16 ♗xd5+ ♔b6 – Yusupov) 13...♘e4+ 14 ♔e1 (14 ♔d3 is met by 14...♘c5+!! 15 dxc5 ♗f5+! 16 ♖xf5 ♕e4+ and Black wins) 14...♕h4+ 15 g3 (Smerdon-Solomon, Gold Coast 1999) and now Black can play

15...♕xh8 16 ♗xe6+ ♔d6 17 ♗xd5 (or 17 h3 ♖e8 18 ♗f4 g5 19 ♗f5 gxf4 20 ♖xe8 ♕xd4 21 ♗xe4 fxg3 and Black wins) 17...♕xh2 18 ♗xe4 ♕g1+ 19 ♔e2 ♕xc1 when White's position is critical.

b2) 12 ♗g8! ♕h4 (or 12...♘e4+!? 13 ♔d1 ♗xg8 14 ♘g6 ♕xe5 15 ♘xe5 ♗d6 and Black has some compensation for his pawn) 13 ♗f7+! ♔d8 14 ♖xe6 ♕g5+ 15 ♔e2 ♕xg2 and the position is completely unclear.

c) 7 ♕e2

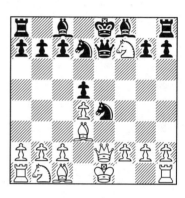

and now:

c1) 7...♔xf7?! 8 ♕h5+ ♔f6 (after 8...♔e6 9 ♗xe4 dxe4 10 d5+ ♔d6 11 ♗f4+ ♘e5 12 ♘c3 the attack also seems to be very dangerous) 9 0-0 ♕f7 10 ♕h4+ g5 11 ♗xg5+! ♘xg5 12 f4 ♔e6 (12...♕e7 13 fxg5+ ♔g7 14 ♘c3 also gives White a winning attack) 13 fxg5 ♕g7 14 ♘c3 ♘b6 15 ♖f6+ ♔d7 16 ♖af1 ♗e8 17 ♖f7 ♕xf7 18 ♖xf7 ♔xf7 19 g6+ ♔e6 20 ♕e1+ 1-0 Gurgenidze-Bellin, Tbilisi/Sukhumi 1977.

c2) 7...♕xf7 8 f3 ♘df6 9 ♘d2! (less energetic is 9 fxe4 ♗g4 10 ♕e3 dxe4 11 ♗xe4 0-0-0 12 0-0 ♕d7!? 13 ♗d3 – but not 13 c3? ♖e8 14 ♘d2 ♘xe4 15 ♘xe4 ♗f5 16 ♖f4 g5 and White is on the ropes – 13...♕xd4 14 ♕xd4 ♖xd4 15 ♗e3 ♗c5 with level chances) 9...♕h5 10 fxe4 ♗g4 11 ♕e3 dxe4 12 ♘xe4 0-0-0 with a further split:

c21) 13 ♘xf6 gxf6 14 0-0 ♗d6 15 g3 (or 15 h3 ♖hg8!? 16 ♕h6 – but not 16 hxg4 ♕h2+ 17 ♔f2 ♕h4+ 18 ♔e2 ♖de8 19 ♗e4

♖xg4 20 ♗f5+ ♔d8 21 ♗xg4 ♕xg4+ 22 ♔d3 ♖xe3+ 23 ♗xe3 f5 and White has a lot of defending to do – 16...♗xh3! 17 ♕xh5 ♖xg2+ 18 ♔h1 ♖h2+ with a draw) 15...♖he8 (15...♖de8 16 ♕h6 would benefit White). After 15...♖he8 Black has enough play, for example 16 ♕h6 ♗c5! 17 dxc5 (17 ♕xh5 ♗xd4+ 18 ♔g2 ♗xh5 is equal) 17...♕xc5+ 18 ♔h1 ♕d5+ and Black delivers perpetual check.

c22) 13 0-0 is stronger: 13...♘d5 (after 13...♘xe4?! 14 ♗xe4 ♗d6 15 h3 ♖hf8 16 ♗d2 White is simply a pawn ahead) 14 ♕g5 ♘b4 15 h3 (15 ♘f2 ♘xd3 16 ♘xd3 ♖xd4 was played in Zhao Zhong Yuan-Solomon, Gold Coast 1999; following 17 ♕xh5 ♗xh5 18 ♗e3 ♖e4 19 ♖ae1 the position looks even) 15...♗e2 16 ♗xe2 ♕xe2 17 ♕f5+ ♔b8 18 ♗f4 and we slightly prefer White.

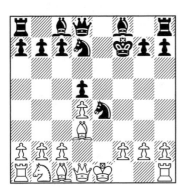

7 ♕h5+ ♔e6!?

The adventurous approach. Also possible is 7...♔e7 and now:

a) 8 ♕xd5?! is known to be bad after 8...♘df6 9 ♕b3 (9 ♕e5+? ♔f7 10 ♗xe4 ♗b4+ 11 c3 ♖e8 and Black wins) 9...♗e6 10 ♕xb7 ♔f7!? (Yusupov) 11 0-0 (11 ♗xe4 ♖b8 12 ♕c6 ♖b6 13 ♕a8 ♕xd4 and Black wins) 11...♗d6! 12 f3 ♗xh2+! 13 ♔xh2 ♕d6+ 14 ♔g1 ♕xd4+ 15 ♔h2 ♕e5+ 16 ♔g1 ♘g3 and Black has the advantage.

b) 8 ♕e2 ♔f7 (8...♗d6? 9 ♗f4+ ♔c6 10 ♗xe4 dxe4 11 ♘c3 a6 12 ♕c4+ ♔b6 13 ♗xc7+! and White wins – Olthof; 8...♔f6 9

♕f3+ ♔e6 could still transpose to the game, though it looks risky with the king on f6) 9 ♕h5+ with a repetition.

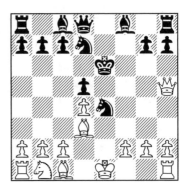

8 ♕e2

8 ♗xe4?! is less reliable: 8...dxe4 9 d5+ ♔e7 10 ♗g5+ ♘f6 11 ♘c3 ♗f5 12 0-0-0 ♔d7 13 ♕h4 ♗d6 and Black is a piece up.

A more serious option is 8 ♕g4+ ♔d6 (8...♔f7 draws) and now:

a) 9 ♗f4+? ♔c6 10 ♕e6+ (on 10 ♗xe4 luckily for Black he has 10...♘f6! 11 ♕g5 h6, winning) 10...♗d6 11 ♗xe4 ♘f6 and White's queen is trapped.

b) 9 ♗xe4?! dxe4 10 ♕xe4 (10 ♗f4+ ♔e7 11 ♕g3 ♘f6 and Black is close to winning) 10...♘f6 11 ♗f4+ ♔d7 12 ♕e2 ♗b4+ 13 c3 ♖e8 14 ♗e5 ♗d6 and Black is certainly better.

c) 9 ♕e2 ♕h4 10 g3 ♕e7 11 c4 when White has compensation, but is it enough?

8...♗d6 9 f3 ♕h4+

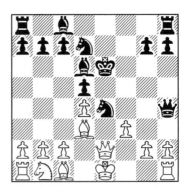

10 g3?

This is already the losing mistake – White must move his king:

a) 10 ♔f1 ♗xh2 11 c4 c6 12 ♘d2 ♗e5 13 ♖xh4 ♘g3+ 14 ♔f2 ♘xe2 15 ♔xe2 ♗f6 16 ♖xh7 ♖xh7 17 ♗xh7 ♗xd4 would probably lead to a draw.

b) 10 ♔d1 ♔f7 (or 10...♘e5 11 fxe4 ♘xd3 12 exd5+ [12 cxd3 ♖f8 is a mess] 12...♔d7 13 ♕xd3 ♕g4+ 14 ♕f3 ♕xd4+ 15 ♗d2 with chances for both sides) 11 fxe4 ♘f6 (after 11...dxe4?! 12 ♖f1+ ♘f6 13 ♗c4+ ♔e7 14 h3 White is better) 12 ♘d2 dxe4 13 ♘xe4 ♗g4 14 ♘g5+ ♔f8 15 ♘f3 ♕h5 and Black has good play for the pawn.

10...♗xg3+ 11 ♔d1

After 11 ♔f1 ♗f4 White is doing very badly.

11...♘df6 12 fxe4 ♔f7 13 ♕g2 ♗g4+ 14 ♗e2

14 ♔d2 ♗f4+ 15 ♔c3 ♗h3 16 ♕f3 ♗xc1 17 ♖xc1 dxe4 18 ♗c4+ ♔f8 19 ♕g3 ♕xg3+ 20 hxg3 ♖e8 also gives Black a material edge.

14...♗xe2+ 15 ♔xe2 ♕xe4+

Or 15...♘xe4 16 ♖f1+ ♔g8 17 ♘d2 ♕xh2 18 ♕xh2 ♗xh2 19 ♘xe4 ♖e8 and Black should win, though it will take some work.

16 ♕xe4 ♘xe4 17 c4 ♖ae8 18 ♗e3 ♘f2

Another option is 18...♗d6!? 19 cxd5 ♘f6.

19 ♖f1 ♗f4 20 ♖xf2 ♖xe3+ 21 ♔f1 g5

The endgame is horrible for White and, in correspondence chess. almost impossible to hold.

22 ♘c3 dxc4 23 ♘e2 ♖e4 24 ♖c1 ♖he8 25 ♘xf4 gxf4 26 ♖xc4 c6 27 ♖c5 ♖xd4 28 ♖f5+ ♔g6 29 ♖5xf4 ♖xf4 30 ♖xf4 ♖e5 31 ♖g4+ ♔f6 32 ♖g2 a5 33 b3 ♖c5 34 ♔e1 ♖g5 35 ♖f2+ ♔e6 36 ♔d2 ♖h5 37 ♔c3 b5 38 ♖d2 c5 39 ♖g2 ♖h3+ 40 ♔c2 ♔d5 41 ♖e2 b4 42 ♔b2 ♔c6 43 a3 a4! 44 axb4 ♖xb3+ 45 ♔a2 cxb4 46 ♖e4 ♔c5 47 ♖e5+ ♔d4 48 ♖a5 ♖h3 49 ♖xa4 ♔c3 0-1

Summary

In the main line Black has very much switched to 7...♗d6 recently. However, the annotated games prove that 7...♕h4 remains interesting and gives Black excellent counterplay after 8 c4 0-0-0 9 c5 g6, and especially after 9...g5. Nevertheless, the truth is that 7...♕h4 leads to extremely sharp positions that are not to everyone's taste.

As Game 54 shows, 6 ♘xd7 ♗xd7 7 0-0 ♕f6 allows White to win a pawn after 8 ♗xe4 dxe4 9 ♘c3 ♕g6 10 ♘xe4; Black has some compensation, but no more than that. However, if we insert the moves 7...♕h4 8 g3 and now 8...♕f6! 9 ♗xe4 dxe4 10 ♘c3 ♕g6 11 ♘xe4 0-0-0, Black has a full compensation due to the weakened light squares on the kingside.

The brave 6 ♘xf7 (Game 58) has not been played much recently. Black should accept the 'gift' with 6...♔xf7 and following 7 ♕h5+ he should move forward with 7...♔e6! – Black's chances are preferable in the arising complications. On the other hand, White has a plus after 6...♕e7 7 ♕e2! ♔xf7 8 f3 ♘f6 9 ♘d2 ♕h5 10 fxe4 ♗g4 11 ♕e3. The assessment of the Zaitsev-Karpov game has changed and become more precise. At present the best line is considered to be 6...♕e7 7 ♘xh8 ♘c3+ 8 ♔d2 ♘xd1 9 ♖e1 ♘xf2 10 ♗xh7 ♘e5 11 ♖xe5 ♗e6 12 ♗g8 ♕h4 13 ♗f7+ ♔d8 14 ♖xe6 ♕g5+ 15 ♔e2 ♕xg2, which is 'a hell of a mess'.

1 e4 e5 2 ♘f3 ♘f6 3 d4 ♘xe4 4 ♗d3 d5 5 ♘xe5 ♘d7 (D) 6 ♘xd7

6 ♕e2 – *Game 56*; 6 ♘c3 – *Game 57*; 6 ♘xf7 – *Game 58*

6...♗xd7 7 0-0 ♗d6

7...♕f6 – *Game 54*; 7...♗e7 – *Game 55*

7...♕h4 8 c4 0-0-0 9 c5 (D)

9...g6 – *Game 53*

9...g5

10 ♗e3 – *Game 51*

10 f3 – *Game 52*

10 ♘c3 ♗g7: 11 g3 – *Game 49*; 11 ♘e2 – *Game 50*

8 c4

8 ♘c3 – *Game 48*

8...c6 9 cxd5 cxd5 (D) 10 ♘c3

10 ♕h5 0-0 11 ♕xd5 ♗c6 12 ♕h5 g6 13 ♕h3: 13...♗b4 – *Game 46*; 13...♘g5 – *Game 47*

10...♘xc3 11 bxc3 0-0 12 ♕h5 f5 – *Game 44*

12...g6 – *Game 45*

5...♘d7

9 c5

9...cxd5

CHAPTER SEVEN

3 d4: 5...♗d6 and Fifth Move Alternatives

1 e4 e5 2 ♘f3 ♘f6 3 d4 ♘xe4 4 ♗d3 d5 5 ♘xe5

In the previous chapter we looked at the main line with 1 e4 e5 2 ♘f3 ♘f6 3 d4 ♘xe4 4 ♗d3 d5 5 ♘xe5 ♘d7. Now it is time to study other 5th move options for Black.

Until quite recently the symmetrical response 5...♗d6 (Games 59-62) was as popular as 5...♘d7. After mutual castling White attacks the centre, but this can be done in more than one way. If White develops his queen's knight for this purpose, he should prefer 7 ♘d2 (Game 61) to 7 ♘c3 (Game 62) because it avoids doubled pawns.

However, the main way of attacking the centre is with 7 c4 (Games 59-60). Black has numerous responses against this. Strengthening the d5-pawn with 7...c6 is a bit passive, while the counterattack on the d4-pawn with 7...♘c6 (Game 60) isn't sufficient to equalise in view of 8 ♘xc6 bxc6 9 c5 ♗e7 10 ♘d2 or 10 ♘c3 – the pawn doubling is unfavourable for Black. A sharp and critical position (despite a queen exchange) is reached after 7...♗xe5 8 dxe5 ♘c6 (8...♗e6 does not equalise) 9 cxd5 (the only try for an advantage) 9...♕xd5 10 ♕c2 ♘b4 11 ♗xe4 ♘xc2 12 ♗xd5, and this has been considered a tabiya of the whole 5...♗d6 system for many years. The fate of Black's knight driven into the corner is the main question of this key position, one which is studied in Game 59.

5...♘c6 attacks both White's centralised knight and the d4-pawn. However, this is not the best idea as White can simply swap the knights to inflict doubled pawns on his opponent. Now 6 ♘xc6 bxc6 7 0-0 ♗e7 transposes to 5...♗e7 6 0-0 ♘c6 7 ♘xc6 bxc6 (see Game 63), while 6 ♘xc6 bxc6 7 0-0 ♗d6 transposes to 5...♗d6 6 0-0 ♘c6 7 ♘xc6 bxc6 (see Game 61). However, Bilguer demonstrated that White does not have to castle; 7 ♕e2 creates problems for Black along the e-file, and that's why 5...♘c6 is almost out of use.

The continuation 5...♗e7 (Game 63) does not challenge the e5-knight and is dictated by the wish to complete development as soon as possible. A bit passive, 5...♗e7 has never drawn much attention. However, even after the most natural 6 0-0 0-0 7 c4 c6 it is unclear how White can gain a visible advantage. Probably White should consider Steinitz's recommendation of 7 ♖e1!?.

Game 59
Van Der Wiel-Mellado
Elgoibar 1998

---

1 e4 e5 2 ♘f3 ♘f6 3 d4 ♘xe4 4 ♗d3 d5

5 ♘xe5 ♗d6

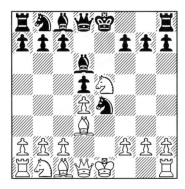

Other options are considered in Game 63.

6 0-0 0-0

Sixth move alternatives for both sides are studied in Game 61.

7 c4 ♗xe5 8 dxe5 ♘c6

8...♗e6 is less reliable. White can put Black under immediate pressure with 9 cxd5 ♕xd5 10 ♕c2 f5 11 exf6 ♘xf6 12 ♘c3 ♕e5 (12...♕c6 13 b3 ♘bd7 14 ♗a3 ♘c5 15 ♗b5 ♕b6 16 ♖ae1 also looks promising for White) 13 ♘e4 ♘g4 14 ♘g3 h5 (14...h6? 15 ♗xh6! ♘xh6 16 ♖ae1 ♕f6 17 ♖xe6! would end the show) 15 ♗d2 ♗d5 (15...h4? 16 ♖ae1 and White takes on e6 again) 16 ♗c3 ♕g5 17 ♗h7+ ♔h8 18 ♕g6 ♕xg6 19 ♗xg6 with a clear plus for White, Liberzon-Hennings, Debrecen 1968.

9 cxd5

White needs to try to refute Black's set-up altogether in order to play for an advantage. Other moves are less critical:

a) 9 f3 ♘c5 10 cxd5 ♘d3 11 ♕xd3 ♘b4 (11...♘xe5 12 ♕d4 ♖e8 13 ♘c3 ♗f5 14 ♗e3 ♕e7 also looks okay for Black) 12 ♕b3 ♘xd5 13 ♖d1 c6 14 ♘c3 ♕b6+ 15 ♕xb6 ♘xb6 16 b3 ♗e6 17 ♔f2 ♖fd8 18 ♖xd8+ ♖xd8 is drawish, Raetsky-Kuznetsov, correspondence 1983,

b) 9 f4 ♗f5 (maybe an even safer way to equalise is 9...♘b4 10 cxd5 ♕xd5 11 ♗xe4 ♕xe4 12 ♘c3 ♕g6 13 ♗e3 ♗g4 14 ♘d5!? ♘xd5 15 ♕xd5 b6) 10 ♘c3 ♘xc3 11 bxc3 ♗xd3 12 ♕xd3 dxc4 13 ♕xc4 ♘a5 14 ♕e4 ♕e7 and Black is okay (Kapengut).

c) 9 ♗f4 ♘b4 10 cxd5 (or 10 ♘a3 ♘c5 11 ♗b1 dxc4 12 ♘xc4 ♗e6 13 b3 ♕xd1 14 ♖xd1 ♖ad8 with equality – Yusupov) 10...♕xd5 11 ♗e2 ♗f5 12 ♘a3 ♖ad8 13 ♗c4 ♕c6 14 ♕b3 a5 15 ♖ad1 ♕g6 16 ♖xd8 ♖xd8 17 ♖d1 ♖f8 18 ♕e3 h6 19 ♘b5 ♘c2 20 ♕e2 c6 21 ♘d6 ♘c5 with an unclear game, Raetsky-Filatov, correspondence 1982.

9...♕xd5 10 ♕c2

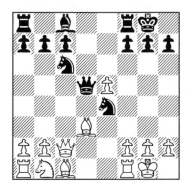

10 ♕f3? is much weaker as Black has 10...♗f5! 11 ♕xf5 ♕xd3 12 ♘c3 ♘c5 13 ♕h5 ♖fe8 14 f4 ♕d4+ 15 ♔h1 ♖ad8 16 ♕f3 ♕c4 when his position is preferable. To make matters worse, White only needs to play 11 ♖e1?! for Black to grab the advantage with 11...♖ad8 12 ♗xe4 ♗xe4 13 ♕g3 ♗xb1 14 ♖xb1 ♘xe5 15 ♗e3 ♖fe8, when Black should convert his pawn, Zelcic-Ascic, Rabac 2003.

10...♘b4

Absolutely the main line, but not the only move in the position because Black can also play 10...♗f5. For example, 11 ♘c3 ♘xc3 12 ♗xf5 ♘d4 13 ♗xh7+ ♔h8 14 ♕d3 ♘ce2+ 15 ♔h1 ♕xe5 16 ♕h3 ♘f4 17 ♗xf4 (17 ♕h4 g5 18 ♕h6 ♕g7 19 ♕xg7+ ♔xg7 20 ♗e4 c6 is very close to equal, if not simply equal) 17...♕xf4 18 ♖ad1 ♕h6 (18...♖fd8?! 19 ♗e4+ ♕h6 20 ♕c3 ♘c6 21 ♖d5 and Black was under pressure in Mi.Tseitlin-Kondali, correspondence 1990) 19 ♕xh6 gxh6 20 ♖xd4 ♔xh7 21 ♖d7 and White has a preferable rook endgame. However, whether this is enough to win is hard to tell.

11 ♗xe4 ♘xc2 12 ♗xd5 ♗f5

12...♘xa1 gives White a slight advantage after 13 ♗e4 (13 e6 ♘c2 14 exf7+ ♖xf7 15 ♖d1 ♗f5 16 ♗xf7+ ♔xf7 17 ♘c3 c6 leads to immediate equality) 13...♖e8 14 ♘c3 ♖xe5 15 ♗d2 ♖xe4 16 ♘xe4 ♘c2 17 ♖c1 ♗f5 18 f3 ♘d4 19 ♖xc7 ♗xe4 20 fxe4 b6 21 ♔f2. The endgame is uncomfortable for Black, though not necessarily impossible to defend. Note that after 21...♘e6 White retains the pressure with 22 ♖e7! ♔f8 23 ♗b4, when 23...♘c5 loses to 24 ♖c7.

13 g4!

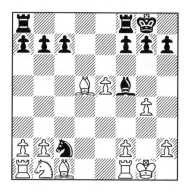

13...♗xg4

Or 13...♗g6 14 f4 and now:

a) 14...♗d3? 15 ♖d1 ♗a6 16 ♗e4! (16 e6 ♘xa1 17 exf7+ ♔h8 18 ♗e3 ♖ad8 19 ♘c3 also looks very promising for White) 16...♘xa1 17 ♗e3 ♗e2 18 ♖e1 ♗xg4 19 ♘c3 and White has good winning chances.

b) 14...c6 15 ♗c4 b5 with a further split:

b1) 16 ♗e2!? h5 17 f5 ♗h7 18 g5 ♘xa1 19 e6 fxe6 20 g6 ♗xg6 21 fxg6 ♖xf1+ 22 ♔xf1 probably leads to a draw, but this line is by no means forced and Black needs to do defend accurately.

b2) 16 f5 ♘xa1?, as in Ginda-Witt, Galati 1973, should have lost quickly to 17 ♗d3 ♖ad8 18 ♗e4 ♖d4 19 ♘d2 when Black will end up with material losses. Instead Black

should accept an inferior position with 16...bxc4.

14 ♗f4

14 ♗e4 ♘xa1 15 ♘c3 is the alternative, but probably less critical (15 ♗f4 simply transposes): 15...f5 16 exf6 ♗h3 17 ♖e1 ♖ae8 18 ♗d2 (18 ♗e3 ♖xe4 19 ♘xe4 ♘c2 20 ♖c1 ♘xe3 21 fxe3 c6 22 ♘g5 ♗f5 23 f7+ ♔h8 with equality, Tal-Timman, Reykjavik 1987) 18...♖xe4 19 ♘xe4 ♘c2 20 ♖c1 ♘d4 21 ♖xc7 ♘f3+ (21...gxf6?! 22 ♗e3 ♘e2+ 23 ♔h1 looks better; 21...♖f7!? 22 ♗xf7 ♘f3+ 23 ♔h1 ♔xf7 24 fxg7 ♔xg7 25 ♗e3 b6 26 ♘d2 ♘xd2 27 ♗xd2 a5 28 f3 a4 29 ♔g1 ♗e6 30 a3 ½-½ Tal-Karpov, Milan 1975 – Black will place his king on f7 and White can never make any progress) 22 ♔h1 ♘xd2 23 ♖xg7+ ♔h8 24 ♘g5 ♗f5! (the most precise; 24...♖xf6 25 ♖xh7+ ♔g8 26 ♖xh3 ♖xf2 still gives White chances – Gipslis) 25 ♘f7+ ♖xf7 26 ♖xf7 ♗e4+ 27 f3 ♗xf3+ 28 ♔g1 ♔g8 29 ♖d7 ♘c4 30 ♔f2 ♗c6 31 ♖g7+ ♔f8 32 ♖xh7 ♘d6 33 ♔e3 ♘e8 and the endgame is drawn, Raetsky-Belomestnykh, correspondence 1982.

14...♘xa1 15 ♗e4

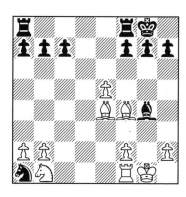

15 ♖c1 has also been tried a few times, but it is less dangerous for Black: 15...c6 16 ♗e4 (or 16 ♗g2 f6!? 17 exf6 ♖xf6 18 ♗e3 ♖g6 19 ♔h1 ♗e6 20 ♘d2 ♗xa2 21 ♖xa1 ♗d5 22 ♗xd5+ cxd5 and Black should not have any trouble at all) 16...f5 (or 16...f6 17 ♘c3 fxe5 18 ♗xe5 ♖ae8 19 f4 g5 20 ♖xa1

gxf4 21 ♗d4 a6 with complete equality) 17 exf6 ♖xf6 18 ♗e3 (Sveshnikov-Tischbierek, Budapest 1988). Now Black could have continued 18...♖e8 19 ♘c3 ♘b3 (19...b5 20 ♗g2 ♖g6 21 ♔h1 b4 22 ♘e4 ♗f5 23 ♘g3 ♖xg3 24 hxg3 ♘c2 25 ♗xc6 looks promising for White – two bishops and a weakened black queenside) 20 axb3 a6 21 ♗d3 ♗f5 and Black's position is at worst marginally inferior; in fact we think it's equal.

15...f5?!

After this move we cannot find a route to full equality. Probably Black should try 15...f6!? 16 ♘c3 fxe5, when his results have been encouraging:

a) 17 ♗g3 ♖ad8 18 ♖xa1 ♗f3 19 ♗xe5 ♖d2 gives good compensation (Yusupov).

b) 17 ♗e3 ♗f3 18 ♖xa1 ♗xe4 19 ♘xe4 b6 20 b4 a5 21 b5 ♖ad8 22 ♖c1 ♖f7 23 a4 h6 24 ♔g2 ♖d3 and Black had sufficient counterplay in Kasparov-Timman, Paris (rapid) 1991.

16 ♗d5+

Much weaker is 16 ♗xb7?! ♖ab8 17 ♗d5+ ♔h8 18 f3 (18 ♘a3?! ♖fd8 19 ♗c4 ♖d4 20 ♗e3 ♘c2! 21 ♗xd4 ♘xd4 and Black's more active pieces mean that he enjoys an advantage in the endgame) 18...♗h3 19 ♖d1 ♖xb2 20 e6 ♖g2+ 21 ♔h1 ♖c8 22 ♗c4 ♖g6 23 ♗g3 f4 24 e7 ♖d6 25 ♖xd6 cxd6 26 ♗xf4 ♗d7, when the responsibility of holding this endgame lies entirely with White.

16...♔h8 17 ♖c1 c6 18 ♗g2

Oddly enough the bishop is best placed here, where it seemingly has little influence. The reason for this is found in the following line: 18 ♗e6 g5! 19 ♗xg5 ♖ae8 20 ♗c4 (or 20 ♗h6 ♖xe6 21 ♗xf8 ♗h3 22 ♘c3 ♖g6+ 23 ♖g3 ♔g8 24 ♗e7 f4 25 ♖xg6+ hxg6 26 ♘a3 f3 27 ♗c5 b6 28 ♗d4 ♗f5 29 b4 ♘c2 30 ♘xc2 ♗xc2 ½-½ Oll-Khalifman, Vilnius 1988) 20...b5 21 ♗f1 f4 (Rozentalis-Ivanchuk, Minsk 1986). After 22 ♗f6+ ♖xf6 23 exf6 ♗f5 24 f7 ♖f8 Black is no worse.

18...♖fd8 19 ♘d2

This is the critical move. 19 f3 ♗h5 20 ♘a3 ♖d4 21 ♗e3 ♖b4 22 ♘c4 (22 ♖xa1 f4 23 ♗f2 ♖xb2 24 ♘c4 ♖c2 25 ♘d6 b6 is not clear) 22...♖a4 23 ♘a3 leads to a repetition, Sax-Yusupov, Thessaloniki 1984.

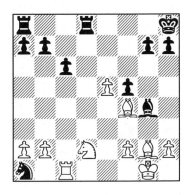

19...h6

19...♖xd2?! has an awful score. Following 20 ♗xd2 ♖d8 21 ♗c3 ♖d1+ 22 ♖xd1 ♗xd1 White should play the following plan: 23 ♗f1! (23 f4 ♘c2 24 ♔f2 ♔g8 25 a4 a5 26 ♗xa5 ♘d4 27 ♗f1 ♗b3 ½-½ Kasparov-Anand, Linares 1991) 23...g6 24 ♗c4 ♔g7 25 b4! (25 e6+ ♔f8 26 ♗f6 ♔e8 27 e7 ♘c2 is unclear – Yusupov) 25...♘c2 26 ♗b3 when it looks impossible for Black to improve his position. Black seemed to lose the following endgame without any real chance: 26...♔f8 27 ♗d2 ♔e7 28 f3 ♔e8 29 ♔f2 b6 30 ♗f4 c5 31 bxc5 bxc5 32 e6 c4 33 ♗xc4 ♘a3 34 ♗d5 ♗a4 35 ♗e3 a6 36 ♗c5 ♘c2 37 ♗c4 a5 38 ♔g3 ♘e1 39 ♔f4 ♗c6 40 ♗e2 h5 41 h3 ♔d8 42 ♔g5 ♗e8 43 e7+ ♔c7 44 f4 ♘g2 45 ♗f1 ♔c6 46 ♗f2 ♔d6 47 ♗xg2 1-0 Mru-gala-Wise, correspondence 1999.

20 h4 ♖d3 21 ♗f1!

This was Timman's improvement on his play in an earlier matchgame with Yusupov: 21 ♖xa1 g5! 22 hxg5 hxg5 23 ♗xg5 (23 ♗f1 gxf4 24 ♗xd3 ♖d8 25 e6 ♖xd3 26 e7 ♗h5 27 ♘b3 b6 28 ♖e1 ♗e8 and Black is fine – Yusupov) 23...♖g8 24 ♗f6+ ♔h7 25 ♘f1 f4 26 ♔h2 ♖g6! 27 ♖e1 ♖h6+ 28 ♔g1 ♖g6 with equality, Timman-Yusupov, 2nd match-game, Linares 1992.

21...♖d4 22 ♗e3 ♖d5 23 ♖xa1 ♖xe5 24 ♘c4 ♖e6

In the stem game Black played 24...♖d5 25 ♗g2 ♖b5?! 26 ♖e1 ♖d8 27 ♗xa7 ♖d1 28 ♖xd1 ♗xd1 29 ♗d4 f4 30 ♗e4 and White enjoyed a clear superiority, Timman-Yusupov, 6th matchgame, Linares 1992. Later Black improved with 25...♖dd8 26 ♖e1 ♔h7 27 ♔h2 ♗h5 28 ♗c5 b6 29 ♗e7 ♖d4 30 ♘d6 ♖d2 31 ♗xc6 ♖b8 32 ♔g3 f4+ 33 ♔xf4 ♖xf2+ 34 ♔g3 ♖xb2 with reasonable drawing chances even though it is still a tough defence, Bucher-Girtz, Biel 1998.

25 f4! ♗f3

25...♖e4 26 ♗d3 ♖ae8 looks tricky, but af-ter 27 ♔f2! ♖4e6 28 ♘e5 White has the ad-vantage.

26 ♘e5 ♗d5

26...♔h7 27 ♔f2 ♗h5 28 ♖c1 also fa-vours White.

27 h5 ♖ae8 28 ♗d3 ♗f3

Also possible is 28...b6 29 ♗f2! (29 ♗xf5?? ♖xe5! wins for Black). Now White has the edge after 29...♗e4 30 ♗c4 ♗d5 31 ♗xd5 cxd5 32 ♖d1.

29 ♔f2 ♗xh5 30 ♖h1 ♗g4 31 ♗xa7 ♖xe5?

This is simply a blunder. Black needs to play 31...♖a8 32 ♗d4 ♖a4 33 ♗c3 ♖xf4+ 34 ♔g3 ♖a4 35 ♗c2 ♖a8 36 ♗b3 when after 36...♖xe5 37 ♗xe5 White has some chances to win the game, though nothing is clear.

32 fxe5 ♖xe5 33 ♖xh6+! ♔g8 34 ♗c4+ ♔f8 35 ♖h8+ ♔e7 36 ♖b8 b5 37 ♖b7+ ♔d8

37...♔f6 38 ♗f1 ♖d5 39 ♖c7 also wins for White.

38 ♗b6+ ♔c8 39 ♖c7+ ♔b8 40 ♖xg7 1-0

Game 60
Shirov-Yusupov
Ter Apel 1997

1 e4 e5 2 ♘f3 ♘f6 3 d4 ♘xe4 4 ♗d3 d5 5 ♘xe5 ♗d6 6 0-0 0-0 7 c4 ♘c6

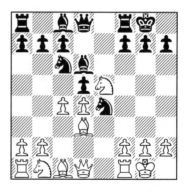

This particular variation, like so many in the Petroff, is a speciality of Yusupov's.

7...c6 is also possible, after which White has a wide range of choices:

a) 8 ♕c2 ♕h4 9 ♘f3 ♕h5 10 cxd5 cxd5 11 ♗xe4 dxe4 12 ♕xe4 ♘c6 and Black has compensation (Yusupov).

b) 8 cxd5 cxd5 9 ♕c2 ♖e8 10 f3 (10 ♗xe4 dxe4 11 ♕xe4 ♕f6 12 ♗f4 ♘c6 looks fine for Black) 10...♘f6 11 ♗g5 h6 12 ♗h4 ♘a6 13 a3 ♗xe5 14 dxe5 ♖xe5 15 ♗f2 and White has compensation for his pawn, although it is difficult to see how Black should ever end up being worse.

c) 8 ♘c3! seems to give White the edge after 8...♗xc3 9 bxc3 and now:

c1) 9...♗e6 10 f4 ♗xe5 11 fxe5 dxc4 12 ♗xh7+!? ♔xh7 13 ♕h5+ ♔g8 14 ♗g5 ♕a5 15 ♖f3 ♘d7 16 ♖g3 looks very dangerous for Black.

c2) 9...♘d7 10 f4!? (10 ♘xd7 ♗xd7 transposes to 5...♘d7 6 ♘xd7 ♗xd7 7 0-0 ♗d6 8 c4 c6 9 ♘c3 ♘xc3 10 bxc3 0-0) 10...♘f6 11 c5 ♗e7 12 f5 ♗d7 13 g4 gave White an attack in Korneev-Y.Hernandez, Mondariz 1997.

c3) 9...♗xe5 10 dxe5 dxc4 11 ♗xc4 ♕e7 (11...♕xd1 12 ♖xd1 ♗f5 13 ♗a3 ♖e8 14 f4 is clearly better for White; it gets even better after 14...♘d7? 15 e6! when White was winning in Maróczy-Marshall, Paris 1900) 12 a4 ♖d8 13 ♕h5 ♖e8?! (13...g6 was sadly necessary although after 14 ♗g5 gxh5 15 ♗xe7 ♖e8 16 ♗d6 Black is in a bad state) 14 ♗a3 ♕d7 15 ♖ad1 ♕f5 16 ♕h4 ♕xe5 17 f4 ♕f6 (17...♕e3+ 18 ♔h1 ♗e6 19 ♗d3 h6 20 a5! and Black's queen is trapped) 18 ♕xf6 gxf6 19 ♖f3 ♗e6 20 ♖g3+ ♔h8 21 ♗e7! h5 22 ♗xf6+ 1-0 Chigorin-Lebedev, Moscow 1900.

8 ♘xc6

This is the right path to an opening advantage. After 8 cxd5 ♘xd4 9 ♗xe4 (9 ♘c4 ♕h4 10 ♘xd6 ♘xd6 11 ♘c3 ♗f5 and Black has equalised – Euwe) 9...♗xe5 10 ♘c3 ♖e8 11 ♖e1 ♘f5 12 ♕f3 g6 13 ♗f4 ♗xf4 14 ♕xf4 ♘d6 15 ♖e3 ♗d7 16 ♖ae1 f5 17 ♗d3 ♕f6 18 a4 ♖xe3 19 ♖xe3 ♖e8 Black is very close to equality, Zelcic-Pavasovic, Nova Gorica 1997.

8...bxc6 9 c5 ♗e7 10 ♘c3

This seems to be the soundest way of playing for White, but it is not the only way:

a) After 10 f3 ♘g5 11 ♘c3 ♖e8 12 ♕a4 ♗d7 13 ♗d2 ♖b8 14 ♖ab1 ♗f6 15 ♔h1 h5 16 ♘e2 h4 17 h3 ♕c8 18 ♗a6 ♕d8 19 ♗d3 ♕c8 20 ♗a6 the game finished with a draw in Kasparov-Yusupov, Horgen 1995. 18 ♘f4!? ♘e6 19 ♖fe1 is interesting, but we believe that Black is okay after the following line: 19...♗g5!? 20 ♗a6 ♕d8 21 ♘xe6 ♖xe6 22 ♖xe6 ♗xe6 23 ♗xg5 ♕xg5 24 ♕xc6 ♗xh3! 25 ♗f1! ♗xg2+! 26 ♗xg2 ♕f5 27 ♖g1 h3 – the game will end in a draw.

b) 10 ♘d2!? looks stronger: 10...♗f6 11 ♘xe4 dxe4 12 ♗xe4 ♗a6 (12...♗xd4 13 ♕d3 ♔h8 14 ♗g5!? ♗xf2+ 15 ♖xf2 ♕xg5 16 ♗xh7 looks slightly better for White) 13 ♖e1 ♗xd4 14 ♕c2 ♖e8 15 ♗e3 ♗xb2 16 ♗xh7+ ♔h8 (Sanchez-Morgado, correspondence 1978) and now after 17 ♕xb2 ♔xh7 18 ♖ad1 ♕e7 19 ♕c3 we think White has some pressure.

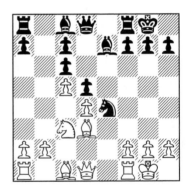

10...f5

Black seems to be unable to equalise here, and it's not due to a lack of trying:

a) 10...♗f5 11 f3 ♘xc3 12 bxc3 ♗xd3 13 ♕xd3 a5 (13...♗g5?! 14 ♕a6! ♗xc1 15 ♖axc1 ♕d7 16 ♖fe1 ♖fe8 17 ♖xe8+ ♖xe8 18 h3 h5 19 ♕xa7 and Black did not have enough for the pawn Shirov-Hübner, Frankfurt [rapid] 1996) 14 ♖b1 ♖e8 15 ♗d2 and White is a bit better.

b) 10...♗f6 11 ♕c2 (11 ♘xe4!? dxe4 12 ♗xe4 transposes to 10 ♘d2 ♗f6 11 ♘xe4 dxe4 12 ♗xe4) 11...♗xd4 12 ♘xe4 dxe4 13 ♗xe4 ♕h4 (13...♗a6?! 14 ♖d1 with a plus;

14...♗xf2+? 15 ♔xf2 ♕h4+ 16 g3! – 16
♔g1?! ♖ae8! is Black's point – 16...♕xh2+ 17
♗g2 and White is winning – Kasparov) 14 g3
♕f6 15 ♗e3! ♗xe3 (15...♗xb2 16 ♖ab1 ♗e5
17 ♗xh7+ ♔h8 18 ♗e4 should also favour
White) 16 fxe3 ♕h6 17 ♖f4 g5 18 ♖f2 ♗h3
19 ♗f5 and in this position White is somewhat better, Ivanchuk-Yusupov, Horgen
1995.

11 f3 ♘g5 12 ♕a4 ♗d7 13 ♗f4

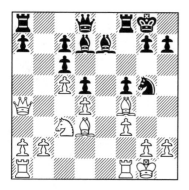

Or 13 ♘e2 ♗f6 14 ♘f4 ♕e7 15 ♗d2 g6
16 ♖ae1 ♕g7 17 ♗c3 h5 18 ♗a6 ♖ab8 19
♘d3 h4 20 ♘e5 with a slight advantage,
Timman-Yusupov, 8th matchgame, Linares
1992.

13...♗f6 14 ♖ae1 ♘e6

14...♘f7 is punished by 15 ♘e2 g6 16
♕a5, when Black cannot defend himself
properly.

15 ♗e5 ♗xe5 16 ♖xe5 ♕h4

16...♘f4 17 ♗b1 ♘g6 18 ♖ee1 ♖e8 was
an alternative, although White's position still
looks more promising.

17 f4!?

Shirov, the great calculator of complicated
lines, naturally takes the chance to enter this
wildly complex position. He suggests that
after 17 ♗xf5 ♖xf5! (17...♘xc5? 18 ♗xh7+
♔xh7 19 dxc5 is good for White) 18 ♖xf5
♘xc5 19 dxc5 ♕xa4 20 ♘xa4 ♗xf5 White
has a slight edge.

After 17 f4 Black has little choice but to
take the challenge.

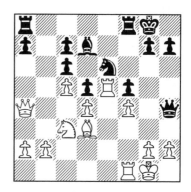

**17...♘xf4 18 g3 ♘h3+ 19 ♔g2 ♕h6 20
♘xd5 f4?**

Black should play 20...♖ae8 21 ♘e7+ ♔h8
22 ♗xf5! ♖xe7 23 ♗xd7! (but not 23 ♖xe7?!
♕d2+ 24 ♔xh3 ♖xf5 25 ♖xf5 ♗xf5+ 26 g4
♗xg4+ 27 ♔g3 ♗h5! 28 ♖e5 ♕d3+ and
Black attains a draw) 23...♖xf1 24 ♔xf1 ♖f7+
25 ♖f5 ♖xf5+ 26 ♗xf5 and White is only
slightly better (Shirov).

21 ♘e7+ ♔h8 22 ♘f5!

It is important that it's the knight that
goes to f5: after 22 ♗f5? fxg3 23 hxg3 g6 24
♗xd7 ♕d2+ 25 ♔xh3 ♖xf1 White is missing
his bishop in defence.

22...♕g5

22...♗xf5 23 ♖xf5 ♖ae8 24 ♕d1! wins for
White according to Shirov – the knight is
simply trapped.

23 ♘h4 ♕h6 24 ♗f5!

24...fxg3

The last chance was probably 24...♗xf5 25 ♘xf5 ♕g6 26 ♕c2 ♕g4 27 ♕d1, when White retains a large advantage but Black can struggle still.

25 hxg3 g6 26 ♗xd7 ♕d2+ 27 ♔xh3 ♖xf1 28 ♗xc6 ♖af8 29 ♗g2

Also winning is 29 ♖e7 ♖e1 30 ♖xe1 ♕xe1 31 ♕b3 ♔g7 32 g4, but the game continuation looks safer despite the complex lines.

29...♖1f2

Black also loses after 29...♖1f7 30 ♖e8 g5 31 ♗d5 ♖f6 32 ♖xf8+ ♖xf8 33 ♘f3, but not 32 ♘f3? g4+ 33 ♔xg4 ♖g6+ 34 ♔h3 ♖h6+ 35 ♘h4 ♖xh4+! 36 gxh4 ♕d3+ when Black escapes with a draw.

30 ♕d7 g5 31 ♖e7 ♕c2 32 ♗e4 ♖h2+ 33 ♔g4 ♖xh4+

Black's attack also runs out of steam after 33...♕e2+ 34 ♘f3 34...h5+ 35 ♔xg5 ♕e3+ 36 ♔g6 ♖g8+ 37 ♖g7 ♕xe4+ 38 ♔h6 ♕e3+ 39 ♘g5, when despite his extra exchange Black is 'out of bullets'.

34 gxh4 ♕e2+ 35 ♔xg5 ♖g8+ 36 ♔f6 1-0

Game 61
Timoscenko-Yusupov
Frunze 1979

---

1 e4 e5 2 ♘f3 ♘f6 3 d4 ♘xe4 4 ♗d3 d5 5 ♘xe5 ♗d6 6 0-0

White has a extensive list of alternatives:

a) 6 ♘c3 ♘xc3 7 bxc3 0-0 8 0-0 ♘d7 transposes to Game 62.

b) 6 ♕f3 0-0 7 0-0 c5!? 8 ♗xe4 dxe4 9 ♕xe4 ♕e7 10 ♖e1 ♖e8 11 ♘d2 cxd4 12 ♘ef3 (12 ♘ec4 ♗b4 13 ♕xe7 ♖xe7 14 ♖xe7 ♗xe7 15 ♘e4 ♘c6 would give Black a preferable endgame) 12...♘c6 13 ♕xe7 ♖xe7 14 ♘e4 ♗c7 15 ♗d2 ♗g4 16 ♘c5 ♗d6 17 ♘e4 ♗c7 with a draw, Raetsky-Mironov, correspondence 1985.

c) 6 ♘d2 ♗xe5 7 dxe5 ♘c5 8 ♘f3 ♘xd3+ (or 8...♗g4!? 9 h3 ♘xd3+ 10 ♕xd3 ♗xf3 11 ♕xf3 0-0 12 ♕g3 ♔h8 13 ♗g5 ♕d7 14

0-0-0 c5 with a very complex position in which White might have an edge) 9 ♕xd3 c6 10 0-0 ♗g4 11 ♘g5 (the less obvious 11 ♗d2 ♘d7 12 ♘d4 ♕b6 13 h3 ♗e6 14 ♘xe6 fxe6 is not easy to evaluate) 11...h6 12 ♕d4 ♗e6 13 ♘xe6 fxe6 14 c4 ♕e7 15 ♗d2 c5 16 ♕g4 d4 and Black has no obvious worries in this unclear position, Raetsky-Y.Aleksandrov, correspondence 1983.

d) 6 c4

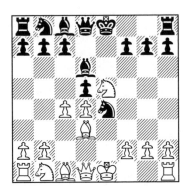

This allows Black to act quickly with 6...♗xe5 7 dxe5 ♘c6 8 0-0 ♘c5 9 cxd5 ♕xd5 10 ♗b5 ♕xd1 (weaker is 10...♗e6 11 ♕xd5 ♗xd5 12 ♘c3 0-0-0 13 ♗e3 ♘e4 14 ♘xd5 ♖xd5 15 ♗xc6 bxc6, when White had an endgame edge in Lindoerfer-Meijers, Schwabisch Gmund 1998) 11 ♖xd1 ♗d7 12 ♘c3 ♘e6 13 f4 ♘ed4 14 ♗a4 0-0-0 and here we can see no argument supporting a white edge.

6...0-0

Or:

a) 6...♗xe5 7 dxe5 ♘c5 is a slightly dubious favourite of the solid GM from Lithuania, Eduardas Rozentalis. Now 8 ♗e2! is probably the right path for White here, for example 8...0-0 9 b3!? ♘c6 (9...c6 10 ♗a3 ♕e7 11 f4 a5 12 ♘c3 ♘bd7 13 ♕d4 gives White a powerful initiative) 10 ♗a3 b6 11 f4 ♖e8 12 ♘c3 d4 13 ♗f3 ♗b7 14 ♗xc5 bxc5 15 ♘a4 ♕e7 16 ♕e2 ♘d8 17 ♕b5 and White has strong pressure, C.Hansen-Rozentalis, Malmö 1997.

b) 6...♘c6 7 ♘xc6 bxc6 8 c4 ♕h4?! (8...0-0, transposing to 6...0-0, is preferable) 9 g3 ♕h3 (9...♕f6 is refuted by 10 ♗xe4 dxe4 11 ♘c3 ♗f5 12 f3! ♕g6 13 fxe4 ♗h3 14 e5! ♗xf1 15 exd6 ♗h3 16 ♕e2+ ♕e6 17 ♕xe6+ ♗xe6 18 dxc7 ♗xc4 19 ♗f4 with a clear advantage for White – analysed by the very reliable duo Yusupov and Dvoretsky) 10 c5 ♗g4 11 ♗e2 ♗xe2 12 ♕xe2 ♗e7 13 f3 ♘f6 14 ♗f4 and Black has achieved little with his kingside actions – White has a slight advantage.

c) 6...c5!? allows White to gain an edge with 7 ♗b5+ ♘d7 8 dxc5 ♗xe5 9 ♕xd5 0-0! (9...♕e7?! 10 c6! would be an unpleasant surprise) 10 ♕xe4 ♕c7 11 ♗d3 g6 12 ♕h4 ♘xc5 13 ♗e2 ♗f5 when Black has some compensation for the pawn, but hardly enough. White could even consider 14 ♘c3!? here.

7 ♘d2

7 ♖e1 is a respectable alternative, after which we have the following possibilities:

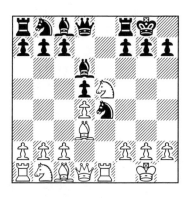

a) 7...♗xe5 8 dxe5 ♘c6 9 ♗f4 f5 10 f3 ♘c5 11 ♗b5 ♘e6 with unclear play (Yusupov).

b) 7...c5 8 c4!? cxd4 9 cxd5 ♗xe5 (9...♘c5 10 ♗c4 ♖e8 11 ♗f4 ♗f5 12 ♘d2 looks good for White, as after 12...f6 13 ♘c6! Black is under attack) 10 ♗xe4 f5 11 ♗f3 ♕d6 12 h3 giving a position balanced on the edge between a slight white plus and equality. In other words, something along the lines of

equality but Black needs to prove it! In Slobodjan-Forintos, Germany 1992, Black failed to do so and following 12...♘d7 13 ♘a3 ♗f6 14 ♘c2 ♘e5 15 ♘xd4 ♘xf3+ 16 ♘xf3 b6 17 ♗g5 ♗b7 18 ♗xf6 ♖xf6 19 ♖e5 White held a clear advantage.

c) 7...♘d7 8 ♗xe4 (8 ♘xd7 leads to an immediate draw after 8...♗xh2+ 9 ♔xh2 ♕h4+ 10 ♔g1 ♕xf2+) 8...dxe4 9 ♘c4 ♘b6 10 ♘xd6 ♕xd6 11 ♖xe4 ♗f5 12 ♖e5 ♕g6 and Black has good counterplay for the pawn.

7...♗xe5 8 dxe5 ♘c5 9 ♘b3

9 ♕h5 does not look dangerous here, 9...♘xd3 10 cxd3 c5 being the most natural reaction. Now 11 b4?! looks unjustified: 11...cxb4 12 a3 bxa3 13 ♗xa3 ♖e8 14 ♗d6 ♘c6 15 ♖a4 ♕d7 16 ♖f4 ♕e6 17 d4 ♕g6 18 ♕f3 ♗e6 with a clear edge for Black, J. Polgar-Kamsky, Groningen 1993. After the more sensible 11 ♘b3 ♕c7 12 ♗f4 ♗e6 Black shouldn't be worse.

9...♘xd3 10 ♕xd3 ♘c6

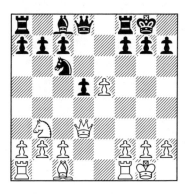

11 ♗f4

11 f4 should probably be met by 11...f6 12 exf6 ♕xf6!? (12...♖xf6 13 f5!? ♘e5 14 ♕h3 ♕f8 15 g4 ♘c4 16 ♘d4 is very complex and difficult to evaluate) 13 ♕xd5+ ♗e6 14 ♕c5 ♖ad8 15 ♗d2!? ♕xb2 16 ♗c3 ♕xc2 17 ♗xg7! ♕xc5+ 18 ♘xc5 ♖fe8 19 ♗c3 (Ljubojevic-Razuvaev, Amsterdam 1975), and now 19...♗c4! 20 ♘xb7 ♗xf1 21 ♘xd8 ♗xg2 22 ♔xg2 ♖xd8 leads to an endgame that Black

will have to defend, but *can* defend with accurate play.

11...♕d7 12 ♖ad1

12 ♗g3 leads to a harmless position after 12...b6 13 ♖fe1 ♘b4 14 ♕d2 c5 15 ♘d4 ♕g4 16 c3 cxd4 17 cxb4 d3 18 ♕xd3 ♕xb4 19 a3 ♕c4 20 ♕d2 (½-½ Grünfeld-Yusupov, Amsterdam 1982).

12...♕g4 13 ♕e3 ♘e7 14 h3

14 ♕c5 ♘f5 15 g3 c6 does not cause any real problems for Black.

14...♕g6 15 c3

15 ♕c5 invites Black to play a pleasing piece sacrifice with 15...♗xh3!? 16 ♗g3 ♘f5! 17 gxh3 ♘xg3 18 fxg3 ♕xg3+ 19 ♔h1 ♕xh3+ 20 ♔g1 ♕g3+ 21 ♔h1 ♖ae8!? (of course a draw was available) 22 ♖d3 ♕h4+ 23 ♔g2 ♖e6, when we fear for the safety of the white king.

15...b6 16 e6?!

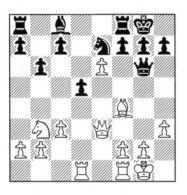

A poor strategic mistake. Black will enjoy the open f-file and develop very quickly. 16 ♘d4 c5 17 ♘f3 ♗b7 18 ♘h4 ♕e6 would give Black plenty of counterplay, but this was still the best option.

16...c5 17 exf7+ ♖xf7 18 ♖fe1 ♗d7 19 ♕g3 ♕c6 20 ♗g5 ♘f5 21 ♕f3 h6 22 ♗c1 ♘e7 23 ♕e2?!

Here the queen is not very well placed. 23 ♕g3 is stronger; following 23...♖af8 White has 24 ♗f4 ♘f5 25 ♕h2 g5 26 ♗e5 with some counterplay, even though Black is better after 26...♕a4.

23...♖af8 24 ♗e3 ♕g6 25 ♔h2 ♘f5 26 ♗f4?

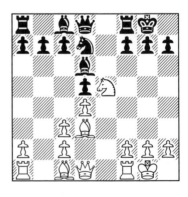

Tougher resistance was possible with 26 ♖f1, though after 26...♗a4 27 ♖c1 ♕c6 28 ♘d2 ♗b5 29 c4 ♗a6 Black is very close to a winning position.

26...♘h4 0-1

Game 62
Anand-Mishra
India 1988

---

1 e4 e5 2 ♘f3 ♘f6 3 d4 ♘xe4 4 ♗d3 d5 5 ♘xe5 ♗d6 6 0-0 0-0 7 ♘c3 ♘xc3

The colourful 7...f5!? 8 f3 ♗xe5 9 dxe5 ♘xc3 10 bxc3 ♕e7 11 ♖e1 ♗e6 12 a4 c5 lead to unclear play in Geller-Yusupov, Vilnius 1980.

8 bxc3 ♘d7

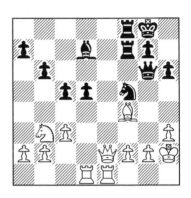

8...c5!? has also been suggested: 9 ♕h5 g6

10 ♕h6 ♘c6!? 11 ♗g5 ♗e7 (11...f6 12 ♗xg6 – 12 ♘xg6? ♖f7! – 12...♕c7 13 ♗xf6 ♖xf6 14 ♗xh7+ ♔xh7 15 ♕xf6 might favour White slightly) 12 ♗xe7 ♕xe7 13 ♖ae1 ♕f6 14 ♘xc6 bxc6 15 dxc5 ♕xc3 16 f4 ♕xc5+ 17 ♔h1 f5 with unclear play (Yusupov). However both 14 f4!? and even 14 ♗b5!? look like reasonable improvements for White.

9 ♖e1

Or:

a) 9 ♘xd7 ♗xd7 transposes to 5...♘d7 6 ♘xd7 ♗xd7 7 0-0 ♗d6 8 ♘c3 ♘xc3 9 bxc3 0-0.

b) 9 f4 c5 10 c4!? cxd4 11 ♘xd7 (11 cxd5?! ♘f6 12 ♗c4 ♗c5 13 ♕f3?! – 13 ♘d3 ♕c7 only leaves Black slightly better – 13...♗f5 14 ♖e1 ♕a5! 15 ♗b2 d3+ 16 ♔h1 d2 and White is in deep trouble, Kupreichik-Dvoretsky, Leningrad 1974) 11...♗xd7 12 cxd5 ♕a5 13 ♕h5 f5 14 ♕f3 ♗b5 and Black should not be worse.

9...♘xe5

9...♗xe5 10 dxe5 ♘c5 is a respectable alternative,

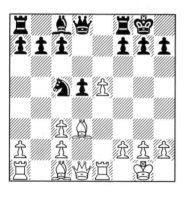

after which White can play:

a) 11 ♖b1 ♘xd3 12 cxd3 b6 looks very solid for Black. It is unlikely that White can squeeze an advantage out of the position, for example 13 ♖b4 f5 14 exf6 (14 d4 ♗e6 15 ♗a3 f4 16 ♖b2 ♖f7 with chances for both sides) 14...♕xf6 15 ♖f4 ♗f5 16 ♗d2 ♕d6 17 ♕f3 ♗d7 18 ♕h5 c6 and Black had equal-

ised, A. Sokolov-Schandorff, Bundesliga 2001.

b) 11 ♗f1 ♖e8 12 ♕h5 ♕d7 13 ♗e3 ♕c6 14 ♖ab1 a6 15 ♖b4 b6 (15...♘e4 16 c4 ♗e6 17 cxd5 ♗xd5 18 c4 ♗e6 19 ♗d3 would give White real threats) 16 ♖h4 h6?! (Chiburdanidze-Schussler, Haninge 1988), and now White had the chance to play 17 c4! dxc4 18 ♗xc4 ♗e6 19 ♗xh6! ♗xc4 20 ♗e3 with a close-to-winning position – 20...f6 21 exf6 ♕xf6 22 ♖xc4, if forced, simply leaves White a piece up. Instead of 16...h6, Black should play 16...♕g6 17 ♕xg6 hxg6 when maybe White has a small plus.

10 dxe5 ♗c5 11 ♕h5 g6 12 ♕h6 ♖e8 13 ♗g5 ♗f8 14 ♕h4 ♕d7

14...♗e7 15 ♗f6 c5!? 16 c4 d4 does not look clear at all. All these positions are really difficult to evaluate, as time after time everything hangs on one move.

15 ♖ab1 ♖b8 16 c4 d4 17 f4

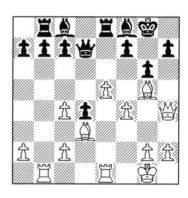

17...♕c6?

First of all, it is not obvious what the queen is doing here. Secondly, Black should not give White a free hand to continue his attack on the kingside. After 17...♕g4 18 ♕f2 c5 Black would at worst only be slightly worse.

18 ♗f6 ♗g7?

Black should not voluntarily part with his only defensive piece. After 18...h6 19 ♕g3 ♔h7 20 ♖f1 ♗f5 21 ♗xf5 gxf5 22 ♕h3 ♕d7 23 ♖f3 things look bleak for Black, but this is still favourable to the game.

19 f5 ♕c5

Or 19...♗xf6 20 exf6 ♗d7 21 ♖f1! and the double threat of fxg6 followed by ♗xg6 combined with ♕h6 ends all speculation about the result.

20 ♗xg7 ♔xg7 21 ♕f6+ ♔g8 22 e6 1-0

Game 63
Aagaard-Legky
Budapest 1996

---

1 e4 e5 2 ♘f3 ♘f6 3 d4 ♘xe4 4 ♗d3 d5 5 ♘xe5 ♗e7

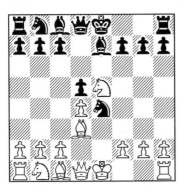

This is a bit passive and Black can easily end up in a slightly worse position.

Another sideline that is no longer popular is 5...♘c6 6 ♘xc6 bxc6 7 ♕e2!? (7 0-0 ♗d6 transposes to 5...♗d6 6 0-0 ♘c6 7 ♘xc6 bxc6, and 7 0-0 ♗e7 transposes to 5...♗e7 6 0-0 ♘c6 7 ♘xc6 bxc6) 7...♕e7 8 0-0 g6 (8...♘d6 may be safer though after 9 ♖e1 ♕xe2 10 ♖xe2+ ♗e6 11 ♘d2 ♔d7 12 ♘f3 f6 13 c3 ♗f5 14 ♘e1 g5 15 ♗xf5+ ♘xf5 16 ♘d3 White retains a very slight edge) 9 ♗xe4 ♕xe4 10 ♕d2!? (this looks more logical than 10 ♕xe4+ dxe4 11 ♖e1 f5 12 f3 ♗g7 13 c3 0-0 14 ♗f4 c5!? 15 dxc5 ♖b8, which gave Black considerable compensation in Pillsbury-Schlechter, Munich 1900) 10...♗e7 11 ♖e1 ♕f5 12 ♕f4 and White has several threats.

6 0-0

6 ♘d2 might be a good way to fight for an advantage. Now Black has two main ways to go:

a) 6...♘d6 7 ♕f3 (7 ♕h5 g6 8 ♗xg6?! does not work on account of 8...fxg6 9 ♘xg6 ♗g4! 10 ♕xg4 ♖g8 11 ♕h5 ♖xg6 12 ♘f3 ♘d7, when White doesn't have enough for the piece) 7...c6 8 ♘f1!? (Kapengut) 8...0-0 9 ♘g3 ♘d7 10 ♘xd7 ♕xd7 11 0-0 ♕g4 12 ♕xg4 ♗xg4 13 ♗f4 and White might have a very tiny edge.

b) 6...♘xd2 7 ♗xd2 ♘c6 (7...0-0 8 ♕h5 g6 9 ♕h6 ♘c6 10 ♘xc6 bxc6 11 0-0-0 ♖e8 12 ♖de1 ♖b8 13 ♖e5 looks better for White) 8 ♘xc6 bxc6 9 0-0 0-0 10 ♕h5 g6 11 ♕h6 ♖b8 12 b3 ♗f6 13 c3 ♖e8 14 ♖fe1 ♖xe1+ 15 ♖xe1 ♗e6 16 ♕f4 ♗e7 17 ♕g3 ♗d6 18 ♗f4 ♗xf4 19 ♕xf4 ♕d6 20 ♕f6 and White had a bit of pressure in Hort-Spassky, Reykjavik 1977.

6...0-0

The safest choice. Others include:

a) 6...♘d7 7 ♗f4 (7 c4 is less dangerous: 7...♘xe5 8 dxe5 c6 9 cxd5 ♕xd5 10 ♕f3 ♗f5! 11 ♘c3 ♘xc3 12 ♕xf5 g6 13 ♕h3 ♖d8 with unclear play – Yusupov; 7 ♘xd7 ♗xd7 transposes to 5...♘d7 6 ♘xd7 ♗xd7 7 0-0 ♗e7) 7...♘xe5 8 ♗xe5 0-0 9 c4 c6 10 ♕c2 and White has an edge according to Euwe.

b) 6...♘c6 also doesn't fully equalise: 7 ♘xc6 bxc6 8 c4 0-0 9 ♘c3 ♘xc3 10 bxc3 dxc4 11 ♗xc4

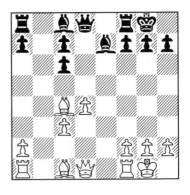

and now:

b1) 11...♗d6 12 ♕d3 ♖b8 13 h3 gives White a slight edge. Holzke-Yusupov, Bundesliga 2000 continued 13...c5?! 14 dxc5 ♗xc5, and here White can play 15 ♗xf7+! ♔xf7 16 ♕c4+ ♗e6 17 ♕xc5 ♕d6 18 ♕xd6 cxd6 19 ♗a3 with good chances of converting the extra pawn into a full point.

b2) 11...♗f5 12 ♗f4 ♗d6 13 ♗g3 ♖e8 14 ♕a4 ♗e4 15 ♖ae1 ♗xg3 (15...h5?! is reckless: 16 f3 ♗d5 17 ♖xe8+ ♕xe8 18 ♖e1 ♕d8 19 ♗xd5 cxd5 20 ♕c6 ♗xg3 21 hxg3 ♖b8 22 ♖e5 with a clear plus for White, Ivanchuk-Yusupov, Novgorod 1995) 16 fxg3 ♗d5 17 ♗d3 ♕g5 18 ♕c2 h6 19 ♕f2 and here we believe there is no argument about White's edge.

7 c4

Maybe the best idea for White is 7 ♖e1!?, as first suggested by Steinitz. After 7...f6 8 ♘f3 f5 9 c4 ♗e6 10 cxd5 ♗xd5 11 ♘c3 ♘xc3 12 bxc3 ♘c6 13 ♘e5 ♘xe5 14 ♖xe5 White was a bit better in Ed.Lasker-Kupchik, New York, 1915.

7...c6

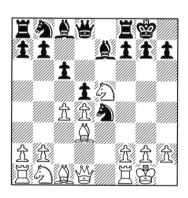

The passive 7...♘f6 does not give real chances for equality after 8 ♘c3 and now:

a) 8...♘c6 9 cxd5!? ♘b4 10 ♗c4 ♘bxd5 11 ♕b3 c6 (11...♗e6?! is a silly invitation: 12 ♕xb7 ♖b8 13 ♕xa7 ♖a8 14 ♕b7 ♖b8 15 ♕c6 ♘b4 16 ♕f3 ♗xc4 17 ♘xc4 ♕xd4 18 ♘e3 ♕e5 19 ♘f5 and White is much better, G.Guseinov-Ekdyshman, St Petersburg 2000) 12 ♖e1 ♗d6 13 ♗g5 with a plus.

b) 8...c6 9 ♖e1 ♘bd7 10 ♗g5 dxc4 11 ♗xc4 ♘b6 (11...♗d5?! is punished by 12 ♗xd5 ♗xg5 13 ♗xf7+! ♖xf7 14 ♘xf7 ♔xf7 15 ♕h5+ ♔f8 16 ♕xh7 ♘f6 17 ♕h8+ ♘g8 18 d5 ♗d7 19 ♖ad1 with a strong attack, Yurtaev-D.Frolov, Tomsk 1998) 12 ♗b3 ♘bd5 13 ♕f3 ♗e6 14 ♖ad1 ♕a5 and Black is only slightly worse (Yusupov).

8 ♘c3

8 cxd5 cxd5 9 ♗xe4 dxe4 10 ♘c3 ♗f5 11 ♖e1 ♘d7 12 ♘xd7 ♕xd7 13 ♘xe4 ♖ad8 gives Black excellent compensation for the pawn, a draw being the likely result.

8 ♕c2 ♘f6 9 c5 is less forcing and therefore also more ambitious: 9...♘bd7 10 ♘c3!? ♘xe5 11 dxe5 ♘d7 12 ♗xh7+ ♔h8 13 ♗f5 ♘xe5 14 ♖e1 ♗f6 (14...f6 is weaker; after 15 ♗e3 ♗xf5 16 ♕xf5 d4 17 ♖ed1 ♗c5 18 ♘a4 ♕e7 19 ♕h3+ ♔g8 20 ♘xc5 dxe3 21 ♕xe3 White enjoys slight pressure) 15 ♗f4 ♖e8 16 ♖e3 ♗xf5 17 ♕xf5 ♘g6 18 ♖h3+ ♔g8 19 ♕h5 ♘h4 20 ♗g3 ♕e7 with a complex battle, Mi.Tseitlin-Karasev, Leningrad 1970.

8...♘xc3 9 bxc3 dxc4

Also possible is 9...♘d7 10 cxd5 (10 f4 dxc4 11 ♗xc4 transposes to 9...dxc4) 10...♘xe5!? 11 dxe5 ♕xd5 12 ♕e2 ♗e6 13 ♖d1 ♕a5 with decent counterplay.

10 ♗xc4 ♘d7

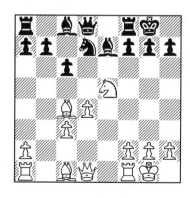

11 ♘xf7!?

A surprising sacrifice. 11 f4 is generally recommended: 12...♘f6 12 ♖b1 (12 ♕b3

②d5 13 f5 f6 14 ②g4 b5 15 ♗e2 a5 with unclear play is not something Black should avoid) 12...♕c7 13 ♕b3 ♗d6 14 ♗a3 ♗xa3 15 ♕xa3 ♗f5 16 ♖be1 ♗e4 17 ②g4 ②xg4 18 ♖xe4 ♖ae8 19 ♖xe8 ♖xe8 20 ♕xa7 ♕e7 with chances for both sides, Popiel-Von Gottschall, Hanover 1902.

11...♖xf7 12 ♗xf7+

Also possible is 12 ♕b3!? ♕f8 13 ♖e1 ♗d6 14 ♗g5 ②b6 15 ♗e7 ♗xe7 16 ♗xf7+ ♕xf7 17 ♖xe7 ♕xb3 18 axb3 ♔f8 19 ♖e5 with a double-edged endgame.

12...♔xf7 13 ♕b3+ ♔f8 14 ♖e1 b6!

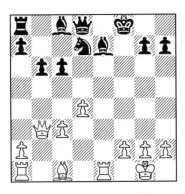

The only move, but good enough to fight on equal terms.

15 c4

This might be too rash a decision. After 15 ♗a3!? ♗xa3 16 ♕xa3+ c5 17 c4 the position is less clear, though it is difficult to believe that Black should be worse.

15...②f6 16 ♗b2 ♗f5 17 d5 ♕d7 18 ♖ad1 ♖e8 19 dxc6 ♕xc6 20 ♗a3 ♗e6

21 ♖d4 ♔f7 22 ♗xe7 ♖xe7

Black is a bit better here.

23 h3 ♖d7 24 ♖xd7+ ②xd7 25 ♖d1 ②e5 26 ♕e3 ②d7?!

This inaccuracy allows White's queen to penetrate Black's queenside and create sufficient counterplay to draw. Though White might have been able to save the draw anyway, it was definitely worth torturing him with 26...②g6 27 ♖c1 ♕c5 with a slight, but enduring, edge.

27 ♕f4+ ②f6 28 ♕b8 a5 29 ♖d6 ♕xc4 30 ♖xb6 ♕xa2 31 ♕c7+ ♗d7

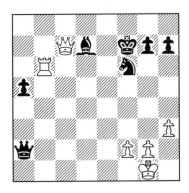

White also achieves a draw after 31...②d7 32 ♖a6 ♕b1+ 33 ♔h2 ♕e1 34 ♕f4+ ②f6 35 ♖a7+.

32 ♖xf6+ ♔xf6 33 ♕xd7 ♕b1+ 34 ♔h2 ♕b4 35 ♕d8+ ♔e6 36 ♕g8+ ♔d6 37 ♕d8+ ♔c6 38 ♕c8+ ♔b5 39 ♕d7+ ♔c4 40 ♕xg7 ♕d6+ 41 g3 a4 42 ♕xh7 a3 43 ♕c2+ ♔b4 44 ♕b1+ ♔a5 45 ♕b3 ♕b4 ½-½

Summary

After 1 e4 e5 2 ♘f3 ♘f6 3 d4 ♘xe4 4 ♗d3 d5 5 ♘xe5, the move 5...♘c6 is unattractive in view of the strategic problems Black faces after the doubling of the pawns. In our view, an interest in 5...♗e7 will be maintained; this continuation is not ambitious and does not have any positional flaws.

After 5...♗d6 interest in the forced line 6 0-0 0-0 7 c4 ♗xe5 8 dxe5 ♘c6 9 cxd5 ♛xd5 10 ♛c2 ♘b4 11 ♗xe4 ♘xc2 12 ♗xd5 will die away as it is thoroughly analysed and does not appear to be more promising for White in terms of gaining an advantage than, for instance, 7 ♘d2!?.

1 e4 e5 2 ♘f3 ♘f6 3 d4 ♘xe4 4 ♗d3 d5 5 ♘xe5 (D) ♗d6

 5...♗e7 – *Game 63*

6 0-0 0-0 (D) 7 c4

 7 ♘d2 – *Game 62*

 7 ♘c3 – *Game 61*

7...♗xe5

 7...♘c6 – *Game 60*

8 dxe5 (D) – *Game 59*

 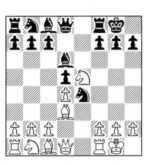 

  5 ♘xe5   *6...0-0*   *8 dxe5*

CHAPTER EIGHT

3 d4: Fourth Move Alternatives

1 e4 e5 2 ♘f3 ♘f6 3 d4 ♘xe4

After the basic opening moves 1 e4 e5 2 ♘f3 ♘f6 3 d4 ♘xe4 the position arising after 4 ♗d3 d5 5 ♘xe5 is considered to be a tabiya. This brief chapter covers deviations by White and Black on move four.

After 4 ♗d3 it first appears that Black must defend his knight with 4...d5. However, in 1993 grandmaster Jacob Murey demonstrated a paradoxical alternative in 4...♘c6!? (Game 64). White can capture the knight but is unable to retain it (5 ♗xe4 d5 and ...e5-e4, or 5 d5 ♘c5 6 dxc6 e4). Since 1993 Murey's idea has been employed on many occasions by modern grandmasters.

4 dxe5 is often played instead of 4 ♗d3. Curiously 4...♗c5, trying to seize the initiative by attacking f2, is unpopular. From our perspective, lines from opening manuals aimed at persuading readers of White's advantage are not particularly convincing (see Game 65).

The continuation 4...d6 transposes to the Philidor Defence (1 e4 e5 2 ♘f3 d6 3 d4 ♘xe4 4 dxe5 ♘e4) and is not discussed here. In the main line with 4...d5 the move 5 ♗d3 (Game 65) is identical to 4 ♗d3 d5 5 dxe5, which is pretty harmless regardless of Black's response (5...♘c5, 5...♗e7 or 5...♘c6). The white pawn on e5 is almost no inconvenience and often becomes an object of attack.

It is more natural to attack the centralised knight with 5 ♘bd2 (Game 66), which is one of the most fashionable variations in the Petroff Defence these days. Black can swap on d2, place his knight to c5, improve its position by means of ...f7-f5 or ...♗f5, or carry on with the development via 5...♘c6 or 5...♗e7 (protecting the queen in case of an exchange on e4). Game 66 shows that all(!) these continuations are quite reasonable.

Game 64
Tiviakov-Forintos
Porto San Giorgio 1994

---

1 e4 e5 2 ♘f3 ♘f6 3 d4 ♘xe4 4 ♗d3 ♘c6!?

This move was a shocking novelty when it first appeared in 1993. Nowadays, of course, it has lost its surprise value.

5 ♗xe4

White has a large number of options:

a) 5 ♘xe5 ♘xe5 (5...♘c6 6 ♗c4 ♘xe5 7 dxe5 d6 8 ♕f3 ♕d7 9 ♗e3 c6 10 ♗xc5 dxc5 11 0-0 favours White, whilst 5...d5 transposes to 4 ♗d3 d5 5 ♘xe5 ♘c6) 6 ♗xe4 d5! 7 dxe5 dxe4 8 ♕xd8+ ♔xd8 9 ♘c3 ♗b4 10 ♗g5+ ♔e8 11 0-0-0 ♗g4 12 ♖d4 ♗xc3 13 bxc3 h6 14 ♖xe4 ♗h3! (a typical Shirov move, here played against him) 15 gxh3 hxg5 16 ♖g1 ♖xh3 17 ♖xg5 ♔f8 18 ♖eg4 ♖e8 19 ♖xg7 ♖xe5 20 ♖g8+ ♔e7 with a likely draw, Shirov-Timman, Wijk aan Zee 1998.

b) 5 dxe5 and now:

b1) 5...d5 6 exd6 ♘xd6 7 0-0 ♗e7 8 ♘c3 ♗g4 9 ♘d5 ♘d4 10 ♗e2 (10 ♖e1 ♗xf3 11 gxf3 ♘e6 12 f4 g6 13 f5 ♘xf5 14 ♗xf5 gxf5 15 ♕f3 leads to a wildly complex position with chances for both sides; note 15...♘d4?? 16 ♘f6+ ♔f8 17 ♗h6 mate!) 10...♘e6 11 h3 ♗h5 12 ♖e1 0-0 13 ♘xe7+ ♕xe7 14 ♘g5 ♗xe2 15 ♕xe2 ♕f6 16 ♘xe6 ♖fe8 17 ♕g4 ♖xe6 18 ♖xe6 fxe6 19 c3 ♖f8 with level chances, Yakovich-Makarychev, Elista 1995.

b2) Also fine is 5...♘c5 6 0-0 ♘xd3 7 ♕xd3 d6 8 ♗f4 dxe5 9 ♕xd8+ ♘xd8 10 ♗xe5 ♘e6 11 ♖e1 ♗d7 12 ♗xc7 ♖c8 13 ♗e5 ♖xc2 14 ♘bd2 ♗c6 15 ♘b3 ♗xf3 (an improvement over 15...♗b4?! 16 ♘fd4 ♗c4 17 ♖ec1 ♖xc1+ 18 ♖xc1 ♔d7 19 a3 ♗e7 20 ♘xc6 bxc6 21 ♖d1+ ♔c8 22 ♘a5 c5 23 ♘c6 with a clear edge for White in Bezgodov-Cs.Horvath, Ljubljana 1995) 16 gxf3 ♗b4 17 ♖e4 ♗c5 18 ♘xc5 ♖xc5 with an equal position.

c) 5 d5 was meant to give White an edge once upon a time, but we cannot see how: 5...♘c5 6 dxc6 e4 7 cxb7 (7 ♗c4 exf3 8 cxd7+ ♗xd7 9 ♕xf3 ♕e7+ 10 ♗e3 ♗c6 11 ♗d5 ♗xd5 12 ♕xd5 ♕e6 13 ♕xe6+ ♘xe6 14 ♘d2 0-0-0 15 0-0-0 was drawn in V. Kotov-Frolyanov, Russia 2003) 7...♗xb7 8 ♗e2 exf3 9 ♗xf3 ♗xf3 10 ♕xf3 ♗d6 11 0-0 0-0

12 ♘c3 c6 13 ♖e1 ♕c7 14 g3 ♘e6 15 ♕d3 ♗e5 16 ♗e3 d5 (Sadvakasov-Koneru, Jodhpur 2003) and now 17 ♗d2 ♖ab8 18 ♖ab1 ♗f6, with a level position, is a possible continuation.

5...d5

6 ♗xh7

6 ♘xe5 dxe4 7 ♘xc6 bxc6 8 0-0 ♗d6 9 ♖e1 0-0 10 ♘d2 (10 ♖xe4 ♗f5 11 ♖e1 ♕h4 12 g3 ♕h3 looks dangerous) 10...f5 11 ♘c4 ♗e6 12 b3 ♕h4 13 ♘xd6 cxd6 14 ♕d2 gives a dynamically balanced position, Hracek-Barua, Moscow 1994.

6 ♗g5 leaves Black with a wide range of choices:

a) 6...f6 7 ♘xe5 dxe4 8 ♕h5+ (8 ♘xc6?! bxc6 9 ♗e3 ♗d6 10 c4 0-0 11 c5 ♗e7 12 ♘c3 f5 13 ♕b3+ ♔h8 14 g3 f4!? 15 gxf4 – or 15 ♗xf4 ♕xd4 16 ♗e3 ♕e5 with attacking chances according to Frolyanov – 15...♗g4 16 ♖g1 ♗f3 and Black had an attack in Yurtaev-Frolyanov, Moscow 2003) 8...g6 9 ♘xg6 hxg6 10 ♕xg6+ ♔d7 11 ♗xf6 (11 ♕f5+ ♔e8 with a draw is of course possible) 11...♖h6 12 ♕xh6 ♗xh6 13 ♗xd8 ♔xd8 14 ♘a3 and we evaluate this endgame as slightly favourable for White.

b) 6...♕d6 7 dxe5 ♕b4+ 8 ♘c3 dxe4 9 a3 ♕a5?! 10 ♘d4 ♘xe5 11 0-0 ♗d7 12 ♘xe4 ♘g6? (Black was in a bad way, but resistance was still possible) 13 ♖e1 ♗e7 14 b4 ♕b6 15 ♗xe7 ♘xe7 16 ♘c5 ♖d8 17 ♕e2 1-0 Palac-Kos, Feldbach 1997. Instead of 9...♕a5,

Black can try 9...♕xb2!? 10 ♘d5 ♗c5 11 ♖b1 ♕xa3 12 ♘xc7+ ♔f8 13 ♘xa8 exf3 14 ♕xf3 ♕xf3 15 gxf3 ♘xe5 with a very unclear position.

c) 6...♕d7 (the normal move) 7 ♗d3 e4 8 0-0 f6 9 ♖e1

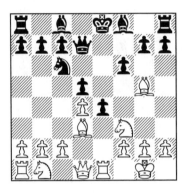

with another branch:

c1) 9...fxg5 10 c4 ♗b4 11 ♘c3 (11 cxd5 ♗xe1 12 ♕xe1 ♘e7 13 ♗xe4 g4 14 ♘e5 ♕d6 15 ♘a3 a6 with an unclear game is given by Murey) 11...0-0 12 cxd5 ♘xd4 13 ♘xd4 exd3 14 ♘e6 ♖f7 15 ♕xd3 favours White.

c2) 9...♗e7 10 ♗f4 exd3 11 ♕xd3 0-0 12 ♘c3 ♗b4 13 ♖e2 (Timman-Hübner, France 1993) and after 13...♕f7 14 ♘b5 ♗a5 the chances are level (Hübner).

6...♖xh7

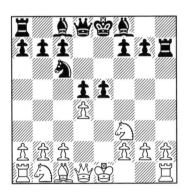

7 dxe5

7 ♘xe5?! is weak: 7...♕e7 8 0-0 ♘xe5 9

♖e1 (or 9 dxe5? ♕h4 10 h3 ♗xh3! and Black wins) 9...♘f3+ 10 gxf3 ♗e6 11 ♕d3 ♖h3 with a very strong attack for Black.

7...♗g4 8 ♗f4 ♕d7

8...g5!? is also enticing: 9 ♗g3 f5 10 exf6 ♕xf6 11 ♘c3 ♗xf3 12 ♕xf3 ♕xf3 13 gxf3 ♗b4 14 0-0 ♗xc3 15 bxc3 0-0-0 with an equal ending; or 9 ♕d3 ♗xf3 10 gxf3 (Alekseev-Bezgodov, Hoogeveen 2002) and after 10...♖h6 11 ♗g3 ♗g7 12 f4 gxf4 13 ♗xf4 ♖e6 Black should have sufficient counterplay.

9 ♘bd2 ♕f5 10 ♗g3 0-0-0 11 0-0 ♗c5 12 a3

12 ♖e1 ♘d4 13 ♘xd4 ♗xd4 14 ♘f3 ♗xb2 15 ♖b1 ♗c3 16 ♖e3 d4 17 ♖d3 ♕g6 18 h3 ♖dh8 gave Black a strong attack in Sveshnikov-Pavasovic, Nova Gorica 1996.

12...♗b6

Or 12...♕h5!? 13 c3 (13 b4? does not work on account of 13...♗d4, with a clear advantage for Black) 13...d4 14 ♕a4 d3 with substantial counterplay.

13 b4 ♕h5 14 ♖e1 ♘d4 15 a4 a6 16 ♖a3 ♘f5!

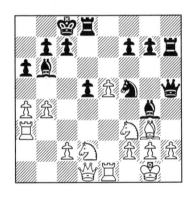

17 ♘f1

17 ♗f4 would be met by 17...g5! 18 ♗xg5 ♖g8 with a strong attack (Forintos).

17...♘xg3 18 ♘xg3 ♗xf3 19 ♕xf3 ♕xh2+ 20 ♔f1 g6 21 ♖d3

Or 21 ♔e2 ♕h4 22 ♖h1 ♕c4+ 23 ♕d3 ♖xh1 24 ♕xc4 dxc4 25 ♘xh1 ♖e8 and the endgame favours Black.

21...♕h4! 22 ♖xd5 ♕c4+ 23 ♖d3 ♖xd3 24 ♕xd3 ♕xb4 25 e6?!

This accelerates an uncomfortable position into more trouble. After 25 ♖e4 ♕c5 26 ♕d2 ♖h8 White is still only 'somewhat' worse.

25...♕f4 26 ♖e2?

The last chance was 26 ♕f3 ♕xf3 27 gxf3 ♖h2 28 ♘e4 fxe6, though Black has every chance of winning the endgame.

26...♕xg3! 27 ♖e3 ♖h1+ 28 ♔e2 ♕g4+ 0-1

Game 65
Nevednichy-Collas
Montpellier 2003

---

1 e4 e5 2 ♘f3 ♘f6 3 d4 ♘xe4 4 dxe5

An unusual move. One further option is 4 ♘xe5, when 4...d6 5 ♘f3 transposes to 3 ♘xe5 d6 4 ♘f3 ♘xe4 5 d4 and 4...d5 5 ♗d3 transposes back to 4 ♗d3 d5 5 ♘xe5.

4...d5

4...d6 transposes to the Philidor Defence (1 e4 e5 2 ♘f3 d6 3 d4 ♘f6 4 dxe5 ♘xe4), which is outside the scope of this book. We will say, however, that White is generally thought to have a slight advantage.

4...♗c5!? leads to very sharp play:

a) 5 ♗c4 ♘xf2 (5...♗xf2+!? 6 ♔e2 ♕e7 7 ♕d3 f5 8 ♘c3 c6 9 ♗e3 ♗xe3 10 ♕xe3 with unclear play is also possible) 6 ♗xf7+ ♔f8 (or 6...♔xf7 7 ♕d5+ ♔e8 8 ♕xc5 ♘xh1 9

♗g5 d6 10 ♕e3 ♕d7 11 ♘c3 h6 12 ♗h4 g5 13 ♘d5 ♔f8 and Black is under attack, but nothing is clear) 7 ♕d5 ♘xh1 8 ♗h5 ♕e7 9 ♗g5 ♗f2+ 10 ♔e2 ♕e6 11 ♘c3 h6 12 ♖d8!? ♘c6 13 ♕xe6 dxe6 14 ♗xc7 with a position almost impossible to understand without dedicating days or weeks of your life to it!

b) 5 ♕d5 ♗xf2+ (5...♘xf2? 6 ♕xc5 ♘xh1 7 ♗g5 f6 8 exf6 gxf6 9 ♗h4 is probably losing for Black)

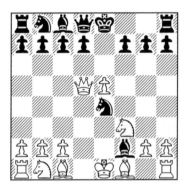

and now:

b1) 6 ♔d1!? f5 7 ♗c4 ♖f8 (after 7...♕e7 8 ♘c3 c6 9 ♕d3 ♗c5 10 ♖f1 b5 11 ♗b3 ♘f2+ 12 ♖xf2 ♗xf2 13 ♕xf5 White has a strong initiative for the exchange) 8 ♘bd2 c6 9 ♘xe4!? (after 9 ♕d3 d5 10 exd6 ♕xd6 11 ♘xe4 ♕xd3+ 12 ♗xd3 fxe4 13 ♗xe4 ♗f5 14 ♗xf5 ♖xf5 the position has rapidly turned drawish) 9...cxd5 10 ♘d6+ ♔e7 11 ♗g5+ ♖f6 (11...♔e6?! 12 ♗xd8 ♖xd8 13 ♘g5+ ♔xe5 14 ♘df7+ ♔d4 15 ♘xd8 ♔xc4 16 ♖f1 and White has the advantage) 12 ♗xd5 ♘c6 13 exf6+ gxf6 14 ♘xf5+ ♔e8 15 ♘d6+ ♔e7 16 ♗f4 with very unclear play. Of course White could take a draw by perpetual with 16 ♘f5+.

b2) 6 ♔e2 f5 7 ♘c3 (Black would get away too easily after 7 exf6 ♘xf6 8 ♕e5+ ♔f8 9 ♗g5 ♗b6 10 ♘c3 ♘c6 11 ♕f4 h6 12 ♗xf6 ♕xf6 13 ♕xf6+ gxf6, after which White cannot fully justify the loss of a pawn) 7...c6 (7...♘xc3+ 8 bxc3 ♗h4 9 ♘xh4 ♕xh4

10 g3 ♕e7 11 ♔f2 ♘c6 12 ♗c4 ♕e6 13 ♕c5 with unclear play might be an improvement) 8 ♕d3 0-0 9 ♘xe4 fxe4 10 ♕xe4 d5 11 exd6 ♖e8 12 ♕xe8+ ♕xe8+ 13 ♔xf2 ♗g4 (13...♗e6!? looks safer; after 14 ♗d3 the position remains very unclear) 14 ♗c4+ ♔h8 15 ♖e1 ♕f8 16 ♖e7 ♘d7 17 ♗d2 and White had good attacking chances in Lozenko-Titlianov, Sverdlovsk 1974.

5 ♗d3

5 ♘bd2 is considered in the next game.

5 exd6 makes no sense: 5...♗xd6 6 ♗e2 0-0 7 ♘bd2 ♗f5 8 0-0 ♘c6 9 ♘xe4 ♗xe4 10 ♘g5 ♗g6 11 ♗d3 ♕f6 12 ♗xg6 ♕xg6 13 c3 ♖ad8 14 ♕b3 b6 and Black was a bit better, Karpov-Noakh, Leningrad 1966.

5...♘c6

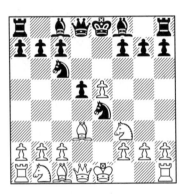

This is the most active move, but Black has reasonable alternatives:

a) 5...♘c5 6 0-0 ♘xd3 7 ♕xd3 ♗e7 8 ♘c3 c6 9 ♘d4 0-0 10 f4 f6 11 ♗d2 ♘a6 12 a3 ♗c5 13 ♗e3 (13 ♔h1 ♗xd4 14 ♕xd4 ♗f5 15 ♖ac1 ♘c7 16 ♘e2 fxe5 17 fxe5 ♘e6 18 ♕b4 ♕d7 gave Black good play in Schiffers-Mason, Breslau 1889) 13...♕e7 14 b4 ♗b6 15 exf6 ♖xf6 is unclear.

b) 5...♗e7 6 0-0 0-0 7 h3 f6!? 8 c4 c6 9 ♕c2 ♘a6 10 ♗xe4 (10 cxd5 cxd5 11 ♗xe4 dxe4 12 ♖d1 ♕c7 13 ♕xe4 ♗e6 is messy) 10...dxe4 11 ♕xe4 fxe5 12 ♘c3 ♕c7 13 ♖d1 ♗f5 14 ♕xe5 ♕xe5 15 ♘xe5 ♗c5 and Black has sufficient counterplay for his pawn, Drazic-Lanzani, Milan 2003.

6 0-0 ♗g4

6...♗e7 is also safe: 7 ♘c3 ♗f5 8 ♕e1!? ♘b4 9 ♘d4 (9 ♘xe4 dxe4 10 ♗xe4 ♘xc2 11 ♗xc2 ♗xc2 is simply equal, but 9 e6!? ♘xd3 10 cxd3 ♘xc3 11 exf7+ ♔xf7 12 ♘e5+ ♔g8 13 ♕xc3 ♗f6 might give White slight pressure) 9...♗g6 10 f4 c5 (or 10...♘xc3!? 11 f5 ♘cxa2!? 12 fxg6 fxg6 13 ♘e6 ♕d7 14 ♘xg7+ ♔d8 15 ♗h6 with a very complex position) 11 f5 ♘xd3 12 cxd3 cxd4 13 fxg6 hxg6 14 ♘xe4 dxe4 15 ♕xe4 ♕b6 16 b3 0-0 17 ♗b2 ♖ad8 with level chances, Nevednichy-Piket, World Championship, New Delhi 2002.

7 ♘c3

7 ♘bd2 ♘xd2 8 ♗xd2 ♘d4 9 ♗e2 ♘xe2+ 10 ♕xe2 ♕d7 11 h3 ♗xf3 12 ♕xf3 ♗c5 13 c4 0-0-0 14 ♖ad1 ♕e6 15 ♗g5 ♖d7 16 ♖xd5 ♖xd5 17 cxd5 was agreed drawn, Romanishin-Makarychev, Frunze 1985.

7...♘xc3 8 bxc3 ♗c5

Or 8...♗e7 9 ♗f4 0-0 10 h3 ♗h5 11 ♖b1 ♕c8 12 g4 ♗g6 13 ♗xg6 (Kurnosov-Skatchkov, St Petersburg 2001) and now best is 13...hxg6 14 ♕xd5 ♕e6 15 ♖fd1 ♖ad8 16 ♕b3 ♘a5 17 ♕a4 b6 with an unclear position. Even so, the text move seems more prudent.

9 ♗f4 0-0 10 h3 ♗h5

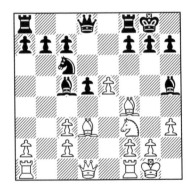

11 g4?!

This is very risky. A more modest approach with 11 ♖b1 ♗b6 12 ♖b5 ♔h8 (12...♘e7? 13 ♗xh7+! would be bad news indeed for Black) 13 g4 ♗g6 14 ♗xg6 fxg6 15 ♖xd5 ♕e7 was called for, reaching a position with chances for both sides.

11...♗g6 12 ♖e1 ♗b6 13 ♗g3

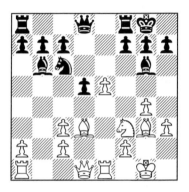

13...f5

13...d4 is weaker: 14 cxd4 ♘xd4 15 ♘xd4 ♕xd4 16 ♗xg6 hxg6 17 ♕xd4 ♗xd4 18 ♖ad1 ♗b6 and White has many ways to secure the advantage in the endgame.

14 ♔g2 ♔h8 15 ♗h4 ♕e8 16 e6 fxg4 17 hxg4 ♖f4

Black can also play the safer 17...♗a5! 18 ♕d2 d4 19 ♘xd4 (not 19 e7? ♖xf3! 20 ♗xg6 hxg6 21 ♔xf3 ♗xc3 22 ♕f4 ♗xa1 23 ♖xa1 ♘xe7 24 ♕xc7 ♘c6 and Black has the advantage) 19...♗d3 20 ♕xd3 ♘xd4 21 ♕xd4 ♕c6+ 22 ♕e4 ♗xc3 23 ♕xc6 bxc6 when although White will have enough compensation for a draw, he will never be able to win.

18 ♔g3 ♗xf2+!?

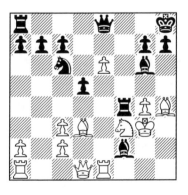

A valid alternative is 18...♖a4!? 19 ♗b5 ♖a3 20 ♕xd5 ♖xc3, when it is probably more pleasant to be Black.

19 ♔xf2?

An understandable mistake as White is scared of allowing his king to go too far into the open. However, this is the worst of the two evils and Black now has a very strong attack.

The alternative is 19 ♔xf4 ♕f8+ 20 ♗f5 ♕d6+ and now:

a) 21 ♖e5 ♘xe5 22 ♗xf2 ♘xg4+ 23 ♔xg4 h5+ 24 ♔h3 ♗xf5+ 25 ♔g2 ♗e4 offers Black compensation, but it is very likely that White will survive the attack.

b) 21 ♔g5! suggests to Black that he should settle for a draw, as after 21...♕e7+ 22 ♔f4 ♗xh4?! (22...♕d6+ is perpetual check) 23 ♘xh4 ♕xh4 24 ♖h1 ♕f6 25 ♕xd5 ♖d8 26 ♕c5 it is not so obvious that Black has sufficient compensation for the exchange. The White king looks strange, but Black's pieces are not that active.

19...♗e4 20 ♗g5

20 ♗e2 ♕xe6 21 ♗g3 ♖f7, with ... ♖af8 to follow, does not help White at all.

20...♖xg4

Or 20...♖xf3+!? 21 ♕xf3 ♗xf3 22 ♔xf3 d4 and Black has good chances. However, the game continuation makes more sense.

21 ♖g1 ♕xe6 22 ♖xg4

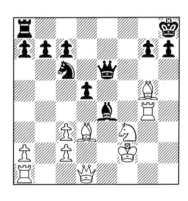

Black's attack is also irresistible after 22 ♗xe4 dxe4 23 ♘h4 e3+ 24 ♔e2 ♖f8.

22...♕xg4 23 ♗e2 ♖f8 24 ♕g1 ♗xf3 0-1

Game 66
Smirin-Alterman
Haifa 1995

---

1 e4 e5 2 ♘f3 ♘f6 3 d4 ♘xe4 4 dxe5 d5 5 ♘bd2

5...♗e7

Black has many alternatives to this modest move:

a) 5...♘c6 6 ♗b5 ♗d7 7 ♕e2 a6 8 ♗xc6 ♗xc6 9 ♘d4 ♘xd2 10 ♗xd2 ♗d7 11 0-0-0 ♕h4?! (11...♕e7 12 ♖he1 0-0-0 13 f4 may be a bit better for White, but the advantage is not that obvious) 12 e6! ♕xd4 13 exd7+ ♔xd7 (Mainka-Schmidt, Germany 1996) and now after 14 ♗g5 ♕a4 15 ♕f3 White would have a very promising attack.

b) 5...f5 6 exf6 ♘xf6 (6...♕xf6?! 7 ♘xe4 dxe4 8 ♗g5 ♕d6 9 ♕e2 would be bad for Black) 7 c4!? d4 (7...♗d6!? 8 cxd5 0-0 9 ♗e2 ♘xd5 looks equal) 8 ♗d3 ♗e7 9 0-0 0-0 10 ♖e1 c5!? (an improvement over 10...♘c6?! 11 a3 a5 12 ♘g5 ♗d6 13 ♘df3 h6 14 c5! hxg5 15 cxd6 ♕xd6 16 ♘xg5 with a clear edge in Sveshnikov-Raetsky, Podolsk 1992) 11 b4!? cxb4 12 ♕c2 ♘c6 13 c5 and White has compensation for the pawn.

c) 5...♗f5 might not lead to equality, for example:

c1) 6 ♘d4!? ♗g6 7 h4!? ♗c5 8 ♘2b3 h5 9 ♘xc5 ♘xc5 10 ♗e3 ♕d7 (maybe Black

should play 10...♕e7!? 11 ♘b5 ♘ba6 12 ♕xd5 ♖d8 13 ♕c4 ♕xe5 with a messy position) 11 ♘b5 ♘e6 12 c4 a6 13 cxd5 axb5 14 dxe6 ♕xe6 15 ♗xb5+ c6 ½-½ Volokitin-Mikhalchishin, Portoroz 2001. In the final position 16 ♗e2 ♘d7 17 f4 ♖xa2 18 ♖xa2 ♕xa2 19 0-0 appears to offer White some chances.

c2) 6 ♘xe4 ♗xe4 7 ♗d3 ♘c6 8 0-0 ♗e7 9 ♖e1 ♗xd3 10 ♕xd3 ♕d7 11 ♗f4 0-0-0 12 a3 ♕g4 13 ♗d2 f6 14 ♗c3 d4 15 ♗b4 ♖he8 (15...♗xb4?! 16 axb4 ♘xb4 17 ♕c4 ♘c6 18 b4! with a clear plus for White, e.g. 18...♔b8?! 19 b5 ♘xe5 20 ♘xe5 fxe5 21 ♖xa7! 1-0 Glek-Mikhalchishin, Zürich 2001) 16 ♗xe7 ♖xe7 17 exf6 gxf6 18 ♖xe7 ♘xe7 19 ♖e1 ♘g6 20 h3 ♕d7 21 ♖e4 with a slight edge for White (Glek).

d) 5...♘c6 6 ♘b3

and now:

d1) 6...♘xb3 7 axb3 ♗e7 8 ♗d3 ♘d7 9 c3 ♘c5 10 ♗c2 ♗g4 11 b4 ♘e6 12 ♕d3 ♕d7 13 0-0 ♗h5 (the weakening 13...g6?! was played in Ivanchuk-Kasimdzhanov, Elista 1998; now after 14 ♘d4 0-0 15 ♗a4 c6 16 h3 ♘xd4 17 hxg4 ♘e6 18 f4 ♗d8 19 ♔h1 White would have enjoyed a clear edge) 14 ♘d4 ♗g6 15 ♘f5 ♗d8! 16 ♖d1 c6 17 ♘d6+ ♕xd6 18 exd6 ♗xd3 with equal chances (Kasimdzhanov).

d2) 6...♗g4 is also sound: 7 h3 ♗h5 8 ♗e2 ♘c6 9 ♘fd4 ♗xe2 10 ♕xe2 ♘xb3 11 ♘xb3 ♕d7 12 ♗f4 0-0-0 13 0-0-0 ♕e6 14

♖d2 ♗e7 with level prospects, Kharlov-Akopian, Moscow 1991. More complex is 8 c4 ♘xb3 9 ♕xb3 ♗xf3 10 ♕xb7 (10 gxf3 ♘c6 11 cxd5 ♘xe5 with unclear play is possible as well) 10...♘d7 with unclear play, for example 11 gxf3 ♘xe5 12 ♗e2 c6 13 cxd5 ♗c5 14 dxc6 0-0 and Black has good compensation for the pawn.

e) 5...♘xd2 6 ♕xd2!? (6 ♗xd2 ♗e7 gives a standard position that has not been investigated very much; a possible continuation is 7 ♗d3 ♗g4 8 h3 ♗h5 9 0-0 0-0 10 ♖e1 ♘d7 11 c3 ♘c5 12 ♗c2 ♘e6 13 ♗f5 c6 14 g4 ♗g6 15 ♕c2 ♗g5 16 ♖ad1 ♗xd2 17 ♕xd2 ♕e7 with unclear play, Kotsur-Zulfugarli, Istanbul 2000) 6...♗e7 (or 6...c5!? 7 ♗d3 ♘c6 8 c3 h6 9 0-0 ♗e6 10 ♖e1 ♗e7 11 h3 ♕d7 with chances for both sides) 7 ♕f4 (7 ♗b5+ c6 8 ♗e2 0-0 9 0-0 f6 10 c4 fxe5 11 cxd5 cxd5 12 ♘xe5 ♘c6 leads to equality: 13 ♘xc6 bxc6 14 b3 c5 15 ♗a3 ♗b7 16 ♖ac1 ♖c8 17 ♗g4 ♖c7 18 ♖ce1 d4 19 ♕d3 ♗d6 20 ♗c1 ♔h8 21 f4 ♖e7 22 ♖xe7 ♕xe7 23 ♗d2 ♗e4 ½-½ Svidler-Kramnik, Dos Hermanas 1999) 7...0-0 8 ♕g3 ♗f5 (8...f6?! 9 ♗h6 ♖f7 10 0-0-0 ♘c6 11 ♗c4 ♗e6 12 ♗xd5! ♗xd5 13 e6! ♗xe6 14 ♖xd8+ ♖xd8 15 ♗f4 gives White a clear edge) 9 c3 ♖e8 10 ♗e2 ♘c6 11 0-0 ♕d7 and Black seems to be no worse.

6 ♗b5+

More critical is 6 ♘xe4 dxe4 7 ♕xd8+ ♔xd8

and now:

a) 8 ♘g5 isn't dangerous: 8...♗f5 (8...♘c6 9 ♘xe4 ♗f5 10 ♗d3 ♘xe5 11 ♘d6+ cxd6 12 ♗xf5 0-0 13 0-0 ♗b6 14 ♗f4 ♗c5 15 ♖ad1 ♖ae8 16 c3 left White with some chances in Iordachescu-Chi Fengtong, Ulan Bator 2002) 9 ♗c4 ♗xg5 10 ♗xg5 ♘d7 11 ♗f4 ♘b6 12 ♗b3 a5 and we think Black will equalise.

b) 8 ♘d4 8...♗d7 9 ♗f4 ♘c6 10 0-0-0 g5!? (after 10...0-0 11 ♗c4 ♘xd4 12 ♖xd4 ♗f5 13 e6!? fxe6 14 ♖d7 White has obtained an unpleasant pressure) 11 ♗g3 h5 12 ♗b5 h4 13 e6 fxe6 14 ♗xc6 (14 ♘xc6?! hxg3 15 ♘xd8 ♖xd8 16 ♗xd7+ ♖xd7 17 ♖xd7 ♔xd7 18 fxg3 ♔d6 and Black's activity gives him a good endgame) 14...bxc6 15 ♗e5 ♖f8 16 ♘b3 ♖f5 (16...♖xf2 17 ♘c5 ♗c8 18 ♘xe4 ♖xg2 19 ♖hg1 ♖xg1 20 ♖xg1 looks very strong for White) 17 ♗d4 ♗e7 18 g4 ♖f7 19 ♗e3 and White's position was preferable, Zviagintsev-Stohl, Rethymnon 2003. However, instead of 12...h4, Black should probably play 12...♘xd4!? 13 ♗xd7+ ♔xd7 14 ♖xd4+ ♔e6 15 h3 (15 h4!?) 15...h4 16 ♗h2 e3!? 17 fxe3 ♗e7 with compensation for the pawn through the safe, yet active, king.

6...c6

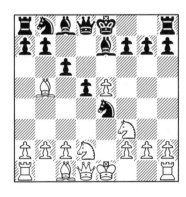

Also possible, although appearing less logical, is 6...♗d7 7 ♕e2 c6 8 ♗d3 ♘c5 9 ♘b3 ♘xd3+ 10 cxd3 c5 with unclear play.

7 ♗d3 ♘c5

7...♘xd2 8 ♗xd2 c5 9 c3 ♘c6 10 0-0 0-0,

with level chances, is simpler.

8 ♗e2 ♗g4 9 ♘d4 ♗xe2 10 ♕xe2 ♘bd7 11 0-0 ♘e6

11...0-0 12 f4 ♘e6 13 ♘2b3 ♘xd4 14 ♘xd4 ♘c5 is 'calmer', although the position remains terribly double-edged.

12 ♘xe6 fxe6 13 ♕g4 ♘xe5

Black must take accept the challenge. 13...♔f7 gives White the initiative after 14 ♘f3 ♕c7 15 ♗g5 ♖he8 16 ♖fe1 – Black's king is not really safe.

14 ♕xg7 ♘g6 15 ♘f3 ♔d7

After 15...♕d6 16 ♘g5 ♗xg5 17 ♗xg5 ♕d7 18 ♕c3 White is slightly better according to Greenfeld.

16 c4

16...♕g8?!

Black should probably play 16...♕f8 17 ♕c3 ♖g8 18 ♖e1 ♗b4 19 ♕b3 dxc4 20 ♖d1+ ♔c7 21 ♕c2 ♗c5 with a very unclear position (but not 19...♗xe1? 20 ♕xb7+ ♔d6 21 c5+ ♔xc5 22 ♗e3+ ♔d6 23 ♗c5+! and mate is imminent).

17 ♕d4 ♖f8!?

17...♗d6 18 cxd5 exd5 19 ♖e1 looks to give White a slight edge.

18 ♕xa7 ♖xf3 19 ♕xb7+ ♔d6

After 19...♔e8? 20 ♕c8+ ♗d8 21 ♕xc6+ ♔f7 22 cxd5 White's position is crushing.

20 ♖e1 e5

20...♖d3? would lose to 21 c5+! ♔xc5 22 ♗e3+ ♔d6 23 ♗c5+! ♔xc5 24 ♖ac1+ with mate to follow – a very nice line.

21 b3 ♖d3?!

21...♖f6! is best, although this can be strongly met by 22 f4!? (22 ♗a3+ ♔e6 23 ♕xc6+ ♔f5 24 ♕d7+ ♔e6 25 g4+ ♔xg4 26 ♕xe6+ ♖xe6 27 cxd5 ♗xa3 28 dxe6 ♔f5 looks fine for Black) 22...♖xf4! (22...e4 is weaker due to 23 ♗a3+ ♔e6 24 f5+! ♖xf5 25 ♕xc6+ ♔f7 26 ♖f1! ♘f4 27 ♖xf4! ♖xf4 28 ♕c7 and Black is lost) 23 cxd5 ♕c8 24 ♕b6 ♗d8 25 ♗a3+ ♔xd5 with unclear play. Our computer prefers Black, but that assessment can change in an instant!

22 ♗a3+

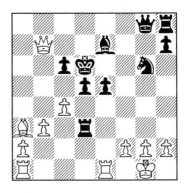

22...c5?

Black is better off playing 22...♔e6. After 23 cxd5+ ♖xd5 24 ♕xc6+ ♗d6 25 ♖ad1 ♘e7 26 ♖xe5+ ♔xe5 27 ♗xd6+ ♔f5 Black seems to survive miraculously. However, the stronger 23 ♗xe7 ♘xe7 24 ♖xe5+ ♔xe5 25 ♕xe7+ ♔d4 26 ♖e1 gives White a very dangerous attack.

23 ♗xc5+! ♔xc5 24 ♖ac1 dxc4

24...♔d6 25 c5+ ♔e6 26 ♕a6+ would pick up the rook.

25 ♖xc4+ 1-0

Summary

Experience has proven that in the case of 4 dxe5 d5 5 ♘bd2 (and 5 ♗d3) Black maintains equilibrium in various ways. However, like in some other systems of the Petroff Defence, it is difficult for Black to move from a solid equalisation to seizing the initiative. That's why we recommend trying the sharp 4...♗c5!? – we can't find any advantage for White after either 5 ♕d5 or 5 ♗c4.

Murey's brilliant discovery (4...♘c6!?) looks artificial and poor at first sight. In fact, it is unclear how White can gain even a slight advantage. In any case, 5 ♗xe4 d5 6 ♗xh7 (as in Game 64) cannot be recommended for White since it gives Black active counterplay.

1 e4 e5 2 ♘f3 ♘f6 3 d4 ♘xe4 4 dxe5 (D)

4 ♗d3 ♘c6 (D) – *Game 64*

4...d5 (D) 5 ♗d3 – *Game 65*

5 ♘bd2 – *Game 66*

4 dxe5   *4...♘c6*   *4...d5*

CHAPTER NINE

3 d4: Black Plays 3...exd4

1 e4 e5 2 ♘f3 ♘f6 3 d4 exd4

In this chapter we will discuss 3...exd4, Black's main alternative to 3...♘xe4. Firstly though, let's briefly go over a couple of other tries for Black. The move 3...d6 simply transposes to the Philidor Defence, which is outside the scope of this book. The symmetrical reaction 3...d5 drew players' attentions as far back as 1900 (Pillsbury-Marshall), but became especially noticeable after the Stein-Bronstein game (Tbilisi 1966). At the same time, this game contributed to the decline of 3...d5. It has been proven that White doesn't have to transpose to the other lines of the Petroff Defence with either 4 dxe5 or 4 ♘xe5 ♘xe4 5 ♗d3. Instead, the continuation 4 exd5! exd4 5 ♗b5+ breaks the symmetry in White's favour (see the notes to Game 67).

Moving onto 3...exd4, let's leave aside the Urusov Gambit (4 ♗c4), since this is the Bishop Opening (1 e4 e5 2 ♗c4 ♘f6 3 d4 exd4 4 ♘f3), or the Two Knights Defence (if 4...♘c6 is played). Instead the games in this chapter are devoted to the tabiya after 4 e5 ♘e4.

White's main choice is the obvious 5 ♕xd4 (Game 67-69). After 5...d5 6 exd6 ♘xd6 Black faces a dreary prospect of fighting for equality with only a slight chance of seizing the initiative. This is why one of the numerous ideas from Morozevich, 5...f5!?, is an enticing option (see the notes to Game 67). Bacrot appears to have chosen a correct reply, with his position being preferable after 6 ♗c4 ♗c5 7 ♕xc5!? ♘xc5 8 ♗g5.

Let's get back to the main line 5...d5 6 exd6 ♘xd6. The specific features of this position are the two open files in the centre, the queen on d4 that is vulnerable but puts pressure on the enemy camp, and the black knight on d6 that has gained stability but prevents Black's development. To avoid confusion with the transposition of moves, we collected all the lines where White declines to play the most natural move 7 ♘c3 in Game 69. In this case it is interesting to contrast the typical fianchetto ....♗f8-g7 with the manoeuvre ♗c1-d2-c3.

Black has various ways to protect himself after 7 ♘c3 ♘c6 8 ♕f4, three of which are studied in Game 67. The arrangement with ....♗e7 and ....♗e6 is effectively met by the queenside castling plan. The attack on the c2-pawn by ....♗f5 is not popular in view of 9 ♗b5, but White doesn't seem to have a substantial advantage. The main part of Game 67 concentrates on the surprising 8...♘f5!? – the knight moves for the fourth time out of eight to prepare attacking the enemy queen with ....♗d6. This idea was tried for the first time during the Kasparov-Karpov match (New York, 1990). A fourth option, the very fashionable fianchetto of the black bishop with 8...g6, is covered in Game 68. Here castling long looks more risky for White than against 8...♗e7, but White still stands better.

The paradoxical 5 ♗b5 attracted our attention (Tal employed it a few times) and is covered in the annotations to Game 70. Black can turn the game into the Berlin Defence of the Ruy Lopez by means of 5...♘c6, transposing to a line that is harmless for Black (1 e4 e5 2 ♘f3 ♘c6 3 ♗b5 ♘f6 4 d4 exd4 5 e5 ♘e4). A worthy alternative is 5...c6 6 ♕d4 ♕a5 7 c3 ♘xf2 (Keres) 8 0-0 ♘h3! (Euwe) – another in-between move that destroys White's pawn chain.

The main part of Game 70 concentrates on the interesting move 5 ♕e2. Steinitz discussed this move in his book *Modern Chess Instructor* (1889). White attacks the centralised knight from the e-file in order to prevent Black from strengthening the knight with either the d- or the f-pawn. However, after 5...♗b4+ 6 ♔d1!? (Steinitz) it is possible to improve support the knight with 6...d5 7 exd6 f5, when Black has the initiative. That's why White prefers the calmer 6 ♘bd2, while Black often retreats with 5...♘c5 after 5 ♕e2. Black's play in the opening in Game 70 is still considered to be a perfect model.

Game 67
Cabrera-Collas
Malaga 2003

---

1 e4 e5 2 ♘f3 ♘f6 3 d4 exd4

3...d5?! is inferior:. 4 exd5! (4 dxe5 ♘xe4 transposes to 3...♘xe4 4 dxe5 d5) 4...exd4 (after 4...e4 5 ♘e5 ♘xd5 6 ♗c4 ♗e6 7 0-0 ♗d6 8 ♗xd5 ♗xd5 9 ♘c3 c6 10 ♕e2 White has a clear advantage – Yusupov) 5 ♗b5+ c6 6 dxc6 bxc6 (6...♕a5+ is critical but White is much better after 7 ♘c3 bxc6 8 ♘xd4! cxb5 9 ♕f3 ♕c7 10 ♘dxb5!? ♕e7+ 11 ♗e3 ♗b7 12 ♕f4 – Znosko-Borovsky) 7 ♗e2 ♗c5 8

c3 dxc3 9 ♕xd8+ ♔xd8 10 ♘xc3 ♔e7 11 0-0 ♖d8 (Stein-Bronstein, Tbilisi 1966) and here Stein could have obtained a sizeable advantage with 12 ♘a4 ♗b6 13 b3 ♗c7 14 ♗e3.

4 e5

4 ♗c4 transposes to the Bishop's Opening (2 ♗c4 ♘f6 3 d4 exd4 4 ♘f3).

4...♘e4

The only sensible move. If 4...♘d5?! then 5 ♕xd4 c6 6 ♗c4 ♘b4 7 0-0 ♘xc2 8 ♗xf7+! ♔xf7 9 ♕c4+ ♔e8 10 ♕xc2 and White's advantage is clear-cut.

5 ♕xd4

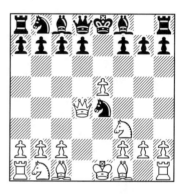

5...d5

Morozevich has risked the remarkable 5...f5!? here:

a) After 6 exf6 ♘xf6 7 ♗g5 ♘c6 8 ♕h4 ♕e7+ 9 ♗e2 ♕b4+ 10 ♕xb4 ♗xb4+ 11 ♘bd2 0-0 it is doubtful that White has any advantage.

b) 6 ♗c4 ♗c5 7 ♕xc5!? (the queen sacrifice is, of course, only temporary; instead 7 ♕d5 ♗xf2+ 8 ♔e2 ♕e7 9 ♘bd2 ♘f6 10 ♕d3 d5 11 ♗b5+ c6 12 ♔xf2 ♘g4+ 13 ♔e2 cxb5 is very complicated) 7...♘xc5 8 ♗g5 ♕xg5 9 ♘xg5 ♘c6 10 0-0 ♘e6 11 ♘xe6 (11 ♘f3 b6 12 ♗d5 ♗b7 13 c4 0-0-0 14 ♘c3 h6 15 ♖ad1 g5 gave Black good counterplay in Bacrot-Morozevich, Biel 2003) 11...dxe6 12 f4 a6 13 ♘d2 and Black's position is slightly cramped.

6 exd6 ♘xd6 7 ♘c3 ♘c6 8 ♕f4 ♘f5

Other than 8...g6 (see Game 68), Black has two inferior options:

a) 8...♗e7 9 ♗d3 (also good enough is 9 ♗e3 ♗e6 10 0-0-0 0-0 11 ♘g5 ♗xg5 12 ♕xg5 ♕e7 13 ♕xe7 ♘xe7 14 ♗c5 ♖fd8 15 ♗e2, when White's bishop pair will be useful) 9...♗e6 10 ♗e3 ♘f6 11 0-0-0!? ♗xc3 12 bxc3 ♕f6 (after 12...♗xa2 13 c4 ♕f6 14 ♖he1 White keeps the initiative) 13 ♕xf6 gxf6 14 ♘d4 ♘xd4 15 ♗xd4 ♔e7 16 ♖he1 b6 17 f4 c5 18 ♗f2 f5 19 g4!? and Black was under severe pressure, Parkanyi-Krivolapov, Gyongyos 1998.

b) 8...♗f5 9 ♗b5

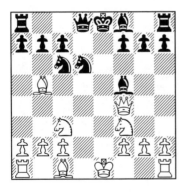

and now:

b1) If 9...♗xc2? then 10 ♘e5 wins instantly.

b2) 9...♘xb5? 10 ♘xb5 ♕e7+ 11 ♔f1! and c7 drops.

b3) 9...♗e7 10 ♗xc6+ bxc6 11 ♘e5 0-0 12 ♘xc6 ♕e8 13 ♘xe7+ ♕xe7+ 14 ♗e3

♗xc2 15 ♖c1 ♗d3 16 ♘d5 ♕d8 17 ♕d4 ♗a6 (after 17...♗g6 Sax gave 18 0-0 ♘f5 19 ♕c5 ♘xe3 20 ♘xe3 as clearly better for White) 18 ♘xc7 ♖b8 (Sax-Yusupov, Rotterdam 1988). Now White should play 19 ♘xa6! ♕a5+ 20 ♘b4 ♘f5 (not 20...♖xb4? 21 ♕xd6! ♖d4+ 22 b4, winning immediately) 21 ♖c5! ♘xd4 22 ♖xa5 ♖xb4 23 0-0 with good winning chances.

b4) 9...♕e7+

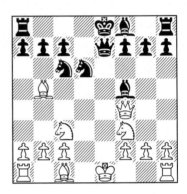

with a further split:

b41) 10 ♔f1 ♗e4 11 ♗xc6+ ♗xc6 12 ♘e5 ♕e6 13 ♘xc6 bxc6 14 ♕f3 ♕c4+ 15 ♔g1 ♗e7 16 b3 ♕a6 17 ♗b2 0-0 and White has a slight edge. Instead Klovans-Harman, correspondence 1967 continued 12...0-0-0?! 13 ♘xc6 bxc6 14 ♕a4 ♘b5 15 ♕a6+ ♔b8 16 ♗e3 ♕b4 17 ♕xc6 ♘d4 18 ♕a6 ♗c5 19 a3 ♕b7 20 ♕xb7+ ♔xb7 21 ♖c1 ♗b6 22 g3 when White was simply a pawn up.

b42) The simple 10 ♗e3 is also promising: 10...♘xb5 11 ♘xb5 ♕b4+ 12 ♕xb4 ♗xb4+ 13 c3 ♗d6 (not 13...♗a5?! 14 b4 ♗d3 15 a4 a6 16 ♘bd4! ♗b6 17 ♘xc6 bxc6 18 ♗xb6 cxb6 19 ♘e5 0-0-0 20 ♘xc6 ♖he8+ 21 ♔d1 ♖d5 22 ♘d4 and White is a pawn up) 14 ♘xd6+ cxd6 15 0-0-0 ♗e6 16 ♖xd6 ♗xa2 17 ♗c5! 0-0 18 ♖xc6 bxc6 19 ♗xf8 ♔xf8 20 ♘d2 ♗d5 21 f3 ♖e8 22 ♔c2 and White's better structure gave him the edge in Matulovic-Kholmov, Sochi 1968.

9 ♗d2

White has a range of options, but Black

should be fine in all cases:

a) 9 ♘b5 ♗b4+ 10 c3 ♗a5 11 ♕e4+ ♕e7 12 ♕xe7+ ♘cxe7 13 ♗f4 ♘d5 14 ♗e5 f6 15 0-0-0 a6 16 ♖xd5 axb5 17 ♗f4 c6 and the position is level.

b) 9 ♗c4 ♗d6 10 ♕e4+ ♗e7 (10...♕e7 is what White wants: 11 ♗d2 ♕xe4+ 12 ♘xe4 0-0 13 0-0-0 ♗e6 14 ♗xe6 fxe6 15 ♖he1 ♖ae8 16 ♘fg5 e5 17 ♗c3 a5 18 a4 b6 19 f3 h6 20 ♘xd6 ♘xd6 21 ♘e4 ♘f5 22 b3 with a pleasant advantage, Berzinsh-Neiksans, Riga 2003) 11 ♗d2 0-0 12 ♗d5 ♗f6 13 0-0-0 ♘cd4 14 g4 ♖e8 15 ♕f4 ♘xf3 16 ♕xf3 ♘d4 17 ♕g2 c5 (the more passive 17...c6 leaves White with the initiative after 18 ♗e4 ♗e6 19 g5 ♗e5 20 ♗e3) 18 ♗e3 ♕b6 19 ♘e4 ♗e7 20 c3 ♗e6 21 ♗xe6 ♘xe6 was unclear in Tiviakov-Ye Rongguang, Groningen 1997.

c) 9 ♗b5 ♗d6 10 ♕e4+ ♗e7 11 ♗g5 f6 12 ♗d2 ♗d7 13 0-0-0 ♕xe4 14 ♘xe4 ♗e7 15 g4 a6?! (more accurate is 15...♘d6 16 ♘xd6+ ♗xd6 17 ♖de1+ ♗f8 18 ♖hg1 ♖e8 19 ♖xe8+ ♗xe8 with equality – Azmaiparashvili) 16 ♗xc6! (instead 16 ♗c4 ♘d6 17 ♘xd6+ ♗xd6 18 ♖de1+ was agreed drawn in Kasparov-Karpov, World Championship [Game 10], New York 1990) 16...♗xc6 17 ♖he1 ♗xe4 18 ♖xe4 ♘d6 19 ♖e2 ♗f7 20 ♘d4 ♘c4 21 ♗f4 and White has an edge.

9...♗d6 10 ♕a4 ♕e7+

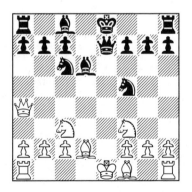

10...♗d7 11 0-0-0 ♘cd4 12 ♖e1+ ♗f8 13 ♕c4 with equality is also acceptable.

11 ♗e2 ♗d7 12 0-0-0 ♘cd4 13 ♘xd4!?

A bold and unclear queen sacrifice. The simple 13 ♗b5 leads to equality after 13...♘xb5 14 ♘xb5 0-0 15 ♖he1 ♕f6 16 ♕b3 ♗c6.

13...♗xa4 14 ♘xf5 ♕d7 15 ♘xg7+ ♗d8

Instead 15...♗e7?! 16 ♖he1 ♗f6?! walks into trouble: 17 ♘h5+ ♗g6 18 g4 and Black will lose too much material in escaping from the mating net.

16 ♗g5+ ♗c8 17 ♖d4! ♖g8?!

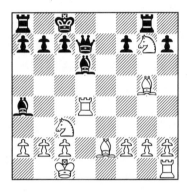

Now White regains the sacrificed material with interest. Black should play 17...♕c6 and now:

a) Not 18 ♖xa4? ♕xg2 19 ♗g4+ f5! and Black wins more material.

b) Also weak is 18 ♘xa4?! ♕xg2 19 ♗g4+ ♗b8 (19...f5?! 20 ♘xf5 ♕xh1+ 21 ♖d1 ♕xh2 22 ♘xd6+ ♗b8 23 ♘f7 is unclear) 20 ♖e1 h5! 21 ♘xh5 b5! 22 ♘c3 ♖xh5! and Black is much better.

c) Best is 18 ♖hd1! 18...♖g8 19 ♗g4+ ♗b8 20 ♗h6 ♕xg2 with a massively complicated position.

18 ♗g4 ♖xg7 19 ♗xd7+ ♗xd7 20 ♗f4 ♖xg2 21 ♗xd6 cxd6 22 ♖xd6 ♗c7 23 ♖hd1

The game has simplified leaving White with a useful extra pawn.

23...♗c6 24 ♖f6 ♖xh2

Or 24...♖f8 25 h4 and White keeps his material advantage.

25 ♖xf7+ ♗b6 26 ♘d5+ ♗a5

Now the king is in danger. Black had to

take the knight, even though the rook ending is probably lost.

27 a3 罩h8 28 b4+ 含b5 29 罩d4

29...a5

The king is also caught after 29...a6 30 c4+ 含a4 31 含b2 盒xd5 32 罩xd5 b6 33 罩ff5 b5 34 罩f6 罩a8 35 cxb5 axb5 36 罩dd6.

30 a4+ 含xa4 31 公c3+ 含a3 32 b5 罩h1+ 33 含d2 1-0

Game 68
Stefansson-Yusupov
Eupen 1994

---

1 e4 e5 2 公f3 公f6 3 d4 exd4 4 e5 公e4 5 豐xd4 d5 6 exd6 公xd6 7 公c3 公c6 8 豐f4 g6 9 盒e3

Preparing to castle long without worrying about the prospect of doubled pawns. Alternatively:

a) Getting ready for kingside castling with 9 盒b5 is also reasonable: 9...盒g7 10 0-0 0-0 11 盒xc6 bxc6 12 盒e3 罩b8 13 罩ab1 a5 14 a3 (it's unclear after 14 盒c5 罩e8 15 公d4 盒e5 16 豐f3 盒b7 17 罩fd1 豐g5) 14...罩e8 15 盒a7 罩b7 16 盒c5 (16 盒d4 gives Black the option of 16...g5!? 17 豐c1 f6 18 h3 盒f5 with a sharp position) 16...盒f5 17 豐a4 公e4 18 罩bd1 豐c8 19 盒d4 公xc3 20 盒xc3 盒xc3 21 bxc3 罩b5 and White may have a tiny advantage, Romanishin-Smyslov, Leningrad 1977.

b) 9 盒d2, like 9 盒e3, prepares castling queenside, but this time preventing the possibility of doubled c-pawns, although of course the bishop is slightly less active: 9...豐e7+ 10 盒e2 盒e6 11 0-0-0 盒g7 12 h4 h6 13 罩he1 0-0-0 14 盒d3 豐f6 15 豐xf6 盒xf6 16 盒xg6 罩dg8 (this is the right rook; instead 16...罩hg8 17 h5 盒g4 18 盒h7 罩h8 19 盒d3 盒xh5 20 盒e2 盒g6 21 公d5 盒g7 22 盒c3 盒xc3 23 公xc3 罩he8 24 公h4 gave White an edge in Geller-Smyslov, Moscow 1991) 17 h5 公e7 18 盒f4 盒xc3 19 bxc3 公xg6 20 hxg6 罩xg6 21 公h4 罩g4 22 g3 h5 and the position is level.

9...盒g7 10 0-0-0

10 盒d3 is a worthwhile alternative. For example, 10...盒e6 11 0-0-0 豐f6 12 公g5 豐xf4 13 盒xf4 0-0-0 (Yusupov assessed 13...盒xc3 14 bxc3 0-0-0 15 公xe6 fxe6 16 罩he1 罩hf8 17 盒g3 罩de8 18 f3 as a bit better for White) 14 罩he1 盒xc3 15 bxc3 盒xa2 16 c4 (Black has an edge after the weaker 16 盒xd6 罩xd6 17 c4 罩d4 18 公xf7 罩g8 19 公e5 公xe5 20 罩xe5 罩gd8) 16...h6 17 公e4 公xe4 (less accurate is 17...公a5 18 公xd6+ cxd6 19 c5! d5 20 罩e7 罩d7 21 罩xd7 含xd7 22 盒b5+, as in Raetsky-Rodionov, correspondence 1982; now 22...含c8 23 罩e1 盒c4 24 罩e8+ 罩xe8 25 盒xe8 would have been marginally in White's favour) 18 罩xe4 罩he8 19 罩de1 罩xe4 20 罩xe4 g5 21 盒d2 盒b3 22 h4 and White has reasonable compensation for the pawn.

10...盒e6

This is more flexible than 10...0-0, which

perhaps commits the king a move too early: 11 h4 h6 12 ♗c5!? ♗e6 13 ♗b5 a6 14 ♗xc6 bxc6 15 ♗d4! (the greedy 15 ♗xd6 cxd6 16 ♖xd6 allows Black dangerous counterplay after 16...♕b6 17 ♘d4 ♖ab8) 15...f6 16 ♗c5 ♖f7 17 ♖he1 ♗d7 18 ♘d4 ♕c8 19 ♕g3 ♘b7 20 ♘a4 g5 21 ♕b3 ♘a5 22 ♕d3 and White had a powerful bind in Ivanchuk-Akopian, Lucerne 1997.

11 ♘g5

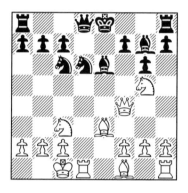

A promising alternative is 11 ♗b5!? ♗xc3 12 bxc3 0-0 13 ♘g5 ♕e7 14 ♗c5 when White's activity compensates for his weakened structure.

11...0-0 12 h4 ♗e5 13 ♕f3 h5

Grabbing a pawn with 13...♗xc3 14 bxc3 ♗xa2 leads to great danger after 15 h5 ♘e5 16 ♕f4.

14 ♘xe6 fxe6 15 ♕h3 ♕f6 16 ♗g5 ♗f4+

Or 16...♕xf2 17 ♗d3 ♗xc3 18 bxc3 ♘f5 19 ♗c4 and White's initiative continues.

17 ♗xf4 ♕xf4+ 18 ♔b1 ♖ae8

If 18...♘f5 then 19 f3 consolidates White's edge.

19 ♗e2 ♘e5

Taking the f-pawn is still risky: 19...♕xf2 20 ♖hf1 ♕c5 21 ♖xf8+ ♔xf8 22 g4 with a powerful attack.

20 ♖he1 ♖f5 21 f3 ♕b4 22 a3 ♕b6 23 g4 ♖f4 24 gxh5 ♘dc4 25 ♗xc4 ♘xc4 26 b3 ♘xa3+ 27 ♔c1 ♕f2

If 27...♕c6 then 28 ♕g2 ♖f7 29 ♘e4 with

a winning attack for White.

28 ♖e2 ♕xf3 29 ♕xf3 ♖xf3 30 ♔b2 c6?

Now White wins by force. 30...gxh5 31 ♖d3 ♖xd3 32 cxd3 ♖d8 would have given Black some drawing chances.

31 ♘e4 ♘b5 32 c4 ♘c7 33 ♖d7 ♘a6 34 hxg6 ♖ef8 35 g7 ♖8f7 36 ♖d8+ ♔xg7 37 ♖g2+ ♔h7 38 ♘g5+ 1-0

1 e4 e5 2 ♘f3 ♘f6 3 d4 exd4 4 e5 ♘e4 5 ♕xd4 d5 6 exd6 ♘xd6 7 ♗d3

White's other alternatives to the usual 7 ♘c3 are:

a) 7 ♗f4 ♘c6 8 ♕d2 ♕e7+ 9 ♗e2 ♘e4 10 ♕e3 ♘b4 11 ♕c1 ♗f5 (chasing material with 11...♕c5 is risky: 12 0-0 ♘xc2 – or 12...♕xc2 13 ♕e1!? with an unclear position – 13 ♘c3 ♘xc3 14 ♕xc2 ♘d5 15 ♕e4+ ♗e6 16 ♖ac1 and White has a dangerous initiative) 12 0-0 0-0-0 with a double-edged position.

b) 7 ♗g5

and now:

b1) 7...♘c6 8 ♕e3+ (or 8 ♕c3 f6 9 ♗f4 ♕e7+ 10 ♗e2 ♗e6 11 0-0 0-0-0 and Black has equalised) 8...♗e7 9 ♘c3 ♘f5 10 ♗xe7 ♘cxe7 11 ♕e5 0-0 12 ♖d1 ♘d6 13 ♗d3 ♘g6 14 ♕g3 ♕e7+ 15 ♔d2 ♘f5 16 ♗xf5 ♗xf5 17 ♔c1 ♖ad8 18 ♘d4 ♗c8 19 ♖he1

♕b4 was level in Konstantinopolsky-Smyslov, Sverdlovsk 1993.

b2) Black should seriously consider the direct 7...f6. For example, 8 ♗f4 ♘c6 9 ♕d2 ♗f5 10 ♗e2 ♕e7 11 0-0 0-0-0 12 ♖e1 ♘e4 13 ♕c1 g5 14 ♗d3 ♗h6!? 15 ♘c3 (the wild 15 ♘h4!? leads to unclear play after 15...gxh4 16 ♗xh6 ♖hg8; note that White must avoid 17 ♕f4? ♖xg2+! 18 ♔xg2 ♖g8+ 19 ♔h1 ♘g3+) 15...gxf4 16 ♗xe4 ♗xe4 17 ♖xe4 ♕g7 18 ♕f1 ♖hg8 19 ♖ae1 ♕g4 20 ♔h1 ♗f8 was unclear in Steinitz-Pillsbury, St Petersburg 1895. However, after 12...♕f7!? 13 ♗d3 ♗g4 Black has a slight plus.

7...♕e7+

Also interesting is 7...♘c6 8 ♕f4 g6 9 0-0 ♗g7 and now:

a) 10 ♖e1+ leads nowhere after 10...♗e6 11 ♘g5 0-0 12 ♘xe6 fxe6 13 ♕g3 (Hübner-Segal, Dresden 1969 continued 13 ♕g4?! ♕f6 14 ♕g3?! ♘b4 15 ♖f1 ♘f5 16 ♕xc7? ♖ac8 17 ♕xb7 ♘xd3 18 cxd3 ♘g3! 19 hxg3 ♖xc1! 20 ♖xc1 ♕xf2+ 21 ♔h1 ♕xg3 22 ♕e7 ♕e3! and Black won) 13...♗d4 14 ♖e2 (not 14 ♖f1? ♘e4! 15 ♗xe4 ♗xf2+! and Black wins immediately) 14...♗f5 15 ♕h3 ♘e5 and Black has excellent counterplay.

b) This sacrificial 10 ♗d2!? is the only way to cause Black trouble: 10...♕f6 (White has good compensation if Black tries 10...♗xb2 11 ♗c3 ♗xa1, for example 12 ♗xa1 0-0 13 ♗f6 ♕d7 14 ♕h6 ♘e8 15 ♗g7! ♘xg7 16 ♘g5 ♖e8 17 ♕xh7+ ♔f8 18 ♕h8+ ♔e7 19 ♕xg7 ♕d5 20 ♗xg6 and the king is in real danger) 11 ♕xf6 ♗xf6 12 ♗c3 ♗xc3 13 ♘xc3 and White may have a tiny advantage.

8 ♗e3 ♘f5?!

This wastes too much time – instead Black should develop with 8...♗f5. For example, 9 ♘c3 ♘c6 10 ♕f4 ♗xd3 11 cxd3 ♕e6 12 0-0-0 ♗e7?! (instead 12...♕g6 13 ♖he1 0-0-0 is unclear) 13 d4 ♕f5 14 d5 ♘b8 15 ♕xf5 ♘xf5 16 ♗f4 ♘a6 17 g4! ♘h4 18 ♘xh4 ♗xh4 19 d6! 0-0-0 20 ♘b5 c6 21 d7+! ♖xd7 22 ♘d6+ ♖xd6 23 ♗xd6 and White was much better in Spassky-Kholmov, Rostov on Don 1960.

9 ♗xf5!? ♗xf5 10 ♘c3 ♕b4

White's lead in development is significant whichever way Black plays:

a) 10...♗xc2 11 ♖c1 ♘c6 12 ♕f4 ♘b4 13 0-0 and the initiative continues. For example, 13...♘d3?! 14 ♕c4 ♘xc1 15 ♖xc1 and, with ♘d5 also threatened, White is winning.

b) 10...♘c6 11 ♕f4 ♕b4 12 0-0-0 and c7 is again impossible to defend.

11 ♕e5+ ♗e6 12 0-0-0 ♘c6 13 ♕xc7 ♖c8 14 ♕f4 ♕a5

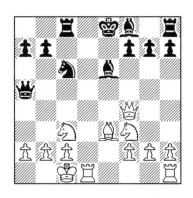

14...♕xf4 is met by 15 ♗xf4 ♗b4 16 ♘e4 and White is a pawn up.

15 ♕g5

Simple is best. Instead 15 ♘g5 ♗xa2 16 ♘xh7?! leads to trouble after 16...♖xh7! 17 ♕e4+ ♗e6 18 ♕xh7 ♕a1+ 19 ♘b1 ♘b4 when Black's attack is very dangerous.

15...♕a6 16 ♖he1 ♘b4?

Now Black is losing. 16...h6 17 ♕h5 ♗e7 18 ♗g5! 0-0 19 ♗xe7 ♘xe7 20 ♘d4 is unpleasant but at least Black can play on.

17 ♘d4 ♖xc3

Allowing a beautiful finish. 17...f6 18 ♕h5+ g6 19 ♕b5+ ♔xb5 20 ♘dxb5 would have lost slowly and painfully.

18 ♕d8+!!

A mating combination that exploits the power of discovered checks.

18...♔xd8 19 ♘xe6+ ♔e7

Or 19...♔e8 20 ♘xg7+! ♗xg7 21 ♗g5+ ♔f8 22 ♖d8 mate.

20 ♗g5+ f6 21 ♘d8+! 1-0

Game 70
Tal-Kholmov
Alma Ata 1968

---

1 e4 e5 2 ♘f3 ♘f6 3 d4 exd4 4 e5 ♘e4 5 ♕e2

A rare alternative to 5 ♕xd4. White has another unusual try in 5 ♗b5 c6 (5...♘c6 transposes to the Ruy Lopez: 1 e4 e5 2 ♘f3 ♘c6 3 ♗b5 ♘f6 4 d4 ed4 5 e5 ♘e4) 6 ♕xd4 ♕a5+ (less active is 6...♘c5 7 ♗c4 ♘e6 8 ♕e4 d5 9 exd6 ♗xd6 10 0-0 when White has a tiny edge) 7 c3 ♘xf2!? 8 0-0 (White should consider 8 ♕xf2 ♕xb5 9 a4 ♕d5 10 ♗e3 ♗e7 11 0-0 0-0 12 ♘a3 with good play – Yusupov) 8...♘h3+! 9 gxh3 ♕xb5 10 ♕f4 ♕d3 11 ♘d4 ♕g6+ 12 ♔h1 d5 with a complex position, Zapata-Castro, Colombia 1999.

5...♘c5

This simple move is more reliable than 5...♗b4+

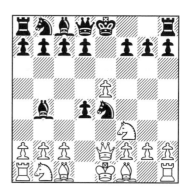

and now:

a) Steinitz suggested the strange 6 ♔d1, for example 6...d5 7 exd6 f5 8 ♘g5 (after 8 dxc7 ♕xc7 9 ♘xd4 ♘c6 10 c3 ♘xd4 11 cxd4 ♗d7 Black has a tremendous initiative) 8...0-0 9 ♘xe4 fxe4 10 ♕c4+ ♔h8 11 dxc7 (Lipschutz-Showalter, USA 1896 continued 11 ♕xb4 ♗g4+ 12 ♗e2 ♗xe2+ 13 ♔xe2 ♘c6 14 ♕e1?! ♕xd6 15 ♔d1 ♖ae8 16 b3 e3 17 ♗a3 ♕f4 and Black had a wonderful position) 11...♕e7 12 cxb8♕ ♖xb8 and Black obviously has a powerful initiative – Porreca.

b) 6 ♘bd2 ♘xd2 7 ♗xd2 ♕e7 8 0-0-0 ♘c6 9 ♗xb4 ♕xb4 10 ♕e4 b6 11 ♘xd4 ♗b7 12 ♗b5 0-0-0 13 a3 ♘xd4 (or 13...♕c5 14 ♘xc6 ♗xc6 15 ♗xc6 dxc6 16 f4 and White has a definite edge) 14 axb4 ♘b3+ 15 cxb3 ♗xe4 16 ♖d4 ♗f5 17 f4 and despite his bizarre queenside structure White was a little better in Rodriquez Andres-Ginzburg, San Martin 1995.

6 ♘xd4 ♘c6 7 ♗e3

This is more testing than 7 ♘xc6 dxc6 (the correct recapture; instead 7...bxc6 8 ♗e3 ♕h4 9 ♕c4 ♕xc4 10 ♗xc4 ♘a4 11 ♗b3 ♘b6 12 ♘d2 a5 13 a3 a4 14 ♗a2 ♗a6 15 ♗xb6 cxb6 16 ♘e4 left White a touch better in Spassky-Vistinietzki, Tallinn 1959) 8 ♘c3 ♗f5 9 ♗e3 h5!? 10 f4 ♘e4 11 ♘xe4 ♗xe4 12 ♕f2 ♕d5 and Black has good counterplay.

7...♘xd4

Safer than 7...♘xe5?! 8 f4 ♘g6 9 ♘b5 ♘a6 10 ♗d4+ ♕e7 11 f5 ♕xe2+ 12 ♗xe2 ♘h4 13 f6 g6 14 0-0 when, despite the exchange of queens, White has a dangerous initiative.

8 ♗xd4 ♕h4

A more active approach than 8...♘e6 9 ♗c3 d5 10 exd6 ♕xd6 11 ♘d2 ♗d7 12 ♘c4 ♕e7 (or 12...♕c5 13 ♘e5 with a promising attack, e.g. 13...♖d8? 14 ♕f3 ♕e7 15 0-0-0 c6 16 ♗c4 h5 17 ♖he1 ♖h6 18 ♗b4 was already winning for White in Raetsky-Varlamov, correspondence 1983) 13 ♘e5 0-0-0 14 ♕e3 and White has a pleasant edge.

9 ♗e3 ♕b4+ 10 c3

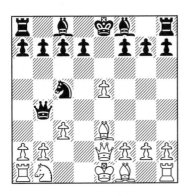

10...♕e4

Not 10...♕d3+? 11 ♕xd3 ♕xb2 12 ♕b5! ♕xa1 13 ♗c4 ♗e7 14 0-0 0-0 15 ♕b3 when the queen is trapped.

11 f4 d5 12 ♘d2

Or 12 exd6 ♗xd6 13 ♘d2 ♕e6 14 f5 ♕e7 15 f6 gxf6 with an unbalanced position.

12...♕g6 13 ♘f3 c6 14 0-0-0 ♗e7 15 ♖g1 h5 16 ♕f2 ♘e4

Black can also consider 16...b6, for example 17 ♘d4 ♘e4 18 ♕c2 0-0 19 ♗d3 c5 20 ♘f3 ♗f5 21 ♘d2 ♖fd8 22 c4 d4 23 ♘xe4 (not 23 ♗xe4?! d3! 24 ♕c3? ♗xe4 25 ♘xe4 ♕xe4 26 ♖de1 b5! when Black was much better in Raetsky-Matsukevich, correspondence 1985) 23...dxe3 24 ♘f6+ gxf6 25 ♗xf5 ♕h6 with a murky position.

17 ♕c2 b5!?

Instead the slow 17...0-0 is marginally in White's favour after 18 ♗d3 ♗g4 19 ♖df1 h4 20 ♘d2.

18 ♗d3

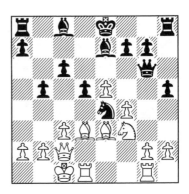

18...f5?!

Black should continue the queenside pawn storm with 18...a6!? 19 ♖df1 c5 when he has a strong attack.

19 exf6 ♗xf6 20 ♗c5

20 ♘d4!? ♗d7 21 f5 with the initiative is also good.

20...♗f5 21 ♖ge1 ♔f7 22 ♘d2

And here the simple 22 ♖e3 a5 23 ♖de1 is promising.

22...♘xc5

Black had to be very careful: 22...♖he8?! allows a nasty trick after 23 ♘xe4 ♗xe4 (not 23...dxe4? 24 ♗xe4 ♗xe4 25 ♕b3+ ♗d5 26 ♖xd5 ♖xe1+ 27 ♖d1+ ♗e6 28 ♖d7+ and White wins) 24 ♖xe4 and White has an edge because 24...dxe4? loses to 25 ♕b3+ ♖e6 26 ♗xb5 ♗e5 27 ♖f1!.

23 ♗xf5 ♕xg2 24 b4

The aggressive 24 ♖g1 allows Black to escape with a safe edge after 24...♕xh2 25 ♗g6+ ♔e7 26 ♖de1+ ♔d8 27 ♕f5 ♔c7 – the king is no longer in danger.

24...♘b7 25 ♕d3 ♖ae8 26 ♖g1 ♕e2 27 ♗g6+ ♔f8 28 ♖ge1 ♕xe1 29 ♖xe1 ♖xe1+ 30 ♔c2 ♘d6 31 ♘f3 ♖e7 32 ♘d4 ♖h6 ½-½

Tal gave the explanatory variation 33 ♘c6 ♖g6 34 ♕g6 ♖e2 35 ♔d3 ♖h2.

Summary

Statistically 3...♘xe4 has not scored overwhelmingly better than 3...exd4. However, the examples shown here after 3...exd4 were mainly played more than a decade ago.

The continuations 4 e5 ♘e4 5 ♗b5 and 5 ♕e2 do not worry Black any longer, but with 5 ♕xd4 the situation is more serious. It appears that after 5...d5 6 exd6 ♘xd6 7 ♘c3 ♘c6 8 ♕f4 ♘f5!? Black maintains equilibrium. However, with the symmetrical pawn structure and easier development, White has many aggressive possibilities that Black needs to be ready for. Consequently, the general interest in 3...exd4 has dropped, but Morozevich's experiment with 5...f5 is interesting.

1 e4 e5 2 ♘f3 ♘f6 3 d4 exd4 4 e5 ♘e4 (D) 5 ♕xd4

    5 ♕e2 – *Game 70*

5...d5 6 exd6 ♘xd6 (D) 7 ♘c3

    7 ♗d3 – *Game 69*

7...♘c6 8 ♕f4 (D) ♘f5 – *Game 67*

    8...g6 – *Game 68*

4...♘e4

6...♘xd6

8 ♕f4

CHAPTER TEN

Third Move Alternatives For White

1 e4 e5 2 ♘f3 ♘f6

After 2...♘f6 White has two equally important continuations: 3 d4 and 3 ♘xe5. Theory pays much less attention to other white possibilities, but statistics prove that White often chooses 3 ♗c4, 3 d3 and especially 3 ♘c3. In this case the positions reached are not always in the domain of the Petroff Defence, as other openings can also arise.

After 3 ♘c3 (Games 71-72) Black is of course able to transpose into the Four Knights (with 3...♘c6). However, Pillsbury employed the move 3...♗b4, Alekhine calling this continuation the 'Ruy Lopez for Black'. The extra tempo ♘g1-f3 plays a significant role here, but it has to be used properly. 4 ♗c4 (Game 72) is best met by 4...♗xc3 5 dxc3 d6 with comfortable development for Black's pieces. More promising is 4 ♘xe5 (Game 71), after which it is easy for Black to win his pawn back but it is more difficult to achieve an equal position. After 4...0-0 5 ♘d3 ♗xc3 6 dxc3 ♘xe4 7 ♗e2 the modest 7...d6 can put Black under long-term positional pressure. Black should play 7...d5 and ...c7-c6 with good prospects of equalising.

The continuation 3 ♗c4 (Game 73) offers Black the interesting opportunity to play 3...♘f6 with the transposition into the Two

Knights Defence, but 3...♘xe4 seems to be strongest move. After 4 ♘c3 Black can return to the Two Knights again with 4...♘c6 (by the way, this variation is favourable for Black). However, it is even more promising to hold onto the extra pawn with 4...♘xc3 5 dxc3 f6. After this Black's pawn chain becomes a formidable force. It is especially useful to activate the pawn chain with ...c7-c6 and ...d7-d5, neutralising the bishop on c4. White should aim to undermine the chain tactically by taking advantage of the insecure position of Black's king (especially with the push f2-f4). Objectively speaking, Black's chances are preferable in these sharp positions. However, he must be very careful: there are numerous examples of Black facing rapid defeats in this line.

After the modest 3 d3 (Game 74) we have a position that also arises from the Alekhine Defence (1 e4 ♘f6 2 d3 e5 3 ♘f3) – in effect White is playing the Philidor Defence with an extra tempo. In this manoeuvring battle White is rarely able to gain an advantage. Black can maintain the symmetry with 3...d6, but 3...♘c6 followed by ...d7-d5 is more promising. Black can develop the dark-squared bishop to c5, e7 or g7, although he normally delays the choice until move six (after 4 c3 d5 5 ♘bd2 a5 6 ♗e2). In general

Black does not have any difficulties and often maintains a small space advantage.

Game 71
Svidler-Akopian
World Team Ch., Lucerne 1997

---

1 e4 e5 2 ♘f3 ♘f6 3 ♘c3

White is trying to escape to the Four Knights, but Black will not allow it!
3...♗b4

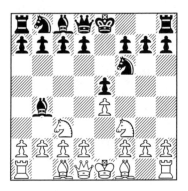

4 ♘xe5

The critical move. 4 ♗c4 is discussed in the next game, while in Ragozin-Kan, Leningrad 1936 White played 4 ♘d5 ♘xd5 5 exd5 e4 6 ♘d4 0-0 7 c3 ♗c5 8 d3 ♗xd4 9 cxd4 ♕e7 10 ♗e3. Now after 10...d6!? 11 ♗e2 ♗f5 12 ♖c1 c6 Black should be okay.
4...0-0

Also possible is 4...♕e7 5 ♘d3 (5 ♘g4!?) 5...♗xc3 6 dxc3 ♘xe4 7 ♗e2 d5 8 0-0 0-0 9 ♘f4 c6 (but not 9...♖d8? 10 ♘xd5 ♕e5 11 c4 c6 12 ♗f4 ♕e6 13 ♗g4! f5 14 ♗xf5 and White wins – Alekhine) 10 c4 dxc4 11 ♗xc4 ♗f5 12 ♕e2 ♖e8 13 ♖e1 ♕d7 14 ♗e3 and White was slightly better in Alapin-Alekhine, Carlsbad 1911.
5 ♘d3 ♗xc3 6 dxc3 ♘xe4 7 ♗e2

This is the critical line (although there is a limit to how critical such a position can be). Instead Galdunts-Raetsky, Aachen 1994 continued 7 ♗e3 ♖e8 8 ♕f3 d6 9 0-0-0 ♘d7 10 h3 (or 10 ♘f4 ♘df6 11 h3 ♗d7 12 ♗c4 ♗c6

and Black is fine) 10...a6 11 ♗e2 b5 12 ♕f4 ♗b7 13 ♗f3 ♘df6 14 ♘c5 ♘xc5 15 ♗xc5 ♗xf3 16 ♕xf3 ♘e4 17 ♗e3 ♖e6 18 ♕f5 ♖e5 19 ♕g4 ♕c8 20 ♗d4 ♕xg4 21 hxg4 ♖e6 and a draw was agreed. If anyone should feel relieved in the final position, it is White.

7...d5

Very natural. Black has also played 7...♖e8 8 0-0 d6 and now:

a) 9 ♖e1 ♘c6 10 ♗f1 ♗f5 11 f3 ♘f6 12 ♗g5 ♘e5 13 ♕d2 h6 14 ♗h4 g5 15 ♗f2 ♘d5?! (15...♘c4 16 ♕c1 ♖xe1 17 ♘xe1 ♘b6 18 a4 would have left White only slightly better) 16 ♘xe5 dxe5 17 ♖ad1 ♘f4 18 ♖xe5! ♕xd2 19 ♖xe8+ ♖xe8 20 ♖xd2 and Black didn't have any compensation for the pawn deficit, Lau-Raetsky, Bad Ragaz, 1994.

b) 9 ♘f4 ♘c6 (or 9...♘d7 10 c4 ♘f8 11 a4 a5 12 ♗e3 ♗d7 13 ♘d5 ♗c6 14 ♖e1 ♘g6 15 ♗f1 h6 16 f3 ♘f6 17 ♕d2 b6 18 b3 and White has an edge in Solleveld-Piket, Bundesliga 2002) 10 c4 ♗f5 11 ♘d5 h6 12 b3 ♘e7 13 ♗b2 ♘xd5 14 ♕xd5 ♕g5 15 ♗d3 (15 f4 ♕g6 16 ♕xb7 ♘c5 17 ♕f3 ♗xc2 leaves Black in a solid condition) 15...c6 16 ♕d4 ♗e6 17 h4 ♕g6 18 ♖ae1 ♖ae8 19 ♗e3 and White is slightly better, Chudinovskikh-Raetsky, Orel 1992.
8 0-0 c6 9 ♘f4 ♖e8

Black is also doing okay after 9...♗f5, for example 10 c4 d4 11 ♗d3 ♖e8 12 f3 ♘d6 13 c5 ♗xd3 14 ♕xd3 ♘b5 15 a4 ♘c7 16 c3 (16 b4 a5 17 b5 cxb5 18 axb5 ♘d7 gives Black excellent counterplay) 16...dxc3 17 ♕xc3 a5 18 ♘h5 f6 19 ♗h6 ♘d5 20 ♕c4 g6 21 ♘g3 ♘d7 22 ♖fe1 f5 23 ♗d2 ♖xe1+ 24 ♖xe1 ♕f8 and Black has equalised, Adams-Rozentalis, Copenhagen 1997.

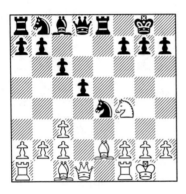

10 c4

10 ♗e3 is best met by 10...♘d6 (10...♘d7 11 c4 dxc4 12 ♗xc4 ♘e5 13 ♕xd8 ♖xd8 14 ♗e2 ♗f5 15 g4 ♗d7 16 f3 ♘d6 17 ♖ad1 ♘dc4 18 ♗c1 ♗e8 19 b3 ♘b6 20 ♗b2 gave White a bit of pressure in Biro-Chetverik, Nagykanizsa 1995) 11 ♗d3 ♗f5 12 ♕h5 g6 13 ♕h6 ♗xd3 14 cxd3 ♘f5 15 ♕h3 ♘d7 16 ♖ae1 ♕f6 17 ♗d2 ♘e5 18 d4 ♘c4 19 ♗c1 ♖e4 with level chances, Benjamin-Yusupov, Munich, 1994.

10...d4

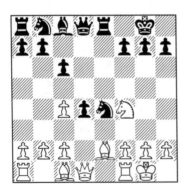

11 ♗d3

After 11 ♗f3 ♘g5 12 ♗g4 ♘e6 13 ♖e1 ♘a6 (13...♘xf4 14 ♖xe8+ ♕xe8 15 ♗xf4

♗xg4 16 ♕xg4 c5 17 ♗h6 g6 18 ♔f1 may be slightly better for White) 14 ♗xe6 ♗xe6 15 ♘xe6 ♖xe6 16 ♖xe6 fxe6 17 ♗d2 ♕f6 the game is level, Adams-Hübner, Dortmund 1996.

11...♘a6 12 c3

12 f3 ♘ec5 13 ♖e1 ♘xd3 14 cxd3 ♗f5 might even preferable for Black.

12...♗f5!?

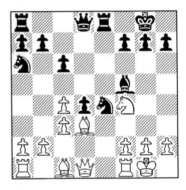

An interesting pawn sacrifice. After 12...c5 13 ♕c2 ♘f6 14 ♗d2 White has a pull.

13 g4 ♗g6 14 f3 ♘g5 15 ♗xg6 hxg6 16 cxd4

Black can answer the alternative capture 16 ♕xd4 with 16...♕c7!?.

16...b5

The alternative 16...♕f6!? 17 d5 ♖ad8 18 h4 ♘h7 19 g5 ♕e5, with play for the pawn, is also strong.

17 cxb5

17 ♕d3 is powerfully met by 17...♕d6 18 cxb5 ♘b4 19 ♕b3 ♕xd4+ 20 ♔h1 cxb5 21 a3 ♘a6 22 ♕xb5 ♘c5 when Black is very active.

17...cxb5 18 d5

Or 18 h4 ♘e6 19 ♘xe6 ♖xe6 20 ♗g5 ♕d6 21 ♕d2 ♖ae8 22 ♗f4 ♕d5 with sufficient play for the pawn.

18...♖c8 19 d6

19 ♗d2 ♖c4 20 ♔g2 ♘c7 gives Black good play, while after 19 h4 ♘h7 20 g5 ♘b4 Black's active pieces also promise him a pleasant game.

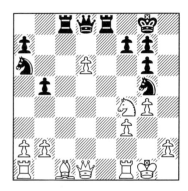

19...♖c6 20 d7 ♖e7 21 ♕d5 ♖c5!

This is stronger than 21...♕xd7?! 22 ♕xg5 ♕d4+ 23 ♔h1 ♖e5 24 ♕h4 g5 25 ♕g3 gxf4 26 ♗xf4, after which Black looks a bit worse.

22 ♕d6?

22 ♕b3 ♖xd7 23 ♗e3 ♖e5, with a complex position, was the right path.

22...♖xd7

Black misses a direct win with 22...♖c2! 23 ♕d3 (23 ♕xa6 ♘xf3+! 24 ♖xf3 ♖e1+ 25 ♖f1 ♕xd7! and Black wins; or 23 h4 ♖xd7 24 ♕e5 ♘xf3+! 25 ♖xf3 ♖e7 26 ♖d3 ♕c7 and White loses his queen) 23...♘b4 24 ♕xb5 ♖xd7! 25 ♗e3 (25 ♕xb4 ♖d1! and White has no defence) 25...♖dd2!!

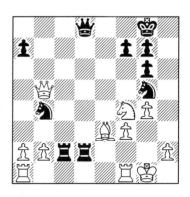

(maybe it was this brilliant move the players overlooked) 26 ♕xb4 ♘h3+ 27 ♘xh3 ♖g2+ 28 ♔h1 ♖xh2+ 29 ♔g1 ♖cg2 mate.

23 ♕xa6 ♘xf3+?

Black could still have gained the advantage

with 23...♖c2! 24 ♗e3 (24 ♕xb5 ♘xf3+! 25 ♖xf3 ♖d1+ and Black wins) 24...♖dd2! 25 ♖f2 ♖d1+ 26 ♔g2 ♖xf2+ 27 ♗xf2 ♖xa1 and Black has all the chances.

24 ♖xf3 ♖d1+ 25 ♔g2 ♕h4, 26 ♘e2 ♖c2 27 ♖f2 ♕xg4+ 28 ♘g3 ♖xf2+ 29 ♔xf2 ♕d4+ 30 ♔g2 ½-½

Game 72
Lev-Alterman
Ramat-Gan 1992

---

1 e4 e5 2 ♘f3 ♘f6 3 ♘c3 ♗b4!? 4 ♗c4

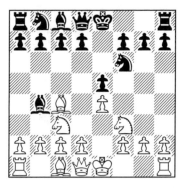

4...0-0

Black has reasonable alternatives here:

a) 4...♗xc3 5 dxc3 d6 6 ♕e2 ♘bd7 7 h3 ♘c5 8 ♗d3 0-0 9 0-0 ♖e8 10 c4 ♗d7 11 b4 ♘e6 12 ♖e1 a5 13 b5 c6 14 c3 ♕c7 with equal prospects, Gaponenko-Raetsky, Krasnodar 1995.

b) 4...d6 5 0-0 ♗g4 6 h3 ♗h5 7 g4 ♗g6 8 d3 c6 (safer is 8...♗xc3 9 bxc3 ♘c6 10 a4 0-0 11 ♖b1 ♖b8 when Black is close to equality) 9 ♘e2 ♘bd7 10 c3 ♗a5 11 b4 ♗c7 12 ♗b3 ♘f8 13 ♘g3 ♘e6 14 g5 ♘h5 15 ♗xe6 fxe6 16 ♘xe5 dxe5 17 ♘xh5 0-0 and Black had good compensation in Chernyshov-Yusupov, Ohrid 2001.

5 0-0

5 ♘d5 is rather unexciting: 5...♘xd5 6 ♗xd5 c6 7 ♗b3 d5 8 0-0 ♗g4 (or 8...dxe4 9 ♘xe5 ♘d7 10 d4 ♘xe5 11 dxe5 ♕xd1 12 ♖xd1 ♗g4 13 ♖d4 ♖fd8 14 ♖xd8+ ♖xd8 15

♗e3 with level chances) 9 h3 ♗h5 10 d3 dxe4 11 dxe4 ♘d7 12 ♕e2 ♕c7 with an equal position, Spielmann-Marshall, Budapest 1928.

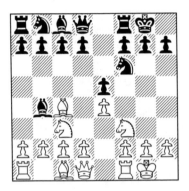

5...♗xc3

Black usually uses this chance to inflict double pawns on White, but he can also try 5...d6!?, for example 6 d3 ♗g4 7 h3 ♗e6 8 ♘d5 ♗xd5 9 exd5 h6 10 c3 ♗a5 11 d4 exd4 (our improvement over 11...e4 12 ♘h4 c6 13 dxc6 ♘xc6 14 ♘f5 d5 15 ♗b3 ♗c7 16 f3 when we prefer White, Priehoda-Chetverik, Martin 1996) 12 ♘xd4 ♘bd7 13 ♘f5 ♘e5 14 ♗b3 ♗b6 with more or less level chances.

6 dxc3

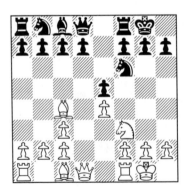

Black has nothing to fear after 6 bxc3 ♘xe4 7 ♘xe5 d5 8 ♗b3 a5 9 a4 ♖e8 10 ♘d3 ♘c6.

6...d6

6...♘xe4?! 7 ♘xe5 is better for White.

One line continues 7...c6 8 ♖e1 d5 9 ♖xe4! dxc4 (9...dxe4? 10 ♗xf7+ ♔h8 11 ♕h5 ♗f5 12 ♘g6+! ♗xg6 13 ♗xg6 leads to mate) 10 ♖d4 ♕e7 11 ♘xc4 and White was a pawn up in L.Guliev-Smougalev, Moscow 1995.

7 ♗g5

Practice has also seen 7 ♕e2 ♘bd7 8 ♗g5 h6 9 ♗h4 ♘c5 10 ♖ad1 ♕e7 11 ♘d2 g5 12 ♗g3 ♔h8 13 h4 (this does not seem logical) 13...♗d7 14 hxg5 hxg5 15 f3 ♔g7 16 ♔f2 ♖h8 17 ♖h1 ♘h5 18 ♘f1 ♕f6 and Black had the initiative in Kofidis-Alterman, Komotini 1992.

7...h6 8 ♗h4 ♗g4

8...g5 can be met by 9 ♘xg5!? hxg5 10 ♗xg5 with the idea of meeting 10...♗e6 with 11 ♗d3 ♘bd7 12 f4!, after which White has a very strong attack – the absence of Black's dark-squared bishop is really felt.

9 h3 ♗h5 10 ♕d3 ♘bd7 11 b4 ♕e8

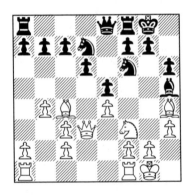

Also interesting is 11...g5 12 ♗g3 ♘b6 13 ♗b3 ♗g6 14 ♖fe1 a5 when Black has good counterplay.

12 ♕e3 ♗g6 13 ♘d2 ♘h5

Or 13...c6 14 ♖fe1 d5 15 exd5 ♘xd5 (15...cxd5 16 ♗b5 a6 17 ♗xf6 axb5 18 ♗xe5 ♘xe5 19 ♕xe5 ♕xe5 20 ♖xe5 would leave Black with a tedious endgame in which he is slightly worse) 16 ♗xd5 cxd5 17 c4 d4 18 ♕f3 and the position is rather unclear.

14 a4 ♔h8 15 a5 f5 16 exf5 ♗xf5 17 a6 b6 18 g4 ♕g6 19 ♗d5 ♘f4 20 ♗xa8 ♖xa8 21 ♔h2 ♗xc2

Black has escaped from the opening with adequate play for the exchange.

22 c4 ℤf8 23 ♗g3 h5 24 f3 ♕h7 25 ♗xf4 ℤxf4 26 ♔g3 ♕h6 27 ℤae1 c5 28 b5 ♘f8?!

28...♘f6!?, with good play, would have been better.

29 ♘e4 ♗xe4 30 fxe4 ♘e6 31 gxh5 ♕xh5 32 ♔g2 ♕f7 33 ♕d3 ♕g6+ 34 ♕g3 ♕h6 35 ℤxf4 exf4 36 ♕g4 ♘d4 37 h4?!

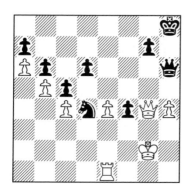

37 ♔h2! would have kept an edge for White.

37...f3+?

Black misses his chance. After 37...♘c2! the game would most likely have ended in a draw.

38 ♔h3 ♔h7 39 ℤg1 f2 40 ℤf1 ♕e3+ 41 ♔g2 ♘c2 42 ℤxf2 ♘e1+ 43 ♔f1 ♘d3 44 ℤf7 ♕e1+ 45 ♔g2 ♕d2+ 46 ♔g1 ♕c1+ 47 ♔h2 ♕b2+ 48 ♕g2 ♕e5+ 49 ♕g3 ♕b2+ 50 ♔h3 ♔g8 51 ♕f3 1-0

Game 73
Morphy-Barnes
London 1858

---

1 e4 e5 2 ♘f3 ♘f6 3 ♗c4!?

A romantic gambit.

3...♘xe4 4 ♘c3 ♘xc3 5 dxc3 f6!

This should lead to an advantage for Black. Alternatively:

a) 5...d6? loses to 6 ♘g5 ♗e6 7 ♗xe6 fxe6 8 ♕f3 (Bilguer).

b) 5...♗e7 is met strongly by 6 ♘xe5 0-0 7 ♕f3 ♗f6 8 ♘g4 ♗e7 9 ♘h6+!? gxh6 10 ♗xh6 with a powerful attack.

c) 5...c6!? leads to equality after 6 ♘xe5 d5 7 ♕e2 ♗e6 8 ♗d3 ♘d7 9 f4 ♘xe5 10 ♕xe5 ♕d6 11 ♕e2 ♗e7 12 0-0, as in San Claudio-Bonati, Mislata 2001.

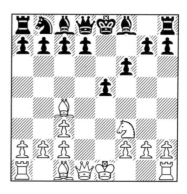

6 0-0

6 ♘h4 g6 7 f4 is probably less dangerous (7 0-0 transposes to 6 0-0 g6 7 ♘h4). Play continues 7...c6! 8 f5 d5 9 fxg6 (9 ♗b3 ♔f7 10 c4 d4 is better for Black) 9...dxc4 10 ♕h5 ♔d7 11 g7 ♗xg7 12 ♕g4+ ♔d6! (12...♔c7?! 13 ♕xg7+ ♘d7 14 ♗h6 ♕e8! 15 0-0-0 ℤg8 16 ♕xh7 ℤh8 is 'only' equal) 13 ♕xg7 ♕f8 14 ♕g3 (or 14 ♕xf8+ ℤxf8 15 ♗e3 ♗e6 16 0-0-0+ ♗d5 and Black dominates the board) 14...♗e6 15 ♗e3 ♘d7 16 0-0-0+ ♔c7 17 ℤhf1 ℤg8 18 ♕f2 b6 19 ♘f5 ℤd8 and Black has a small plus, Tribushevsky-Raetsky, correspondence 1982.

6...♘c6

Or:

a) 6...c6? is now strongly met by 7 ♘xe5! d5 8 ♕h5+ ♔e7 9 ♗d3 with a winning attack.

b) 6...g6 7 ♘h4 ♕e7 8 ♔h1 c6 9 f4 d5 10 ♗b3 e4 is worth thinking about – we prefer Black here.

c) 6...♕e7 7 ℤe1 d6! (7...c6?! is met by 8 ♘xe5!? fxe5 9 ♕h5+ g6 10 ♕xe5 d5 11

♕xe7+ ♗xe7 12 ♗g5 0-0 13 ♗xe7 dxc4 14 ♗xf8 ♔xf8 15 ♖ad1 and the endgame looks good for White) 8 ♘d4 c6 9 f4 g6 10 f5 d5 11 ♗d3 ♕g7 also looks better for Black.

d) 6...d6 7 ♘h4 g6 8 f4 ♕e7 9 f5 ♕g7 should be better for Black. Now 10 ♗e3 c6 11 ♕e2 d5 12 ♗b3 g5 13 c4!? gxh4?! 14 cxd5 c5 15 d6! ♗xd6?! 16 ♖ad1 gave White tremendous compensation in Crepan-Rezonja, Bled 2000. However, stronger is 13...d4! 14 ♗xd4 gxh4 when Black has a clear plus.

7 ♘h4 ♕e7

Or:

a) 7...♘e7?! is very well met by 8 ♗d3 g6 9 f4, when White has a powerful initiative. One game continued 9...♗g7 10 fxe5 fxe5 11 ♗g5 c6? 12 ♘f5! gxf5 13 ♕h5+ ♔f8 14 ♖xf5+ 1-0 Saburov-Lutze, correspondence 1906.

b) 7...g6 8 f4 f5 9 ♘f3 e4 10 ♘g5 ♗c5+ 11 ♔h1 ♕f6 12 ♕d5 (12 ♗f7+ ♔e7 13 ♗d5 d6 14 ♖e1 ♔f8 15 g4 ♘e7!? 16 gxf5 ♘xd5 17 ♕xd5 gxf5 is even worse, Black having a clear plus in Schlechter-Marco, Berlin 1897) 12...d6 13 ♘xh7 ♕e7 14 ♘g5 ♘d8 and we prefer Black even if it is not entirely clear.

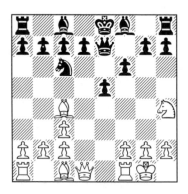

8 ♘f5?!

8 ♕h5+ ♔d8 9 ♘f5 (9 ♘g6? ♕e8 and Black wins) 9...g6 10 ♘xe7 gxh5 11 ♘xc8 ♖xc8 12 ♗e3 is better, giving White good compensation for the pawn.

8...♕c5 9 ♗b3 d5 10 ♗e3 ♕a5 11 ♘h4

Black's position is also more pleasant after 11 ♘g3 ♗e6 12 ♕h5+ g6 13 ♕h4 ♗e7.

11...♗e6 12 ♕h5+ g6

12...♗f7 13 ♕g4 g6, with a slight edge, was also possible.

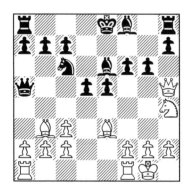

13 ♘xg6?!

Risky. After 13 ♕e2 0-0-0 14 f4 ♗c5 15 ♕f2 ♗xe3 16 ♕xe3 White is maybe only slightly worse.

13...♗f7 14 ♕h4 ♗xg6 15 ♕xf6 ♖g8 16 ♖ad1 ♗e7

Not 16...♘e7? 17 ♖xd5! ♘xd5?! 18 ♕xe5+ ♗e7 19 ♗xd5 when White wins because of the threat of ♗f7+.

17 ♕e6 ♗f7 18 ♕h3 ♘d8

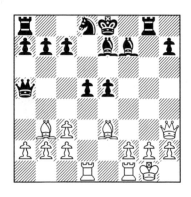

18...♖d8!? 19 ♕xh7 ♖d6 looks good, White not having enough for the piece. After 18...♘d8 the trend starts to change.

19 f4 e4 20 ♖xd5

20 ♗xd5!? is an interesting option: 20...♗xd5 21 ♕h5+ ♘f7 22 ♖xd5 ♕xa2 23 ♖e5 and White has an attack.

20...♗xd5 21 ♕h5+

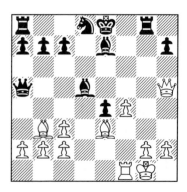

21...♔f8?!

Much stronger is 21...♖g6 22 ♗xd5 ♗c5 23 ♔h1 ♕a6 (23...♗xe3 24 ♗f7+ ♘xf7 25 ♕xa5 leaves White slightly better) 24 ♖e1 ♗xe3 25 f5 ♕f6 26 fxg6 hxg6 27 ♕g4 and the game is still very unclear.

22 ♗xd5 ♖g7

22...c6? loses to 23 ♕f5+ ♔g7 24 ♗d4+.

23 b4 ♕a6 24 f5!

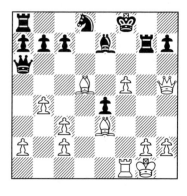

24...♘f7?

24...♕f6 25 ♗d4 ♕g5 26 ♗xg7+ ♔xg7 27 ♕e8 was necessary, when White's attack is fearsome, but the game goes on.

25 f6! ♗xf6 26 b5! ♕d6 27 ♗xf7+ b6

27...♖xf7 28 ♗c5 is the end.

28 ♗h6 ♔e7 29 ♗xg7 ♗xg7 30 ♗b3 ♖f8 31 ♖f7+ ♖xf7 32 ♕xf7+ ♔d8 33 ♕xg7 ♕d1+ 34 ♔f2 ♕d2+ 35 ♔g3 e3 36 ♕f6+ ♔c8 37 ♗e6+ ♔b7 38 ♕f3+ 1-0

Game 74
Svetushkin-Miles
Alushta 1999

1 e4 ♘f6 2 d3 e5 3 ♘f3

For our purposes, the Petroff move order would have been 1 e4 e5 2 ♘f3 ♘f6 3 d3.

3...♘c6

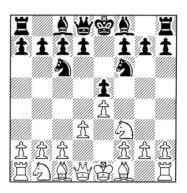

4 c3

4 g3 is also harmless: 4...d5 5 exd5 ♘xd5 6 ♗g2 ♗c5 7 0-0 0-0 8 ♖e1 ♖e8 9 h3?! (9 ♘c3 ♘xc3 10 bxc3 ♗g4 would transpose to the so-called Glek Variation of the Four Knights Opening – the chances are equal) 9...♗f5 10 ♘h4?! (10 ♘bd2 is better, although we prefer Black after 10...f6 11 ♘e4 ♗b6) 10...♗e6 11 ♘d2 ♘f4! (this surprising move leaves Black with a substantial plus) 12 gxf4 ♕xh4 13 ♘e4 ♗xh3! (a nice sacrifice) 14 ♘xc5 ♗xg2 15 ♔xg2 exf4 16 ♘e4 ♘d4 17 f3 ♖e6 18 ♘f2 ♕g3+ 19 ♔f1 ♖g6 0-1 Manik-Oral, Trencin 1995.

4...d5 5 ♘bd2 a5 6 ♗e2 ♗c5

Black has also tried 6...g6 7 b3 (7 0-0 ♗g7 8 ♖e1 0-0 9 ♗f1 ♖e8 10 b3 b6 11 ♗a3 ♗a6 12 ♕c2 ♕d7 13 ♖ad1 ♖ad8 looks pretty standard and pretty level) 7...♗g7 8 ♗a3 ♘h5 9 0-0 ♘f4 10 ♖e1 ♘xe2+ 11 ♕xe2 ♗e6 (or 11...d4!? 12 cxd4 exd4 13 ♖ac1 ♘b4 with equality – Makarychev) 12 exd5 ♕xd5 13 c4!? ♕d7 14 ♗b2 ♗g4 15 d4 0-0-0!? 16 dxe5 ♖he8 17 ♕e3 f6 and Black had good compensation in Morozevich-Makarychev, Moscow 1992.

7 0-0 0-0 8 a4

Other moves to consider are:

a) 8 ♕c2 a4!? 9 ♖b1 ♖e8 10 b4 axb3 11 axb3 ♘h5 12 ♖e1 ♘f4 13 ♗f1 with equal chances.

b) 8 b3 ♖e8 9 a3 ♗a7 (or 9...d4 10 ♗b2 dxc3 11 ♗xc3 ♗g4 with equality) 10 ♖b1 dxe4 11 dxe4 ♘h5 12 ♘c4 ♕f6 13 b4 axb4 14 axb4 ♘f4 15 ♗xf4 ♕xf4 16 b5 with unclear play, Gelashvili-Hellsten, Korinthos 2002.

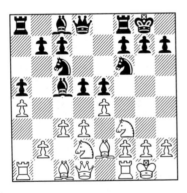

8...♖e8

8...h6 9 ♕c2 ♗e6 is also a very sensible way to play. The following continuation looks promising for Black: 10 exd5 ♘xd5 11 ♖e1 ♕d7 12 ♗f1 f6 13 ♘e4 ♗a7 14 b3 ♗g4 (14...♖ad8 15 ♗a3 ♖fe8 is a sound alternative; we prefer Black) 15 ♗e2 f5 16 ♘g3

♖ae8 17 h3 e4!? 18 dxe4 fxe4 19 ♘xe4 ♗f5 20 ♗c4 ♔h8 21 ♗a3 ♗xh3! 22 ♗xf8 ♕g4 23 ♘h4 ♗xg2 24 ♘g3 ♗e4! (Lein-Kupreichik, Hastings 1982/83). Now after 25 ♖xe4 ♕xg3+ 26 ♔h1 ♕h3+ the game would have ended with a draw.

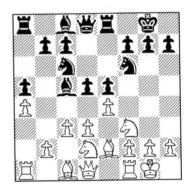

9 exd5

White has also played 9 ♕c2 ♗g4 10 ♖e1 h6 11 ♘f1 ♕d7 12 ♗e3 ♗f8 (or 12...d4 13 cxd4 ♗xf3 14 d5!? ♗xe2 15 dxc6 ♕xc6 16 ♖xe2 ♗xe3 17 ♘xe3 ♕d7 with level prospects) 13 ♖ad1 ♖ad8 14 ♘g3 d4 15 ♗c1 (after 15 cxd4 ♗xf3 16 ♗xf3 ♘xd4 17 ♗xd4 ♕xd4 18 ♕xc7 ♗c5 19 ♖f1 b6 Black has fantastic play for the pawn) 15...♗c5 16 ♘h4 ♗e6 17 ♘hf5 ♔h7 18 ♗f3 ♘g8 19 ♘e2 ♗f8 and Black was a bit better, Veselovsky-Sergeev, Ceske Budejovice 1997.

9...♘xd5 10 ♘e4

10 ♘c4 ♗f5 11 ♕b3 ♕d7 12 ♘g5 ♖ab8 also gives a fair share of chances to both players.

10...♗f8

Or 10...♗b6!? 11 ♘fd2 f5 12 ♘g3 ♗e6 13 ♘c4 ♗c5 with unclear play.

11 ♖e1 h6 12 ♕b3?!

This is the path to destruction. White was better off playing 12 ♘fd2 ♘f4 13 ♘c4 ♘xe2+ 14 ♕xe2 ♗f5, though Black has easy equality.

12...♗e6! 13 ♕xb7?!

13 ♕b5 was better, though after 13...♕c8 14 ♗f1 ♖a6 White is still struggling.

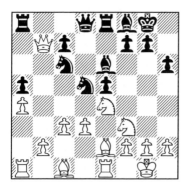

13...♘b6!?

Maybe even stronger is 13...♕d7!? 14 ♕b5 ♖eb8 15 ♘c5 ♕e8 16 ♘xe6 ♖xb5 17 axb5 ♘cb4! (the hidden point) 18 cxb4 ♗xb4 with a clear plus for Black.

14 ♕xc6

Forced. After 14 ♗e3? ♗d7! 15 ♗xb6 cxb6 followed by ...♖a7 Black wins the queen for a rook.

14...♗d5 15 ♕xe8

The queen is trapped, and after 15 ♕b5 c6 it would be sold more cheaply.

15...♕xe8 16 ♗d1 c5 17 c4

17 d4 also leads to a black edge after 17...cxd4 18 cxd4 ♗b4 19 ♗d2 ♗xd2 20 ♘exd2 e4.

17...♗c6 18 ♘c3 f6 19 b3 ♕d8 20 ♗e2 g5!? 21 ♘d2 ♘c8 22 ♗b2 ♘e7 23 ♘de4 ♘f5 24 ♘d5 ♗e7

After the inferior 24...♗xd5?! 25 cxd5 ♘d4 26 ♗xd4 cxd4 27 ♗g4 White has excellent counterplay on the light squares.

25 ♗g4 ♘g7 26 ♗f3 g4 27 ♘xe7+ ♕xe7 28 ♗e2 h5

It is safe to say that White is far from having sufficient compensation.

29 ♗d1 ♘e6 30 g3 ♖d8

31 f4?!

The only chance was 31 ♖e3 f5 32 ♘c3 ♘g5 although Black still has all the fun.

31...♖xd3

Simpler was 31...♗xe4! 32 ♖xe4 ♖xd3 33 fxe5 ♘g5 34 ♖e1 ♕b7 and Black wins.

32 ♘f2 ♖d8 33 fxe5 f5! 34 ♗c1 ♗a8!

After this there is no defence.

35 ♖a2 ♕b7 36 ♔f1 ♕g2+ 37 ♔e2 ♗f3+ 38 ♔e3 ♗xd1 0-1

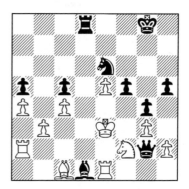

Summary

In practice White's deviations from the main continuations on move three quite often transpose to other openings. The least justifiable is 3 d3, since White gives away his advantage of the first move. Those who enjoy attacking the king should study 3 ♗c4 ♘xe4 4 ♘c3 ♘xc3 5 dxc3, which is especially recommendable for rapid and blitz tournaments. Unfortunately, 4...♘f6 cools down White's ardour.

3 ♘c3 ♗b4 leads to quite another type of position with a slow, manoeuvring fight and White having the advantage of two bishops (often in the endgame). Like in many other basic variations of the Petroff Defence, Black has to neutralise White's pressure with careful play.

1 e4 e5 2 ♘f3 ♘f6 3 ♘c3
    3 ♗c4 (D) – *Game 73*
    3 d3 – *Game 74*
3...♗b4 4 ♘xe5 (D) – *Game 71*
    4 ♗c4 (D) – *Game 72*

3 ♗c4

4 ♘xe5

4 ♗c4

INDEX OF COMPLETE GAMES